Global Civil Society 2012

Global Civil Society yearbook

Global Civil Society 2001
Editors: Helmut Anheier, Marlies Glasius and Mary Kaldor

Global Civil Society 2002
Editors: Marlies Glasius, Mary Kaldor and Helmut Anheier

Global Civil Society 2003
Editors: Mary Kaldor, Helmut Anheier and Marlies Glasius

Global Civil Society 2004/5
Editors-in-chief: Helmut Anheier, Marlies Glasius and Mary Kaldor

Global Civil Society 2005/6
Editors-in-chief: Marlies Glasius, Mary Kaldor and Helmut Anheier

Global Civil Society 2006/7
Editors-in-chief: Mary Kaldor, Martin Albrow, Helmut Anheier
and Marlies Glasius

Global Civil Society 2007/8
Editors-in-chief: Martin Albrow, Helmut Anheier, Marlies Glasius,
Monroe E. Price and Mary Kaldor

Global Civil Society 2009
Editors-in-chief: Ashwani Kumar, Jan Aart Scholte, Mary Kaldor,
Marlies Glasius, Hakan Seckinelgin and Helmut Anheier

Global Civil Society 2011
Executive Editors: Martin Albrow and Hakan Seckinelgin
Editors: Helmut Anheier, Marlies Glasius, Mary Kaldor, Gil-Sung Park,
Chandan Sengupta

Global Civil Society 2012

Ten Years of Critical Reflection

Editors: Mary Kaldor, Henrietta L. Moore and Sabine Selchow

Managing Editor: Tamsin Murray-Leach

First published 2012 by
PALGRAVE MACMILLAN

Palgrave Macmillan in the UK is an imprint of Macmillan Publishers Limited, registered in England, company number 785998, of Houndmills, Basingstoke, Hampshire RG21 6XS.

Palgrave Macmillan in the US is a division of St Martin's Press LLC, 175 Fifth Avenue, New York, NY 10010.

Palgrave Macmillan is the global academic imprint of the above companies and has companies and representatives throughout the world.

Palgrave® and Macmillan® are registered trademarks in the United States, the United Kingdom, Europe and other countries

ISBN: 978–0–230–36787–6   paperback

This book is printed on paper suitable for recycling and made from fully managed and sustained forest sources. Logging, pulping and manufacturing processes are expected to conform to the environmental regulations of the country of origin.

A catalogue record for this book is available from the British Library.

A catalog record for this book is available from the Library of Congress.

10 9 8 7 6 5 4 3 2 1
21 20 19 18 17 16 15 14 13 12

Printed and bound in Great Britain by Scotprint

To the protestors of 2011

CONTENTS

LIST OF BOXES, MAPS, FIGURES AND TABLES

BOXES

MAPS

FIGURES

TABLES

ACKNOWLEDGEMENTS

Consultations

Chapter 4, '"Lost in Transformation": The Crisis of Democracy and Civil Society' and Chapter 7, 'Pro-Roma Global Civil Society: Acting For, With or Instead of Roma?' were produced in consultation with Corvinus Univerity, Budapest; the Institute for Social & European Studies Foundation (ISES), Kőszeg; and the Central European University (CEU), Budapest. Particular thanks goes to Ferenc Miszlivetz and Andrea Krizsan.

Other Input

Special thanks to Khaled Mattawa for the kind permission to reprint his poem, 'Now That We Have Tasted Hope'.

Thanks also to Al Jazeera for permission to reprint 'Al-Qaeda is its Own Worst Enemy' by Alia Brahimi, and to OpenDemocracy.net for permission to reprint 'The Road to Europe', by Donatella della Porta.

Text Box Authors

Omar Benderra, Alia Brahimi, Renjie Butalid, Giuseppe Caruso, Donatella della Porta, Aurore Fauret, Magda Fried, Paolo Gerbaudo, Johan Hellström, Radhika Hettiarachchi, Michael Hoelscher, Jungmin Jamie Kim, Thomas Kirk, Alison Locke, Gustave Massiah, Katie McKenna, Francine Mestrum, Richard Moyes, Mario Pianta, Heba Raouf Ezzat, Brian Rappert, Remy Reymann, Max Richman, Andrea Römmele, Erin Saltman, Henrik Schober, Hajnalka Szarvas, Marika Theros, Gavan Titley, Francis Ward, Erik Wilson.

Research and Editorial Assistance

Renjie Butalid, Thomas Kirk, Anaël Labigne, Tim Meijers (research assistants); Aurore Fauret, Jungmin Jamie Kim, Erik Wilson and Jon Wiltshire (interns); Claire Alleaume and Aurore Fauret (translators); Sally Stares (data editor and designer); Max Richman (data design assistant).

Others Who Provided Input or Support

Catherine Fieschi, Marlies Glasius, Denise Mahon, Hakan Seckinelgin and Neha Sinha.

Financial Support

We gratefully acknowledge the financial support of the following organisations:

Jamsetji Tata Trust
Paresh Kanani
Open Society Foundations

Helmut K. Anheier holds a chair of Sociology at Heidelberg University and serves as Academic Director of the Center for Social Investment. From 2001 to 2009, he was Professor of Public Policy and Social Welfare at UCLA's School of Public Affairs and Centennial Professor at the London School of Economics. Professor Anheier founded and directed the Centre for Civil Society at LSE and the Center for Civil Society at UCLA. Before embarking on an academic career, he served as social affairs officer to the United Nations. He is currently researching the nexus between globalisation, civil society, and culture and is interested in policy analysis and methodological questions.

Bolette B. Blaagaard is a research fellow at the Centre for Law, Justice and Journalism at City University, London. She works in the interdisciplinary field of journalism, media and cultural studies and has published in Nordic as well as in international journals on issues of Nordic colonialism, multiculturalism, civil society, cosmopolitanism and new media.

Sean Deel is a researcher in the Department of International Development at the London School of Economics and Political Science.

Bernard Dreano is a member of the Centre d'études et d'initiatives de solidarité internationale (CEDETIM) in Paris, and of the Helsinki Citizens' Assembly (HCA).

Marlies Glasius is a senior lecturer in international relations at the University of Amsterdam. Before returning to Amsterdam in 2008, she worked at the London School of Economics and Political Science as a lecturer in Global Politics. She was previously the managing editor of the Global Civil Society yearbook (2001–03), coordinator of the Study Group on European Security (2003–04), and a lecturer in the management of non-governmental organisations (2004–06) at the LSE. Marlies holds a PhD with distinction from the University of Utrecht in association with the Netherlands School of Human Rights Research. She is the author of *The International Criminal Court: A Global Civil Society* (Routledge, 2006) and co-editor of *Bottom-Up Politics: An Agency-Centred Approach to Globalization* (Palgrave MacMillan, 2012). Her research interests focus on civil society, international law, authoritarian and democratic rule, and human security. Current projects concern the legitimacy of international criminal courts, and authoritarian rule in a global age.

Mary Kaldor is Professor of Global Governance and director of the Civil Society and Human Security Research Unit in the Department of International Development at the London School of Economics and Political Science. She has written widely on security issues and on democracy and civil society, and is a founder and executive editor of the Global Civil Society yearbook series. Her recent books include *Human Security: Reflections on Globalisation and Intervention* (Polity Press, 2007) *New and Old Wars: Organised Violence in a Global Era* (Polity Press, 2nd edn 2006) and *Global Civil Society: An Answer to War* (Polity Press, 2003). Most recently, she co-authored *The Ultimate Weapon is No Weapon: Human Security and the Changing Rules of War and Peace* (PublicAffairs, 2010) with Colonel Shannon D. Beebe. Mary was a founder member of European Nuclear Disarmament (END), and founder and co-chair of the Helsinki Citizens' Assembly. She is convenor of the Human Security Study Group, established at the request of Javier Solana, then High Representative for Common Foreign and Security Policy of the European Union, and in 2009–10 was a member of the UK Defence Advisory Forum.

Angéla Kóczé is a sociologist and the former funding director of the European Roma Information Office (ERIO) in Brussels, as well as the former director of the human rights education programme at the European Roma Rights Centre (ERRC) in Budapest, Hungary. She was the founding director of the Romaversitas program in Budapest, which offers scholarships and mentorships for Roma university students. She is active in the movement for the emancipation of Roma in Europe, and has a particular research and policy interest in issues of women's political representation and social justice. Angéla is a research fellow at the Institute of Ethnic and Minority Studies of the Hungarian Academy of Sciences, Budapest.

Ferenc Miszlivetz is Jean Monnet Professor and director of the Institute for Social and European Studies at the University of West Hungary, and scientific advisor of the Institute for Political Sciences at the Hungarian Academy of Sciences (HAS) in Budapest. In 2009 he was appointed as the academic director of the postgraduate Institute for Global and European Integration Studies established by the Corvinus University in Kőszeg, Western Hungary. Additionally, he lectures at several European universities, including at the University of Bologna, where he has been a permanent guest professor in the MIREES program since 2008. His research interests include transition, democratisation, and changing values as well as European integration, cross-border regional cooperation and global and European civil society. His articles have been published in ten languages, and his latest book is *The European Construction from a Central European Perspective* (HAS, forthcoming). A former dissident, Ferenc was an active participant in the new social movements of the 1980s, co-founding the European Network for East-West Dialogue as well as the Network of Free Initiatives. He is co-founder with Elemér Hankiss of a new initiative for social dialogue: 'Re-inventing Europe, re-inventing Central Europe, re-inventing Hungary'.

Henrietta L. Moore is the William Wyse Chair of Social Anthropology at the University of Cambridge. She has held numerous Visiting Appointments in the United States, Germany, Norway and South Africa, among other places. Recent research has focused on virtual worlds, new technologies and the relationship between self-imagining and globalisation. She has worked extensively on Africa, particularly on gender, livelihood strategies, social transformation and symbolic systems. She has written and lectured on Social Theory, Epistemology, Feminist Theory, Space, Robots, Sociality, Development and Social Enterprise. She is a Fellow of the British Academy, a Fellow of the Royal Society of Arts and Academician of the Learned Societies for the Social Sciences.

Robin Murray is an industrial and environmental economist. His recent work has focused on new waste and energy systems and on projects in the social economy. He has coupled spells in academic teaching and research with work in local, regional and national governments, and was co-founder and later chair of Twin Trading, the fair trade company. Formerly a Fellow of the Institute of Development Studies at the University of Sussex, he is now a Senior Visiting Fellow at the Civil Society and Human Security Research Unit, London School of Economics and Political Science. He is also a Fellow of the Young Foundation, where he has recently completed work on methods of social and environmental innovation.

Thomas Nash serves as joint Coordinator for the International Network on Explosive Weapons, established in March 2011. He is the director of Article 36, a UK-based initiative monitoring the use and impact of weapons, and has been a member of the board of the International Action Network on Small Arms since November 2010. From 2004 to 2011, Nash served as Coordinator of the Cluster Munition Coalition, acting as strategist and spokesperson throughout the global campaign that resulted in the 2008 Convention on Cluster Munitions. Nash has undertaken numerous research and advocacy missions including in Kosovo, Lebanon, Vietnam and Lao PDR, and previously worked for the New Zealand and Canadian Foreign Ministries in Geneva and Ottawa respectively.

Geoffrey Pleyers is an FNRS researcher at the University of Louvain, Belgium. He holds a PhD in sociology from the Ecole des Hautes Etudes en Sciences Sociales (EHESS, Paris) and teaches sociology of globalization and social movements at the EHESS and at the University of Louvain. He is the author of *Forums sociaux mondiaux et défis de l'altermondialisme* (Academia, 2007) and *Alter-globalization. Becoming Actors in a Global Age* (Polity Press, 2010), and edited the books *Movimientos sociales. De lo local a lo global* (Anthropos, 2009) and *Consommation critique* (Desclée de Brouwer, 2011).

Márton Rövid is a PhD candidate at the International Relations and European Studies Department of Central European University, Budapest. His research considers cosmopolitan theories and the notion of transcendence of national citizenship in the light of the case of Roma, an allegedly non-territorial nation. Márton holds an MA in International Relations and Economics (Budapest University of Economic Sciences) and a DEA in Relations Internationales (Institut d'Etudes Politiques de Paris). He has worked for NGOs both as a researcher (European Roma Rights Center, East-Central-European Cultural Observatory) and as a volunteer (primarily with Roma communities). Márton has been a visiting fellow at the Sociology Department of Yale University, the Hungarian Institute of International Affairs, and the Research Institute of Ethnic and National Minorities of the Hungarian Academy of Sciences.

Sabine Selchow is a researcher in the Civil Society and Human Security Research Unit in the Department of International Development at the London School of Economics (LSE). She holds a PhD in Government from LSE.

Sally Stares is a research fellow in the Methodology Institute at LSE. She completed her PhD in the Institute of Social Psychology at the LSE, and has been a member of the yearbook team for a number of years, both as an author and contributor to the presentation of quantitative data. Her research interests are largely methodological in focus, including survey design and analysis, and social measurement broadly speaking, particularly in comparative perspective. Substantively, these interests are directed towards studies of social values and attitudes, including public perceptions of science and technology, and various aspects of civil society.

Jill Timms is completing a doctorate in the Department of Sociology, LSE, on the role of corporate social responsibility (CSR) discourse in campaigns for workers' rights. She lectures at Brunel University, is an external tutor for the Centre for Labour Market Studies at Leicester University, an examiner for the University of London's International Programme, and is also on the committee of the Global Studies Association. Her main research interests include CSR, ethical consumerism, labour movements and globalisation, social forums, and campaigns related to the Olympics. Jill coordinated the Chronology of the Global Civil Society yearbook from 2001 to 2009, and related publications include: 'Trade Union Internationalism and a Global Civil Society in the Making' co-authored with Peter Waterman in *Global Civil Society 2004/5* (Sage, 2005); 'The Role of Social Forums in Global Civil Society: Radical Beacon or Strategic Infrastructure?' co-authored with Marlies Glasius in *Global Civil Society 2005/6* (Sage, 2006); and 'Global Organisation in Civil Society: The Effects on Poverty' co-authored with Jan Aart Scholte in *Global Civil Society 2009* (Sage, 2009).

Now That We Have Tasted Hope

Now that we have tasted hope,
Now that we have come out of hiding,
Why would we live again in the tombs we'd made out of our souls?
And the sundered bodies that we've re-assembled with prayers and consolations,
What would their torn parts be other than flesh?

Now that we have tasted hope,
And dressed each other's wounds with the legends of our oneness,
Would we not prefer to close our mouths for ever shut
On the wine that twirled inside them?

Having dreamed the same dream,
Having found the water that gushed behind the thousand mirages,
Why would we hide from the sun again,
Or fear the night sky after we've reached the ends of darkness,
Live in death again after all the life our dead have given us?

Listen to me, Zawiya, Bayda, Ajdabiya, Tobruk, Nalut, Derna, Misrata, Benghazi, Zintan,
Listen to me, houses, alleys, courtyards and streets that throng my veins,
Someday soon, in your freed light, and in the shade of your proud trees,
Your excavated heroes will return to their thrones in your martyrs' squares.
Lovers will hold each other's hands.

I need not look far to imagine the nerves dying,
Rejecting the life that blood sends them.
I need not look deep into my past
To seek a thousand hopeless vistas
But now that I have tasted hope
I have fallen into the embrace of my own rugged innocence

How long were my ancient days?
I no longer care to count.
How high were the mountains and my oceans' fathoms?
I no longer care to measure
How bitter was the bread of bitterness?
I no longer care to recall

Now that we have tasted hope,
Now that we have lived on this hard earned crust,
We would sooner die than seek any other taste to life
Any other way of being human

Khaled Mattawa

To an extent, this yearbook breaks with the tradition of the *Global Civil Society* series. As the tenth edition it is more of a pause, a moment of reflection upon reflection. But our authors are not merely surveying the past and examining where we stand at the present; they are taking the experiences of the last decade to look forward: sometimes prescriptively, sometimes simply with an eye to what may pass.

Mary Kaldor, Helmut Anheier and Marlies Glasius open this edition with a discussion both of the momentous events of 2011, and of the lessons and insights that ten years of the *Global Civil Society* yearbook have provided. They discuss the potential of the protests of 2011 to create lasting political, economic and societal change, in the context of the mobilisations and social organisation of the recent past. And they ask whether, in the first year of this new decade, we are witnessing a new beginning – the start of a new political movement.

Taking up the invitation to understand the concept of global civil society as an 'island of meaning' that asks for constant reconceptualisation, with which the editors opened the very first edition of the yearbook series (Anheier et al. 2001: 3), Henrietta L. Moore and Sabine Selchow focus on the internet as one of the conceptual ingredients of the notions of 'globalisation' and 'global civil society'. In their Chapter 2, they suggest moving away from understanding the internet as a 'tool' or a 'space', as it is usually done, towards thinking of it as a 'process of becoming'; aiming to provide the ground for a reconfiguration of the conceptual architectures of the notions of 'globalisation' and 'global civil society' that leaves space for new questions to emerge.

In Chapter 3, Bernard Dreano opens the section on Democracy and Citizenship with a survey of the uprisings and the politics of the Arab Spring, documenting both what came before and what now may come. While rich in this factual accounting of actors, events, institutions and other forces at work in the region, his chapter also – along with many of the additional boxes throughout this yearbook that touch on the Arab Spring – helps us to make another conceptual shift: from one of Arab exceptionalism to one that revitalises the normative hopes of the first yearbook of 2001, and the promise of a universal politics from below.

In Chapter 4, Ferenc Miszlivetz takes us back even further in time to the heady hopes of Eastern Europe in 1989 and asks what has happened today to the promises of democracy. He suggests that democracy is dangerously divided, updating the traditional dichotomy of liberal democracy between freedom and equality into one presently existing between dignity and human rights and the good life and economic democracy, and argues that civil society needs to find ways of reuniting the two forces in order to pull through the crisis in which we now find ourselves.

Bolette Blaagaard, in Chapter 5, also takes some of the classic dichotomies of liberal democracy, specifically in the context of the media – those of freedom of speech and incitement, the public and the private, objectivity and subjectivity – and injects them with passion: the passion of global civil society, mediated over the past decade in the voices of citizen journalists, able through both technology and passion to challenge the status quo.

Mary Kaldor begins a section on Peace and Justice by moving from Blaagaard's voices of individuals to civil society at the level of global politics. In Chapter 6, Kaldor examines the past decade of the 'War on Terror' and the gradual implementation of the Responsibility to Protect (R2P), revisiting the chapter that she wrote for the first yearbook, on the prior decade of humanitarian intervention (Kaldor 2001). In reflecting upon the interventions of the past decade, and particularly those in Afghanistan, Iraq, Darfur and Libya, she analyses to what extent the humanitarian ideal has been tarnished – and how far, with the emergence of norms like R2P, it has actually advanced, despite many opinions to the contrary.

In Chapter 7, Angéla Kóczé and Márton Rövid, both scholars of and participants in pro-Roma civil society, question the norms and problems associated with the institutions of global civil society. In an in-depth examination of the development of pro-Roma context, they look at how the approaches of self-determination, of human rights and of social and economic inclusion have helped and hindered this development, and how both regional bodies (the European Union) and international ones (the United Nations) have reacted to a supranational movement of peoples.

Thomas Nash, former Coordinator of the Cluster Munition Coalition (CMC), brings a positive account of civil society practices to the yearbook. In Chapter 8 he traces the success of the coalition, from establishment and growth to the achievement of the 2008 Covenant on Cluster Munitions and beyond, and in doing so offers a primer for the establishment of a highly successful global NGO network.

In the section on Economy and Society, Robin Murray, unlike many other current analysts of economics, paints another positive picture: in Chapter 9 he discusses the many innovations that have emerged from global civil society over the past decade, presenting a thorough survey of the state of the civil economy as a precursor to *Global Civil Society 2013*, which will tackle the politics of transition from an oil-based economy to one of knowledge and sustainability.

In Chapter 10, Geoffrey Pleyers takes further an issue that has been discussed throughout the yearbook series: the World Social Forums (WSF). His insightful analysis of the first decade of the WSF reveals that, unlike the accepted theoretical expectations of social movements, these alter-global actors and their loose networks have resisted institutionalisation, and in fact deepened horizontal connections and participatory openness.

Following on from this analysis of a particular set of global civil society actors, institutions and events, Sally Stares, Sean Deel and Jill Timms widen the lens in Chapter 11, reviewing the exhaustive attempts to document the many facets of empirically-existing global civil society that have been undertaken by contributors to the Records section of the yearbook over the past decade. This chapter again concludes with a forward-looking section, introducing a new data-collection platform for the upcoming decade.

Finally, as both a snapshot of history and inspiration for the future, Jill Timms presents an abridged retrospective of global civil society events that we have documented, with the help of our global network of correspondents, over the past ten years.

Tamsin Murray-Leach

References

Anheier, Helmut, Glasius, Marlies and Kaldor, Mary (2001) *Global Civil Society 2001*. Oxford: Oxford University Press.

Kaldor, Mary (2001) 'A Decade of Humanitarian Intervention: The Role of Global Civil Society' in Helmut Anheier, Marlies Glasius and Mary Kaldor (eds), *Global Civil Society 2001*. Oxford: Oxford University Press.

PART I

Looking Back, Thinking Forward

CHAPTER 1

THE GLOBAL CIVIL SOCIETY YEARBOOK: LESSONS AND INSIGHTS 2001–2011

Helmut Anheier, Mary Kaldor and Marlies Glasius

We no longer have political movements. While thousands of us may come together for a rally or march, we are bound together on such occasions by a single shared interest. Any effort to convert such interests into collective goals is usually undermined by the fragmented individualism of our concerns. Laudable goals – fighting climate change, opposing war, advocating public healthcare or penalising bankers – are united by nothing more than the expression of emotion. In our political as in our economic lives, we have become consumers: choosing from a broad gamut of competing objectives, we find it hard to imagine ways or reasons to combine these into a coherent whole. We must do better than this. (Judt 2010: 134–5)

Tony Judt's book, *Ill Fares the Land* (2010), and a pamphlet by Stéphane Hessel entitled *Indignez-Vous!*, or 'Time for Outrage' (see Box 1.2) have been circulating among the European protestors of 2011. Both are passionate pleas for indignation against the overwhelmingly ideology of free markets and greed. Both are appeals to the young from older people close to their end – Judt knew he was dying when he wrote the book and Hessel, a hero of the French Resistance, is in his nineties. And both books are, perhaps not surprisingly, nostalgic, reinforcing Marx's argument that when people try to change their circumstances they dress up in the clothes of the past; both yearn for a time in the post-war period, when people believed in universal welfare and in the possibility of a benign state guiding a creative market – the Social Democratic vision.

These trenchant critiques of neoliberal policies cannot be faulted; they are just what is needed in this selfish and unequal era. But they tend to neglect some of the achievements of the of the post-1968 social movements. Contemporary society is far more conscious of environmental and human rights and the importance of gender equality, and far more inclusive in terms of race, language, religion or sexual orientation than in the 1950s and 1960s.

Not only in the West, but also in growing parts of Asia and Latin America, Africa and the Middle East, today's generation are the children of the internet, the mobile phone and cheap air travel – the 'globalisation generation'. They know that the world is a singular fragile eco-system – and that while the national state does have a role to play, it is part of a broader global community. And above all, as has become so movingly obvious in Tahrir Square, on the streets of Syrian towns or even in the Yemen, most believe in non-violence as a fundamental guiding principle (see Box 4.4). It is true, as Judt suggests, that up to now these new preoccupations have been fragmented; that we have lacked a political movement, that is to say, a movement that has the potential to change the way human affairs are managed. Thus the question that we pose in this yearbook is whether the protests of 2011, in both the Middle East and Europe, represent the seeds of a more coherent emancipatory agenda, one which combines the post-1968 issues with a more global demand for social justice. In other words, is this a new beginning – the start of a new political movement?

This *Global Civil Society* yearbook is the tenth edition of the series. It is an opportunity to look back over a decade of trying to explain, interpret, conceptualise, describe and measure the phenomenon we decided to call global civil society, to reflect critically on what we have learned as a result of the research that was undertaken to produce the yearbooks.

From the beginning we conceived global civil society as a 'fuzzy and contested concept' with both descriptive and normative content, and we envisaged the yearbook project as a journey into unknown territory where we would discover unconventional ideas and sources of information, and different ways of seeing the world. For operational purposes, we adopted an empirical definition of global civil society as 'the sphere of ideas, values, institutions, organisations, networks, and individuals located *between* the family, the state, and the market and operating *beyond* the confines of national societies, polities, and economies' (Anheier et al. 2001: 17). As the journey progressed, we became increasingly critical of the dominant associational notion of global civil society often equated with international NGOs. In the pages of the yearbook, we began to experiment with different, more normative versions of the concept; communicative power, for example, or the space where justice is deliberated, or a realm of civility and non-violence. We developed partnerships with a range of academic and civil society institutions in Africa, Asia and Latin America, and our contributors raised new critiques concerning the Eurocentric nature of the concept of global civil society, the hegemony of the global market, or the way that global civil society erodes procedural democracy at a national level. In particular, our collaboration with the University of Cairo raised questions about the Western narrative that underpins most concepts of civil society, jumping from Aristotle to John Locke and through to Hegel and Gramsci, and entirely bypassing the tradition of classical Islam.

In what follows, we start by describing what happened in 2011, relating it to various definitions or aspects of global civil society that we have elaborated in previous yearbooks. We then try to locate the events of 2011 in a broader historical context, based on a decade of analysing global civil society. In the final section we draw together the data collection effort of past yearbooks and what this shows for our analysis.

The Events of 2011

2011 has been a turbulent year both climatically and in social and political terms. It has been a year of popular uprisings – emancipatory and civil, as in the Arab Spring or the Indian anti-corruption movement, as well as reactionary and uncivil, as in the case of the American Tea Party movement and the English riots respectively. The balance between what is emancipatory and what is reactionary is often difficult to assess and varies from place to place, but it seems as though the new movements tend to be more emancipatory in the Arab and Asian world and more reactionary in Europe and America.

Our first yearbook was published a few days before the events of 9/11; in the ensuing decade, interest in global civil society has waned, even though new forms of activism, such as the Social Forums (see Chapter 10), were emerging. The protestors in different parts of the world tend to talk of themselves as 'the people' rather than as civil society; indeed, civil society is often viewed warily as the associational realm. Nevertheless, the events

of 2011 do give new meaning to the concept of global civil society.

Democracy and Communicative Power

In *Global Civil Society 2008*, Albrow and Glasius wrote that the 'multiple uses to which human communication can be put … have not fundamentally changed with the advent of global communications technology. But it may have eroded the force of monolithic messages from a single (state or religious) entity' (Albrow and Glasius 2007: 2). The subtitle of the same yearbook suggests that global civil society can be defined as 'communicative power' as opposed to the power of force or money.

A desperate act of self-immolation by a Tunisian street trader set in motion a series of events that rocked a region long considered by Western commentators as politically stagnant and incapable of democratisation, overdetermined by national and especially international obstacles to change. In particular, Western support for dictators in the region has been underpinned by orientalist assumptions about the incompatibility of Islamic societies with democracy and civil society. The protestors in Tunisia, Egypt, Syria, Yemen and elsewhere have disproved these theories. They have displayed extraordinary dignity and self-restraint. With the exception of Libya, the protestors have refused to be drawn into violence in spite of huge provocation. This determined stance in Syria, where at the time of writing, some 2,200 people have been killed, is truly inspirational. They have shown an exemplary degree of self-organisation, with people's committees springing up everywhere. They have refused to be framed as sectarian or Islamist; Muslims and Christians, Sunni and Shi'a, women in veils and women with their hair streaming behind them have stood together in Tahrir Square, Pearl Square and many other places. They have shown great ingenuity, creativity and humour, as Dreano shows in Chapter 3. 'Leave already' proclaimed a placard in Tahrir Square, 'My arm is beginning to hurt.'

Like the crowds in Prague or Berlin in 1989, the protestors are showing that they can be the agents of history. However these events unfold, an active civil society has begun a movement for democracy across the region. Even Israelis have been affected by this mood of expressing indignation and taking charge of destiny: tent cities have sprung up all over Israel, inspired by Tahrir Square. Although focused primarily on social demands, these tent city protests could have implications for the peace process as the demonstrators, who include both Jewish and Arab Israelis, make the point of contrasting the

July 2010
Wikileaks releases more than 92,000 confidential documents on the war in Afghanistan to newspapers *The Guardian*, *The New York Times* and *Der Spiegel*. Almost 400,000 documents concerning Iraq follow in October, with U.S. State department diplomatic cables published from November 2010, and files relating to Guantanamo Bay from April 2011.

23 January 2011, Belgium
On the 250th day of deadlocked negotiations between Flemish and Walloon parties, between 20,000 and 30,000 attend a rare pro-government protest organised by university students in Brussels, in support of national unity and against the ongoing state of uncertainty. At the time of going to press, Belgium is still without a government.

17 December 2010, Tunisia
A vegetable salesman sets himself on fire after the police seize his goods. His action sparks huge protests in Tunisia, and marks the start of the 'Arab Spring'. President Ben Ali flees the country on 14 January 2011.

15 March 2011, Syria
Though protests against the regime of President Bashar al-Assad have been mounting since January, today marks a Day of Rage across the country, and an escalation of violent clashes between police and protestors.

16–17 February 2011, Libya
Following a Day of Rage in Benghazi against the regime of Colonel Qadhafi, protests spread across the country. Qadhafi refuses to step down and the country plunges into civil war, with citizens taking over the running of all public services in the Benghazi area.

28 December 2010–11 January 2011, Egypt
Huge protests in Cairo and elsewhere against the regime of Husni Mubarak. After a series of crackdowns and the subsequent occupation of Tahrir Square, the president resigns.

9–16 January 2011, South Sudan
Monitored by domestic and international volunteer observers, the people of southern Sudan vote in a referendum for independence. The Republic of South Sudan is declared an independent state on 9 July 2011.

13 February 2011, Italy
Thousands of Italian women protest against the chauvinism of President Silvio Berlusconi, marching in more than 60 towns and cities across Italy, and as far away as Tokyo. In a referendum held on 14 June 2011, Italians vote against immunity for cabinet ministers, in a move seen as an attack on Burlusconi's future.

6–15 April 2010, Kyrgyzstan
President Bakiyev resigns after a week of popular uprisings against government corruption, alleged election-rigging and rising utility bills.

8 October 2010, China
Arrested and imprisoned in 2008 for authoring the Charter 08 manifesto, which demanded democratic reform and an end to the one-party system, Liu Xiaobo is awarded the 2010 Nobel Prize. This causes a diplomatic row, and immediate censorship of the announcement.

14 February 2011, Bahrain and Iran
Following the example of Egypt and Tunisia, protests bring unrest to the Gulf and, in the largest demonstrations since the disputed elections of 2009, to Tehran.

18 March 2011, Yemen
Government snipers kill 52 protesters in the bloodiest day of unrest witnessed in the country since protests against President Ali Abdullah Saleh began in January. Although resignations from the government follow, Saleh remains in power, despite being injured in a bomb attack on 3 June.

12 April 2011, Swaziland
Pro-democracy rallies are held in Africa's last absolute monarchy; unionists and journalists are beaten and arrested.

31 May 2010, Palestine
The Israeli Defense Force attacks the 'Gaza Freedom Flotilla', consisting of 6 boats carrying humanitarian aid from Turkey, before it reaches the Gaza strip. Nine activists die and several – both soldiers and activists – are wounded. The incident sparks a diplomatic row between Turkey and Israel, and leads to anti-Israel protests around the world.

Box 1.1
Tahrir Square: A Narrative on the Civility of Non-State Spheres

Tahrir Square is the heart of downtown Cairo. This vast square, whose corners hold representations of the different pillars of Egyptian civilisation, is now the icon of the 25 January 2011 revolution.

Located at one end of the square, the Egyptian Museum is the symbol of ancient Egypt. The Arab League headquarters stands as a mark of Arab identity and Arab nationalism; the location of the old Ministry of Foreign Affairs signifies the relationship between Egypt and the world; and the Omar Makram Mosque announces the call for prayer five times a day, as in any Muslim country. The huge *Mogama'a* bureaucratic building represents the modern state, and the old campus of the American University in Cairo reminds us of how modernisation efforts have focused on education, and how the West has played a conflicting and contested role in this process.

I live on Tahrir Square.

I was born in 1965. At the age of four I started walking down the road to reach my school, a German missionary school located in the Bab-el-Louk neighbourhood nearby, and have been part of that locale ever since. From the balcony of my parents' flat that overlooks the square, I have watched the masses crossing the street in tears to attend Nasser's funeral in 1970, the bread riots of 1977, the national security soldiers riots of 1986, and the massive demonstrations in 2003 on the day of the fall of Baghdad. I have been writing political columns since 1988, but 2003 marked my initiation into political demonstrations. I protested against the invasion of Iraq, and have stayed on the political street since that moment, joining demonstrations of all sorts of political groups and coalitions, all leading, eventually, to this revolution.

It was on the annual national day of the police, 25 January, that hundreds of thousands of Egyptians demonstrated across squares in Egypt, responding to a Facebook page entitled 'We are all Khaled Said'. The page was founded after the death of a young man in Alexandria, who was physically abused by police on the street, despite having no record of political engagement. The page got thousands of 'fans', becoming a very popular source for pacifist youth dissent. Choosing this particular day was a signal that people would no longer accept such police violations.

After taking over Tahrir Square, demonstrators prepared to stay overnight. Security forces responded by storming the square with tear gas, gun shots and sniping, which resulted in heavy casualties and some fatalities. Similar occurrences took place in other governorates. These demonstrations and confrontations continued almost round the clock until 28 January, the peak of the revolution, when, after massive demonstrations following Friday prayer, the police forces opened fire. Clashes escalated around police stations in many parts of the country, leading to the declaration of curfew and military tanks taking to the streets.

In Cairo, demonstrators responded by liberating the square, turning it into the eye of the revolutionary hurricane until Mubarak stepped down on 12 February. During that period Tahrir witnessed repeated violent attacks by thugs, especially on the famous 'black Wednesday', 2 February. All that time, the tanks of the army circulated the entrances of the square without interfering.

The square became a public space of a very unique nature. Under the threat that loomed over the heads of the tens of thousands of demonstrators, who remained in the square for long days and nights, a sense of solidarity emerged, with stories of Christian participants waking orthodox Muslims for early morning prayers, and Muslim brothers hosting Coptic Sunday ceremonies. National songs from the socialist Sixties were chanted all day, and not a single sexual harassment case was reported until 12 February. The paradox is that the absence of the state and of political competition, as well as hegemony in the revolutionary moment, allowed individual civility to flourish; this could be interpreted as the return of the nobility of human nature, as described by Rousseau.

After the fall of the president, the political engine started moving again, bringing to the square moments of confrontation between different political groups, as well as repeated clashes between demonstrators and military police. Yet the layers of meaning in the overlapping political, social and spiritual spheres that the days of the revolution witnessed have remained as a powerful legacy, inspiring the political imagination with new and renewed notions of agency, human nature and the power of the peaceful masses to change history.

Heba Raouf Ezzat is a Lecturer of Political Theory at Cairo University.

huge settlement programme in the Palestinian territories with inadequate social housing inside Israel.

The outcome of the protests has varied from country to country, depending on the role played both by state institutions and by outside powers. In Egypt and Tunisia it was the military and other state institutions that ensured the possibility of peaceful change: the shift of stance made by Western powers that had previously supported the dictators was also significant, especially in Egypt. Of course, in both countries the transition is difficult; in particular the role of the military is a huge obstacle to change, and shadowy forces appear to be fomenting divisions, for example, among Muslims and Christians. Nevertheless, a process has begun that can never be completely reversed. Where state institutions are weak and do not restrain violence, as in Syria, Libya or Yemen, the end result is likely to be not the survival of regimes but low-level pervasive violence, in which the sectarianism and Islamism that the regimes warn of could become a self-fulfilling prophecy. The Bahraini regime is the only one that appears to have successfully crushed the revolution – with support from Saudi Arabian and Western powers – although even there, protests are continuing. And the liberal monarchies and the Gulf states have been able to respond to more minor protests with some degree of reform.

These varied outcomes also illustrate the argument made in the chapter about illiberal regimes in *Global Civil Society 2008* (Kaldor and Kostovicova 2008). In an era of globalisation, where it is almost impossible to sustain closed societies, authoritarian states depend on consent. When that consent is withdrawn they cannot survive. They can, however, try to reproduce consent through the mobilisation of fear, and this leads not to stability but to anarchy, lawlessness and violence.

In analyses of the Arab Spring, there has been much attention to the extent to which the use of Facebook, Twitter and social media allowed immediate diffusion of information about mobilisation and repression. This was profoundly important. But equally important was the role of satellite television channels in Arabic, particularly al-Jazeera, which disseminated information picked up from social networking sites. These transnational Arabic channels have already contributed to an emerging pan-Arabic civil society and, by the same token, their role in the revolutions has enormously enhanced their status and popularity.

The internet may also, of course, be used for less benign purposes. Authoritarian states, for example,

use the internet to track down previously anonymous critics. A year before the Arab revolts, Google reversed its controversial decision to offer a censored version of its search engine in China, after a cyber attack which it believes was aimed at gathering information on Chinese human rights activists (Helft and Barboza 2010). On the side of society, too, of course, the technology itself has no politics, but enables all sorts of purposes, as evidenced by the use of text messages, Facebook and Twitter to facilitate looting in London in August 2011.

There has been much less attention to the *content* of what civil society has been diffusing, communicating and receiving, in the Arab region and beyond, than to the media by which they did so. If the Arab revolts can in part be understood as a cacophonous communications war, it would be important to understand not only the means of communication, but also, what is being communicated, and who is being heard. More particularly, comparisons may be drawn between the language and methods of the protests in Tunisia, Syria and especially Egypt, and those in Greece and Spain. In both Tahrir Square, Cairo and Syntagma Square, Athens, there has been an emphasis on human dignity which is constructed as requiring fulfilment of basic socio-economic needs, treatment with respect by authorities, and participation in determining one's fate (Droz-Vincent 2011: 5, Vote of the People 2011). On both sides of the Mediterranean, participants have reported that they believed themselves to be 'doing democracy' on the square itself.

The communications aspect of the Arab revolts could also be understood as part of a wider global civil society trend of simultaneously utilising and demanding transparency against secretive or corrupt organisations, not just in authoritarian settings and not just at the state level. Wikileaks is a prime example in this context: while it has existed and posted classified information since 2006, Wikileaks shot to fame in April 2010, when it showed a video of a 2007 US airstrike on Baghdad in which journalists were mistakenly fired at. In 2010 and 2011, it has continued to publish many thousands of classified documents, most notably US diplomatic cables (Chesterman 2011). Wikileaks' stated motivation for the releases, itself subject to much speculation and debate on the internet, is that

transparency creates a better society for all people. Better scrutiny leads to reduced corruption and stronger democracies in all society's institutions, including government, corporations and other organisations. A

22 April–12 June 2010, United States
An explosion at the BP drilling rig Deep Water Horizon on April 22 results in the largest offshore oil spill in US history. International outrage ensues: 39 civil society groups post a letter to the US Senate urging them to reconsider off-shore drilling and over 800,000 people join the Facebook group 'Boycott BP', which, along with other mobilizations, culminates in an international day of protest. Cleanup and litigation expected to take many years.

29 November–10 December, 2010, Mexico
A coalition of civil society organisations call for a 'democratic, transparent and participatory process at the UN climate talks' at the COP16 in Cancun, but the deals that come out of the talks are critiqued as rescuing UN credibility rather than the environment.

15 October 2010, Haiti
Residents and civil society groups protest against the renewal of the UN peacekeeping mission (MINUSTAH), established following the January earthquake. Protesters claim that it is akin to an occupation, with donated funds going to humanitarian workers rather than to real reconstruction.

19–22 April 2010, Bolivia
Around 30,000 people attend the World Peoples Conference on Climate Change in Cochabamba, which coincides with the worldwide celebration of 'Earth Day'.

25 April 2011, Germany
Following the March 11 tsunami in Japan and subsequent leaks at the Fukushima nuclear plant, large protests against nuclear energy sweep across Germany and France. As a result of popular pressure, Chancellor Merkel announces that Germany will be free of nuclear energy by 2022. Subsequently, Italians vote against the resumption of their country's nuclear power programme, in a referendum held on 14 June 2011.

4 October 2010, Hungary
Toxic mud is leaked from the Ajka alumina plant in the worst chemical spill in the country's history, leading to an outcry by environmental NGOs.

26 July–September 2010, Pakistan
Two months of abnormally heavy rains cause repeated flooding in the Indus basin. 2,000,000 people are affected – civil society rallies to organise help for the victims.

15 March 2011, East Africa
A regional food security alert from the Famine Early Warning Systems Network joins the rising clamour of voices from NGOs and UN agencies predicting famine in East Africa. Although 'the worst drought in 60 years' is blamed, with climate change fingered as the culprit, observers also point to rising food prices, continued regional conflict, systemic poverty and the failure of states to honour aid promises. The reluctance of the UN to define a critical situation as a famine is also criticised. At the time of going to press, the food crisis has affected more than 12 million people in Djibouti, Ethiopia, Kenya, Somalia and Southern Sudan, with famine officially declared by the UN in areas of Somalia in July.

healthy, vibrant and inquisitive journalistic media plays a vital role in achieving these goals. We are part of that media. (Wikileaks 2011)

In February 2011, Wikileaks' founder was arrested in the UK, and at the time of writing is appealing against a warrant for extradition to Sweden in relation to a sexual assault investigation. Whilst Wikileaks has since been the subject of internal dissension and accusations of secretiveness that mar its transparency mission, it has spawned other initiatives including Brussels Leaks, TradeLeaks, Balkan Leaks, Indoleaks, RuLeaks and Spanish PPLeaks and PSOELeaks.

Other recent arenas of struggle between secrecy and accountability have included the spate of scandals concerning the systematic cover-up of child sexual abuse in the Catholic church, the handling of bribe-taking charges by FIFA officials, and the phone-hacking by *News of the World* journalists facilitated by corrupt British police officers.

Risk, Complexity and Disaster

Another way in which a past edition of the yearbook has defined global civil society is as 'the medium through which the consciousness and perceptions of risk are shaped and new methods of protection are promoted' (Glasius et al. 2005: 1). This aspect of global civil society was clearly demonstrated in the rapid change of views on nuclear power after the radioactive leakage from the Fukushima plant caused by the Tohoku earthquake in Japan in March 2011. In Italy, the return to nuclear power was overwhelmingly rejected in a referendum, and in Germany and Switzerland nuclear power is being phased out (Faris 2011). There remains, of course, a debate about whether this could mean greater reliance on traditional energy sources as alternatives to nuclear power, which could have a detrimental effect on climate change. Nevertheless, what these path-breaking decisions showed was that, over the long-term, social movements like the anti-nuclear movement can bring about fundamental changes in attitudes, and ultimately, policy. What began as isolated protests in 1970s Western Europe has effectively toppled the technocratic-economic duopoly that the nuclear and petro industries once had on the world's energy policy.

The 2010 earthquake in Port-au-Prince, Haiti, raised a very different set of questions about how global disaster relief should be done when state capacity is severely lacking. The earthquake came almost exactly five years after the Asian tsunami, long enough for all humanitarian agencies to have done their evaluations and lessons to have been learnt. Billions were once again raised from compassionate publics. But the Haiti relief effort displayed all the same ironies: a rat-race for photogenic victims, inappropriate aid, lack of coordination and lack of information (let alone participation) for victims, distortion of the local economy, and a gap between emergency aid and long-term infrastructural projects (Van Hoving et al. 2010, Zanotti 2010, Bolton 2011). Unleashing a hotchpotch of international, bilateral and non-governmental agencies is the only disaster response mechanism the international community has at present, but it is hardly a recipe for success. Civil society as risk mediation is not always benign. A year after the earthquake, frustrated Haitians launched a series of violent protests directed at the United Nations (UN), and foreigners generally, following an outbreak of cholera thought to have originated with Nepali peacekeepers (Carroll 2010).

By contrast, the BP oil spill in the Gulf of Mexico highlighted the creative aspect of civil society in pioneering new methods of protection: the company took the unusual step of asking the public for advice on how to clean up the oil – and was then unable to cope with the 120,000 responses that poured in (Brown 2010).

Justice

In our last yearbook, Albrow and Seckinelgin, paraphrasing Nancy Fraser, defined global civil society as a 'dynamic of claims and counterclaims for justice that extends far beyond the discursive frame of the conventional nation state' (Albrow and Seckinelgin 2011: 1). This dynamic has been particularly pronounced in 2011, with virulent claims and counterclaims pertaining to international criminal justice as well as social justice.

- In May 2011, in his speech announcing the death of Osama bin Laden, President Obama referred to the operation to shoot him and throw his body into the sea as 'an operation to get Osama bin Laden and bring him to justice' ('Osama bin Laden Killed' 2011). In New York and Washington DC thousands took to the streets to celebrate this 'justice'. In other places, including Berlin, Cairo, Istanbul, Java, Kashmir, London and different cities of Pakistan, protest demonstrations were held ('Reaction to the Death of Osama' 2011).
- The Yugoslavia tribunal convicted former Croatian general Ante Gotovina to 24 years'

Box 1.2
Indignez-Vous!

Between October and December 2010, a slim pamphlet by a pensioner sold more than 600,000 copies; enough to propel it to the top of the bestseller list in France. Entitled *Indignez-Vous!*, or, in the English translation that followed, *Time for Outrage* (2011), it is a clarion call to those 'who will create the twenty-first century' (2011: 37) by a man who has lived through the twentieth.

Born in 1917, Stéphane Hessel is a former prisoner of war, member of the French Resistance and diplomat. He regards the first decade of the millennium with a similar eye to the authors of Chapter 1: in many ways a period of regression, due in part to the US reaction to 9/11, in which there has been a marked failure to respond to either the economic crisis or the environmental crisis.

Hessel talks of 'the principles and values' fought for by those in the Resistance, determined to achieve a democratic Free France – including social welfare, nationalised energy, a free press and the redistribution of wealth. Perhaps unsurprisingly, given his involvement in the drafting of the Universal Declaration of Human Rights (UDHR; 1948), he believes that the rights of 'justice and freedom' are universal; an unfashionable belief in some circles, but one now supported by the demise of Arab exceptionalism, one of the first false idols to fall in the Arab Spring (see Chapter 3).

And in decrying the greed of those in power and the mixed messages of neoliberal growth and austerity, Hessel echoes the cries of so many of those protesting over the past year: the students, the unions, the marginalised and the dictated:

> They have the nerve to tell us that the state can no longer cover the costs of these social programmes. Yet how can the money to continue and extend these achievements be lacking today, when the creation of wealth has grown so enormously since the Liberation, a time when Europe lay in ruins? It can only be because the power of money, which the Resistance fought so hard against, has never been as great and selfish and shameless as it is now, with its servants in the very highest circles of government ... The gap between rich and poor has never been so wide, competition and the circulation of capital never so encouraged. (2011: 22)

He identifies 'two great new challenges' (2011: 26) for defenders of his cherished principles and values: to stop the inequality gap growing ever larger; and to ensure that the norms of the UDHR become reality. In attempting to meet these challenges, he praises the traditional actors of civil society, and is positive about the growth of NGOs (see Figure 1.1).

But it is to each individual that he directs his call to action. He admits that the path is not always clear; that the world is interconnected, and that there is no single small elite to form an easy nemesis. But he believes that indifference is no answer, and asks the young to notice those 'concrete situations to provoke you to act as a real citizen' (2011: 29), including the topic of Chapter 7: 'the treatment of ... Roma people' (2011: 29). And although he is vehement in his believe that 'the future belongs to non-violence' (2011: 32), he sums up the mood of 2011 with the emotion that he claims was the driver of the Resistance: outrage.

> Take over, keep going, get angry! ... When something outrages you, as Nazism did me, that is when you become a militant, strong and engaged. You join the movement of history, and the great current of history continues to flow only thanks to each and every one of us. (2011: 22–3).

Tamsin Murray-Leach

Indignez-Vous! is published in the original French by Indigène editions, Montpellier (2010). Quotes here are taken from the English edition, *Time for Outrage* (2011) translated by Damion Searls and published by Charles Glass Books, an imprint of Quartet Books.

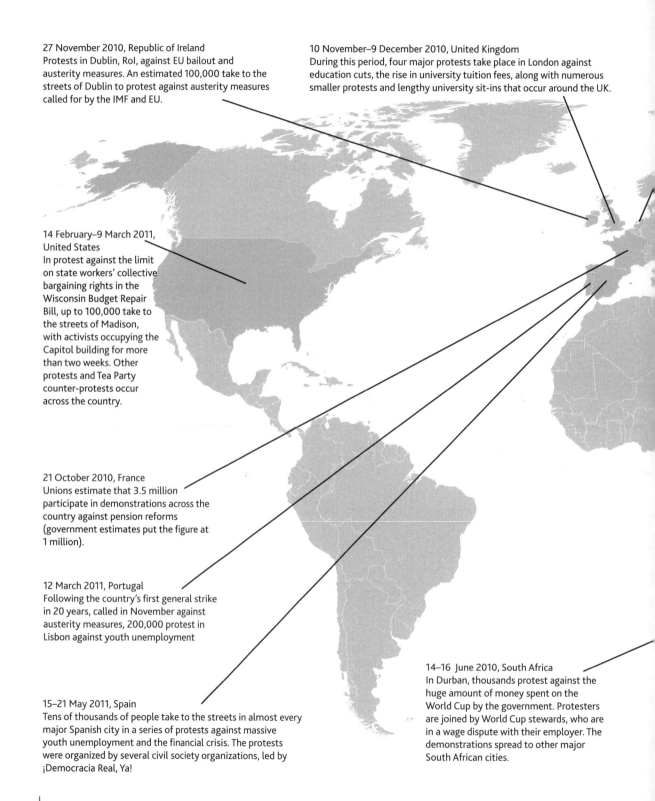

27 November 2010, Republic of Ireland
Protests in Dublin, RoI, against EU bailout and austerity measures. An estimated 100,000 take to the streets of Dublin to protest against austerity measures called for by the IMF and EU.

10 November–9 December 2010, United Kingdom
During this period, four major protests take place in London against education cuts, the rise in university tuition fees, along with numerous smaller protests and lengthy university sit-ins that occur around the UK.

14 February–9 March 2011, United States
In protest against the limit on state workers' collective bargaining rights in the Wisconsin Budget Repair Bill, up to 100,000 take to the streets of Madison, with activists occupying the Capitol building for more than two weeks. Other protests and Tea Party counter-protests occur across the country.

21 October 2010, France
Unions estimate that 3.5 million participate in demonstrations across the country against pension reforms (government estimates put the figure at 1 million).

12 March 2011, Portugal
Following the country's first general strike in 20 years, called in November against austerity measures, 200,000 protest in Lisbon against youth unemployment

14–16 June 2010, South Africa
In Durban, thousands protest against the huge amount of money spent on the World Cup by the government. Protesters are joined by World Cup stewards, who are in a wage dispute with their employer. The demonstrations spread to other major South African cities.

15–21 May 2011, Spain
Tens of thousands of people take to the streets in almost every major Spanish city in a series of protests against massive youth unemployment and the financial crisis. The protests were organized by several civil society organizations, led by ¡Democracia Real, Ya!

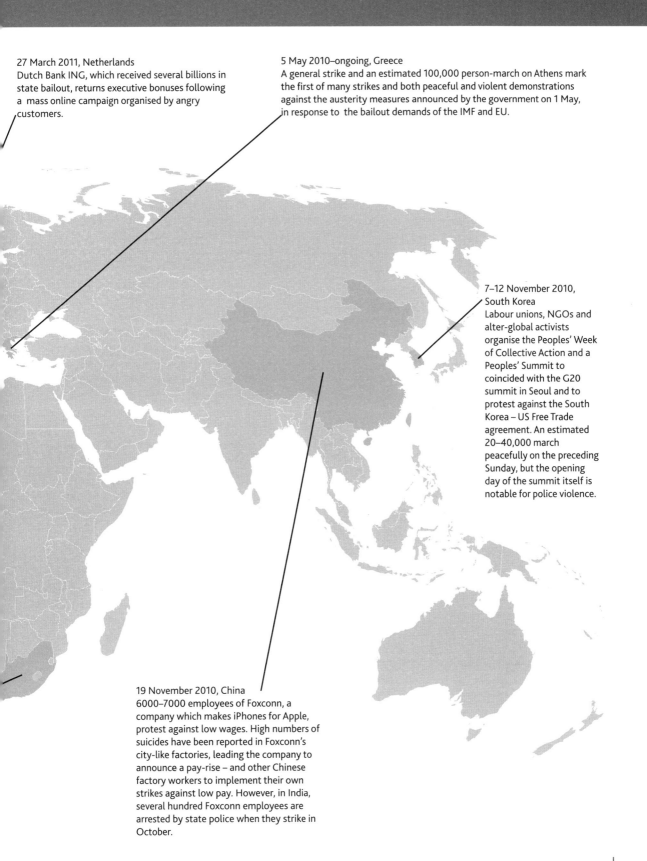

27 March 2011, Netherlands
Dutch Bank ING, which received several billions in state bailout, returns executive bonuses following a mass online campaign organised by angry customers.

5 May 2010–ongoing, Greece
A general strike and an estimated 100,000 person-march on Athens mark the first of many strikes and both peaceful and violent demonstrations against the austerity measures announced by the government on 1 May, in response to the bailout demands of the IMF and EU.

7–12 November 2010, South Korea
Labour unions, NGOs and alter-global activists organise the Peoples' Week of Collective Action and a Peoples' Summit to coincided with the G20 summit in Seoul and to protest against the South Korea – US Free Trade agreement. An estimated 20–40,000 march peacefully on the preceding Sunday, but the opening day of the summit itself is notable for police violence.

19 November 2010, China
6000–7000 employees of Foxconn, a company which makes iPhones for Apple, protest against low wages. High numbers of suicides have been reported in Foxconn's city-like factories, leading the company to announce a pay-rise – and other Chinese factory workers to implement their own strikes against low pay. However, in India, several hundred Foxconn employees are arrested by state police when they strike in October.

imprisonment for murder and war crimes, causing several thousand people to protest the verdict and war veterans to go on hunger strike in Zagreb ('Thousands of Croatians Protest' 2011). A month later, his Bosnian Serb counterpart Ratko Mladic was arrested in Serbia, causing thousands of people to protest in Belgrade ('Thousands Protest in Belgrade' 2011).

- The trial of former Egyptian president Hosni Mubarak, and more specifically the controversial decision by the judges to stop televising the proceedings, has led to clashes between Mubarak supporters and opponents (Kirkpatrick 2011). The trial contains elements of social justice as well as criminal justice, as Mubarak and his sons stand accused not only of responsibility for the death of demonstrators but also for corruption and illegal business deals (Shenker 2011).

- The protests that brought hundreds of thousands of people to the street in Spain, Greece, Portugal, Israel and Ireland are also about social justice: they protest against unemployment, wage cuts and other austerity measures, but beyond that also about having been lied to by politicians and being disproportionally targeted by austerity cuts while bankers were bailed out.

Civility

In the 2006/07 yearbook, Kaldor and Raouf Ezzat defined global civil society in terms of 'preemptive civility' (2006). Indeed, one of the most remarkable features of the Arab Spring, as well as the Greek, Spanish and Israeli protests, has been the combination of civil disobedience with an extraordinary level of civility. None of the protests succeeded in remaining completely free of violence, but all succeeded in projecting a mainstream message of non-violence. After violence against Copts in Egypt, even before the democracy protests took off, thousands of Muslims joined Christmas services to protect them (El-Rashidi 2011). In Greece, violence eventually marred the protests after a month of non-violent demonstrations, strikes and blockades by the Indignant Citizens Movement and others in Athens, Thessaloniki and other cities. The Syrian government has gone to great lengths to suggest that the opposition is plagued by sectarian violence, but the opposition debunked fake footage and organised spokespersons and coordinated slogans to emphasise its inclusive character (Syria Seminar 2011). In all these cases, the police and security forces have been using overwhelming force against the public.

The most spectacularly uncivil act of 2011 to date must have been the bombing of government buildings and shooting of 69 teenagers by Anders Behring Breivik in Norway. If we do take the word 'civil' in the definition of global civil society to have any import at all, then this act must lay outside its realm. At the same time, it must be acknowledged that the ideological formation of Breivik, like that of his al-Qaeda counterparts, belongs to 'the sphere of ideas, values, institutions, organisations, networks, and individuals located between the family, the state, and the market and operating beyond the confines of national societies, polities, and economies', our original operational definition of global civil society (Glasius et al. 2001: 17). But normatively, it was the antithesis of what Kaldor and Raouf Ezzat imagined and what the bulk of the 2011 street movements epitomised. It was a global, and in its targeting of youth arguably pre-emptive, strike against civility. Brievik seems to have had links with right-wing anti-immigrant parties in Western Europe like, for example, the English Defence League and the British National Party in the UK, the National Front in France, the Danish People's Party, and Gerd Wilders Party for Freedom in the Netherlands – some of which have been gaining electoral support in the past year (see Box 4.2).

Other ambiguous phenomena include the spectacular growth of the right-wing Tea Party in the United States and the English riots. The Tea Party has often been described as an 'astroturf' movement as opposed to a grassroots one, since funding and organisers have been provided by wealthy supporters like David Koch. Yet given the extent of its mobilisation, it has evidently touched some populist chord – in a weird combination of ideas including nostalgia for a 'pure' white America, conservative 'family values', a distorted conception of freedom that involves cutbacks in the role of the federal government (except for the military) and in taxation, as well as opposition to the wars in Iraq, Afghanistan and Libya and support for greater decentralisation. An innovative response to the Tea Party has been the glitterati, a gay movement that targets members of the Tea Party with glitter bombs.

The English riots are ambiguous in another sense. The looters were young; many were drawn from the excluded and marginalised unemployed, but their ranks also included some middle-class workers. They had no overt political message, except that the looting began as a reaction to police brutality, and that, as many commentators have pointed out, they saw themselves as part of a broader culture of looting or getting rich that began with the scandal of MPs' expenses and the various hacking scandals. They were uncivil in their destructiveness and lawlessness, but they have had a submerged emancipatory message.

Looking Back

The revolutions of 1989 could be viewed as the culmination of the post-1968 movements. In contrast, the revolutions of 2011 may represent a new beginning.

One way to interpret civil society is as the medium through which individuals participate in public affairs, through which they endorse or challenge the dominant discourse. It is a constantly shifting medium – sometimes characterised by consensus and sometimes by sharp polarisation and struggle, sometimes it changes slowly and sometimes, in revolutionary moments, dramatically. Its concrete manifestations – as coffee houses or market places in the eighteenth century, town hall meetings and party conferences in the twentieth century, or Facebook and tent cities most recently – vary according to time and place.

The cycle of social movements and how they interact with centres of political authority is at the core of understanding this changing medium. In the early stages, social movements experiment with new forms of organisation and new but often inchoate ideas. The spread of movements is a learning process through which narratives and organisational forms evolve. At the height of the cycle, movements either succeed in challenging the dominant discourse or they fail. Succeeding means that political authorities assimilate at least part of their agenda and they themselves are transformed into social institutions that reproduce the newly emerging discourse. If they fail, they disappear and/or sometimes turn to violence.

The end of the Second World War marked a revolutionary moment for the pre-war workers' movements. Social Democrat or Socialist parties came to power, at least in Europe, and professional trades unions became the negotiating partners of states and governments. Something similar happened later to the anti-colonial movements that transformed themselves into ruling parties in post-colonial states. The subsequent two or even three decades were a period of consolidation for the political agenda of state intervention planning and welfare articulated by workers' movements in the pre-war period.

The challenge to the state that started in the late 1960s came from both left and right. The right challenged the state's role in the economy and pressed for a neoliberal programme of markets and deregulation. The so-called new social movements that had their beginnings in the revolutions of 1968 were more concerned with those emancipatory issues that had been excluded from the compact with labour. Actually, at the beginning, their demands were clothed in rather traditional Marxist terms. It was only as the movements developed during the 1970s and 1980s that coherent narratives began to develop around the coming together of peace and human rights, multiculturalism, gender and the environment. What these movements had in common was a new kind of horizontal form of organisation and a commitment to a radicalisation of democracy. They were not anti-state; they wanted to change the relationship between state and civil society.

In our yearbooks, we demonstrated that the 1990s were a period of consolidation for the post-1968 movements. This was a time when a new post-1968 generation came to power and when the end of the Cold War fatally weakened the dominant ideologies of socialism and post-colonialism. It can be argued that the 1989 revolutions opened the space for the new narratives of the post-1968 movements, and indeed the very idea of global civil society – a kind of radical democratisation – could be said to be the big idea of the 1989 revolutions. In the aftermath of 1989, many of the actors in the new social movements transformed themselves into NGOs. If workers' movements had turned into national institutions, then the new movements consolidated themselves within a more global environment. Our records showed a dramatic increase in the number of international NGOs during this period (see Figure 1.1). Furthermore, much of the agenda of the post-1968 movements was formally adopted. Our yearbooks described how global civil society had contributed to a new global consensus on human rights (Glasius 2007), leading to the new norm of humanitarian intervention (Kaldor 2001), the establishment of the International Criminal Court (Glasius 2002), or to new treaties like the Land Mines Treaty (see also Chapter 8 this volume). Likewise, the emerging importance of climate change (Newell 2006), or of dealing with AIDS/HIV (Seckinelgin 2002), can be treated as global civil society achievements.

At the same time, of course, this was also a time of triumph for the neoliberal ideas of the right. Both the global market and global NGOs were agents in the intensifying process of interconnectedness. The new humanitarian discourse effectively was displacing an earlier discourse about social justice and was interpreted

Box 1.3
Global-Local-Glocal Consciousness in Hungary

Hungary at first glance may not seem like a beacon of global consciousness or community awareness. Many Hungarian NGOs do not address or involve large segments of the population; nor, on first examination, do the so-called 'globally conscious' movements. However, a different perspective emerges if Hungary is examined from its grassroots and localised projects and organisations. The diversity in Hungarian global, 'glocal' and alter-global movements, particularly in those led by youth, shows evidence of citizens engaged in modern and innovative social networks used to develop knowledge and awareness of issues impacting local, national and international society.

The process of resurrecting civil society in Hungary began in the 1990s, after decades of communism throughout Central and Eastern Europe. New NGOs became a symbol of regenerating social connective tissues among the people and in the short period between 1990 and 1993 the number of NGOs grew from a few hundred to over 30,000 (HCSO 2011). Large economic and political changes left a gap in certain state functions which NGOs filled, giving them both legitimacy and status. However, despite this complementary role, NGOs have remained somehow suspect in the eyes of those in power – perhaps a leftover sentiment from the communist era, when they were considered a potential threat by politicians and prevented from becoming independent from the state. Although access into the European Union has diversified funding options, to the chagrin of NGO members most organisations remain largely dependent on state finances.

Meanwhile, the introduction of neoliberal economic policies after the transition, seen as the deliberalisation of markets and the introduction of neoliberal economic policies, has led to discontent for many over a market that seems to favour big business, foreign investors and banks (Gowan 1995, Robertson 2004, Ost 2009). In Hungary, as in other countries around the world, the negative effects of globalisation have largely affected local producers and those living in marginalised situations. This has led to the rise in alter-global consciousness in Hungary. Arguably, it is a combination of this growth in desire for alternatives to globalisation along with the state restrictions on larger, traditional NGOs that has led to a new sphere of localised projects with an alter-global stance, as evidenced in the emergence of 'global' NGOs, advocacy organisations and apolitical democracy projects. Here we define 'glocal' as local representations of globally recognised intentions.

Local civil society building is at the root of many of the current 'glocal' projects in Hungary. The Foundation for Democratic Youth (Demokratikus Ifjúságért Alapítvány), founded in cooperation with Youth Service International, aims to teach democratic awareness and enhance community commitment through volunteer projects. Similarly, the Foundation for Active

Citizenship works to improve democratic participation and knowledge of citizens. Világfa Szövetség (Alliance of the World Tree) is another glocal organisation. This network of intellectuals design decision-making processes for individual Hungarian towns in order to realise genuine democratic participation within their communities. The 'Soproni Kékfrankos' (Blue Frank of Sopron) project has created a local town currency with the aim of strengthening local economies in order to decrease exposure to the global financial processes and machinations of neoliberalism. With the success in Sopron, other towns and communities have also begun to plan the introduction of local currencies.

In recent years Hungary has also developed a strong network of 'cultural creatives' who refuse to adopt mainstream consumerist lifestyles and instead utilise globally and environmentally conscious decision-making. Organisations by this set of cultural creatives set out to develop globally conscious societies and values by raising consumer awareness and changing patterns of consumption. Hangya (www.hangyaszov.hu) and Szatyor (www.szatyor.org), for example, help to connect local producers of organic foods directly to customers. Organisations working to create more immersive globally conscious lifestyles include the network of Ecovillages (www.ecovalley.hu) and the urban youth movement Reclaim the Fields, a part of a broader European network of deindustrialisation, which encourages people to move back to the countryside. The Ecovillage networks create and reshape villages with the aim of making them 100 per cent sustainable. These communities use renewable energy sources, harvest their own food sources and recycle their waste to develop a self-supplying lifestyle. Along these lines, NGO Szövet (www.elotiszaert.hu) works to preserve natural resources and values with several projects that are helping local producers to ensure unified trademarks and preserve environmental ethics.

Alter-global consciousness in Hungary has furthermore directed attention towards injustice and inequality within the national political sphere. Anti-political and radicalised movements aiming to force awareness and change upon society have amassed large support networks. Targeting the recent controversial 2010 Media Law, the social movement One Million for the Freedom of Press in Hungary (nicknamed Milla) drew attention to the law's potential infringement on the freedom of the press, and more generally freedom of speech, as counter to fundamental human rights. Milla used online social forums as a tool to spread information about demonstrations and rallies, acquiring over 85,000 members on Facebook. On 15 March 2011 tens of thousands joined publicly to defend the free press in Hungary (Egymillióan a magyar sajtószabadságért 2011).

Other anti-political globally conscious groups have chosen humour to draw attention to what they consider political absurdity in society. The Hungarian Garlic Front (Magyar Fokhagymafront) was founded in early 2011 by a group of young Hungarians consciously using the prototype of a similar satirical anti-fascist group abroad, the German Apple Front. Dressed in all black, carrying their flag and beating drums, the group stages realistic looking but humorous events – mocking the recent rise in radical-right paramilitary groups in Hungary or calling attention to political policies and decisions they find problematic. Rallies calling for the pension age to be risen to 100 and demanding 'death to all vampires' have made news in several national journals and television exposés.

In Hungary, as elsewhere, globally conscious and glocal movements can also be seen developing within the roots of radical-right culture, particularly within the party Movement for a Better Hungary (Jobbik), and in its related organisations. Founded in 2003, the young radical party has focused much attention on the negative social outcomes of globalisation, calling for the need to protect landscapes, save rural areas and develop small communities and villages, and arguing for a new Eco-Social National Economy:

> Economic growth produced an enormous amount of profit but the beneficiaries have been a thin layer of multi-million-aires, as opposed to the rest of humanity that both physically and spiritually have been broken by the system that created growing inequalities among people and bred conditions that pushed people to the edge of global revolt. (Jobbik 2011)

Even the controversial grassroots paramilitary organisation associated with Jobbik, the Hungarian Guard (Magyar Gárda), has been active in helping local communities. Known mainly for their links to racism, violence and authoritarianism, the Guards have also set up local food donations for the poor, secured houses during floods and helped to evacuate people during the 2010 toxic waste spills.

The Sixty-Four Counties Youth Movement (HVIM), an irredentist youth group which helps to organise radical-right events and forums, has also followed these global-glocal trends. Closely linked with Jobbik, their work includes the creation of summer camps and social clubs to develop spaces for the Hungarian youth. Their largest event, the Hungarian Island Festival (Magyar Sziget; www.Magyarsziget.hu), started in 2001 as a Hungarian music and culture festival that includes nationalist concerts, conferences, crafts and cavalry. Although seemingly xenophobic and insulated, the structure of the organisation and its event are surprisingly 'glocal', inviting nationalist organisations and political activists from other countries to come to their forums in order to discuss ways in which a nation can preserve its cultural identity and values.

Ecological preservation, local economic innovation, volunteer groups, human rights defenders, anti-fascist satire, cultural protection and radicalised eco-social policies are just a few examples of how global consciousness has manifested itself in Hungary. Recent research shows that up to 35 per cent of Hungarians can be considered 'cultural creatives' (Székely et al. 2011). Lost in larger statistics of political disillusionment, Euroscepticism and youth apathy, one often forgets to look at the grassroots level to evaluate the diverse developments of a nation. Hungary has a growing spectrum of alter-global projects with a particularly active youth base ensuring the continuation and spreading of community awareness and greater global consciousness on a local and national level.

Erin Saltman is a PhD candidate at University College London researching youth political socialisation in Hungary, and is an affiliate of Corvinus University, Hungary.

Hajnalka Szarvas is an international relations expert, and has worked at Eötvös Loránd University, the Hungarian Academy of Sciences and the Society for Organisational Learning, Hungary.

by some as a form of co-option – a way for the neoliberals to salve their consciences about inequality.

In successive yearbooks, we developed a framework for analysing positions on globalisation. These positions comprised: supporters (those who considered all forms of globalisation – economic, political, cultural – as positive), rejectionists (those who opposed all forms of globalisation), regressives (those who favoured globalisation as long it benefited their group) and reformers (those who favoured globalisation as long as it benefited the majority). It can be argued that the period of the 1990s was a period dominated by supporters and reformers; those who favoured the global market as well as the spread of multilateral arrangements and humanitarian norms.

It was only towards the end of the 1990s that a new anti-capitalist movement emerged. The protests at the G20 meeting in Seattle in 1999 represented the first dents in the so-called Washington consensus. The events of 9/11 and the proclamation of the 'War on Terror' represented a profound setback to the humanitarian agenda and a resumption of notions of sovereignty and unilateralism. Subsequently, in contrast to the 1990s, the first decade of the new millennium was one of political and social polarisation, in which movements, especially the Social Forums, mobilised both against the 'War on Terror' and against the dominance of the global market. In terms of the positions on globalisation, it could be said that the early 2000s were dominated by regressives and rejectionists (neoliberals, global warriors and jihadists, and those who favour a return to the nation state and sovereignty).

The mobilisations of 2011 appear typical of the early stages of a social movement; the involvement of a new generation, experimentation with forms of organisation, new and sometimes inchoate ideas, and, above all, excitement. In terms of composition, Droz-Vincent (2011: 12) writes of the crowds in Egypt and Tunisia that many were drawn from 'a large cohort under thirty that has borne the brunt of exclusion from the labour market, social life, and that has been devoid of any political voice', but the same characterisation applies also to the movements in Europe, for instance in Spain, where youth unemployment stands at 46 per cent (Eurostat Newsrelease 2011). At the same time, the crowds also included women, professionals and even families, reflecting a long-term trend of participation in street demonstrations becoming more respectable in all walks of life (Van Aalst and Walgrave 2001).

The use of NICTs (new information and communication technologies) by the 2011 movements, for quick mobilisation on the one hand and dissemination of news to the wider world on the other, may have been unprecedented in scale, but rests on antecedents built up over the decade. The anti-corporate globalisation movement has used the internet to report on summit protests since the WTO meeting in Seattle in 1999 (Juris 2005); mobile phones generated mobilisations in the Philippines, Spain and South Korea in the middle of the decade (Castells et al. 2005); the Kefaya movement in Egypt used a combination of mobile phones and the internet to disseminate evidence of state brutality; and the Iranian Green Movement explored the use of Twitter, Facebook and YouTube. Both the worldwide demonstrations against the war in Iraq in 2003 and the World Social Forums were important vehicles of dissemination of ideas about horizontality, and about how to combine ideological pluralism with an anti-neoliberal stance (Glasius 2005) as well as opportunities to learn about the political uses of communications innovations.

Another much remarked-upon feature of the 2011 mobilisations is their 'leaderlessness' and lack of visible rooting in the sustained interaction familiar to social movement scholars. The movements have sprung up outside political parties and (with the exception of Tunisia) large external organised civil society organisations such as NGOs and trade unions. These elements too have antecedents in the last decade, ranging from the '"submerged networks" which come to the fore only around certain campaigns or exercise resistance through a particular lifestyle' described by Desai and Said (2001: 69) in the context of the anti-capitalist movement to the 'non-movement' of Iranian women that pre-dated the Green Movement (Bayat 2007). The lack of visible leadership partly has a protective element: the survival of the Syrian opposition movement to date, for instance, may in part be attributed to its anonymity. But it is also presented as a value in itself, akin to the emphatic rejection of leadership by the Social Forums (Glasius and Timms 2005: 224; Chapter 10, this volume) and is particularly striking against the background of the traditional patriarchal political cultures on both sides of the Mediterranean.

Because the movements attempt to transcend left-right distinctions (in Europe) and secular-Islamist distinctions (in the Arab world) they get portrayed as post-political (Tambakaki 2011) or non-ideological. But this may just be because the language used is not recognisable in terms of either traditional left-wing, Islamist or even liberal ideologies. To dismiss the Greek demands of 'equality, justice and dignity' or the Egyptian cry for 'bread, freedom, dignity, humanity' as non-ideological would be the same as calling the French Revolution's 'equality, freedom, brotherhood' non-ideological. Yet admittedly these aims are very broad. The movements of 2011 appear to be committed to 'thick' democracy as a method, but they have not to date articulated clear substantive aims; for instance in relation to regulation of the global economy, social justice or sustainable development.

Empirical Portraits of Global Civil Society

A core objective of the yearbook has been the development of an empirical base of what constitutes global civil society. Beginning in 2001, we tracked the infrastructure of global civil society, events, the prevalence of cosmopolitan values, and various other facets. Looking back over the last decade, we observe five major changes:

1. The rise in the number of international non-governmental organisations (INGOs) continues but has slowed down

As Figure 1.1 shows, in 2010 the Union of International Associations (UIA) database listed nearly 56,000 INGOs, compared to just over 22,200 in 1990. When we started work on the first volume of the yearbook, in 2000, the number of INGOs had more than doubled within a decade after 1989, adding over 23,000. After 2000, the numbers kept rising but in smaller increments. Whereas in the 1990s, UIA reported typically an additional 1,500–2,000 INGOs per year, that number dropped to 1,000–1,500 in the subsequent decade.

In other words, growth in the number of INGOs as documented by UIA shows a stable, consolidated growth pattern. It is difficult to fathom if we are dealing with first signs of a saturation effect or if some other factors are at play. What seems likely, however, is that the factors which propelled the significant growth of INGOs in the 1990s have lost some of their momentum: political opportunities in a broadened political space, institutional weakness of the state and transnational regimes, and easier and less costly communication.

Indeed, we argued in previous yearbooks that the 1990s brought a political opening and a broad-based mobilisation of unknown proportion and scale (see also 'The Ideas of 1989' in Kaldor 2003: 50–77), which coincided with the reappraisal of the role of the state in most developed countries, and growing disillusionment with state-led multilateralism in the developing world among counter-elites (Edwards 1999). In addition, favourable economic conditions, the vastly reduced costs of communication and greater ease of organising facilitated the institutional expansion of global civil society in organisational terms (Anheier and Themodo 2002). Much of this has changed or levelled off in terms of its impact on INGO growth.

The slower growth in INGOs comes with only marginal changes in the way INGOs are distributed around the world. Figure 1.2 shows that five countries account for four out of ten INGOs, although Belgium, France and the UK have experienced slight decreases in recent years. In terms of countries gaining INGOs, China and South Africa stand out, but not in any major way. For example, while there are more INGOs in China in 2010 (152) than ten years ago (104), these numbers pale in comparison to the US (2000: 7,625; 2010: 8,395) and other INGO centres like France or the United Kingdom. Overall, the pattern is one of stability, rather than of major shifts in INGO presence.

This stability is also seen in Table 1.1, which relates changes in the number of organisational memberships countries have in INGOs to changes in the density of INGOs per 1 million population between 1998 and 2008 (the most recent available year). Whereas the first figure indicates the extent to which a particular country is part of the INGO global infrastructure, the second reveals its intensity relative to population size. The results show that the great majority of countries (138) experienced a positive change in both extensity and intensity of INGO presence, and that about one-third (76) saw increases in extensity but not intensity. The latter combination refers to many African and Middle Eastern countries that have more INGO memberships, but not relative to their fast-growing populations. The reverse combination applies to Zimbabwe only, with a fewer number of INGOs serving a population that has shrunk even more, hence the density increase. Finally, in only 13 countries, among them war-torn nations like Liberia and the Democratic Republic of Congo, but mostly small island states, have both the presence and the density of INGOs declined.

Table 1.1 Changes in INGO Memberships and Density per 1 Million Population, 1998–2008, by Number of Countries

	Density Increase	Density Decrease
Membership Increase	138	76
Membership Decrease	1	13

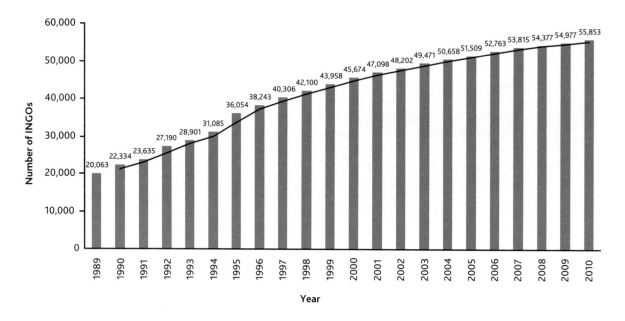

Note: The trend line joining the bars highlights the general increase in numbers of INGOs, smoothing over minor fluctuations in counts year to year.
Source: Union of International Associations (2010: based on their Figure 2.9) *Yearbook of International Organizations 2010/2011. Statistics, Visualizations and Patterns*. München: De Gruyter Saur.

Figure 1.1   Total Number of INGOs Counted between 1989 and 2010

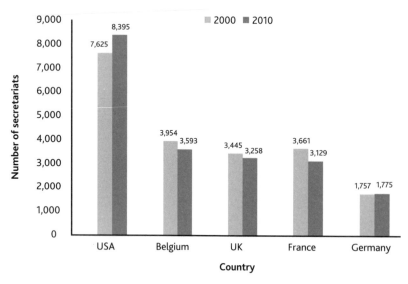

Note: Secretariats include Headquarters as well as other offices.
Sources: Union of International Associations (2001, 2010) *Yearbooks of International Organizations 2000/2001 and 2010/2011. Statistics, Visualizations and Patterns*. München: De Gruyter Saur.

Figure 1.2   International Secretariats 2000–10

2. New form developments

The second major finding concerns form developments, and in two ways: form changes in the NGO infrastructure itself, and new forms of organising outside the NGO universe. Looking at NGOs first, the trend towards NGO form changes that we first observed in 2002 has continued. NGOs that are neither conventional membership organisations nor corporate NGOs increased from 7 per cent in 1981 to 15 per cent in 2001 and further to 18 per cent in 2011. This category includes a very broad spectrum: from foundations to information networks and from diaspora organisations to hybrids such as 'informal quasi-organisations'. The data lend some support to the growing role of hybrids in civil society arenas. Dot.causes are one part of the emerging non-NGO civil society infrastructure. The use of Tweets and other phone-based messaging is another form of mobilisation, for example in the case of the Iranian election in 2009 (Figure 1.3). Indeed the Web and handheld mobile devices have facilitated a new activism, which Van Laer and Van Aelst (2009: 233) see as internet-based and internet-supported forms that vary by the threshold involved.

Some forms require little effort, others significant dedication and investments on behalf of activists. The first dimension is about the role of the internet, and differentiates between internet-supported ('facilitating function') and internet-based roles (exist only because of the internet). The second dimension is about the scale of the threshold involved in becoming

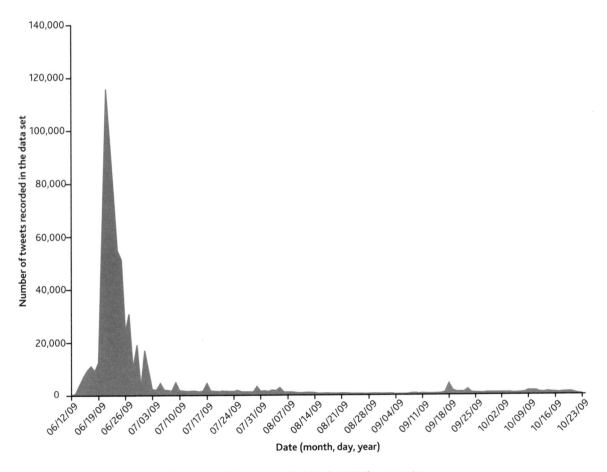

Source: Gaffney, D (2010) *#IranElection: Quantifying the Role of Social Media in 140 Characters or Less.* Senior Thesis, Bennington College, Bennington, VT.

Figure 1.3   Twitter During the Iranian Election of 2009: Tweet Volume Per Day

active which gives us a typology of four different combinations (Van Laer and Van Aelst 2009: 236–42):[1]

- Internet-supported activism with low threshold: donation of money, legal demonstration.
- Internet-supported action with high thresholds: transnational demonstrations and meetings, and obstructive action forms such as sit-ins or blockades. Here the idea is that the internet lowers the practical barriers by changing the organisation and especially the coordination of events.
- Internet-based action with low thresholds: an 'Email bomb' which comprises large amounts of emails sent to one account. A typical example of a receiver would be a minister or corporate CEO, although a system may be the target, with the aim of shutting down the mailing server. A less aggressive option would be an online petition.
- Internet-based action with high thresholds, such as 'alternative media sites'. The first independent media centre (IMC), Indymedia, was set up in the wake of the Seattle WTO protests in 1999. 'Culture jammers' are exemplified by the Nike Email Exchange Campaign: an MIT student requested that the personalisation on his customisable Nike iD shoes read 'sweatshop'. The company's refusal and the subsequent email exchange then generated unexpected media attention and thousands of reactions worldwide.

3. The rise in cosmopolitan values has levelled off

The growth and expansion of global civil society as a phenomenon in the 1990s seemed closely associated with a major shift in cultural and social values that took hold in most developed market economies in the 1970s. This shift saw a change in emphasis from material security to concerns about democracy, participation and meaning, and involved, among others, a formation towards cosmopolitan values such as tolerance and respect for human rights (see Inglehart 1990). These values facilitated the cross-national spread of social movements around common issues that escaped conventional party politics, particularly in Europe and Latin America, and led to a broad-based mobilisation in social movements, with the women's, peace, democracy and environmental movements the best examples of an increasingly international 'movement industry' (Diani and McAdam 2003, McAdam et al. 2001).

Table 1.2 Tolerance and Respect for Others, 1981–2008

Country	1981	1990	2000	2008
Argentina	44	78	70	72
Belgium	45	67	84	82
Canada	53	80	82	83
Denmark	58	81	87	87
France	59	78	84	87
Germany	42	76	73	75
Hungary	31	62	65	71
Iceland	58	93	84	86
Ireland	56	76	75	74
Italy	43	67	75	71
Japan	41	60	71	75
Mexico	39	64	72	79
Netherlands	57	87	90	85
Norway	32	64	66	90
South Africa	53	59	74	78
South Korea	25	55	65	57
Spain	44	73	82	81
Sweden	71	91	93	91
Great Britain	62	80	83	79
United States	52	72	80	79
Average	48	73	78	79

Source: World Values Survey (2011) http://www.worldvaluessurvey.org/.

However, this, we remind ourselves, was the diagnosis in the 1990s. What has happened since then? Data are available across the four waves (1981, 1990, 2000 and 2008) of the World and European Value Surveys. While we saw that 'tolerance and respect for others' became a more frequently cited core value between 1980 and 1990, levels reached then are comparable to what we observe nearly a decade later. With very few exceptions the real increase took place in the 1980s – namely from 48 per cent to 75 per cent, with a levelling off in the 2000s at fairly high levels.

4. The changing pattern of events

Values represent one way of capturing the empirical content of global civil society that goes beyond counting NGOs. Another way to discover what is happening is through an effort to describe and measure the changing pattern of events. This approach highlights the dynamic nature of global civil society. In past yearbooks, we have published an annual chronology of global civil society events and have also included data on the prevalence and make-up of parallel summits. In this yearbook we survey what has been learned from this data collection effort (see Chapter 11). We include a retrospective ten-year chronology (see p. 204) which suggests a gradual rise in popular mobilisation over the last decade, mainly focused on opposition to neoliberalism. In Box 11.2 on parallel summits, Mario Pianta shows that global events (parallel summits and conferences) peaked in 2005. The new manifestations are much more local and national, even though more extensive. And, looking forward, we consider how digital technology can be used to develop a more ambitious database of events.

5. New positioning and innovations

We argued in 2003 that global civil society is likely to enter a new phase of restructuring in coming to terms with a changed and uncertain geopolitical situation. This process would involve both different outcomes for major policy positions and actors, and innovations like Social Forums, new kinds of alliances and coalitions, and increased use internet-based forms of communicating and organising. Indeed, we pointed to the striking contrast between the 1990s and the 2000s.

The 1990s represented a period of consolidation, the construction of which appears to be a sturdy infrastructure of civil society, represented by the rapid growth of INGOs, and a growing emphasis on what we have described as the public management and corporatisation approaches to global civil society. At the beginning of the twenty-first century, by contrast, we witnessed a renewed mobilisation of people and movements and a renewed emphasis on self-organisation and activism. This has indeed been the case, especially in the extent to which new forms of communication and organising were facilitated by new technologies that did not exist just a few years ago.

What is more, in the 1990s, the predominant political force behind globalisation was a coalition between supporters and reformers, in transnational corporations as well as in governments and intergovernmental organisations, and in global civil society. To us, the Davos World Economic Forum represented an annual expression of this coalition. It was the combination of supporters and reformers that pressed for the globalisation of the rule of law and of technology, as well as the economy, although there was disagreement on the globalisation of people. This combination, mainly associated with the corporate and the new public management manifestation of global civil society, discussed above, came to be seen by many as depoliticising and co-opting global civil society. However, it also contributed to the growth and solidification of its infrastructure.

For the decade that has just begun, we foresee continuing political turbulence – a period not of consolidation but of experimentation and mobilisation, in which civility and uncivility, emancipation and reaction struggle to shape the discourse of the next phase of human development.

Conclusion

How this struggle plays out depends to a large extent to whether the newly emerging emancipatory social movements can transform themselves into a political movement. Can they develop a political agenda capable of constructing new sources of political authority with the capacity to address the big issues of our time?

The workers' movements and the anti-colonial movements of the early twentieth century provided the political basis for the strengthening of the state in the late twentieth century. The post-'68 movements had a far-reaching cultural impact and also contributed to democratisation, as well as to the consolidation of

Table 1.3 Developments of Global Civil Society

Decade	Infrastructure growth	Composition/Fields	Form innovation	Value changes	Participation
1970s	Medium growth	Economic, research and science	Humanitarian membership-based INGOs	Rise of post-materialism	Slow increase, largely in West
1980s	Acceleration of growth	Value-based	INGOs linked to International Social Movement	Cosmopolitan values	Higher increase, West and Central and Eastern Europe
1990s	High growth	Value-based; service-provision	Corporate and public management NGOs	Consolidation	Slower increase
2000s	Moderation of growth	Anti-capitalism; opposition to war	Social Forums; dot. causes	Resilience	Slower increase
2010s	Moderate growth	Democracy, social justice	Web-based activism; Tweets	Repoliticisation	Higher increase, more global

Box 1.4
Wutbürger in Wonderland?

German civil society is on the move. A type of citizen that has existed for many years is, all of a sudden, receiving attention: the *wutbürger* ('angry citizen'). They first publicly appeared when the city-state of Hamburg was about to introduce a far-reaching school reform; the protest of *wutbürgers* (www.wir-wollen-lernen.de) led to a referendum, and the reform was cancelled. They then showed up in Bavaria, where they urged the government to strengthen the existing law to protect non-smokers (www.nichtraucherschutz-bayern.de). Again, a referendum was held, leading to very strict non-smoking legislation. The *wutbürgers'* most important appearance, however, was in Stuttgart, the capital of Baden-Württemberg (www.kopfbahnhof-21.de). It was during the protest against the plan to expand the city's railway network and move the central station underground – or 'Stuttgart 21', as the project is known – that the term '*wutbürger*' was coined. It has since made its way into German dictionaries, and the German Language Society named it the word of the year in 2010.

The issue of Stuttgart 21 is still up for debate. The political impact of the protests, however, has already been huge. After more than 50 years in office, the governing Christian Democrats, along with their coalition partner, the Free Democrats, had to give way to a new government after the state elections in early 2011. Since then, the Greens and the Social Democrats have governed Baden-Württemberg, led by the first ever Green prime minister of a German state.

This is not to say that *wutbürgers* necessarily vote for leftist parties. The cases mentioned above illustrate that not only do they care about political decisions, but they also believe that expressing discontent can make a concrete difference. When protesting against certain issues, they might occasionally take sides with political parties, but they do not build coalitions. There is no *wutbürger* ideology other than a certain belief in the liberal state order and the political rights that such an order provides. This is why the movements were joined by greens, conservatives and social democrats alike.

What is newsworthy about the *wutbürgers* is not the fact that they protest, but their attitude towards protesting. Contrary to other activists, many wutbürgers do not pursue any overarching goal or mission. They feel rather that pointing at shortcomings in policy making is part of their civic duty. Accordingly, *wutbürgers* acknowledge that the government's scope is limited, and try to offer feasible alternatives along with their criticism.

This notwithstanding, the crucial question remains: when – and how – did their activism turn into a phenomenon? One possible explanation goes as follows: the increasing number of protests and the intensity of the arguments led to huge media coverage, with '*wutbürger*' merely a term coined by the media. However, there have been intense and well-covered protests before, such as those in the long-lasting debate on the civil use of nuclear energy. This topic, however, has been closely connected to certain political camps right from the start, even leading to the birth of a new party, the Greens. The new *wutbürger* movements, on the contrary, attract a broad range of citizens who are not necessarily involved with traditional party politics.

Political leaders acknowledging these efforts have begun to offer ways for citizens to provide input on certain topics. Citizens now have the chance to state their arguments eye-to-eye with politicians, in sessions broadcast on national television. *Wutbürgers* in Wonderland? Not really. As far as the railway project is concerned, the anti-Stuttgart 21 coalition has partly eroded, with some of the activists returning to the streets after their televised mediation, while others accepted the settlement.

The next big issue, the debate on nuclear energy, brought another setback for the *wutbürgers*. This topic has been on the public agenda for decades and has led to huge political clashes again and again. Nevertheless, it was finally decided without hearing the *wutbürgers*, in the traditional way: politicians and business leaders agreed on a strategy to end the use of nuclear power. And the commission which publicly negotiated the question consisted of well-known experts, not citizens.

So did public protests influence political decision-making? In the case of Stuttgart 21 it certainly did. The decision on nuclear energy, however, is a mixed picture, showing both the potential and the limitations of grassroots activism. The question of whether the style of political discourse in Germany is sustainably changed remains open. There is still much left to do on the *wutbürgers'* agenda …

Andrea Römmele is Professor for Communication in Politics and Civil Society at the Hertie School of Governance and an advisor to political parties and NGOs.

Henrik Schober is the editorial manager of the *Journal for Political Consulting and Policy Advice* and co-founder of an initiative to foster civil society in eastern Germany.

humanitarian, human rights and peacekeeping institutions at an international level.

The protests of 2011 have the potential to re-instil public morality and to help build institutions at regional and global levels that can tackle such issues as global inequality and or environmental necessity, although at present they seem largely focused on national and local levels. Already there are some largely unnoticed but significant innovations at a non-national institutional level. The German and French leaders agreed in August 2011, for example, on a European tax on financial transactions – something long demanded by Social Forum activists. The International Monetary Fund has uncharacteristically reacted to the Arab Spring and the European sovereign debt crisis with political concerns about how to sustain social cohesion.

In other words, there is what sociologists call a political opportunity structure (Kriesi 1995). The next decade will be a dramatic learning process for the new global generation. Can they articulate a shared political agenda that has the potential to save their successors from the dire consequences of deprivation, climate change and war? In future yearbooks, we plan to track the answers to this question: how twenty-first century social organisation and mobilisation evolves, and how this evolution influences the dominant discourse.

Note

1. Collom (2003) found empirical evidence that people engaging in unconventional political activity with higher intensity (for example, demonstrations) were likely to have already participated in low-intensity forms of actions, like signing petitions, and thereby put the logic of an 'activism hierarchy' to the test.

References

Anheier, Helmut, Glasius, Marlies and Kaldor, Mary (2001) 'Introducing Global Civil Society', in Helmut Anheier, Marlies Glasius and Mary Kaldor (eds), *Global Civil Society 2001*. Oxford: Oxford University Press, pp. 3–22.

Anheier, Helmut K. and Themudo, Nuno (2002) 'Organisational Forms of Global Civil Society: Implications of Going Global', in Marlies Glasius, Helmut Anheier and Mary Kaldor (eds), *Global Civil Society 2002*. Oxford: Oxford University Press.

Albrow, Martin and Glasius, Marlies (2007) 'Democracy and the Possibility of a Global Public Sphere', in Martin Albrow et al. (eds), *Global Civil Society 2007/8*. London: Sage Publications.

Albrow, Martin and Seckinelgin, Hakan (2011) 'Globality and the Absence of Justice', in Martin Albrow and Hakan Seckinelgin (eds), *Global Civil Society 2011*. Basingstoke: Palgrave Macmillan.

Bayat, Asef (2007) 'A Women's Non-Movement: What it Means to Be a Woman Activist in an Islamic State', *Comparative Studies of South Asia, Africa and the Middle East*, Vol. 27 No. 1: 160–72.

Bolton, Matthew B. (2011) *Human Security After State Collapse: Global Governance in Post-Earthquake Haiti*. LSE Global Governance Research Papers, RP 01/2011. London: London School of Economics and Political Science.

Brown, David (2010) 'As Cleanup Suggestions Pour in, BP Pays Little Heed', *Washington Post*, 3 July.

Carroll, Rory (2010) 'Protesters in Haiti attack UN Peacekeepers in Cholera Backlash', *Guardian*, 16 November.

Castells, Manuel, Fernandez-Ardevol, Mireia, Linuchan Qiu, Jack and Sey, Araba (2005). 'Électronic Communication and Socio-Political Mobilisation: A New Form of Civil Society', in Marlies Glasius, Mary Kaldor and Helmut Anheier (eds), *Global Civil Society 2005/6*. London: Sage Publications, pp. 266–85.

Chesterman, Simon (2011) 'Wikileaks and the Future of Diplomacy', 14 June, available at SSRN: http://ssrn.com/abstract=1864661.

Collom, Ed. (2003) 'Protest Engagement in America: The Influence of Perceptions, Networks, Availability, and Politics'. Paper presented at the American Sociological Association, Chicago.

Desai, Meghnad and Said, Yahia (2001) 'The New Anti-Capitalist Movement: Money and Global Civil Society', in Helmut Anheier, Marlies Glasius and Mary Kaldor (eds), *Global Civil Society 2001*. Oxford: Oxford University Press, pp. 51–78.

Diani, M. and McAdam, D. (eds) (2003) *Social Movements and Networks: Relational Approaches to Collective Action*. Oxford: Oxford University Press.

Douzinas, Costas (2011) 'In Greece, We See Democracy in Action', *Guardian*, 15 June.

Droz-Vincent, Philippe (2011) 'Authoritarianism, Revolutions, Armies and Arab Regime Transitions', *International Spectator*, Vol. 46 No. 2: 5–21.

El-Rashidi, Yasmine (2011) 'Egypt's Muslims Attend Coptic Christmas Mass, Serving as "Human Shields"', *Al Ahram*, 7 January.

Edwards, M. (1999) 'Legitimacy and Values in NGOs and Voluntary Organisations: Some Sceptical Thoughts', in D. J. Lewis (ed.), *International Perspectives on Voluntary Action: Reshaping the Third Sector*. London: Earthscan.

Egymillióan a magyar sajtószabadságért (2011), Facebook Page, http://www.facebook.com/sajtoszabadsagert.

Eurostat Newsrelease (2011) 'Euro Area Unemployment Rate at 9.9%', 1 August.

EVS (2010). European Values Study 2008, 4th wave, Integrated Dataset. GESIS Data Archive, Cologne, Germany, ZA4800 Data File Version 2.0.0 (2010-11-30).

Faris, Stephan (2011). 'Italy Says No to Nuclear Power – and to Berlusconi', *Time* Magazine, 14 June.

Gaffney, D. (2010). 'Iran Election: Quantifying the Role of Social Media in 140 Characters or Less'. Senior thesis, Bennington College, Bennington, VT.

Glasius, Marlies (2001) 'Expertise in the Cause of Justice: Global Civil Society Influence on the Statute for an International Criminal Court', in Marlies Glasius, Mary Kaldor and Helmut Anheier (eds), *Global Civil Society 2002*. Oxford: Oxford University Press.

Glasius, Marlies (2007) 'Pipe Dream or Panacea? Global Civil Society and Economic and Social Rights', in Mary Kaldor, Martin Albrow, Helmut Anheier and Marlies Glasius (eds), *Global Civil Society 2006/7*. London: Sage Publications.

Glasius, Marlies, Kaldor, Mary and Anheier, Helmut (2005) 'Introduction', in Marlies Glasius, Mary Kaldor and Helmut Anheier (eds), *Global Civil Society 2005/6*. London: Sage Publications, pp. 1–34.

Glasius, Marlies and Timms, Jill (2005) 'Social Forums: Radical Beacon or Strategic Infrastructure', in Marlies Glasius, Mary Kaldor and Helmut Anheier (eds), *Global Civil Society 2005/6*. London: Sage, 191–238.

Gowan, Peter (1995) 'Neo-liberal Theory and Practice for Eastern Europe', *New Left Review*.

Helft, Miguel and Barboza, David (2010). 'Google Shuts China Site in Dispute over Censorship', *New York Times*, 22 March.

Hessel, Stéphane (2011) *Time for Outrage*. London: Quartet Books.

Heydemann, Steven and Leenders, Reinoud (2011) 'Authoritarian Learning and Authoritarian Resilience: Regime Responses to the "Arab Awakening"', forthcoming, *Globalizations*, Vol. 8 No. 5.

Hungarian Central Statistics Office (HCSO) (2011) http://portal.ksh.hu/portal/page?_pageid=38,119919&_dad=portal&_schema=PORTAL.

Inglehart, R. (1990). *Cultural Shift in Advanced Industrial Society*. Princeton, NJ: Princeton University Press.

Jobbik (2011) 'Eco-Social National Economics', Jobbik.com, http://jobbik.com/en_pol_economics.html.

Judt, Tony (2010) *Ill Fares the Land*. London: Penguin.

Juris, Jeffrey S. (2005) 'The New Digital Media and Activist Networking within Anti-Corporate Globalization Movements', *Annals of the American Academy for Political and Social Science*, No. 597, January: 189–208.

Kaldor, Mary (2001) 'A Decade of Humanitarian Intervention: The Role of Global Civil Society', in Helmut Anheier, Marlies Glasius and Mary Kaldor (eds), *Global Civil Society 2001*. Oxford: Oxford University Press.

Kaldor, Mary (2003) *Global Civil Society: An Answer to War*. Cambridge: Polity Press.

Kaldor, Mary and Raouf Ezzat, Heba '"Not Even a Tree": Delegitimising Violence and the Prospects for Pre-emptive Civility', in Mary Kaldor, Martin Albrow, Helmut Anheier and Marlies Glasius (eds), *Global Civil Society 2006/7*. London: Sage Publications, pp. 18–41.

Kaldor, Mary and Kostovicova, Denisa (2008) 'Global Civil Society and Illiberal Regimes', in Martin Albrow et al. (eds), *Global Civil Society 2007/8*. London: Sage Publications.

Kirkpatrick, David (2011) 'Judge Orders Televising of Mubarak Trial to End', *New York Times*, 15 August.

Kriesi, Hanspeter (1995) 'The Political Opportunity Structure of New Social Movements: Its Impact on Their Mobilization', in J. Craig Jenkins and Bert Klandermans (eds), *The Politics of Social Protest*. Minneapolis: University of Minnesota Press.

McAdam, D., Tarrow, S. and Tilly, C. (2001) *Dynamics of Contention*. New York: Cambridge University Press.

Newell, Peter (2006) 'Climate for Change? Civil Society and the Politics of Global Warming', in Marlies Glasius, Mary Kaldor and Helmut Anheier (eds), *Global Civil Society 2005/6*. London: Sage Publications.

'Osama bin Laden Killed: Barack Obama's Speech in Full' (2011), *Telegraph*, 2 May.

Ost, David (2009) 'The Politics of Tripartite Cooperation in New Democracies', *International Political Science Review*, Vol. 30, March, 141–62.

'Reaction to the Death of Osama bin Laden' (2011), *The Economist*, 7 May.

Robertson, M. M. (2004) 'The Neoliberalization of Ecosystem Services', *Geoforum*, Vol. 35 No. 3, May: 361–73.

Seckinelgin, Hakan (2002) 'Time to Stop and Think: HIV/AIDS, Global Civil Society and People's Politics', in Marlies Glasius, Mary Kaldor and Helmut Anheier (eds), *Global Civil Society 2002*. Oxford: Oxford University Press.

Shenker, Jack (2011), 'Mubarak Trial: Toppled Dictator Denies All Charges', *Guardian*, 3 August.

'Syria Seminar' (2011), Knowledge Programme Civil Society in West Asia, Amsterdam, 5 July.

Székely, Polgár and Takács (2011) 'Values and Culture of Sustainable Consumption', *Sustainable Consumption 2011*, Budapest, January.

Tambakaki, Paulina (2011), 'Greek Protest in Syntagma Square: In Between Post-politics and Real Democracy', openDemocracy, 28 June, available at http://www.opendemocracy.net/paulina-tambakaki/greek-protest-in-syntagma-square-in-between-post-politics-and-real-democracy.

'Thousands of Croatians Protest Against Gotovina Verdict' (2011), *Balkan Insight*, 16 April.

'Thousands Protest in Belgrade Against Mladic Arrest' (2011), *Balkan Insight*, 29 May.

Union of International Associations (2001) in *Yearbook of International Organisations 2000/2001. Statistics, Visualisations and Patterns*. München: De Gruyter Saur.

Union of International Associations (2009) in *Yearbook of International Organisations 2009/2010. Statistics, Visualisations and Patterns*. München: De Gruyter Saur.

Union of International Associations (2010) in *Yearbook of International Organisations 2010/2011. Statistics, Visualisations and Patterns*. München: De Gruyter Saur.

Van Aelst, Peter and Walgrave, Stefaan (2001) 'Who is that (Wo)Man in the Street? From the Normalisation of Protest to the Normalisation of the Protester', *European Journal of Political Research*, Vol. 39 No. 4: 461–86.

Van Aelst, P. and Van Laer, J. (2009) 'Cyber-Protest and Civil Society: The Internet and Action Repertoires of Social Movements', in Y. Jewkes and M. Yar (eds), *Handbook on Internet Crime*. Willan Publishing.

Van Hoving et al. (2010) 'Haiti Disaster Tourism – A Medical Shame', *Prehospital and Disaster Medicine*, Vol. 25 No. 3: 201–2.

Vote of the People's Assembly of Syntagma Square (2011), Athens, 27 May, available at http://en.wikipedia.org/wiki/File:Vote_of_the_People%27s_Assembly_of_Syntagma_Square.svg.

Wikileaks (2011) http://www.wikileaks.org/About.html.

Zanotti, Laura (2010). 'Cacophonies of Aid, Failed State Building and NGOs in Haiti: Setting the Stage for Disaster, Envisioning the Future', *Third World Quarterly*, Vol. 31 No. 5: 755–71.

CHAPTER 2

'GLOBAL CIVIL SOCIETY' AND THE INTERNET 2012: TIME TO UPDATE OUR PERSPECTIVE

Henrietta L. Moore and Sabine Selchow

Interwoven Concepts

To date, there are around 2 billion people using the internet (see Chapter 5 this volume, Figure 5.1). The 750 million active users of the social network site Facebook share more than 30 billion pieces of content each month (Facebook Statistics 2011). Each minute more than 48 hours of video are uploaded to YouTube (YouTube Blog 2011) and 3,000 new pictures are shared on Flickr, which in September 2010 had a stock of 5 billion images (Flickr Blog 2010). Each day around 200 million 140-character-messages are sent via Twitter; this is the equivalent of a 10-million-page book per day, or 8,163 copies of Leo Tolstoy's *War and Peace* (Twitter Blog 2011). Perhaps even more astonishing is the speed with which this volume of tweets has been growing, from 2 million per day in January 2009 to 65 million in June 2010, and 200 million only a year later (Twitter Blog 2011). Social media services, such as Twitter, have not only become an integral part of people's daily lives, but these days also guide military strategies, such as the NATO strikes in Libya (Norton-Taylor and Hopkins 2011), and play a considerable role in contemporary mass activism (see Chapter 3 this volume). As an Egyptian activist explained during the 2011 protests in Cairo's Tahrir Square: '[W]e use Facebook to schedule the protests, Twitter to coordinate, and YouTube to tell the world' (UNOG 2011).

Given its apparent and growing relevance in people's lives in general, and in political activism in particular, it is not surprising that the internet is of increasing interest in the analysis of contemporary politics. It is promoted as a potential solution for a number of (democracy-related) problems that scholars detect within the contemporary global context; and academic and public debates about supposed 'Facebook revolutions' and 'Twitter revolutions' revive and sharpen with each new civil society upheaval (see Box 2.1). However, the internet is more than an increasingly popular point of reference in empirical studies of contemporary politics and civil society; it is also

– although this is rarely problematised – a fundamental *conceptual ingredient* in the constitution of one of the dominant frames through which many scholars and practitioners make sense of the contemporary world in general and politics in particular. This dominant frame is 'globalisation'.

When the notion of 'globalisation' came to prominence in public and academic discourses at the beginning of the 1990s, it was at the centre of rich and interdisciplinary debates. Yet, over time, it became 'tamed' by mainstream political analysts in the sense that it became naturalised as a 'material-structural' thing that transforms our world (see Bisley 2007). Today, it is widely treated as something akin to a 'second nature'. Foundational to the mainstream understanding of this second nature is the notion of an unprecedented degree of worldwide interconnectedness between people and socio-economic systems. It is this increasing interconnectedness that is usually seen as *the* new and determining development of our times and justifies the invention of a neologism – the term 'globalisation'. And new information and communication technologies (NICT) – with the internet as one of the most prominent – are understood as a central driving factor in this development. Consequently, there is rarely any commentary on 'globalisation' that does *not* mention the internet in one way or other.[1]

Putting this differently, the idea of the internet is *inscribed* in the concept of globalisation. This is the case no matter whether scholars who operate with, and through, the frame of 'globalisation' are aware of this conceptual knot or not, and no matter if the internet actually plays an *explicit* role in their various empirical investigations; the idea of the internet is there, conceptually weaved in. Consequently, to some extent, the held understanding of the internet plays into the construction of the conceptual frame of 'globalisation', which then, in turn, not only reinforces the held idea of the internet but also, of course, shapes the view of the world more broadly, with all the material consequences that worldviews entail.

Box 2.1
The Internet Debate: Freedom or Delusion?

It is not unusual for scholars to disagree with one another. While the disagreements between Clay Shirky and Evgeny Morozov have played out in standard academic arenas such as book reviews and magazine articles, much of their ongoing debate takes place on Twitter, blogs, and in the online comments boards of articles written by other authors. This use of the internet for debate, and especially in social media, is fitting given that the academic disagreements between Shirky and Morozov revolve around the use of the internet and online tools by protestors.

Shirky, author of *Here Comes Everybody: The Power of Organizing Without Organizations* (2008) and *Cognitive Surplus: Creativity and Generosity in a Connected Age* (2010a) has been involved with online media for many years, from overseeing the internet strategies for advertising campaigns to providing advice to the US government on computer technologies. A Professor of New Media at Hunter College and Partner at The Accelerator Group, he was recently described by Morozov as 'the man most responsible for the intellectual confusion over the political role of the internet', due to his depiction of the internet as a tool for positive social change, particularly within authoritarian societies (Morozov 2009). In contrast, Morozov, who is the author of *The Net Delusion: The Dark Side of Internet Freedom* (2011) is sceptical of the internet's role, pointing to the ways in which authoritarian regimes use the internet to increase their power. Born in Belarus, Morozov worked as the Director of New Media at Transitions Online, a media development NGO that works in former Soviet countries, before moving to the United States and academia; he is currently a Visiting Scholar at Stanford.

Although their arguments vary depending upon the context in which they are published, Morozov and Shirky's discussion on the 2009 protests in Iran encapsulates the broader views of each author that are present throughout many of their debates. However, when stepping back from the specifics, it can seem as though they are arguing for argument's sake and not truly engaging with the arguments of the other.

Digital Activism and Iran

Shirky takes the 2009 protests in Iran as reinforcement of his view that social media improves the way in which people can communicate with and rally others. He believes that 'it also represents a new dynamic within political protest, which will alter the struggle between insurrectionists and the state, even if the state wins in any given clash' (Shirky 2010b). As such, he contends that while social media did not trigger the protests, it did play an important role in shaping the events. Even though the Iranian regime eventually cut off activists from social media, Shirky argues that by this time the spread of information and level of coordination was at a level which no longer required those tools, and that in the end, 'the net value of social media has shifted the balance of power in the direction of Iran's citizens' (Shirky 2010b).

Taking issue with Shirky's optimistic view of the events in Iran, Morozov contends that instead of the protests leading to a more democratic state, the regime became even more authoritarian. As evidence for his broader view that like protestors, authoritarian regimes can also use the internet to promote their interests, Morozov points to the fact that the Iranian revolutionary guards used the internet as a way for pro-Ahmadinejad Iranians to help them identify the protestors (Morozov 2009).

Argument for Argument's Sake?

As demonstrated by their debate on Iran, Morozov's focus is on the cause and effects of protests, while Shirky emphasises the process of protest, not the outcome. As in many of their other disputes, the two scholars seem to be advancing their own point of view but not engaging with the specific arguments of the other. Additionally, despite his negative view on the internet as a tool for democracy promotion, Morozov contends that 'even a sceptic like me can see the upside' of projects that use the internet to promote democracy, although he argues that the 'digital democracy push' must be improved (Morozov 2009). Based on this statement, it seems as though fundamentally, Morozov and Shirky agree that the internet can be used as a tool for the advancement of democracy. So is it time for a new debate, or are these scholars just trying to demonstrate to the world how the internet can be used as a forum for discussion?

Magda Fried is currently completing her MSc in Global Politics and Global Civil Society at the London School of Economics, where her research focuses on the democratic nature of digital activism.

If we acknowledge the above, a further step can follow, which brings us to the core of this present publication: as a foundational conceptual ingredient of the 'globalisation'-frame, the idea of the internet is also automatically inscribed in the concept of *global civil society*. This suggestion becomes evident if we think about the rationale that gave birth to the concept of global civil society. The idea of global civil society emerged out of the understanding that civil society is now situated within a 'global' world, that is, a world shaped by globalisation. 'What is new about the concept of civil society since 1989 is globalization', explains Mary Kaldor (2003: 1) and – through the application of the attribute 'global' – she and others write globalisation (including the idea of the internet as one of its foundational conceptual ingredients) into this 'new' conception of 'civil society' (see further Selchow 2010).

With these theoretical considerations in mind, this chapter addresses mainstream political analysts and aims to put forward an understanding of the internet that is an alternative to the one that they commonly hold. Two conceptual steps are central to this endeavour. First, instead of conceptualising the internet as a virtual space and/or tool for activism, or indeed as a 'new type of territory' (McEvoy Manjikian 2010: 383), we follow theorists of digital culture (for example, Manovich 2001, Miller 2011) in reconceptualising the internet as a *'process of becoming'*. In other words, we understand the internet as a set of resources, engagements and structures through which the world is constantly renewed; it is not a material object or a single entity but a set of interactions and processes. Second, instead of thinking of the internet as a thing separate from the 'real' world, in other words, instead of working with the notion of a 'great divide' between the offline and the online (real/virtual, material/symbolic), we suggest acknowledging that the internet today 'has become enmeshed within the enduring structures of our society' (Miller 2011: 1).

The value of our chapter is a conceptual one. Our aim is not to provide 'better answers' to the questions that are usually asked by political analysts about global politics, global civil society and the internet. Rather, we aim to provide theoretical ground on which we can start re-imagining the concepts of global politics and global civil society in order to find a position alternative to the mainstream one, which will help us to delineate new questions to be asked. In general, given the enmeshed and mutually imbricated nature of existing concepts, any change in the coordinates that constitute a conceptual frame inevitably affects its shape, and hence opens the possibility of alternative perspectives. In particular, to understand the internet as a process of becoming inevitably forces us to engage with notions such as flux, imagination, and creativity, which are usually not dealt with nor deployed in mainstream understandings of, and approaches to, global civil society.

The Contemporary Internet as a Process of Becoming

In 2004, Democratic contender Howard Dean stunned observers and political opponents in the US presidential race by using the internet to mobilise supporters and to raise money for his campaign in what was, at the time, a hitherto unimaginably effective way. Although the $53 million Dean raised was considerably less than, for instance, George W. Bush's $367 million (Federal Electoral Commission 2011), it was perceived as remarkable and 'revolutionary' that, in a political environment such as the US, in which money plays a crucial role, an 'internet insurgent' (Anderson 2004) could shake up the scene and could start '[c]hanging the formula: from the power of money to the money of the powerless' (Castells 2009: 379) by relying heavily on small donations. Yet, not even four years later, in 2008, Dean's celebrated e-insurgency appeared wholly outdated as electioneering in the US was rocked by another so-called e-revolution in US politics. Barack Obama's presidential campaign, with its novel and systematic use of Web 2.0 services,[2] was able not only to raise 60–90 per cent (Castells 2009: 381) of its record $779 million (Federal Electoral Commission 2011) via the internet, it was also able to mobilise the grassroots in the US and capture a global audience to an unprecedented degree. Some evidence of this was the extent to, and enthusiasm with, which supporters independently produced and distributed online material in support of Obama; the most prominent example was the award-winning YouTube video 'Yes, We Can' (2008), which was produced by will.i.am and quickly established Obama's 'Yes, We Can' slogan as a catchphrase with global resonance. All this led commentators to see Obama's campaign, and his eventual victory, as nothing less than the birth of a new kind of presidency, 'the first wired, connected, networked presidency' (Joe Tippi, quoted in Miller 2008). But today, less than four years later, Obama's highly celebrated 2008 Web 2.0 campaign is already outmoded, appearing like 'something out of the era of America Online and 56k modems' (Herb 2011). In the 2012 campaign, we are told that location-based services will be 'the killer app' (Wassermann 2011); microblogging tools, such as Obama's Townhall @ The White House (2011) held on 6 July 2011, are becoming normality, and campaign supporters' spirits are bolstered by the option of earning virtual badges, as seen on Republican candidate Tim Pawlenty's online platform PawlentyAction (2011). As Obama's campaign manager, Jim Messina, promises those joining the Obama campaign: '[F]orget everything you know about politics. I can tell you that the next year and a half will be like nothing you've seen from a campaign' (Messina 2011). In other words, there seems to be yet another 'e-revolution' on the horizon.

It is often this propensity for change, the degree and speed of innovation of the contemporary internet that amazes and seduces observers and commentators. Innovations that were recently celebrated as innovations are in no time re-innovated, and what was moments ago perceived as an e-revolution is in no time e-revolutionised. There is a constant stream of new applications and services, which provide ever new possibilities to be picked up by users worldwide. Countless crowd funding platforms enable us to be arts funders (for example, We Did This 2011); it only takes a mobile phone (-camera) these days to turn one into a 'citizen journalist' (see Chapter 5 this volume) or a blog to catch media attention worldwide by pretending to be a lesbian blogger reporting from Damascus (Whitaker 2011). And instead of relying on the mediating role of charities, we can simply visit one of the many social marketplaces and, with a few clicks and the equivalent of around three cups of Starbucks coffee, around $10, we make an immediate 'impact' by 'buy[ing] enough fabric for women affected by HIV to make and sell 5 purses in the market for income' in Cambodia. If we top up the investment with another $15, we can provide 'a workshop for one individual to start a community bank' in Mexico (GlobalGiving.org Microfinance 2011). Alternatively, we can download the iPhone game *Raise the Village* (2011) and enter the aid business: whatever we decide to purchase when we build our personal virtual village is delivered in actuality to help develop Kapir Atiira, a real village in Uganda. Who would have thought only a few years ago that an iPhone is all one needs for African development?

Leaving aside the problems that we might feel are implied in trends and services such as *Raise the Village* (see the discussion in Box 2.2) and the mushrooming array of so-called 'serious games', there is still little doubt that much is to be gained from a focus on the innovations that are spawned by the contemporary internet. And it is the

very interest in them that leads to the development of further ideas, thus potentially fostering social innovation. Yet there is more to the internet than individual technical innovations, although this is often overlooked by political analysts and commentators – overshadowed as it is by the magic attraction that the endless stream of innovations seems to spark. The contemporary internet is not only an array of distinct and concrete innovations which emerge, and which inevitably change over time, but the internet as such, and in itself, is constituted and takes form through ceaseless innovation. To put it more appropriately, getting away from the term 'innovation', whose meaning has been indelibly marked by the discourse of modern market thinking, the internet is a continuous *process of becoming* in and of itself, rather than an entity that changes from one fixed state of being to another. To support this suggestion is a straightforward task; all it needs is to recall the nature of two main features of the contemporary internet: its digital nature in general and the ethos of Web 2.0 in particular. Let's look at both aspects in turn.

The determining characteristic of the digital is that it is immaterial, in the sense that it is a numerical or mathematical – as opposed to an analogue – representation of information. While '"[a]nalogue" refers to the way in which one set of physical properties can be stored in another "analogous" physical form …, [i]n a digital media process the physical properties of the input data … are converted not into another object but into numbers; that is, into abstract symbols rather than analogous objects and physical surfaces' (Lister et al. 2003: 14–15). For something to be digital then means, by its very nature, that it is open to manipulation and alteration; 'digital media can be "tinkered with" in a way that is extremely difficult with traditional analogue media' (Miller 2011: 15). Obviously, it is much harder to change the background colour of da Vinci's painting *Mona Lisa* when it is displayed in the Palais du Louvre than to produce visual 'evidence' that *Sesame Street*'s Bert has not only been at Woodstock, and in the *Jerry Springer Show*, but that he is simply 'evil', befriended by almost all the dictators in world history. This openness to change means that something that is digital can be imagined as being in a 'state of permanent flux' (Lister et al. 2003: 17), and being digital means by default being in process; it means never being done. This feature of the (dematerialised) digital as constituting a state of flux is one of the two aspects that accounts for the process-character of the contemporary internet; the second aspect is subsumed under the label Web 2.0.

Box 2.2
Serious Gaming

'Transform lives through an iPhone!' declares *Raise the Village*, an interactive game that allows users to create and develop a virtual African village on their mobile devices. The twist? When players use their credit cards to purchase goods like mosquito nets, soap and food within the game, the developers send real-world versions of those goods to Kapir Atiira – what the game cheerfully describes as a 'REAL village in Uganda'.

Raise the Village is a member of the emerging wave of 'serious games', loosely defined as games designed to educate, inform and train their players, with the intention of creating positive real-world outcomes. These games can cover almost any topic, but generally focus on education, health, government, media and activism ('games for change').

So what is driving the trend towards the 'gamification' of real-world social issues? Games, the argument goes, have a powerful track record of inspiring player effort, rewarding hard work, facilitating large-scale collaboration, and motivating people to stick with challenges over time (McGonigal 2011). The result is an industry projected to be worth US$68 billion, with more than 500 million daily players engaged for over an hour a day. 'What if', asks gaming guru Jane McGonigal, 'we decided to use everything we knew about game design to fix what's wrong with reality?' (2011: 7).

Funders, academics and non-profits are beginning to ask the same question. In the United States, the Woodrow Wilson Center for International Scholars founded the Serious Games Initiative (www.seriousgames.org) to use games to develop new policy education and management tools. The New York-based Games for Change (www.gamesforchange.org) hosts an annual festival, development lab and awards for social impact games from around the globe. And universities in Europe, Canada and the US are beginning to offer certificates in serious game design.

But the good intentions of serious games do not always play out well in the real world. In 2011, *The City that Shouldn't Exist*, a game in which players competed for the chance to win an all-expenses-paid trip to Kenya's Dadaab refugee camp, was pulled from the web after claims that it dehumanised refugees and was in bad taste. Other games have been critiqued for over-simplifying complex issues, presenting players with an artificially 'big picture' perspective on ground-level problems, and commodifying the lives of people in the developing world.

The serious games industry is young, and the jury is still out on the degree to which games will, in fact, 'transform lives' in the real world. When asked to comment on *The City that Shouldn't Exist*, 25-year-old Ethiopian refugee Biru Okoth summed up the dilemma exactly: 'It's not good if you are just playing a game with our lives … this game will help only if you put it into practice' (Elkington 2011).

'Serious Games'

3rd World Farmer. Confront the frustrations of poverty, trade and conflict as an African farmer in this 'classic' serious game. www.3rdworldfarmer.com (free).

Against All Odds. The UNHCR-sponsored simulation that lets you experience life as a refugee. www.playagainstallodds.com.

Darfur is Dying. Experience a 'faint glimpse' of the dangers of life as a displaced person in Darfur through your cartoon avatar; engage in real-world activist challenges. www.darfurisdying.com (free).

Evoke. 'An urgent call to innovation.' Funded by the World Bank, Evoke helps players around the globe become 'social innovators' and share their world-changing ideas through the online community. www.urgentevoke.com (free).

FreeRice. A quiz game that rewards correct answers with real-world donations to the United Nations World Food Programme. http://freerice.com (free).

PeaceMaker. Solve the Middle East conflict as either the Israeli Prime Minister or the Palestinian President. www.peacemakergame.com (free demo).

Raise the Village. Donate goods to the citizens of Kapir Atiira, Uganda, by developing your own 'virtual village' online. www.raisethevillage.com (Freemium).

Katie McKenna is a graduate of the London School of Economic's Global Politics MSc programme, and producer of the award-winning disaster relief simulation *Inside the Haiti Earthquake* (http://insidethehaitiearthquake.com).

David Gauntlett (2011: 6) neatly summarises the key characteristic of Web 2.0: instead of being about 'searching and reading', as was Web 1.0 with its static web presentations, Web 2.0 is about 'writing and editing'. In fact, Web 2.0 is what distinguishes the 2004 Dean campaign from the Obama one in 2008; it does not simply address an audience 'out there', but it 'invites users in to play' (Gauntlett 2011: 7). Web 2.0 is about categorising, commenting, liking, mapping, sharing, labelling, producing, reproducing, collaborating, posting, customising, tagging, listing. It is about initiatives like the earlier mentioned 'Yes, We Can' video and its viral existence, or the online encyclopaedia Wikipedia and other crowd-sourcing initiatives, such as Ushahidi-Haiti @ Tafts University (2011) or GuttenPlag (2011), a platform via which a crowd revealed a total of 10,421 plagiarised lines in German Defense Minister Karl Theodor Freiherr von und zu Guttenberg's doctoral thesis, and, by doing so, played a key role in his 2011 resignation; 'net defeats minister', cheered Christian Stöcker (2011). Web 2.0 is about Facebook, Twitter, and Foursquare; it is about customised playlists and feedbacks on Amazon. In fact, it is also about many of the technological innovations that capture our attention these days (such as those discussed in the earlier mentioned context of the presidential campaigns), as they are often the (collaborative) product of Web 2.0. However, for our purposes here it is particularly important to realise that Web 2.0 is not 'simply a particular kind of technology, or a business model, and it certainly isn't a sequel to the Web as previously known. Web 2.0 describes a particular kind of *ethos* and *approach*' (Gauntlett 2011: 5; italics added).

There is a wide range of critical discussions about the contemporary internet in general, and Web 2.0 in particular, provided by cultural and media studies scholars. These discussions, in contrast to those available in political science, address the various problems entailed when the 'established differences between author and reader, performer and spectator, creator and interpreter become blurred and give way to a reading writing continuum that extends from the designers of the technology and networks to the final recipient, each one contributing to the activity of the other – the disappearance of the signature' (Pierre Levy, quoted in Lister et al. 2003: 17). New terminologies such as 'prosumer' and 'produsage' (Bruns 2008) have come out of these debates. A particularly prominent concern are the problems entailed in automated customisations and the so-called 'filter bubble' argument as discussed by Eli Pariser (2011) (see Box 2.3).

Leaving aside the many exciting aspects of its logic that invite discussion, the relevant issue for our purposes here is to understand that in addition to being digital – that is dematerialised and open to manipulation – it is the *ethos* of Web 2.0 that turns the contemporary internet into a permanent process of production. So, in addition to the fact that – as a consequence of their digital nature – things *can* be altered, changed and manipulated, it is in the very discourse, structures and logics of the contemporary internet that things *should* be altered, changed and manipulated – reason enough for us to be inspired by some theorists of digital culture and to imagine the internet as a process of becoming.

Tool, Space, Participation, Deliberation and the 'Great Divide v2': the Taming of the Contemporary Internet

The notion of the internet as a process of becoming differs from those understandings that are commonly held and applied by mainstream political analysts. There is of course always something problematic about categorisations; nevertheless, it is worth distinguishing here between two primary conceptions that dominate and shape the knowledge production of mainstream political studies. Most commonly, the internet is conceptualised as a *tool*, a (new kind of) medium that is used by political actors to do something. The growing body of scholarship which builds on this idea of the internet is rich and covers a very broad set of issues. The focus of these studies ranges from the use of the internet by diasporas (for example, Hiller and Franz 2004, Parham 2004), via issues such as political communication and e-government (for example, Henman 2010), to its use by activists in the context of anti-corporate campaigns, as is, for instance, systematically studied by Baringhorst et al. (2010). A particularly popular focus of interest has been the role of the internet in the context of political organisation, that is, the potential of the internet for (large-scale) networking and mobilisation. John Naughton (2001: 155–6), in his overview chapter on the internet and global civil society in the first edition of the *Global Civil Society* yearbook, stresses this aspect, and, of course, the earlier mentioned (arguably more popular than academic) debate about 'Twitter revolutions' falls into this category too (see Box 2.1). Given that some of the analysts who investigate the various uses of the internet as a new kind of tool see it as something that brings to contemporary activities a distinct and new quality, a number of new labels have come out of this scholarship, such as cyberactivism (McCaughey and Ayers 2003), cyberprotest (Van de Donk, Loader, Nixon and Rucht 2004) and web campaigns (Mosca and Santucci 2009).

Alternatively, the internet is conceptualised as a (new kind of) *space*, a sphere in which (new) things happen. Looking through this conceptual lens, scholars see and investigate those activities which they perceive as specific to, and only taking place on, the internet, such as hacktivism (for example Jordan and Taylor 2004). In particular, there is a considerable body of literature which deals with the internet as a distinct sphere of debate and knowledge production, such as in the extensive discussions about the deliberation potential, the above mentioned 'produser' debate, or in the context of citizen journalism (see Chapter 5).

The existing body of scholarship is rich and multifaceted, but despite its diversity, mainstream political analysts have two interlinked and mutually re-producing and re-enforcing things in common. First, they approach the internet with questions that are shaped by the norms and concerns that are 'naturally' perceived as specifically relevant within their discipline. In the widest sense, these questions are predominantly about the internet's (potential) *impact on* politics. In a narrower sense, most of the mainstream studies are driven by the question of whether or not the internet can help to overcome the specific (normative or realist) problems that political analysts diagnose as shortcomings in and of contemporary democracies. Of particular interest here are issues of participation and deliberation. On the one side, many scholars set out to investigate whether the internet can improve the style and level of political participation. In addition to general studies (for example, Polat 2005), the focus on young people – as a social group that is seen as 'increasingly apathetic and reluctant to exercise their civic responsibilities' (Banaji and Buckingham 2010: 15) but at the same time open for new media – is particularly popular; studies in this field are mushrooming (for example, Bennett 2008, Dahlgren and Olsson 2007, Loader 2007). On the other side, there is a sense (and hope) that the internet could serve as a (Habermasian) public sphere.

Consequently, the first thing that mainstream studies have in common is that the questions with which they address the internet are shaped by predetermined, discipline-specific concerns; these are mainly issues concerning participation and deliberation. The second

thing that mainstream studies have in common is that they work with a notion of the internet as something that is separate from the 'real' world. More often than not, this conceptual separation is implicit and naturalised, and is, for example, apparent when analysts ask for the 'impact of the internet on' (for example, Kalathil and Boas 2003). This categorical distinction between the offline and the online appears like a v2 of the notion of the 'great divide', which has been one of the key foundational notions of International Relations theory (Clark 1998).

Acknowledging these two trends in mainstream approaches to the internet by political analysts – discipline specific questions of participation and deliberation, and the offline/online binary – is important because analytically and discursively, they frame a specific understanding of the internet as an object of analysis. The idea of the internet that informs the work of mainstream political analysts is trimmed through the norms and concerns 'natural' to the discourse. The internet is shaped by the questions and assumptions that are used to frame analyses which, in their turn, are the natural-ised products of mainstream political analyses. In other words, the internet that political analysts examine in their attempts to find solutions to the problems that they perceive is already a product of their pre-existing concerns; it is a specific kind of internet that they describe, investigate and construct.

While there is no doubt that mainstream political analysis provides us with important insights concerning the use and significance of the internet, and that much can be gained from current work, the question we might more profitably be asking is what is it that is *not being* investigated and interrogated? Given the prominence of the internet in contemporary life, and in the construction of globalisation as a powerful conceptual frame that guides our view of the world, it is legitimate to ask what is discursively and analytically excluded as a result of certain working assumptions about the internet.

From a Tool and a Space to Creativity and Imagination

The binary between the offline and the online, the real and the virtual, the material and the symbolic, which is central to mainstream approaches to the internet, is something that is deeply embedded in the common worldview held within the political science discourse. It is something naturalised within the political science discourse, which – more than many other contemporary academic discourses – continues to be shaped by a focus on 'objective reality' (essence) rather than 'textuality'

Box 2.3
Eli Pariser's *Filter Bubble*

Did you realise that you and your doppelganger best friend might get a completely different search result when Googling, say, 'civil society'? Bringing to light the invisible algorithms that underpin the architectures of the largest websites – such as Facebook, Google, Yahoo, Amazon – lies at the heart of Eli Pariser's recent publication, *The Filter Bubble* (2011). These algorithms present users with the information that they are 'likely' to want, extrapolated from extensive personal data such as past clicks and public profiles. Pariser's primary concern is that such 'personalisation' of the internet space is resulting in each individual being trapped in his or her own universe of information: the 'filter bubble'.

The ramification of Pariser's argument cannot but be considerable in an era in which online activities are a large part of many people's lives. Half of the 400 million Facebook users are known to log in on a daily basis (Zuniga and Valenzuela 2010: xxxi), and 36 per cent of Americans under the age of 30 get their news through these social networking sites (Pariser 2011: 8). In such a context, Pariser is concerned that the public's skewed exposure to information not only deprives people of different life options at the individual level, but it also connotes a significant cultural impact at the societal level.

The internet is often championed as a tool for enhancing civic participation and democracy. However, Pariser views that the open and free exchange of varied opinions in online space is being hindered by 'filter bubbles', as corporate motivations dictate the designs of the web algorithms. In the process large amounts of personal information is being transacted without individuals' consent. Pariser calls for government intervention directed to injecting a sense of civic responsibility into the architectures of the web. Governance on the internet may sound paradoxical, as its purportedly unfettered nature has been considered by many to be its greatest boon. Yet a global-level multi-stakeholder discussion on the administration of the internet has been ongoing for the past decade in the World Summit on Information Society forums, reflecting a growing awareness that unregulated technology may cause more harm than good.

Acknowledging this, Pariser incisively remarks that 'in the fight for control of the Internet, everyone's organized but the people' (Pariser 2011: 242). His most imperative call is directed to the people who he believes hold the key to the mobilisation of governments and corporations. Indeed, he himself is a dedicated activist, co-founder of the successful global campaigning website Avaaz (www.avaaz.org) and Board President of its US fundraising and advocacy partner, MoveOn (www.moveon. org). Since the publication of his book, he has been rallying the public's attention to the 'filter bubble' through lecture series and using online media, such as the popular TED Talks (www. ted.com). As a matter of fact, bringing to the public sphere an issue that has been lurking invisible is what has garnered *The Filter Bubble* the most commendation. The ramification of the 'search engine bias' has been scrutinised over the past decade within the academic community, but *The Filter Bubble* has re-illuminated the issue at a timely moment for the public, who perhaps are the biggest stakeholders.

Jungmin Jamie Kim is an MSc candidate in Development Studies at the London School of Economics.

(discourse). More generally, it is a discourse in which the symbolic structures that make the world meaningful are widely ignored, hence, in which questions such as 'when can a purely textual presence actually cause political change?' (McCaughey and Ayers 2003: 5) are natural questions to ask. Of course, somewhere at the very base of this are ontological issues which require philosophical analysis. However, in the case of the internet, the categorical distinction between the offline and the online is a somewhat unhappy one not because of any ontological concerns but because it simply does not reflect lived reality (anymore). A number of recent studies show that in the contemporary moment 'offline' and 'online' have come to be enmeshed in a way that throws into question the analytical validity of this dichotomy. For example, in a systematic study on 'How Young People Participate in Civic Activities Using Internet and Mobile Technologies' in Australia, the authors demonstrate that young people move between offline and online seamlessly (Ohlin et al. 2010). Hirzalla and van Zoonen (2010) come to similar findings in their analysis of civic actitivities in the Netherlands; they too discover a signifcant convergence between the offline and the online, and hence they suggest looking 'beyond the online/offline divide'. A profound enmeshment of the internet with the 'real' world is also highlighted by studies that look at the construction and stylisation of the (online) self (for instance, via avatars and profiles on social networking platforms), and, more broadly, in those which look at the relationship between the body and virtuality (for example, Boellstorff 2008, Miller 2011, Moore 2011). As Sabina Misoch (2007) suggests, while, for a long time, scholars have focused on the notion of disembodiment and the idea that it is 'cyber existences' (Misoch 2007: 1744, referring to Hofmann 1997) that interact in the virtual, recent studies show that it is more and more apposite to speak of a *transference* of the body into the virtual sphere. This is due not least to the increasing multimedialisation of the internet, which enables presentation strategies that go beyond (in a narrow sense) textual ones. Similarly, much of the literature from the past decade or so that looks at the stylisation of the self in online environments has stressed the play with identities; how individuals take on different identities online and/or hide what they consider to be undesirable identity features (for example, Turkle 1996, McKenna et al. 2002). Yet recent studies of online social networking environments, such as Facebook, show that a significant play with identity is no longer the norm, as users 'show rather than tell' their identities (Zhao et al. 2008: 1876) –

and as these environments are not anonymous (anymore). As Vincent Miller (2011: 182) finds, social networking environments play a significant role in ('offline') identity construction, and 'social networking profiles in particular have become tools to represent and aid "offline" selves. As a result, there has been an integration of "offline" and "online" frames or lifeworlds'.

Staying with Miller (2011: 1), we can conclude that

[t]he internet has now become a major part of work, leisure, social and political life, for most people in advanced economic nations. It is no longer its novelty, uniqueness, or potential to transform life, but its mundane nature and pervasiveness that now gives the internet its significance. Not in the sense that it has profoundly 'changed' the world, but in the sense that it has become enmeshed within the enduring structures of our society. As such, the online sphere is no longer a realm separate from the offline 'real world', but fully integrated into offline life.

All of the above holds two interlinked implications for the scholarly imagination of political analysts. Once we decide that the distinction between the offline and the online does not easily reflect contemporary reality (anymore), the internet needs to take a position in our thinking that is different from the one that it has in mainstream political analyses. Instead of asking how or if the internet has the potential to improve the 'real' world, we need to consider it as a part of this 'actual' world. This means that assessments of the internet that are based on comparisons with (an ideal state in) the 'actual' world are unhappy ones. In other words, being guided by pre-set questions, which arise out of the idea of a categorical distinction between the offline and the online, cannot be fully satisfying (anymore). But this is of course not all; the above also brings along a set of guiding concepts that are very different from and, arguably, less tangible, than the ones which shape the majority of existing approaches by mainstream political analysts. Understanding the internet as a *process of becoming* throws into question the usefulness of the concepts of 'tool' and 'space', since questions about what is happening 'on' the internet and how the internet is used by whom, and with what impact, on the 'actual' world do not give sufficient analytical purchase anymore. As a process of becoming, the internet can be understood as a process in which 'people are rejecting the givens and are making their world anew' (Gauntlett 2011: 20), which, in turn, requires working with alternative concepts such as the notion of flux and – importantly – the concepts of creativity and imagination.

Rebuilding the 'Island of Meaning'

When the *Global Civil Society* yearbook series was born in 2001, it was with the aim of establishing 'global civil society' as a new '"island of meaning" in the conceptual landscape of modern social science and policy-making' (Anheier et al. 2001: 3). As the editors of the first edition stressed, they understood the addition of the term 'global' to the concept of 'civil society' to be a move which takes 'civil society' and 'places it into a framework that ultimately transcends conventional social science categories' (2001: 3). In this sense, they invited their audience to actively participate 'in a journey of discovery', understanding the yearbook series as 'a terrain for developing ideas, investigating issues, and gathering information that does not readily fit existing categories, cannot be found in conventional sources' (2001: 3). Following this invitation, we believe that the establishment of a new 'island of meaning' cannot only mean to develop new ideas and gather new and unconventional information, but importantly requires the shake-up of the conceptual frames through which we look at, experience, and assess the world. But, of course, this is anything but an easy task, since there is hardly anything more 'political' and 'powerful' than conceptual frames which are thick discursive formations, consisting of a complex interplay of other conceptual frames, reflecting, producing and reproducing dominant and (pre)naturalised worldviews. We see this in the concept of 'globalisation' which has come to be captured by the mainstream as a material-structural 'creature'. The concept of globalisation is particularly interesting and important in the contemporary moment. This is both because it has come to be constructed as a second nature, and, as we suggested at the beginning of this chapter, because through the adjective 'global' it is written into other conceptions, such as 'global civil society' and 'global politics'.

We began our chapter by highlighting the interwoven nature of the concepts of globalisation and the internet, suggesting that the internet can be seen as a *conceptual ingredient* of the globalisation frame. As such, both concepts play into and construct one another. In order to escape this mutual construction, in our chapter we stepped outside the discourse of mainstream political analysis and, inspired by writing from digital culture

theorists, reshaped the concept of the internet in two important ways. First, we questioned the strict offline/online dichotomy that underlies mainstream approaches to the internet; hence, we suggested understanding the contemporary internet as 'being' the world. Second, we conceptualised the internet as a 'process of becoming', a process in which the world is constantly renewed. With that, we brought into play the guiding concepts of 'imagination' and 'creativity', replacing the mainstream ones of 'tool' and 'space', which shape current approaches by mainstream political analysts.

We need to remind ourselves here that metaphors, and therefore analytical concepts, do not describe the world as it is, but rather the way that we talk about it. Thus, any reshaping of our models and understandings of politics and the political requires close attention to the conceptual frameworks and 'pre-theoretical commitments' (Moore 2004: 75) underlying contemporary analyses of the internet in political science. It is for this reason that we attend in this paper to the meta-analysis of how political scientists conceptualise and analyse the internet.

By default, the reconceptualisation of the internet that we have presented in this chapter has an impact on the conceptual architecture of the globalisation frame, since it reshapes it in a way that leaves space for new questions to emerge. Playing into the concept of 'global civil society', it forces us to ask much more of the strategies of how the world is *imagined* and *symbolically* renewed; not least it moves aesthetics into the focus of political scientists. The particular value of this kind of shift in conceptual frames is that it fosters and, in fact, builds into the very concept of 'global civil society' 'a type of reflective understanding that emerges not from systematically applying the technical skills of analysis which prevail in the social sciences, but from cultivating a more open-ended level of sensibility about the political' (Bleiker 2009: 2). So, as Bleiker (2009: 2) suggests, '[w]e might then be able to appreciate what we otherwise cannot even see: perspectives and people excluded from prevailing purviews, for instance, or the emotional nature and consequences of political events.'

Notes

1. We use the term 'internet' here in a broad way as encompassing all sorts of contemporary virtual services, and prominently the World Wide Web.
2. By July 2008 the Obama campaign had spent around $7.26 million on internet media; in contrast, Clinton's internet media expenditure until that time was $2.9 million and McCain's was $1.7 million (Castells 2009: 392).

Box 2.4
Glossary

Crowdsourcing: refers to the mobilisation of a crowd to create content (Wikipedia.org), solve a particular problem, or to accomplish a particular task (such as mapping dark matter for NASA; see www.challenge.gov).

Foursquare: a location-based social networking tool for mobile users that allows them to 'check-in' at locations and share their whereabouts with others.

Internet: a worldwide system of computer networks facilitating information exchange and communication based on the standard Internet Protocol Suite (TCP/IP).

Location-based services: mobile application services that identify the current location and uses it to provide information for the user, such as directions and local recommendations.

Microblogging: the act of posting short sentences onto microblogs that convey diary-type messages, such as Twitter or Facebook status updates.

Second Life: an internet-based virtual world created by Linden Research Inc. in 2003.

Social media: an inclusive term to refer to online applications and tools that enable content creation and consumption by users.

World Wide Web (www): a collection of internet resources that can be accessed by browsers based on standards such as Hypertext Transfer Protocol (HTTP).

Web 1.0: the state of the World Wide Web before the introduction of the Web 2.0 technologies, characterised by static websites rather than constantly-updated weblogs and social networking tools.

Web 2.0: a term for advanced internet technology and applications that support interoperability, user-centred designs, and participatory information exchange, such as in blogs, wiki, RSS and social bookmarking.

Wiki: a type of user-controlled website of which the contents are created, edited and organised by the users, as in Wikipedia.

References

Anderson, Kevin (2004) 'Internet Insurgent Howard Dean', BBC News Online, 14 January, http://news.bbc.co.uk/1/hi/world/americas/3394897.stm (accessed 30 June 2011).

Anheier, Helmut, Glasius, Marlies and Kaldor, Mary (2001) 'Introduction', in Helmut Anheier, Marlies Glasius and Mary Kaldor (eds), *Global Civil Society 2001*. Oxford: Oxford University Press.

Banaji, Shakuntala and Buckingham, David (2010) 'Young People, the Internet, and Civic Participation: An Overview of Key Findings from the CivicWeb Project' *International Journal of Learning and Media*, Vol. 2 No. 1.

Baringhorst, Sigrid, Kneip, Veronika, Maerz, Annegret and Niesyto, Johanna (2010) *Unternehmenskritische Kampagnen: Politischer Protest im Zeichen digitaler Kommunikation*. Wiesbaden: VS Verlag.

Bennett, W. L. (ed.) (2008) *Civic Life Online: Learning how Digital Media can Engage Youth*. Cambridge, MA: MIT Press.

Bisley, Nick (2007) *Rethinking Globalization*. London: Routledge.

Bleiker, Roland (2009) *Aesthetics and World Politics*. London: Palgrave Macmillan.

Boellstorff, Tom (2008) *Coming of Age in Second Life: An Anthropologist Explores the Virtually Human*. Princeton University Press.

Bruns, Axel (2008) *Blogs, Wikipedia, Second life, and Beyond: From Production to Produsage*. New York: Lang.

Castells, Manuel (2009) *Communication Power*. Oxford: Oxford University Press.

Clark, Ian (1998) 'Beyond the Great Divide: Globalization and the Theory of International Relations', *Review of International Studies*, Vol. 24: 479–98.

Dahlgren, Peter and Olsson, Tobias (2007) 'From Public Sphere to Civic Culture: Young Citizens' Internet Use', in Richard Butsch (ed.), *Media and Public Spheres*. London: Palgrave Macmillan.

Elkington, Natasha (2011). 'Dadaab Facebook Refugee Game Pulled from Web Amid Claims of Poor Taste'. Available at http://www.trust.org/alertnet/news/worst-vacation-ever-win-a-trip-to-worlds-largest-refugee-camp/ (accessed 24 August 2011).

Facebook Statistics (2011) http://www.facebook.com/press/info.php?statistics (accessed 26 July 2011).

Federal Electoral Commission (2011) http://www.fec.gov/finance/disclosure/srssea.shtml (accessed 15 July 2011).

Flickr Blog (2010) http://blog.flickr.net/en/2010/09/19/5000000000/ (accessed 26 July 2011).

Gauntlett, David (2011) *Making is Connecting: The Social Meaning of Creativity, from DIY and Knitting to YouTube and Web 2.0*. Cambridge: Polity Press.

Gil de Zúñiga, Homero, and Valenzuela, Sebastián (2010) 'Who Uses Facebook and Why?', in D. E. Wittkower (ed.), *Facebook and Philosophy*. Chicago: Open Court.

GlobalGiving.org (2011) Microfinance http://www.globalgiving.org/dy/v2/content/themes.html?themeName=Microfinance (accessed 14 June 2011).

GuttenPlag Wiki (2011) http://de.guttenplag.wikia.com/wiki/GuttenPlag_Wiki (accessed 14 June 2011).

Henman, Paul (2010) *Governing Electronically: E-Government and the Reconfiguration of Public Administration, Policy and Power*. London: Palgrave Macmillan.

Herb, Jeremy (2011) 'In 2012, a New World for Online Campaigning', *Star Tribune*, 10 April, http://www.startribune.com/politics/national/119575059.html?page=all&prepage=1&c=y#continue (accessed 14 June 2011).

Hiller, Harry H. and Franz, Tara M. (2004) 'New Ties, Old Ties and Lost Ties: The Use of the Internet in Diaspora', *New Media & Society*, Vol. 6 No. 6: 731–52.

Hirzalla, Fadi and van Zoonen, Liesbet (2010) 'Beyond the Online/Offline Divide: How Youth's Online and Offline Civic Activities Converge', *Social Science Computer Review*, Vol. 4.

Hofmann, Ute (1997) 'Die erträgliche Leichtigkeit des Seins: Subjektivität und Sozialität in der Netzwelt', in Gerd-Günter Voß (ed.), *Subjektorientierte Soziologie*. Opladen.

Jordan, Tim and Taylor, Paul (2004) *Hacktivism and Cyberwars: Rebels with a Cause?* London: Routledge.

Kalathil, Shanthi and Boas, Taylor C. (2003) *Open Networks, Closed Regimes: The Impact of the Internet on Authoritarian Rule*. Carnegie Endowment for International Peace.

Kaldor, Mary (2003) *Global Civil Society: An Answer to War*. Cambridge: Polity Press.

Lister, Martin, Dovey, Jon, Giddings, Seth, Grant, Iain and Kelly, Kieran (2003) *New Media: A Critical Introduction*. London: Routledge.

Loader, Brian D. (ed.) (2007) *Young Citizens in the Digital Age*. London: Routledge.

Manovich, Lev (2001) *The Language of New Media*. Cambridge: MIT Press.

McCaughey, Martha and Ayers, Michael D. (eds) (2003) *Cyberactivism: Online Activism in Theory and Practice*. London: Routledge.

McEvoy Manjikian, Mary (2010) 'From Global Village to Virtual Battlespace: The Colonization of the Internet and the Extension of Realpolitik', *International Studies Quarterly*, Vol. 54: 381–401.

McGonigal, J. (2011) *Reality is Broken: Why Games Make Us Better and How They Can Change the World*. New York: The Penguin Press.

McKenna, K. Y. A., Green, A. S. and Gleason, M. E. J. (2002) 'Relationship Formation on the Internet: What's the Big Attraction?', *Journal of Social Issues*, Vol. 58 No. 1: 9–31.

Messina, Jim (2011) *You're in*, email to S. Selchow, 28 July 2011.

Miller, Claire Cain (2008) 'How Obama's Internet Campaign Changed Politics', *New York Times*, 7 November.

Miller, Daniel (2011) *Tales from Facebook*. Cambridge: Polity Press.

Miller, Vincent (2011) *Understanding Digital Culture*. London: Sage.

Misoch, Sabina (2007) 'Der Koerper im Netz: Inszenierungen selbstverletzenden Verhaltens durch Jugendliche' in Tagungsband zum 33. Kongress der Deutschen Gesellschaft fuer Soziologie in Kassel 2006.

Moore, Henrietta L. (2004) 'Global Anxieties: Concept-metaphors and Pre-theoretical Commitments in Anthropology', *Anthropological Theory*, Vol. 4 No. 1: 71–88.

Moore, Henrietta L. (2011) *Still Life: Hopes, Desires and Satisfactions*. Cambridge: Polity Press.

Morozov, Evgeny (2009) 'How Dictators Watch Us on the Web', *Prospect*, Vol. 165, December 2009, http://www.prospectmagazine.co.uk/2009/11/how-dictators-watch-us-on-the-web/ (accessed 11 July 2011).

Mosca, Lorenzo and Santucci, Daria (2009) 'Petitioning Online. The Role of E-Petitions in Web Campaigning', in Sigrid Baringhorst, Veronika Kneip and Johanna Niesyto (eds), *Political Campaigning on the Web*. Bielefeld: Transcript Verlag.

Naughton, John (2001) 'Contested Space: The Internet and Global Civil Society', in Helmut Anheier, Marlies Glasius and Mary Kaldor (eds), *Global Civil Society 2001*. Oxford: Oxford University Press.

Norton-Taylor, Richard and Hopkins, Nick (2011) 'Libya Air Strikes: Nato Uses Twitter to Help Gather Targets', *Guardian*, 15 June, http://www.guardian.co.uk/world/2011/jun/15/libya-nato-gathers-targets-twitter (accessed 2 July 2011).

Ohlin, Jackie, Heller, Allison, Byrne, Susan and Keevy, Nicky (2010) 'How Young People Participate in Civic Activities Using Internet and Mobile Technologies'. Report to the National Youth Affairs Research Scheme (NYARS), http://www.deewr.gov.au/Youth/Programs/NYARS/Documents/NYARSReport2010.pdf (accessed: 2 August 2011).

Pariser, Eli (2011) *The Filter Bubble: What The Internet Is Hiding From You*. London: Viking.

Parham, Angel A. (2004) 'Diaspora, Community and Communication: Internet Use in Transnational Haiti', *Global Networks*, Vol. 4: 199–217.

PawlentyAction (2011) http://action.timpawlenty.com/m/ (accessed: 28 June 2011).

Polat, R. K. (2005) 'The Internet and Political Participation: Exploring the Explanatory Links', *European Journal of Communication*, Vol. 20 No. 4: 435–59.

Raise the Village (2011) http://www.raisethevillage.com/apps.aspx (2 July 2011).

Selchow, Sabine (2010) 'The "Global"-isation of Politics: A Theorisation of the Oomnipresence of "Global" in Contemporary Discourses'. PhD thesis, Government Department, London School of Economics.

Shirky, Clay (2008) *Here Comes Everybody: The Power of Organizing Without Organizations*. New York: Allen Lane.

Shirky, Clay (2010a) *Cognitive Surplus: Creativity and Generosity in a Connected Age*. London: Penguin Books.

Shirky, Clay (2010b) 'The Twitter Revolution: More than Just a Slogan', *Prospect*, Vol. 166, January 2010, Web exclusive, http://www.prospectmagazine.co.uk/2010/01/the-twitter-revolution-more-than-just-a-slogan/ (accessed 11 July 2011).

Stöcker, Christian (2011) 'Netz besiegt Minister' *Spiegel Online*, 1 March 2011, http://www.spiegel.de/netzwelt/netzpolitik/0,1518,748358,00.html (accessed 30 June 2011)

Townhall @ The White House (2011) http://askobama.twitter.com/ (accessed 15 July 2011).

Turkle, S. (1995) *Life on the Screen: Identity in the Age of the Internet*. New York: Simon & Schuster.

Twitter Blog (2011) http://blog.twitter.com/2011/06/200-million-tweets-per-day.html (accessed 2 July 2011).

UNOG (2011) 'World Press Freedom Day: UN Expert Says that at this Historic Juncture, Governments Must Choose Reform Over Repression', United Nations Office at Geneva, 2 May, http://www.unog.ch/80256EDD006B9C2E/(httpNewsByYear_en)/E58F3A9FD4BAC2A7C1257884003 5D164?OpenDocument (accessed: 2 July 2011).

Ushahidi-Haiti @ Tafts University (2011) http://haiti.ushahidi.com/# (accessed 15 July 2011).

Van de Donk, Wim, Loader, Brian D., Nixon, Paul G. and Rucht, Dieter (eds) (2004) *Cyberprotest: New Media, Citizens, and Social Movements*. London: Routledge.

Wassermann, Todd (2011) 'Why Location-Based Services Will be the Killer App of the 2012 Elections', http://mashable.com/2011/05/01/2012-election-killer-app/ (accessed 14 June 2011).

We Did This (2011) http://www.wedidthis.org.uk/ (accessed: 28 July 2011).

Whitaker, Brian (2011) 'Gay Girl in Damascus was an Arrogant Fantasy', *Guardian*, 13 June, http://www.guardian.co.uk/commentisfree/2011/jun/13/gay-girl-in-damascus-hoax-blog?intcmp=239 (accessed: 2 August 2011).

'Yes, We Can' (2008) http://www.youtube.com/watch?v=SsV2O4fCgjk (accessed 1 July 2011).

YouTube Blog (2011) http://youtube-global.blogspot.com/2011/05/thanks-youtube-community-for-two-big.html (accessed 2 August 2011).

Zhao, Shanyang, Grasmuck, Sherri and Martin, Jason (2008) 'Identity Construction on Facebook: Digital Empowerment in Anchored Relationships', *Computers in Human Behavior*, Vol. 24: 1816–36.

PART II

Democracy and Citizenship

CHAPTER 3

THE ARAB AWAKENING: THE CRISIS OF DICTATORSHIP AND CIVIL SOCIETY

Bernard Dreano

In the Muslim world and in particular in the 'Arab world' the repercussions of any kind of shaking taking place in any point is extremely fast. Its effects can be felt everywhere in a vast area. The speed is almost electric.
(Francis Charmes, Member of the French parliament, speaking in a debate about the opportunity for the French to join the British military expedition in Egypt in 1882)

In the middle of March 2011, Saudi and Emirati troops invaded Bahrain to stop the movement begun several weeks before in the small Gulf kingdom. The rallying point of the pro-democracy demonstrators, the magnificent Pearl Monument, was toppled down; King Hamad Bin Isa al-Khalifa considered that the white pearl, standing on its six sail-shaped cement pillars, had been 'dishonoured' by the demonstrations.

Precisely at the same moment, the shiny fighter aircrafts of Qatar and the United Arab Emirates were sent to the Mediterranean, joining NATO forces in airstrikes against the Libyan leader Colonel Qadhafi. The colonel was attempting to crush his own peoples' rebellion. So: cracking down on the uprising in Bahrain, yet supporting the one in Benghazi?

The contradiction is only superficial. The wave of protests now known as the Arab Spring, which began towards the end of 2010 in Tunisia, disturbed the whole region. It became necessary to restore order. A victory of the Great Leader of the Great Libyan Arab Jamahiriya, after a massacre of civilians – which would likely have taken place in Libya – would have been disturbing to international public opinion and destabilising for the region; that was the opinion in Paris, London and Washington, and Riyadh agreed. At the same time, the democratic evolution of Bahrain would have been destabilising for the other states of the Arabic peninsula; at least, that was the mood in Riyadh and Washington. London and Paris let Riyadh put an end to it.

After the fall of Zine el-Abidine Ben Ali in Tunisia and Hosni Mubarak in Egypt, presidential elections were expected to bring back order. A few reforms put forward by kings Mohammed VI in Morocco, Abdullah in Jordan and President Bouteflika in Algeria were intended to appease potential demonstrators. The Saudis and their partners of the Gulf Cooperation Council were going to find a solution assuring political stability in Yemen. Nobody was expecting anything to happen in Syria.

But things did not work out that way. The immovable Assad clan in Syria was shaken by an immense wave of protest despite bloody retorts. Turmoil continues in Yemen. In Tunisia and in Egypt people wanted more than a change of leader, and they have returned to the streets to demand this vocally. Arab populations are awakened. The second wave of Middle East uprisings – Libya, Yemen, Bahrain and Syria – is characterised by the same quest for universal values as in Egypt and Tunisia: freedom of expression, democratic reforms, an end to economic and political corruption, and a determined resistance to sectarian splits (Baun and Hudson 2011). Whatever short-term results will be, whatever specific outcomes in the different countries will result, this *shawa* (awakening) will have long-term effects. The moment is comparable to the European 'spring of the people' in 1848; it is a major historical event in the twenty-first century.

From the Atlantic Ocean to the Gulf Sea the Ground Shifts under the Tyrants' Feet

The Arab Spring started at the beginning of winter in the small Tunisian town of Sidi Bouzid, with the ordeal of a young fruit seller who could stand no more misery and humiliation. Then a movement of protest spread across the whole region of central Tunisia (a region forgotten by the 'Tunisian economical miracle'), and then to the entire country. With a lag of two weeks, the Egyptian people were confronted by the same type of autocratic, corrupted regime, and also began to demonstrate, especially on Tahrir (Liberation) square in Cairo (see Box 1.1). and continued to demonstrate, until the enormous victories: the fall of Ben Ali (on 17 January), and then of Mubarak (on 11 February).

The same kind of pro-democracy *intifada* (uprising) had already begun in Yemen and Bahrain; there were smaller mobilisations in Algeria, Oman, Jordan, Iraq. Then, after violent clashes in the little town of Deraa, the Syrian people went out on the street. There was even some kind of protest in Saudi Arabia. Demonstrators protesting against confessionalism in Lebanon and against division in Palestine explicitly referred to the Arab Spring.

Elsewhere in the world, from the social movements in Wisconsin to the *indignados* in Spain, other activists quoted the slogan of the Arabs demonstrations ... however, this *shawa* is Arabic.

Some Western experts, surprised by the fall of Ben Ali and Mubarak, explained that 'at least' there was a democratic movement taking place in the Arab states. They opportunely forgot all the previous movements which have taken place in the twentieth century, from the democratic and constitutionalist movements of Egypt (1919), the national liberation struggles against the French and the British that continued until 1967, the building of independence in the 1960s and 1970s, the participation in the movements of 1968 of Tunis, Casablanca, Beirut, Amman, Aden or Oman (see Box 4.4), and the demands for democracy and freedom in the late 1980s in Palestine, Algeria, Jordan, Yemen. Today is the turn of a new generation; as the old Algerian leftist Sadek Hadjeres says, 'from the Atlantic to the Gulf the ground shifts under the feet of tyrants' (Hadjeres 2011).

Contrary to the movement of the mid-twentieth century, this one is not a pan-Arabic one of Arab nationalism. Very few slogans are circulating about the 'United Arab Fatherland'. It is not pan-Islamist, either. Of course people are shouting *Allah Ouakbar* ('God is mighty') in front of the bullets and bombs – but not slogans like 'Islam is the solution, Quran the constitution, *jihad* the way'.

In every country, people have been waving their national flag, sometimes together with another, symbolic one (such as one from Tunisia or Palestine). Yet everywhere the demands were the same, as underlined by Tariq Ramadan (2011): 'requiring the implementation of five unalienable principles: rule of law, equal citizenship, universal suffrage, elective mandate, and separation of powers'. And the slogans and methods were also the same: peaceful demonstrations and gatherings, *Irhal!* (Leave!) – or as the Tunisians say '*Dégage!*', '*Es Chaab yourid isqat al nizam!*' (The people want the fall of the regime) on the rhythm of the famous Chilean motto '*El pueblo unido, jamás será vencido*'.

It was said during the time of Nasser that the Arab world was the space of the fans of the great Egyptian singer Oum Kalthum. Today one could say it is the space

of the viewers of al-Jazeera television in Arabic. It is a cultural and linguistic unity, even if the local dialects are very different from one another and if a significant number of people have another mother tongue than Arabic (such as the Tamazight and the Kurds) or do not consider themselves Arabs.

But what unifies the region stretching from the Atlantic Ocean to the Persian-Arabian Gulf is probably a common destiny. In 1992 the Moroccan Fatima Mernissi diagnosed 'a lost and economically defeated Arab World' because of its 'non democratic management', and the Arab societies as being paralysed by the fear of power and traditions, and by the *ta'a* (obedience) to the rulers (Mernissi 2010). Just before his assassination in 2005, the Lebanese journalist Samir Kassir described an 'Arab misfortune', noting that 'the lack of democracy is not specifically an Arab disease, but the Arab world is the only regional system where this defect is shared by almost all these countries', and that 'it would be a mistake to attribute the citizenship crisis to a cultural predisposition. First of all this is the effect of another crisis, the crisis of the State' (Kassir 2004). And the Arab Human Development Report published by the United Nations Development Programme (UNDP) in 2009 underlined three major deficits: education, womens' rights, and, above all, political freedom.

Freedom had been limited by external pressure: colonial domination but also imperialism after independence. It had been limited also through internal constraint by authoritarian regimes, by so-called 'progressive' republics as well as by 'reactionary' monarchies; by those that had been granted independence, from Amman to Oman, and those that were heirs of the national liberation struggles, from Algiers to Baghdad. The latter were historically legitimate (Nasser, Bourguiba, the Algerian National Liberation Front (FLN)) and had been able to provide a certain level of prosperity. But they had lost their popular footholds, giving up independence, developing inequalities, scrapping public services and organising corruption, with police everywhere and justice nowhere.

Such corrupt governing exists in other parts of the world. In the Arab world it simply added itself to collective humiliations. Humiliation provoked by the numerous defeats and betrayals: betrayal by the British and the French in the Arab uprising after the First World War; defeat against Israel from the *Nakba* (the catastrophe) of 1948 to the *Naksa* (the new defeat) of 1967; unpunished Israeli invasions of Lebanon; the smothering of the first Palestinian intifada; and the retraction of the Peace Process. Iraqi wars and invasions, not to speak of

Box 3.1
Five Lessons from the Revolutionary Uprisings in the Maghreb-Mashreq Region

Besides their many appellations, the Arab revolutions have already brought us much. They constitute a phenomenon, one which could hardly have been predicted, and one that opens up new horizons. Here, I will highlight five lessons that are already apparent.

The first lesson is that the situation can indeed perhaps qualify as revolutionary

It was already believed that the world was in crisis: a crisis of neoliberalism as a phase of capitalist globalisation; a crisis of the foundations of the capitalist system; a crisis of Western civilisation and of its hegemony. The uprisings of the people of the Maghreb-Mashreq region show that this is something more than a crisis. Rather, it becomes revolutionary in the sense that Lenin and Gramcsi define a revolutionary situation; 'when those below no longer want to be governed, and those above can no longer govern'.

The second lesson is the assertion of major demands: for freedom, for independence, and for the end of corruption

This is a confirmation of the many conflicts inherent in the current situation: the predominance of social conflicts between the working classes and the oligarchies, the explosion of social inequalities and corruption; ideological conflicts surrounding the fundamental question of liberties; geopolitical conflicts linked to Western hegemony. Ecological conflicts are not absent, notably the issues of raw material, land and water, but they are not as explicitly present as in other movements in South America or Asia.

The uprisings bring the evolution of social conflicts to light. They reveal the fact that the oligarchies have divided the dominant classes. In the Maghreb-Mashreq, these have become profit-driven clans who have relied on the police, militia and secret services in order to detach themselves from the armies that put them in power. The uprisings highlight the fact that corruption, resulting from the concentration of extraordinary amounts of money in the hands of the oligarchy, is a structural result of neoliberalism, and one that has a negative effect on the economy and on world politics.

The third lesson is that by rebelling in its own way, a new generation has taken up the revolutionary torch

It is not so much a case of the youth defined by an age bracket than by a cultural generation that is absorbed in a situation and transforms it. It shows the deep social changes linked to educational opportunity, which translates into a brain drain, on the one hand, and to unemployed graduates, on the other. Migration and diaspora expose this generation to the world and its conflicts in terms of consumption, of cultures and of values. While this exposure sets up more conflicts of expectations and experience, it does reduce isolation and confinement; these unemployed graduates are building a new alliance between the children of the working classes and those from the middle classes.

This new generation is building a new political culture. It is modifying the determining factors of social structures: social strata, religion, national and cultural references, affiliations to gender and age, migrations, diaspora and territories. It is experimenting with new forms of organisation through the command of digital and social networks, and through attempts at horizontal self-organisation. It attempts to define, in different situations, forms of autonomy between the political movements and the political authorities. Through its demands and its ingenuity, it reminds us of Frantz Fanon's powerful words: 'Each generation must discover its mission, fulfil it, or betray it.'

The fourth lesson is that the issue at stake is the democratisation of the whole Maghreb-Mashreq region

From national situations – first, the Tunisian detonator and then the Egyptian conflagration – the uprising spread, particular to each nation and yet regional. It is crucial to understand that, at a certain point, the people were no longer scared of rebelling, and that this revolt of the masses was on a regional scale. They revealed the nature of their own dictators while questioning the role meted out to them by Western hegemony. They showed the reality of the four functions that these dictatorships performed [for the West]: the guarantee of access to raw materials; the guarantee of military agreements, and particularly of treaties with Israel; the containment of Islamism; and the control of migration. The revolt of the people is a revelation and an awakening, bringing about the abolition of impossibilities. A new approach is now both essential and possible.

Democratisation spreads at the level of geocultural regions, as has been observed elsewhere. However, the individual uprisings are national, and are not abolished by their regional scale. It is at a national scale that relationships with states, institutions and other political organisations are defined, that alliances are formed and old structures undone, and where transitions are built. However, the regional scale is of great importance. Just as people are shaped through the history of their struggles, a region is also shaped by its transformations and the convergence of its people's actions. The construction of the Maghreb-Mashreq region is now in progress.

It is interesting to look at the example of Latin America, which was rife with dictatorships only 30 years ago. Popular revolutions overthrew these dictatorships. Democracies succeeded them. However, these democracies were controlled by the bourgeoisie, who put regimes of neoliberal growth in place, following the prevailing logic of the times. The result was a little democratisation, and a lot of social struggle. The United States changed its hegemonic strategy, moving from the control of dictatorships to the control of democracies. Yet within this process, new social and civic movements developed, changing the situation in many countries in the region. This type of evolution cannot be witnessed on the scale of a few months, but rather of a generation. What are the new social and civic movements that will emerge in the Maghreb-Mashreq? (cf. Box 10.3).

The fifth lesson is that this new era opens up the possibility of a new phase of decolonisation

Neoliberalism began with an offensive against the first phase of decolonisation: a project of recolonisation built by the G7, the G5 at that time, a club of the old colonial powers, bent on control of raw materials and domination of the global market. This offensive was built around the management of debt, on Structural Adjustment Programmes, of International Monetary Fund (IMF), World Bank and World Trade Organisation interventions, not to mention military operations. This recolonisation relied on the repressive and oligarchic regimes of decolonised countries, born from the breach of national liberation alliances between the people and the elite. This subjugation of people from the global South preceded the attacks on workers in the North, themselves subjected to precariousness through unemployment and the gradual withdrawal of social welfare and public services.

A new phase of decolonisation would mark the transition from the independence of states to self-determination of the people. As specified in the International Covenant of Civil and Political Rights (1976), all peoples have the right of self-determination. They not only have this right against any form of domination from an external source; they also have the right to internal self-determination, that is to say a democratic regime, in the sense of a regime that guarantees individual and collective liberties. This new phase of decolonisation needs a new form of international solidarity, a solidarity built on a converging belief that another world is possible. It begins with the convergence of movements: of labourers, of office workers, of peasants, of women, of human rights activists, of young people, of indigenous people, of environmentalists, of the stateless, of migrants and the diaspora, and so on. This convergence has developed in the space of the World Social Forums around a strategic orientation: to create equal rights for all on a world scale and to affirm the democratic imperative (see Chapter 10). Many movements in the Maghreb-Mashreq have taken an active role in such convergences; what is brought to light by the revolutions in this region is the great importance that such unions hold.

This text is taken from a speech given by **Gustave Massiah** at the Solidarity Meeting with the Revolutions in the Arab World, 2 May 2011, at the Bourse du Travail in Paris. The transcription was first published on the Facebook page of the Solidarity Inter-Collective with the People's Uprisings in the Arab World (www.facebook.com/pages/Comité-de-Solidarité-avec-la-Lutte-du-Peuple-Egyptien/186252268073586#!/pages/Intercollectif-de-solidarité-avec-les-luttes-des-peuples-du-monde-arabe/121147407964720) and on http://egyptesolidarite.org. It is translated here from the original French by **Claire Alleaume**.

Lebanese, Algerian and Iraqi civil wars. The double-standard approach of the international community, the disdain of the major powers, the *hogra* (contempt in North African dialect) of the Arab oligarchy towards the situation of Arab populations. And as a consequence of all this, cultural decline – with the collapse of the former centres of artistic creation and festivals, Beirut, Cairo and Tunis.

Week after Week, 'Days of Anger' after 'Days of Dignity', Revolt becomes Revolution

How does a revolution start? Why can people suddenly not bear the unbearable anymore? Why does the martyrdom of the previously-unknown Mohamed Bouazizi cause a general revolt?

Of course, in Tunisia, as in Egypt, there were plenty of warning signs: the courageous struggles of human rights defenders, including demonstrations of lawyers, hunger-strikes, and so on; peasant revolts; workers' strikes, especially the Egyptian textile workers of Mahalla in 2006 and the Tunisian phosphate mine-workers of Gafsa in 2008; political protests against falsified elections and lack of freedom, particularly in 2005, and both in Tunisia and Egypt. There was also the evident rise of a youth movement, a new internet generation. Such phenomena were also apparent in Morocco, Algeria, Bahrain, and elsewhere across the region.

The situation was not identical in all the Arab countries, but everywhere one could notice the signs of a new social situation. A whole new generation, enjoying a much higher level of education than the previous one, faced a wall built by a privileged caste, state conservatism, and the massive growth of unemployment, including for those with university degrees. These young people were looking for jobs but also for autonomy in a mutating society. Muslim societies in general, including almost all of the Arab societies, are in the process of a demographic transition, with illiteracy and birth rates decreasing to levels similar to those of Western societies, and a diminishing difference in the level of schooling between boys and girls (Courbage and Todd 2007).

And everywhere one sees the growth of economic inequality. Through the policies of *infitâh* (economic opening) and the process of privatisation, the coherence of the system built post-independence in Tunisia, Algeria, Egypt, Iraq and Syria has vanished. Neoliberalism has deepened the differences between rich and poor. For the oligarchies, privatisation was not only the opportunity to plunder and control the benefits of oil and other raw materials, but also to win the grants of foreign aid (from North America, Europe and the Gulf). Of course corruption had always existed (*backshich*), but not at such a level: it became the main system of redistribution. And, as time elapses, the clans also controlling the state have taken increasing portions of the cake: Mubarak and son in Egypt, the Assad-Shawkat clan in Syria, Saleh in Yemen and, of course, the arrogant Ben Ali-Trabelsi family in Tunisia.

In each country the gap between oligarchy and society has widened, and rage has accumulated. Rage of the young unemployed graduates and their families, cheated after years of working to give a good education to their children. Rage of workers and peasants living in ever more precarious conditions, and making less and less from their work. Rage of middle-class business owners and professionals, being racketed by the ruling mafias.

Revolt became revolution when the 'days of anger' and the 'days of dignity' brought together people with common goals: educated youth, salaried middle class and small entrepreneurs, the peasants and workers, residents of marginalised areas. Such a coalition was built in Tunisia, beginning with the marginalised centre-south and then on to the coast and the capital. The same scenario occurred in Egypt, with the convergence of Cairo and Alexandria youth movements and the workers from Suez and Mahalla. In Bahrain it started with the (relatively) poor and obviously marginalised Shi'a population. In Yemen, with the youth from the capital, Sanaa, and the people of the South (Taiz and Aden) and the North (Saadah); in Libya from the neglected eastern province of Cyrenaica; in Syria from Deraa in the south, then rapidly spreading across the whole country.

Protests remained discrete in the eastern province of Hasa in Saudi Arabia and in the city of Sohar in the sultanate of Oman, although everybody knew about the ongoing revolt of women banned by the state from driving their own cars. The Jordan and Moroccan monarchy had to face much stronger movements. In Morocco the political and social demands of the 'February 20th Movement' had a great support. The movement is a network of young people similar to those in Egypt, and is backed by the leftists and the Islamist Al Adl Wa Al Ihssane (Justice and Charity) party. But the King and the central political power around him *(Makhzen)* kept control of the situation and accepted minor reforms, adopted by referendum with the support of all political and religious forces of the country except the '20th Februarists'. In Iraq, the complex and Lebanese-like system of power (a confessionalist and ethnic system combined with foreign presence) has been challenged by a wave of social demands since the 'day of anger' on 25 February. The situation is very specific in Algeria, where the level of social unrest is extremely high (what Smaïl Goumeziane (2011) calls 'resistance through the riot system') but where the political opposition is weak, divided and often discredited, and where the real power, the military nomenklatura, remains unshaken.

Everywhere, demonstrators ask for justice, dignity, democratisation.

Islamists, Leftists, Democrats

The decline of Arab nationalism after Arab defeat in the Six Day War of 1967 and the evolution of the nationalist regime into illegitimate dictatorship created a political vacuum. From then on, political Islam grew aross the whole region. During the 1970s and 1980s the general attitude of the regimes was to court a certain type of cooperation with the Islamist movements, especially those linked with the Muslim Brotherhood (founded in 1928 by Hassan El-Banna in Egypt), as counterfire against the leftists who were still quite active at that time.

But with the radicalisation of political Islam after the Islamic Revolution in Iran, and the development in the late 1980s of political Islam's jihadist wing, the clashes between Islamists and regimes grew; from Egypt, after the peace treaty with Israel (1978) and the assassination of Sadat (1981), to the suppression of the electoral process in Algeria in 1991 (before the victory of the Islamic Salvation Front) and the bloody civil war (1991–2001). The regimes, with the exception of Syria and Tunisia, have used religion but favoured 'a conservative Islam, in phase with the Salafist streams, emphasising the re-Islamisation of individuals and not the social movements' (Roy 2011): in other words, a conservative apolitical Islam generally supported by Saudi Arabian clerics.

Back in 1992 Olivier Roy had diagnosed 'a failure of political Islam' (Roy 1992), and certainly by the beginning of the twenty-first century Islamist parties of the Muslim Brotherhood type were in a deadlock. The radical strategies had failed, and even more, al-Qaeda global terrorism and, of course, the events of 9/11 had given the Arab regimes the alibi of being at the forefront of the 'War on Terror', the only protection against Barbary. Even the consequences of victories, like the electoral success of Hamas in Palestine in 2006, brought more division and isolation. Islamist parties only had the political space that the regimes permitted; for example, there were 88 Islamist MPs in the Egyptian parliament after the elections of 2005, but none in 2010.

The revolutionary utopian goal of the Islamic state was progressively abandoned; the Islamist parties have been trivialised, progressively transformed into 'conservative political parties accepting the parliamentarian game' (Olivier 2006). And they have ceased to oppose 'Democracy as a Western Concept' and to promote the Quran as constitution. In Morocco, Algeria, Tunisia, Egypt, Jordan and Yemen, these parties are rooted in the urban middle class, supported by professionals, civil servants, and the like, the kind of people who aspire to law and order more than to the turmoil of Islamic revolution.

Such conservative parties could be part of the basis of a post-revolutionary regime, in cooperation with the military (in Egypt), or conservative liberals (in Tunisia), or any kind of conservative coalition after the elections and the 'return to normality' – with the benevolent approval of the Saudis or the US.

But the Islamists are challenged from within. On one side, some of the younger Islamist activists have been struggling together with leftist or liberal secular forces. This is the case in Morocco, with the Justice and Charity party in the February 20th Movement, and with young Muslim Brothers (and Sisters) in Yemen and Syria. In Egypt, some of the young Islamists have created their own party, the Egyptian Current Party (Hizb al-Tayyar al Masry), separate from the official party of the Brotherhood, the Justice and Freedom party (Hizb Al-Horriya Wal-Adala). On the other side, mainstream Islamists are challenged by ultraconservative Salafists, often active within these Islamist mainstream movements. They can perturb the cautious and moderate approach of the leadership of movements like Ennadha in Tunisia, and the 'guidance' of the Muslim Brotherhood in Egypt, and thus frighten potential allies for political coalition. But a challenge also comes from outside, from radical Salafist groups or a radical international pan-Islamist movement like Hizb u Tharir (Party of the Liberation), who, possibly in connection with former security services, are carrying out provocations: attacks against Christians in Egypt and Jews in Tunisia, raids against leftist rallies, violence towards female activists and violent demonstrations.

Nevertheless, Islamist mainstream parties will play an important role in the political life of most of the Arab states. Everywhere secular forces are divided. Movements of a liberal democrat or conservative democratic form are not very strong. The heir of the old Egyptian Wafd party

Box 3.2
Cairo in the Eye of the Cyclone

Introduction

Cairo, June 2011. Four months after the 'revolution', the Egyptian capital still retains its character. The maelstrom of impervious traffic and klaxons make the crossing of streets a dangerous endeavour for pedestrians. Smiles and good-humoured faces inhabit the crowd. The famous Tahrir Square is almost empty, with only a handful of anti-regime protestors chanting under the gaze of policemen. Cairo seems to have returned to its normal pace.

However, the residents of Cairo know that appearances can be deceiving. The transition is uncertain. The government led by Essam Charaf attempts to simultaneously respond to the population's socio-political demands and maintain a system that profits the military and the bourgeoisie.

Despite the current calm, strenuous living conditions and the abyss between rich and poor threaten to fuel further social explosions: socio-economic inequalities persist, prospects for the youth are scarce, and resentment at the ongoing submission to the American order remains high. Tourism, which represents a source of income for the most destitute, has plummeted: the number of foreigners visiting the country has fallen by 36 per cent compared with April 2010. Foreign investment in the Egyptian economy has seen a similar fate. Adding to these difficult economic conditions, rising prices over the past three months have increased the cost of living.

A Political Scene in Reconstruction

Trying to predict the composition of the future parliament is a shot in the dark. Political Islam, in its 'moderate' or 'radical' forms, undeniably plays a central role in Egyptian politics. Islamist movements and parties – led by the new Liberty and Justice party initiated by the Muslim Brotherhood – are very influential, although they played a secondary role in the Tahrir Square demonstrations. The secular right, on the other hand, is less organised (though perhaps not for long) and is embodied in key non-religious figures such as Mohamed El Baradeï, former director general of the International Atomic Energy Agency (IAEA), and the lawyer Ayman Nour. Such important conservative and religious currents are actively supported by the veritable Egyptian institution Al-Azhar. Leftist forces thus remain visibly weak. Various elements of the left, organised in small groups lacking both grassroots bases and strong leadership, came together in May 2011 to constitute the Front of Socialist Forces – but the current legal structure dwarfs emergent political forces.

Against the backdrop of a slowly changing political landscape, the new Egyptian Socialist Party (PSE) embraces a clear anti-globalisation and anti-liberal stance. The PSE, composed of intellectuals and unionists and led by engineer Ahmed Baha'edine Chaabane, held its first congress on 18 June 2011 in order to set out its priorities: it does not, yet, aspire to take part in elections but rather seeks to establish a progressive party in order to consolidate democratic practices.

Leftist actors have long been subject to brutal repression and forced into secrecy. They are only gradually reconstituting themselves in an increasingly vibrant, but still emerging, political society. Progressive movements are directly confronted by both the military and the Muslim Brotherhood, who seek to put a new face on the regime while preserving its defining structures. The PSE is, according to the party's international relations officer, Mamdouh Al Habashi, a key supporter of Tahrir Square's young demonstrators, and will continue to mobilise the population to demand an effective democratisation.

'Put the Poor First, Son of a …!'

The disaffection of a large segment of Egypt's population – those who were long considered a burden by Mubarak's regime – stems from evident inequalities, an unjust redistribution of wealth and economic policies implemented at the expense of the poorest. Egyptians are proud of what they have achieved, and rightly so. Despite the substantial human costs incurred in the struggle against Mubarak's clan, decades of humiliation were erased by his demise. The pride shared by all those who fight for dignity, liberty and better living conditions across the world gains its fullest expression in the conversations amongst a small group of Egyptian friends gathered in a simple restaurant near the El-Hussein mosque.

In this restaurant, a unionist and a journalist from the progressive website Al-Badil leads a heated discussion. The particularly incendiary subject of the debate is the article a young blogger, Mohamed Abou El-Gheit, published on Al-Badil (http://elbadil.net) and on his Facebook page. Entitled 'Put the Poor First, Son of a …!', the article is accompanied by stirring images of the revolution's young martyrs and issues a compelling wake-up call. The author forcefully expresses the opinion of young Egyptians, aggravated by ideological discourses that dominate interminable public debates and which centre exclusively on questions of secularism and religion. He is revolted by the media's portrayal of the revolution as led by the middle class. And he demands a more accurate representation for all the sacrifices made by impoverished young Egyptians in the name of freedom and justice.

Abou El-Gheit reminds us of those youths from 'marginalised' areas – of their courage and determination, their confrontation with brutal anti-riot units, and their Molotov cocktails against armoured vehicles. He applauds them, the poorest of the poor, who protected demonstrators from the police and the *baltadjias*, the regime's thugs:

> These young people did not take to the streets to demand a Constitution or elections. They did not take to the streets for a secular or religious state ... They took to the streets for their daily lives; for the price of food, clothing, and housing. They took to the streets against the policeman who stops their brother's minibus to extort a 50 pound bribe; for the sister they are unable to marry off; for their uncle, unemployed as a result of industrial privatisation; and for their aunt, killed not by her cancer but by the lack of a room in a public hospital ...

The debates around the Constitution and the elections sound like nothing so much as vain chattering to the most marginalised, who made up the bulk of the revolutionary crowd:

> But this does not seem to be a concern for the opposing parties. As a result of recent price hikes, many have discredited the revolutionaries and politicians ... None of the elites have expressed outrage at price increases. Even those that had loudly protested in defence of an assaulted activist did not come to the aid of Al-Salam's inhabitants when two of them died during a five-day sit-in. These people and their trivialities should simply have stayed put in their holes until we had settled our important contentious political issues!

The article concludes, merciless: 'Today, instead of an Egyptian Erdogan, we are blessed with old and dull elitists absorbed in narrow debates on secularism, Islamicism, Constitutions, and elections. To all of them, I say: put the poor first, sons of a ...!'

Transition and Regional Context

A welcome reality check, then, for an Egypt where a post-revolution tranquillity and 'societal debates' conceal uneasiness: 'These are troubled times. We cannot distinguish friend from foe',

claims an ageing resident of Cairo. 'They have us believe that the choice is between theocracy and secularism. But people do not care, they want real dignity: the dignity of work, bread and justice.'

Many Egyptians seem to have a romantic notion of their army (it did not open fire on protesters ...), but many also see through its official neutrality. High-ranking officers stand close to businessmen and the richest, and the army might very well follow a path wherein it would continue to hold the reins while delegating society's affairs to religious parties; a scenario that would resemble Pakistan. The military is managing a transition designed to perpetuate the system, with a few amendments. Entertaining close ties with Washington, the army is seeking to nurture its international alliances.

But for the majority of Egyptians, dignity will come with the restructuring of Egypt's foreign relations – perhaps best embodied by the demand for renewed solidarity with Palestinians. Normalisation of relations with Israel without a clear respect for Palestinians' rights is unthinkable. Mubarak was 'an invaluable ally', according to a Tel Aviv diplomat, and Israel rues the fall of the dictator.

Conclusion

After an active month of January 2011, Egypt has entered the eye of the cyclone. Egyptians refuse to let billionaires, the pillars of the country's power structure, appropriate their revolution. For many activists, a complete overhaul of the political landscape and forceful economic reforms will be the only solution to a profound and complex crisis. Egypt now has an emerging political society that refused submission and demands justice and liberty. It remains for this society to find its own mode of functioning as soon as possible.

Omar Benderra, Foundation Frantz Fanon. This abridged translation from the original French by **Aurore Fauret**, an MSc candidate in Development Management at the London School of Economics.

(dominant in Egypt from 1925 to 1952), the Neo-Wafd (refounded in 1983), is rather marginal and will probably make an electoral alliance with the Muslim Brotherhood. The historical Istiqlal (Independence Party) is still active in Morocco, but is part of the establishment.

On the left, 'Arab socialism', which was supposed to be the ideology of the nationalists (from Nasser to the Baath, and, under other forms, of the Algerian FLN or the Tunisian Neo-Destour), has vanished into the oligarchic system and the reign of corruption; parties like the Baath, Ben Ali RCD (the continuation of Neo-Destour) or Mubarak National Democratic Party became part of the security apparatus meant to control the masses. Today genuine Arab nationalist forces like the Egyptian Nasserite party, Karama (Dignity), are small groups. Only those who did not achieve power, like the Moroccan USFP (Socialist Union of Popular Forces) or the Algerian FFS (Socialist Forces Front) can be, to a certain extent, considered social democratic parties.

It has been said that communists had no influence in the Arab world. Historically, this is not true, considering the importance of the Iraqi Communist Party in the 1950–1970s or the Sudanese Communist Party in the 1960s. Parties in Lebanon or Iraq are still influential. Others became post-communist centre-left parties like the Tunisian Ettajdid, while the Moroccan post-communist members of PPS (Socialist Progressive Party) are considered the 'Communists of his Majesty'. In comparison, the radical left of the 1960s has had more prolific offspring. In the 1960s and 1970s this was composed mainly of far-left groups like Perspectives in Tunisia, also known from its newspaper *Amel Tounsi* (the Tunisian Worker), and *Ilal Amam* (Forwards) and the March 23rd Movement in Morocco. In the Middle East it was mainly the Harakyins, a group belonging originally to the Nasserite National Arab Movement, which radicalised in the late 1960s and formed the Popular and Democratic Front for the Liberation of Palestine (PFLP and DFLP), the Organisation of Communist Action in Lebanon, the National Liberation Front that took power in South Yemen, the Popular Front for the Liberation of Oman, and so on. Some of these movements, like the PFLP, are still active; the NLF is now the Socialist Party of Yemen. Others have been reconstructed, such as the leftist parties PSU (United Socialist Party) and Democratic Way in Morocco, and the social democratic *al-Waad* in Bahrain. And new movements have appeared: the PCOT (Communist Party of the Workers of Tunisia), the Tunisian social democrats of the FDTL (Forum for Democracy,

Labour and Liberty), a few Green parties (in Morocco and Tunisia) and numerous much smaller groups. Former radical-leftist activists became the organisers of some of the new parties, among them Ahmed Néjib Chebbi, leader of the centre-left Tunisian PDP (Democratic Progressive Party) and a serious contender in a recent presidential election.

Active and Autonomous Civil Society

During the 1980s and 1990s, a large number of former activists, departing from party politics, created, from the Atlantic Ocean to the Gulf of Persia, NGOs, women's groups, human rights associations and social movements. Under their influence a strong alter-global movement emerged in the Maghreb, especially in Morocco, and to a lesser extent in Egypt and Palestine. The Maghreb Social Forum in El Jedida (Morocco) in 2008 attracted 2,400 participants, not only from the region, but also from Middle East, Sub-Saharan Africa and Europe (see Box 10.3). Everywhere, more or less, an autonomous organised civil society appeared; the *mujtama' madani* of free associations and volunteers, as opposed to the *moujtama'ahli*, confessional or local-based organisations under the control of the government, and to GONGOs (government-organised non-governmental organisations).[1] In Egypt, for example, French analyst Alain Gresh (2011) noted that 'the past ten years have seen a multiplication of organisations defending homeless people, human rights, and women, that have contributed towards the autonomy of a society facing a police state'.

Totally new forms of action developed in the 2000s. The blog phenomenon took off in Egypt. The self-organised 'Unemployed-Graduate' movement began in Morocco. Internet chats and Facebook became tools for communication and initiating actions. The first network of cyber-dissidence was the April 6th Movement initiated by young bloggers in support of Mahalla's textile workers' struggle on 6 April 2008. Around 70,000 'Facebook friends' connected themselves to the movement, overwhelmingly a majority of young people without any political experience or affiliation. The group became a network of information and initiative, together with another group, We are all Khalid Said (Khalid Said was killed by the police in June 2010). These networks played a decisive role in the early days of the mobilisation on Tahrir Square. And, with others, including some of the Brotherhood of Muslim Youth, they created the Youth Coalition for Revolution.

Because of police pressure, Tunisian bloggers did not possess the capacity to organise such networks, but following the example of Zouhair Yahyaoui's site, the TUNeZINE (jailed and tortured in 2003, he was freed and died later in 2005), they also played a large role in the diffusion of information and slogans. One of them, Slim Amamou, called '@slim404', participated for a few months in the new Tunisian government after the fall of Ben Ali.

Cyber-dissidence flourished in Bahrain, Yemen, Morocco and Syria, helping the constitution of youth networks like the Young People for Revolution in Yemen or the February 20th Movement in Morocco.

Everywhere, except in Libya where it was impossible from the beginning, the movement has been trying to act with *Sulamya* (a peaceful approach), developing a Ghandi-like strategy to 'demilitarise the intifada', despite the casualties (300 people died in Tunisia, 900 in Egypt). This occurred even in an over-armed country like Yemen; even when confronted with the bloodbath imposed by the regime of Bachar al-Assad in Syria.

Women have been notably active during the Arab Spring. Following the end of the colonial period, the promises made by national women's liberation movements were not fulfilled. 'The situation post-independence, decided by men, consisted in the transformation of society by female education and professional women's employment, but at the same time minimised the social and economic impact of this transformation' (Naciri 2006), a frustration that Moroccan Ghita El-Kayata (1988) termed 'the foreclosure of Arab Women'.

Women's liberation movements are not something new in the Arab world. The first feminist publications date from the 1920s, in Egypt. And in the 1980s autonomous women's groups blossomed. They formed coalitions like Collectif 95 Maghreb-Egalité in 1992 in North Africa and, on an international level, the Equality without Reservation coalition to work for the implementation of the Convention on the Elimination of All Forms of Discrimination against Women (CEDAW), adopted in 1979 by the UN General Assembly. The same period saw the beginnings of so-called Islamist Feminism, calling for *ijtihad*, an interpretation and contextualisation of the prescriptions of the Quran; a 'liberation reading', as explained by the Moroccan Asma Lamrabet (2007)[2] to end 'Patriarchal Islam'. Muslim feminists organise regular congresses and have visible defenders in the Maghreb, Egypt, Yemen and even in the Gulf countries.

In March 2011, the Jordanian Leila Hammarneh explained that the events of Tunisia and Egypt had an enormous impact on the other Arab countries 'because of the fact that men and women could demonstrate together', and added that the women of Amman joined the demonstrations too, as they did 'in Libya, Yemen, Bahrain, demanding reforms and particularly legislative reforms in the field of women's rights' (Carroll 2011). In Yemen the young journalist Tawakkul Karman became one of the most visible spokespersons of the movement, inspiring other women to get involved in politics – she is herself a leader of the Islamic party Islah. Prior to the uprisings, when considering the participation of women in public life, the women's associations of the Arab world proposed, in a meeting held in Beirut,[3] a quota of one-third of women presented in elections. The Tunisians have bettered this, imposing strict equality (50:50) for the legislative elections in the autumn of 2011 – a proposition supported by the Islamic party Ennadha and adopted unanimously.

However, as the Egyptian feminist Dina Gami told a *Le Monde* journalist, 'even though women participated massively to the demonstrations, this has had no direct impact on their situation within society' (Mandraud et al. 2011). The struggle continues.

The Arab Spring has a strong social dimension. Before the uprising there were workers' strikes in the mining industry in Tunisia and by textile workers in Egypt. After the fall of Ben Ali and Mubarak there was an unprecedented wave of strikes and social demands, which are still ongoing. The demand to change labour laws 'to fit the rules of the UN International Labour Organization', are common to workers movements in several countries, from Morocco to Iraq.

Everywhere workers have tried to develop new, self-organised structures, either alongside the traditional trade unions or against them. The movement of Independent Trade Unions started in 1990 in Algeria against the official and state-controlled UGTA (General Union of Algerian Workers). New unions were created in Iraq in 2005, under the umbrella of the Federation of Workers' Councils and Unions (FCWUI). At the beginning of 2011, a crucial moment of the Egyptian Spring was the constitution of a dynamic new Egyptian confederation of independent unions, the Centre for Trade Union and Workers Services (CTUWS), confronting the official Egyptian Trade Union Federation (ETUF). Sometimes it was from officially recognised unions that a new fighting spirit emerged, as in the Tunisian General Labour Union (UGTT) or in the different Moroccan confederations. A first meeting of Mediterranean Independent Unions took place in Algiers in 2010, and there will no doubt be others.

The Past is Still Competing with the Future

The political future of Tunisia and Egypt is uncertain. The past and the future are still competing. In Tunisia, social unrest, provocations (from the old security apparatus, perhaps, or from the Salafists) and a bad economic situation might push the electorate towards candidates promising a return to order. Ennadha is hesitating between cooperating or confronting other political parties, probably because of contradictory aspirations of its members, as well as potential voters. In Egypt, the Supreme Military Council is engaged in arm-wrestling with the forces of change – the youth networks, elements of the Left, elements of the Islamic youth – with the Muslim Brotherhood on the sidelines, waiting to reap the benefits of the situation following an expectedly good electoral result.

Preceeding the Islamists, the secular left (or at least elements of it) attempts to unite. In Egypt the old leftist-Nasserite party *Tagammu* (*Hizb al Tagammu' al-Watani al-Taqadomi al Wahdawi*, the National Unionist Progressist Party) seems to be outdated. Some groups have created a Coalition of Socialist Forces: composed of the Democratic and Popular Alliance Party and the Communist Party (former a faction of Tagammu), the Workers' Democratic Party that was created by trade unionists, the Revolutionary Socialists (Trotskyites) and the new Egyptian Socialist Party (alter-globalist). In Tunisia the Democratic and Modernist Pole is composed of eleven small parties including the Ettajdid Party and the Greens (Tunisie verte).

Such a political game is going on in a more tragic and complex mode in Yemen, with a creeping civil war, tribal division and an al-Qaeda offensive – probably pushed from behind by the Saleh regime, and with Saudi interference. The movement is going on in Morocco, even if Makhzen seems to control the situation. And things are moving too in Algeria. Of course, no one yet knows how the civil and international war in Libya will end, even though it is likely that the Qadhafi regime will fall.[4] And nobody now knows how long the Assad regime will hang on, firing and killing.

The short-term fate of the Arab revolution in each particular state will depend on the nuisance capacity of those who would like to limit it or would like to go backwards: all those from outside, especially the Western powers, Saudis and Israelis; and all those from inside, the oligarchies and clans. But whatever happens in the coming months and years, things are not going to go back to what they used to be, and the 2011 awakening of the Arab people will be harvested in the coming decades.

Notes

1. See, for example, in the case of Syria, Ruiz de Elvira (2010).
2. See also Lamrabet (2011).
3. UNDP meeting on Participation of Women in Politics in the Arab World, 9–10 July 2008.
4. At the time of writing Qadhafi was alive; he was captured and killed on 20 October 2011.

References

Baun, Dylan and Hudson, Leila (2011) 'The Arab Spring's Second Wave', *al-Jazeera*, 16 May 2011.

Carroll, Shawna (2011) 'Interview with Leila Hammarneh, Project Director, Arab Women Organization, Jordan; Le droit jordanien doit intégrer les textes internationaux concernant les femmes', 7 March 2011, on the website of the International Federation of Human Rights, http://www.fidh.org (accessed 10 September 2011).

Clark, Helen (2009) *Arab Human Development Report 2009. Challenges to Human Security in the Arab Countries* (forward), UNDP, Regional Bureau for Arab States. New York: United Nations.

Courbage, Youssef and Todd, Emmanuel (2007) *Le Rendez-vous des civilisations*. Paris: Le Seuil.

El-Kayat, Ghita (1988) *Le Monde arabe au feminine*. Paris: L'Harmattan.

Goumeziane, Smaïl (2011) *Algérie, l'Histoire en heritage*. Paris: Non Lieu.

Gresh, Alain (2011) 'Ces organisations qui ont préparé la révolution', on the website of le Monde Diplomatique, July 2011, http://www.monde-diplomatique.fr/2011/07/GRESH/20752 (accessed 10 September 2011).

Hadjeres, Sadek (2011) 'De l'Atlantique au Golfe le sol se dérobe sous les pieds des tyrans', *Le Quotidien d'Oran*, 31 January 2011.

Kassir, Samir (2004) *Considérations sur le malheur arabe*. Paris: Sindbad Actes Sud.

Lamrabet, Asma (2007) *Le Coran et les femmes, une lecture de libération*. Lyon/Paris: Tawhid.

Lamrabet, Asma (2011) *Femmes Islam-Occident: chemins vers l'universel*. Biarritz/Casablanca: Séguier/La Croisée des chemins.

Mandraud, Isabelle, Barthe, Benjamin, Gurrey, Béatrice and Trégan, François-Xavier (2011) 'Les révoltes arabes font-elles progresser la cause des femmes? Quels sont leurs acquis et leurs combats?', *Le Monde*, 29 April 2011.

Mernissi, Fatema (2010) (new edition) *Islam et démocratie*. Paris: Albin.

Naciri, Rabea (2006) *Le Mouvement des femmes au Maroc*, published in 2006 on the website Cinquante ans de développement humain au Maroc, http://www.rdh50.ma.

Ramadan, Tariq (2011) 'Vendredis de la Liberté', 25 February 2011, http://www.tariqramadan.com/Les-Vendredis-de-La-Liberte.html (accessed 10 September 2011).

Roy, Olivier (1992) *L'échec de l'Islam politique*. Paris: Le Seuil.

Roy, Olivier (2006) 'Le passage à l'Ouest de l'Islamisme, rupture et continuité', in Samit Amghar (ed.), *Islamisme d'Occident. Etat des lieux et perspectives*. Paris: Lignes de repères.

Roy, Olivier (2011) 'Révolution post-islamiste', *Le Monde*, 12 February 2011.

Ruiz de Elvira, Laura (2010) 'L'Etat syrien à l'épreuve des organisations non gouvernementales depuis l'arrivée au pouvoir de Bachar al-Assad', *Maghreb-Machrek*, No. 203, Spring.

CHAPTER 4

'LOST IN TRANSFORMATION': THE CRISIS OF DEMOCRACY AND CIVIL SOCIETY

Ferenc Miszlivetz

Introduction: the Symptoms of Crisis and Emerging Ambiguities

In turbulent times often repeated clichés and conventional wisdoms easily become outdated and quickly forgotten. This has happened to the 'end of history' thesis, popular in the early 1990s. Today we not only know that history is not over, but that we are rather seriously challenged by the rapid and constant changes produced by the new course of history in the post-1989 world.

According to another conventional wisdom, closely related to the 'end of history' thesis, 'old' and 'consolidated' democracies serve as models for newly democratising societies and democratic social movements that aim to find alternatives to authoritarian regimes or dictatorships. Taking the consolidated character of West European and North American democracies for granted, and their deep roots as guarantees, only a few envisaged that potential popular movements with freedom and choice aspirations would not automatically follow the Western model but would rather carve out new frames, institutional structures and methods according to their cultural context.

We know very well today that neither history nor politics is over. We are learning almost daily that these aspirations reflect non-conventional and not necessarily Western values that have a rather universal appeal. If anything is over, or at least seriously discredited, it is the neoliberal credo with all of its various social, economic, political and cultural implications. The almighty dogmas of market fundamentalism, supported by media moguls and their global empires, are seriously questioned and rejected by expanding and interconnected popular movements and an emerging global civil society. Bushism and Putinism, as well as Berlusconism and Murdochism, have been eroding, provoking vigorous rejection, both locally and globally, by a well informed and expanding networked public. But the sudden collapse of firm beliefs and the erosion of powerful ideologies are only the byproducts of a deepening and increasingly manifest and manifold global crisis (Held et al. 2009). As Immanuel Wallerstein has convincingly and consequently argued for a long time, this global crisis is a manifestation and part of a fundamental and irreversible transformation of the modern capitalist world system (Miszlivetz 2010).

The crisis of democracy as a set of legal regulations, procedures and institutions is one of the major and most outstanding and surprising symptoms of this robust transformation process. Potentially, an entire set of institutional structures might disappear or get lost in the labyrinths of the global transformation, whereas new forms, structures, procedures, players and institutions might emerge.

From Spain and Portugal via Greece to Turkey, from the new East Central European Union (EU) member states to Russia, from Scandinavia via Ireland and Great Britain to the United States, we can read daily about corruption scandals and decreasing trust in political parties and public institutions, on the one hand, and about the reactions of an increasingly disappointed, exposed, helpless, disoriented and angry public, on the other. There is a growing conscious understanding of the crisis of democracy in general, or about 'the crisis of capitalist democracy' (Posner 2003), or about 'the crisis of parliamentary democracy' (Gilbert 2009). Even global market players and international guardian institutions such as the International Monetary Fund (IMF) have begun to worry about the vulnerability of democracy. However, most of the warning signs of crisis describe symptoms without providing proper diagnoses and, therefore, suggested 'therapies' remain superficial, short-termist and ineffective.

The roots of the present crisis of democracy can be found in the increasingly unequal and imbalanced relationship between representatives of markets, governments and societies – in Marc Nerfin's words, the Merchant, the Prince and the Citizen. (A fourth powerful player, the Media, should be added to the list as the 'Jester'.) As Robert Reich observed, present-day 'supercapitalism' has 'invaded democracy: capitalism has become more responsive to what we want as individual purchasers of goods, but democracy has grown less responsive to what we want as citizens' (Reich 2008). Behind the spectacular crisis of everyday reality there are some less obvious but profound contradictions and ambiguities, such as the tension between global and local non-territorial versus territorial, exclusion versus inclusion, accountability on the local level versus unaccountability on the supranational level, and democracy as an idea versus democracy as a set of legal procedures and formal institutions.

The Idea of Democracy and the Praxis of Democracy

The idea of democracy has grasped the imagination of an overwhelming majority of governments and societies throughout the last century. This process accelerated considerably from the 1960s (see Figure 4.1). As Alain Touraine noted, up until today, most of these countries have adopted democracy as a common good. This fact has serious consequences for both the present crisis and the future of democracies worldwide (Touraine 2009). Expectations – and consequently disappointments – about the democratic performance of political parties, governments and institutions have been spreading and growing since the so-called 'third wave' of democratisation, which gained momentum in the 1970s and peaked in 1989 (see Box 4.1).

Thanks to many coinciding factors, like the globalisation of human rights, the changing geopolitical constellation and the emergence of civil society movements and networks, the 'third wave' resulted in the collapse of Soviet-type dictatorships and the Soviet Union-led 'socialist camp' as a major challenger to the 'free Western world'. Ever since, democratic performance has been measured in comparison to its own standards instead of from the point of view of Communist dictatorships. The disappearance of bipolar logic, the collapse of the ideological, political and the military 'threat of Communism', left democracies alone with their internal problems of self-legitimation and with the increasing expectations of a widening public. Their internal quality and capability to deliver became the only measure and standard, so that public attention has shifted its focus increasingly to the *quality of democracy*. Behind growing expectations, two major driving forces can be identified:

- the increase of freedom and choice aspirations;
- the aspirations for the improvement of life chances or simply for the 'good life'.

These two aspects of human dignity are closely intertwined in reality, even if they have been separated for a long time by mainstream economic and political science theory. There were, and still are, powerful economic and political interests manifested in the daily practice of liberal democracy and consumerism that work to keep this separation intact and alive.

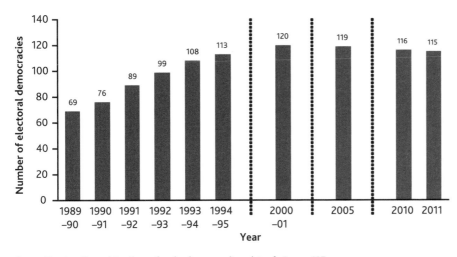

Source: Freedom House http://www.freedomhouse.org/template.cfm?page=637.

Figure 4.1   Number of Electoral Democracies Worldwide, 1989–2011

Box 4.1
Waves of Democratisation

Table 4.1   Four Waves of Democracy?

Wave	Time period	Description
First	1828–1926	The first 'long wave' of democratisation began in the United States in 1828. By 1922, 45 per cent of all nations were categorised as democratic. The first reverse wave of democracy, due in large part to the rise of fascism, the Great Depression and the Second World War, started in 1922 and ended in 1942 (Kurzman 1998).
Second	1943–64	The second 'long wave' of democratisation began at the end of the Second World War, with 32 per cent of all nations being categorised as democratic by 1962. The second reverse wave began in 1964 with the rise of military-led regimes, particularly in Latin America and Asia (Huntington 1991), resulting in a decrease to 25 per cent of nations being democratic by 1973 (Kurzman 1998).
Third	1974–90?[1]	The third wave of democratisation began with the Portuguese Revolution in 1974. As of 1990, 45 per cent of all nations were categorised as democratic (Kurzman 1998). Samuel Huntington's analysis was published in 1991, ending the analysis of the third wave in 1990. However, Larry Diamond notes that by 1996, 57 per cent of all nations were democratic, causing speculation about the end of the third wave (Diamond 1996).
Fourth	2010?	There are different ideas regarding a fourth wave of democratisation. Some consider the period after the fall of the Soviet bloc to be a fourth wave, consisting of regime changes as some countries transitioned to democracy and others to dictatorship (McFaul 2002). As this period was not merely one of democratisation, a better description is needed. More recently, the 2011 Arab Spring is being mooted by some as a fourth wave of democracy, particularly in popular discourse (see, for example, Dobson 2011, Grand 2011, Meijenfeldt 2011).

1   There is considerable discussion as to the actual end date of the third wave of democracy, given that Huntington published in 1991 and democracy continued to increase across the globe until 1996, as indicated by Diamond.

Samuel Huntington's *The Third Wave: Democratization in the Late Twentieth Century* was published in 1991. This table uses Huntington's notion of a 'wave of democratization' which he takes to mean 'a group of transitions from nondemocratic to democratic regimes that occur within a specified period of time and that significantly outnumber transitions in the opposite direction during that period' (Huntington 1991: 15). The notion of a 'wave' also suggests fluctuation, which is embodied in Huntington's idea of a reverse wave, in which the level of democracy across the world would be expected to decrease after a period of expansion. As Charles Kurzman states, 'the three waves of democratization peak at one-third to one-half of the world's nations and trough at one-fifth to one-quarter' (1998: 43). This notion of waves has been challenged over the past two decades. Philippe C. Schmitter, for example, suggests that the periods of time that Huntington lays out are far too lengthy, and that 'the initial impulse or the interactive properties that constitute a wave could (not) have lasted that long' (1993: 349–51). He suggests instead that it is more useful to consider the periods during which efforts to democratise were contained in a specific location for a specific period of time, namely: (1) the 'Springtime of Freedom', 1948–49; (2) the First World War and its aftermath, 1910–20; (3) the Second World War and its aftermath 1943–48; (4) contemporary times 1974–? (1993: 349–51).

Erik Wilson is an MSc candidate in Development Studies at the London School of Economics. Previously he worked with civil society in Nepal, and has recently returned to the region to conduct research on transitional justice.

The complex and deepening global crisis is, among other things, the manifestation of unprecedented social and political tensions created by this artificially-maintained separation. More importantly, it is the manifestation of an accelerating and irreversible global transformation. The entire modern capitalist world system was built upon this separation, and has been functioning and 'developing' accordingly. The tension that arose out of this division produced the dynamics and energy of what we call technical and economic development and innovation, which has both positive and negative consequences. This dynamic was exhausted when the capitalist world system reached its present phase of irreversible imbalance, chaos, uncertainty and unpredictability. Although conventional economic and social science theory (still seen by many as 'mainstream') suggests that our current situation is only one of the more serious and destructive crises to be followed by 'business as usual', there are good reasons to believe that the perspectives and possible outcomes are more severe in the medium and long run. The transformation into something unknown actually began decades ago.

The outburst of the 2007–08 global financial and economic crisis only made this transformation obvious and undeniable. It became crystal clear that the crisis has many interlinked and interdependent aspects, as revealed in the domino effect caused by Tunisia's Jasmine Revolution and the 'Real Democracy!'-type of protest movements throughout EU member states, including in the 'old', 'matured' and 'consolidated' democracies. The decreasing legitimacy and increasing disappointment of voters in these old, or in Schmitter's words 'archeo', democracies (Schmitter 2011), demonstrates that the present system of political and institutional regulations, dominated by nineteenth-century visions of successful Western nation states, is not maintainable and has begun to erode.

Democracy as praxis, as a set of institutions, regulations and legal guarantees, has to face fundamental challenges; already on the way to profound transformation, democracy has to be reinvented. But democracy as an idea has a more profound appeal than the single world economic system and its fragmented political units known as 'democracies': it entails the eternal desire of the individual for freedom and dignity and a deeper recognition of the necessity of human cooperation and mutual support and dependence.

From Annus Mirabilis to Annus Horribilis?

As the ongoing global turmoil demonstrates on a daily basis with surprising frequency, it seems to be more and more self evident that one cannot detach the ever deepening problems that old and new democracies face from the consequences and interdependencies of the equally deepening and complex global economic and financial crisis. The narrow path and space for manoeuvre available to chief executives of nation states is increasingly determined more by major global market players, transnational financial guardian institutions and media moguls than by their own constituencies. Promises of election campaigns are therefore rapidly forgotten, if ever taken seriously, by increasingly sceptical, apathetic and frustrated voters. Nobody is surprised anymore if it turns out that politicians lie in order to be voted into power. But as a consequence, public trust in democratic institutions, especially in the case of political parties, parliaments and politicians, has dramatically fallen during the past decade (see Figures 4.3 and 4.4); elections are becoming empty rituals, with the difference between centre right and centre left disappearing. Rhetoric, style and amusement – a combination of circus and scandal – have taken over the scene, with a strong xenophobic agenda on the far right tacitly but increasingly backed by the conservative middle classes of the 'old and consolidated democracies'. Rapidly strengthening and increasing popular xenophobic and nationalistic political forces are emerging not only in newly democratising societies with recent dictatorial and authoritarian pasts, but also within 'archeo-democracies' with strong democratic credentials, such as Denmark, Sweden or Norway (see Box 4.2).

The Infinite Process of Democratising Democracy

Philippe Schmitter raised a number of highly relevant questions about the future of what he calls the 'REDs', that is, 'in reality existing democracies'. His first concern is with the expression 'RED' itself, which requires further definition. There is little to no consensus among political scientists, experts and practitioners about the definition of democracy (see Box 4.3, which compares various indexes of democracy). As Larry Diamond noted in one of his recent books, 'defining democracy is a bit like interpreting the Talmud (or any religious text): ask a room of ten rabbis (or political scientists) for the meaning, and you are likely to get eleven different answers' (Diamond 2008: 21). Avoiding the hopeless academic hurdles of definition games, Schmitter talks straight about reality, defining 'democracies' as those recognised as such by themselves and by others (primarily by politicians, political scientists and political experts). The number of such entities has

Box 4.2
The Rise of Far-Right Parties Across Europe

The rise of Marine Le Pen, daughter of Jean-Marie Le Pen, whom she succeeded in January 2011 as current leader of France's National Front, has her polling ahead of both President Nicolas Sarkozy and any likely Socialist challenger in the French presidential elections of 2012. As her popularity and credibility as a presidential candidate grows, comparisons are often drawn between Le Pen and extreme-right figures elsewhere in Europe, including Dutch politician Geert Wilders, British National Party leader Nick Griffin, and, before he shed his overt fascist trappings to gain more mainstream influence, Italian Gianfranco Fini.

It is not only France that is seeing a surge in popularity of far-right political parties. In an arc of countries spreading north-east from the Netherlands, populist parties are cutting a swathe through politics, appealing to electorates with various blends of nationalism, Euroscepticism (and euro-scepticism) and outright xenophobia. This is particularly evident in Finland, where the True Finns emerged from relative obscurity on the extreme right to join the government following elections held on 17 April 2011. Surging poll ratings prior to the elections placed the True Finns on a par with Finland's three main parties: the National Coalition, the Social Democrats and the Centre Party (*The Economist* 2011). Following the elections, the True Finns made incredible gains in parliament, winning 39 seats or 19 per cent of the electoral vote, compared to five seats or 4.1 per cent of the electoral vote in 2007 (Reuters 2011). The True Finns have been able to broaden their appeal from its rural base by adopting an anti-immigration stance and hostility towards the European Union: opposing the bailout of eurozone countries and demanding changes in the Portugal package. The party's leader, Timo Soini, has said the party wants to balance public finances by lowering EU member dues and development aid (Reuters 2011).

In Denmark, the leader of the Danish People's Party (DPP), Pia Kjaersgaard, has said that the party hopes to do well in elections that must be held by November 2011 (*The Economist* 2011). Under its influence, the minority centre-right coalition that it has propped up for the past decade has turned Denmark's immigration regime into one of Europe's tightest, all in return for agreeing to the government's budget for next year.

Their Swedish counterparts, the Sweden Democrats – a party with roots in the neo-Nazi movement – enjoyed success at a general election last September 2010, gaining more than 4 per cent of the vote, which enabled them to enter parliament for the first time. For a short while, there was speculation that they would become an ally of the government: the narrowly re-elected four-party centre-right alliance under prime minister Fredrik Reinfeldt, which won just 173 seats out of a possible 349. This is the first time that a Swedish conservative government has been re-elected in about a century; the centre-left Social Democrats have been in power for 65 of the past 78 years and are largely credited with setting up the country's generous welfare state. However, despite being shunned by other parties, with Erik Ullenhag, Sweden's integration minister, recently accusing the Sweden Democrats of intolerance and Islamophobia, poll ratings for the party are holding up (*The Economist* 2011). Immigrants make up approximately 14 per cent of the country's population of 9.4 million, with the largest immigrant group from neighbouring Finland, followed by people from Iraq, the former Yugoslavia and Poland.

In the Netherlands, polls put Geert Wilders anti-immigrant Freedom Party (PVV) second only to the Liberals, whose minority-led coalition with the Christian Democrats Wilders has supported in parliament since last year, in a Denmark-style arrangement. The British National Party has been represented in the European Parliament since 2009, while the Vlaams Belang continues to remain a political force in Belgium's dysfunctional politics. In Central Europe, Jobbik, a Hungarian far-right party, took 15 per cent of the vote in the June 2009 European elections, sending shudders across the continent; it ran on an anti-Roma platform, in addition to stating opposition to Jews and homosexuals. Jobbik joined the ranks of existing right-wing extremists in the region, including the Slovak National Party, which has won seats in every Slovak parliament but one since 1990 and has been part of the government since 2006 – and whose leader, Jan Slota, is known for anti-Hungarian remarks. Bulgaria's extreme-right coalition, Ataka, is known for denouncing the country's Turkish population; it has taken 10 per cent of the national vote since 2005.

And the Viennese Freedom Party, led by the far-right Heinz-Christian Strache, more than doubled its vote to 27 per cent following a xenophobic campaign which featured free computer games which involved firing at mosques, and calls for the city's 'blood to remain Viennese' (Phillips 2011). In some working-class areas of the city, the Freedom Party took 37 per cent of the electoral vote (Traynor 2010).

On a European level, encouraged by their recent successes in the polls, the Austrian and French far-right parties have also pushed for respectability in the European Parliament. Austria's Freedom Party has notably called on the Eurosceptic alliance in the chamber – between the Europe of Freedom and Democracy grouping led by the United Kingdom Independence Party (UKIP) and Italy's Northern League – to let their two MEPs join. Strache and Marine Le Pen have also recently expressed a strong interest in deeper cooperation between their two parties.

Renjie Butalid is an MA student in the ISES Corvinus International Relations programme, Kőszeg, Hungary.

increased dramatically during the past half a century, which can be seen as a result of both changing values and growing freedom and choice aspirations globally, as well as the consequence of hazy rules and vague and abstract criteria. Except for China, North Korea and perhaps Cuba, very few countries remain that do not aspire to being recognised as a democracy. Even within these explicitly non-democratic political units of one-party systems, there is growing fear of the spread of the spirit of democracy and of liberty aspirations. In North Korea, for example, the government recently suspended the functioning of universities for the entire academic year and sent students to the countryside to do agricultural work. In China, the Communist Party attempts to control internet usage, and has banned certain words – such as 'Egypt' – from search engines.

This opens the way in two directions: both for almost limitless governmental cynicism and arbitrariness of self-interpretation and forever-growing popular, bottom-up, self-organising and mobilising civil societies worldwide. The growing gap between aspirations and realities can be interpreted as a 'crisis of democracy'. This leads us to what Schmitter calls the 'great political paradox of our times': exactly at the historic moment of the unexpected blossoming of new democratic aspirations in parts of the world seen previously as hopeless for democratisation, the old established democracies are facing deepening crises and are getting lost in the turmoil of global and national transformation, which they obviously cannot predict, interpret nor control efficiently in harmony with each other.

Following the path of Robert Dahl, Schmitter rightly emphasises the ever-changing forms and content of democracies in terms of size, scale and scope. Some of these 'revolutionary' changes – like the professionalisation of politics or the 'associational revolution' – are recognised and accepted features of democratic regimes, whereas other changes are not yet completely understood or recognised. One of the great challenges is the increasing role, for example, of international 'guardian institutions' such as the World Bank, the IMF, the EU or the European Central Bank. Those new democracies with typically weak and exposed economies, like the democracies of the post-Soviet, post-Communist countries, are especially likely to be perceived as 'no choice democracies' by their respected constituencies. Both local and national politicians, theoretically accountable for their decisions, claim instead that the faraway and unaccountable guardian institutions leave them no choice of decision

in cases of fundamental importance. This tendency has serious and far-reaching consequences:

- first of all, it empties out national sovereignty and delegitimises democracies on the national level;
- it supports the general feeling that 'nobody can be made accountable';
- and consequently further strengthens the tendency of growing mistrust of democratic institutions, political parties and politicians.

The decreasing public trust in politics and democratic institutions is a worldwide tendency that is clearly identifiable in certain neo-REDs, like Hungary (see Figures 4.3 and 4.4). According to a recent opinion poll in Hungary (Civil Szemle 2011), more than 80 per cent of respondents do not trust politicians, political parties, nor even the parliament itself, despite the fact that the present ruling coalition has a vast and unprecedented – more than two-thirds – majority. People have more trust in NGOs and other actors of civil society, or the police and the church.

Although the process of cross-border/regional/ transnational democratisation processes, as well as the establishment of effective and democratic multilevel governance, have been held back, the democratisation of democracy might gain new momentum with the awakening in Middle Eastern and North African (MENA) countries. The Arab Spring has had an unstoppable domino effect throughout the entire Middle East; unexpected freedom and choice aspirations surfaced one after the other from Tunisia through Egypt, Morocco, Bahrain, Yemen, Jordan, Syria and Libya. The great transformation of the Arab world is far from over: political change has not yet crystallised, and violence could not be avoided. It is obviously too early a stage to predict the outcome of the eruption of freedom. But it has been proved clear that the idea of democracy has an undeniable and growing global appeal and that the democratisation of democracy, or rather the reinvention of democracy, is unavoidable on all possible levels.

The European Paradox

Closely connected to the emptying out of democracies and the weakening of the nation state, another important 'revolutionary' change in the scope of democracies is the existence and prospect of multilevel governance. Weaknesses of the nation state could be well compensated by introducing new levels of aggregate decision-making.

This occurred, first of all, in post-WWII Europe, where the process of integration produced concepts and policies directed towards delegating political responsibilities and decision-making on interconnected but separable sub-national, national and transnational levels.

Expectations were high in the early 1990s about the introduction and empowerment of new players on the mezo-level. Regional decision-making, however, was taken over by member states that pursued overwhelmingly centralised national interests. This has created a second, in my words, 'European paradox' of existing democracies. In the case of the European Union, nation states became member states of a larger supranational entity, freely delegating decision-making and, as a consequence, part of their sovereignty at the supranational level. At the same time, their own democratic legitimacy is being emptied out at home while the new supranational entity is unable to reach full democratic legitimacy – the 'democratic deficit' frequently noted in the literature on global civil society and on global governance.

Voters can only hold their elected politicians accountable at the national level for decisions being brought about by the semi-sovereign (the EU) on the supranational level. This discrepancy in the process of European construction of multilevel governance offers the opportunity for national politicians to blame the EU for unpopular decisions, which in turn further alienates citizens from EU institutions and undermines public trust in supranational guardian institutions.

Similarly, there is a tendency among political scientists and analysts of European integration to believe that the EU itself is responsible for the crisis of democracy at the national level. They claim that transnational decision-making weakens the functioning of democratic institutions on the nation state level and, at the same time, does not lead to automatic democratisation at the transnational/European level. There is an undeniable element of truth in this observation. However, presumably we need to dig deeper if we want to find the core of the problem, paying attention to the very roots of multinational governance. One has to remember the wise but often neglected warning of Jean Monnet, concerning the undetermined nature of transnational European political power. Monnet emphasised that European democracies have yet to invent and build up a new kind of political power. It is rather the capability (or lack of capability) of European democracies to construct such a new political power that is at stake.

Obviously, to create multilevel decision-making and 'governance' is not an easy job, especially not under circumstances of crisis, and with such an erosion of public trust in political institutions. This is certainly a task that would require both more time and more serious and concerted efforts, accompanied by political courage and maybe even just good luck, in order for stakeholders to seize the right moment to take action.

Looking at the broader picture, beyond the European orbit, there is no doubt that we are again in a new phase of global turmoil. 2011 reminds many observers and analysts of 1989. Indeed, there are some similarities: although in both cases there were plenty of signs of escalating social and political discontent, these revolutions were seen as unexpected surprises. Superpower and big power interests in keeping the geopolitical status quo were in collision in both cases with bottom-up social movements and self-mobilising civil society aspirations.

Of course, there are many important differences between the Arab Spring of 2011 and the East Central European revolutions of 1989: the pull effect of the West is far less obvious, or possibly even absent in 2011, while European peace movements and cross-border networking for East-West dialogue played a significant role in mobilising democratic dissent within the former Soviet bloc. Although there was a strong media presence in 1989 in East Central Europe, ICT and social media play an unprecedented role in organising demonstrations and sharing information with the largest possible public today. Using these new technologies in creative ways contributes to the emergence of a global public, and to the potential of this public to become an aggregate globalising political pressure group. This will likely have unforeseeable and far-reaching consequences for the future of democracy on global, regional and local levels.

The Legacy of 1989

1989 signalled a paradigm shift in the history of democracies: civil society became an indispensible agent and dynamising engine of democratisation. It heralded the twilight of the exclusive Grand Narrative. It integrated some characteristics of the alternative 'new' social movements such as self-mobilisation, civil autonomy, self-limitation, non-violence, the pluralist understanding of sovereignty and the ethics of disagreement. Altogether the 'Velvet Revolutions' differed in many ways from previous revolutions, and the emergence and self-assertion of civil society has far richer consequences than mainstream social and political sciences have ever recognised.

Civil society's normative programme of self-restriction as the internal brake mechanism preventing violence

Box 4.3
Comparing Democracies

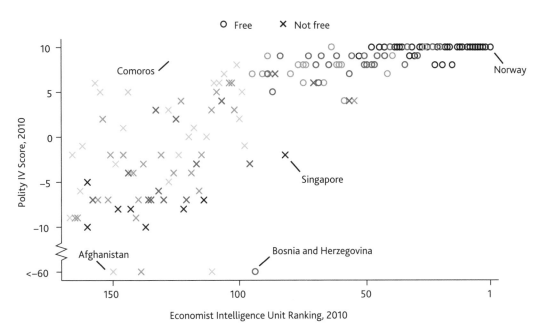

Figure 4.2   Comparisons of Democracies, 2010

Notes: The scatterplot shows how evaluations of countries' polities and economies are associated with each other. Each marker represents a country; we have labelled five countries at key points in the chart for illustrative purposes. Plotting scores from the latest Polity IV data set on the vertical axis (where higher values indicate better outcomes) against rankings from the Economist Index on the horizontal axis (where the lower the number, the better the outcome) shows that the two measures are positively correlated with each other. Countries rated highly by the Economist Index tend also to be rated highly by the Polity IV index (looking at the upper right-hand corner of the plot). Those rated less well by the Economist Index tend to be rated less well by the Polity score – but correspondence between scores is looser at this end of the spectrum (note the greater degree of scatter on the left-hand side of the plot).

    The markers used in the chart give further information about the income level and political system type of the countries. Circles represent those countries that are electoral democracies, according to Freedom House (2011), and crosses those that are not. And finally, lighter shades of marker indicate countries with lower levels of income, and darker shades indicate higher income countries, based on World Bank income rankings (2011). It seems that higher-income countries, with electoral democracies, tend to have higher Polity IV and Economist Index values – but with some exceptions.

    For ease of presentation, four countries (Haiti, Côte d'Ivoire, Bosnia and Herzegovina and Afghanistan) with extremely low scores on the Polity index are presented below a break in the scale of the vertical axis, at the level marked 'less than –60'.

Sources: Economist Index http://graphics.eiu.com/PDF/Democracy_Index_2010_web.pdf; Polity IV http://www.systemicpeace.org/inscr/inscr.htm; Freedom House http://www.freedomhouse.org/template.cfm?page=637; World Bank http://siteresources.worldbank.org/DATASTATISTICS/Resources/CLASS.XLS.

Closer examination of the graph suggests that the EIU seems to provide a more precise measure of democracy than Polity IV. For Polity IV, electoral democracies (upper right hand corner) are all within the numerical range of 5 and 10, while the range for the same countries spans over 100 points for EIU. By providing more nuances in the values allocated to polities, the EIU allows for a greater distinction between each country thus permitting a more detailed comparative study. On the other hand, Polity IV's measure (from –10 to +10) clearly states whether a regime tends towards autocracy or democracy.

    The comparison of the indexes reveals that different definitions of democracy – and their associated normative underpinnings and choice of criteria – result in very different classifications. While Freedom House here provides a measure focused on elections, it is now widely recognised that institutional design and elections are not sufficient conditions for democracy. In the components of their democracy indexes, Polity IV and EIU mention Dahl's eight requirements of polyarchy (Dahl 1971). However, it is interesting to note that the EIU measures political culture, based on surveys, and places civil society attitudes as a central criteria in its index. This could be said to reflect a more substantive notion of democracy, wherein citizens can influence policy decisions and participate in democratic processes (Kaldor 2008).

Research and analysis by **Aurore Fauret**, an MSc candidate in Development Management at the London School of Economics.

and Jacobean revolutionary spirit worked successfully throughout the 1980s. Fundamentalist projects were successfully avoided, but facing up to the past has not yet happened. The particular merit of 1989 is that societies engaged in Velvet Revolutions managed to avoid giving one great and final answer to the flaws, sins and failures of the past. Instead, a dynamic, vibrant and oscillating civil society became engaged in constant self-reflection and self-correction in an effort to prevent the democratisation process from floundering. On the theoretical level, this is substantiated, among others, by the concept of autonomy proposed by Castoriadis. This notion is based on the freedom of different forms of thinking and political action, keeping alive the possibility of questioning and of breaking out from existing institutional frames.

The lesson we can learn in 2011 from 1989 is that no single discourse can claim any more to convey an exclusive truth – today it is hard to question the fact that democracy has many different voices. We can safely declare that one of the most important goals of 1989 has been met. Instead of a uniform frame of discourse regarding liberal democracy, it has become possible to guarantee heterogeneity. Structural conditions of political plurality are in place.

The other great achievement of 1989 was that it did not follow the classical logic of revolutions in so far as it did not invent a mythological 'people' with the right to create the constitutional order of the new political regime. In other words, the homogeneous 'will of the people' and the fiction of the 'sovereignty of the people' did not gain dominance. However, as democracy in its present forms is further eroded, this danger may surface once more. Since democracies are fragile constructions, there are no guarantees against setbacks and relapses.

The Velvet Revolutions left more questions open than they answered by expressing a 'negative' consensus – what they were rejecting was clear, but what they wished to create was not. This is often interpreted as a lack of revolutionary ideas (Offe 1996, Kaldor 2003). However, the lack of a guiding revolutionary idea does not prevent us from claiming that this was a time when a great number of novel ideas, programs and thoughts surfaced. Ulrich Preuss (2001) offers an excellent summary of the main achievements of 1989, noting that these self-restricting revolutions marked a considerable shift from the monistic model of political sovereignty toward a pluralist model, one which prioritises civil society and guarantees a wide arena for its development.

Carrying the idea further, Paul Blokker (2009) draws our attention to the difference and potential tension between legality and legitimacy. He is right to emphasise that democracy cannot be reduced to a simple justification of proceduralism or legalism. However, if we wish to speak in terms of legitimacy instead of mere legality, we need constant endorsement of the society and the permanent re-evaluation of civil society. Consequently, the rule of law cannot be a sufficient condition of democracy. Legal systems – formal democracies – need permanent correction by 'dissenting' citizens so that the rule of law does not become a 'herbal cure-all remedy'.

The New Language of Civil Society

During the 1980s, the activities and new way of thinking of democratic opposition groups and independent actors created a new language which is now, after two decades, able to convey critical thinking even in opposition to those who were the first to use this language. This new discourse of civil society simultaneously represents the idea of legality and insistence on the rule of law, and the position of radical self-restriction and disagreement. It is the self-expression of a new paradigm. This aspect, the 'democratisation of democracy', is perhaps the most innovative and original product of 1989. Civil society as the guarantee of the self-correcting capability of democracy is a new definition, one which goes beyond the criticism of totalitarian regimes and the attempt to overcome them which was characteristic in the 1980s, and one which can become an organic part of a new theory of democracy. It provides a theoretical grip, and may offer a way out for people who have become disillusioned with democracy, potentially leading to the discovery of new ways to rejuvenate democracies and, in doing so, overcome the present crisis which, at least in the case of the 'new democracies', is at the root of much of this disillusionment. Thus interpreted, the concept of civil society will open up the 'democratic space' and leave it open. It will contribute to the plurality of democratic practice and at the same time enhance the democratic legitimacy of democracies.

In this context, civil society is a public arena where different actors, ideas, values, aspirations and interests influence, contradict, alter and enrich each other. It is a sort of creative chaos, a hotbed of reproducing and redefining the temporary and transitory order of the public sphere – or rather, the 'publics'. Although different actors have different ideas of what constitutes the public good, civil society itself is part of the ever-changing

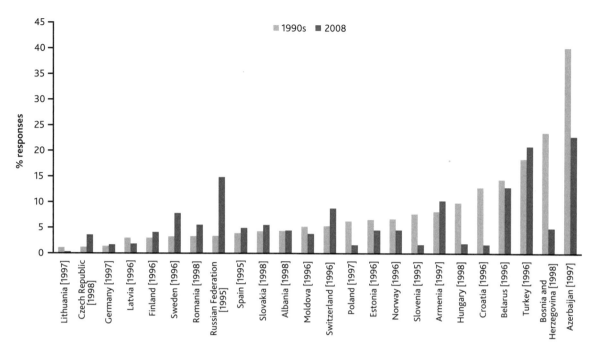

Figure 4.3 Percentage of Survey Respondents Expressing 'A Great Deal of Confidence' in Government
(Years in brackets show the year indicated in comparison to 2008)

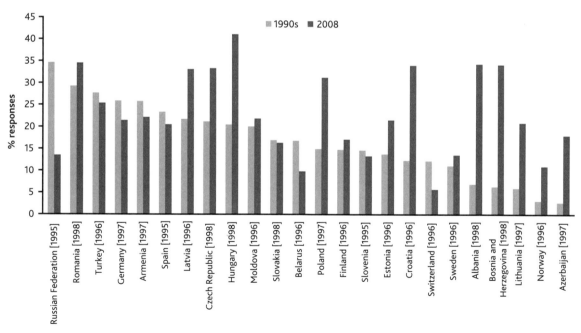

Source: World Values Survey 1981–2008 Official Aggregate v.20090901, 2009. World Values Survey Association (http://www.worldvaluessurvey.org).
Aggregate File Producer: ASEP/JDS, Madrid.

Figure 4.4 Percentage of Survey Respondents Expressing 'No Confidence at All' in Government
(Years in brackets show the year indicated in comparison to 2008)

Box 4.4
The Thread of Non-Violent Protest: 1968, 1989, 2011

A thread of non-violent discourse has run through the revolutions of the late twentieth century and into those of 2011. Indeed, non-violence is now 'a dominant commitment of contemporary social movements' (Kaldor 2003: 83), and groups that resort to armed struggle are generally delegitimised by the international community. Perhaps the most striking commonality between the revolutions of 1968, 1989 and 2011 is their overall adherence to non-violent collective action. The tactics adopted by these movements ranged from peaceful protests, strikes and boycotts, to direct action and civil disobedience. In recognition of their specifically non-violent character, these revolutions were given 'softening' labels, such as 'velvet' in the case of Czechoslovakia and 'singing' for the Baltic states, which can be understood as an attempt to dissociate the word 'revolution' from 'violence' (Garton Ash 2009).

1968 – Counter-Culture as Protest

In the context of the Cold War and the Vietnam War, the 1968 revolutions provided much of the impetus for the profound reconfiguration of politics and culture in the decades to follow. The year of 1968 alone saw demonstrations in Northern Ireland, Germany, Britain, Greece, Italy and Poland, as well as 'Mai 68' in France. 1968 also resonated in the United States, with widespread mobilisation of solidarity in Chicago, New York and San Francisco.

While these peaceful protests were intertwined with violent riots and 'urban guerrillas' – most notably in France and West Germany – some civil society groups emphasised non-violent cultural protest. The French-based Situationistes International (SI), featuring key figures such as Guy Debord, was a prominent intellectual group that inspired the 1968 student movements. The SI fostered a counter-culture through the deployment of subversive messages in the media, a practice known today as 'culture jamming'. The group left a lasting and global legacy for civil society activism and was influential throughout the world, particularly in Italy, Germany and the United Kingdom (Blissett 2002).

1989 – Ending Communism

In 1989, the wave of protests sweeping through Central Europe led to the historic fall of the Berlin Wall and the collapse of twentieth-century communism. That year, the Polish opposition group Solidarity entered the 'Round-table Talks'; Romania, Bulgaria, Slovenia and Albania experienced mass mobilisations;

Georgia's protests planted the seeds for the 'Rose Revolution'; and Czechoslovakia lived the 'Velvet Revolution'. Across the globe, Chinese pro-democracy protestors were massacred in Tiananmen Square.

Influential Czechoslovakian human rights groups of 1989, such as Charter 77 and the Civic Forum, explicitly espoused peaceful tactics. Indeed, members of the Civic Forum explain that 'our weapons are love and non-violence' (Garton Ash 2009). These groups played a key role in the 'Velvet Revolution' and inspired Charter 91 in Hungary (Tismaneanu 1999: 147). Charter 77 also notably forged transnational connections with the peace movements in Western Europe and Solidarity in Poland (Hauner 2008: 3).

In August 1989, political dissidents in Estonia, Latvia, and Lithuania formed the Baltic Council of Popular Fronts (O'Connor 2003: 155) and created the 'Baltic Way': a spectacular human chain that ran through all three nations. This peaceful action drew the world's attention to their demand for autonomy from the USSR.

2011 – Fighting the 'Arab Exceptions'

Throughout the so-called 'Arab Spring' (see Chapter 3), non-violence has been the dominant discourse embraced by global civil society activists. The writings of Gene Sharp, a prominent American thinker, have purportedly shaped the non-violent nature of the recent revolutions (Stolberg 2011). His manual of Ghandian tactics, *198 Methods of Non-Violent Action* (Sharp 1973), has been widely distributed throughout the world and used by pro-democracy protestors in the Middle East and North Africa as a tool for political change.

A multiplicity of networks, in particular those formed on the internet, constitutes the leading actors of the twenty-first-century revolutions. Numerous groups of solidarity with figures on the ground such as Mohamed Bouazizi (Tunisia) and Wael Ghonim (Egypt) appeared on Facebook and provided a virtual base for non-violent mass mobilisation. The wide use of social media has led the movements of the 'Arab Spring' to be popularly referred to as the 'Twitter Revolutions'.

For resources on non-violence, see the International Center on Nonviolent Conflict: www.nonviolent-conflict.org.

Aurore Fauret

consensus about public good. Researchers of the Civil Society Network (CiSONET, organised by the WZB für Sozialwissenschaften as an FP7 (the EC's Seventh Framework Programme) research programme under the leadership of Jürgen Kocka) project concisely summarised the different aspects of this complex notion, accordingly:

> civil society refers (a) to the community of associations, initiatives, movements and networks in a social space related to but distinguished from government, business and private sphere; (b) to a type of social action which takes place in the public sphere and is characterized by non-violence, discourse, self-organisation, civility, recognition of plurality and orientation towards general goals; (c) a project with universalistic claims, which changes while it expands across boundaries ... . (CiSONET 2010)

Michael Edwards clearly distinguishes the three major aspects of civil society: (1) a kind of a 'good society' or utopia; (2) associational life; (3) the public sphere. The real dynamics of civil society lie in the interaction of the different constituting elements, in 'an integrated approach to civil society that unites elements of all three models and thus increases the utility of this idea both as an explanatory tool and as a vehicle for action' (Edwards 2004: 91). This complex and integrated concept of civil society might be useful for the analysis and deeper understanding of the changing relationship between the Merchant, the Prince, the Citizen and the Jester on the global level.

Conceptual Interventionism

During the past two decades of the post-1989 era, resource-rich actors (guardian institutions, the EU and global philanthropists, amongst others) have increasingly promoted the notion of civil society. This conceptual interventionism is partly responsible for the global diffusion of the concept and for the widespread debate surrounding it. Guardian institutions are especially attracted to nominating and listing civil society interlocutors with whom they are eager to enter into public dialogue. The World Bank, the IMF, the World Trade Organisation (WTO) and the Commission of the EU are known for their civil society discourse and 'devotion'. As the Final Report of CiSONET observes, such conceptual interventions are similar to other forms of military, diplomatic or economic interventions that alter the socio-political constellations into which they intervene without being able to predict or control their consequences (CiSONET 2010: 45–6). The

growing discrepancy between words and deeds, between the civil society language used by representatives of the Merchant and the Prince, on the one hand, and by a genuine civil society of self-organising Citizens on the other, has proved to be a creative confrontation. It is an expression of the growing role of civil society in settling global matters.

The pluralistic character and increasing fragmentation and fragility of modern societies demand the further crystallisation of new forms of social imagination that are both self-reflexive and at the same time self-restricting (Miszlivetz and Jensen 2005). Most importantly, this social imaginary needs to view all forms of institutionalised democracy as by nature transitory. These forms must always be open to transformation in the future. This approach radically points beyond the way in which democracy is interpreted today, which is essentially elitist and reduced primarily to questions of the rule of law and legality. It is based on the assumption that legality and formal, procedural stability in themselves cannot constitute a democratic regime in the twenty-first century.

The most innovative achievement of 1989 was perhaps the legitimisation of the 'ethics of disagreement'. Any self-respecting democratic system which accepts and supports autonomy and a broad, emancipatory concept of politics must be open to civil disobedience and at all times respect dissent. It should also reckon with the idea that civil movements, initiatives and social flows, starting up at the peripheries of the political community, are the most promising resources for reviving democracies which are in crisis or emptied out in terms of content: they are our best chance for democratising democracy.

Perspectival Conclusions: Towards a Great Reconnection?

Most democracy theoreticians agree that one of the great and unbeatable characteristics of democracy is its capacity to renew, and even more, to reinvent itself (Keane 2010, Schmitter 2011). Looking at the perplexities and complexities of the present profound transformation and the diverging expectations and aspirations of decisive players, this self-reinvention does not seem to be an easy game, nor an automatic process. Nothing seems to be sure or unquestionable in the arsenal of the post-Second World War economic, legal and social institutions. Nation states, supranational regional institutions such as the EU, international guardian institutions such as the IMF, the World Bank or the European Central Bank, not to speak of powerful and unaccountable media empires, appear to

Box 4.5
The Road to Europe: Movements and Democracy

There is no doubt that the crisis in Europe is a crisis of democracy as well as, or even more than, a financial crisis. Neoliberalism is a political doctrine that brings with it a minimalist vision of the public and democracy – as Colin Crouch demonstrates so well in his *Post-Democracy* (2004). It envisages the reduction of political intervention to correcting the market (with consequent liberalisation, privatisation and deregulation), an elitist concept of citizen participation (electoral only, and therefore occasional and potentially distorted) and an increased influence of lobbies and powerful interests. The evident crisis of a liberal concept and practice of democracy is however accompanied by the (re) emergence of diverse concepts and practices of democracy, elaborated and practiced – among others – by social movements. In today's Europe, they are opposing a neoliberal solution to the financial crisis, accused of further depressing consumption and thereby quashing any prospect for growth – whether sustainable or not.

Austerity measures in Iceland, Ireland, Greece, Portugal and Spain were met with long-lasting mass protests. In part, they took the more traditional form of general strikes and trade union demonstrations, contesting the drastic cuts to social and labour rights.

Another protest also emerged – not opposed to the former, but certainly different and more directly concerned with democracy: the criticism to democracy as it is now, and the elaboration of possible alternatives. '*¡Democracia real ya!*' was the main slogan of the Spanish *indignados* protesters that occupied the Placa del Sol in Madrid, the Placa de Catalunya in Barcelona and hundreds of squares in the rest of the country from 15 May 2011, calling for different social and economic policies and indeed greater citizen participation in their formulation and implementation. Before such a mobilisation in Spain, at the end of 2008 and start of 2009, self-convened citizens in Iceland had demanded the resignation of the government and its delegates in the Central Bank and in the financial authority. In Portugal, a demonstration arranged via Facebook in March 2011 brought more than 200,000 young people to the streets. The *indignados* protests, in turn, inspired similar mobilisations in Greece, where opposition to austerity measures had already been expressed in occasionally violent forms.

Accused by the left of being apolitical and populist (not to mention without ideas) and by the right of being extreme-leftists, these movements have in reality placed what Claus Offe long ago defined as the 'meta-question' of democracy at the centre of their action.

The *indignados*' discourse on democracy is articulated and complex, taking up some of the principal criticisms of the ever-decreasing quality of representative democracies, but also some of the main proposals inspired by other democratic qualities beyond electoral representation. These proposals resonate with (more traditional) participatory visions, but also with new deliberative conceptions that underline the importance of creating multiple public spaces, egalitarian but plural.

Above all, they criticise the ever more evident shortcomings of representative democracies, mirroring a declining trust in the ability of parties to channel emerging demands in the political system. Beginning from Iceland, and forcefully in Spain and Portugal, indignation is addressed towards corruption in the political class, seen in bribes (the dismissal of corrupt people from institution is called for), as well as in the privileges granted to lobbies and in the close connection between public institutions and economic (and often financial) power. It is to this corruption – that is the corruption of democracy – that much of the responsibility for the economic crisis, and the inability to manage it, is attributed to.

If the centrality of the condemnation of corruption has bent some noses out of shape on the left (which still sees anti-politics more in the criticism of corruption than in corruption itself), the slogan 'they don't represent us' is nevertheless also linked to a deeper criticism of the degeneration of representative democracy, linked to the failure of elected politicians to carry out appropriate policies. They are often united in creating the image that no alternatives are available – an image that protesters do not accept. In Spain in particular, the movement has asked for proportional reforms to the electoral law, denouncing the reduced weight given to citizen participation inherent to the majority system (a very pertinent theme for Italy), where the main political parties tend to form cartels, and electors see their choices limited (for this reason equal weight for each vote was called for).

Representative democracy is also criticised for having allowed – to use the metaphor proposed by Mario Pianta in his contribution to this debate – the abduction of democracy, not only by financial powers, but also by international organisations such as the European Union and the International Monetary Fund. Pacts for financial stability, imposed in exchange for loans to troubled countries, are considered as anti-constitutional forms of blackmail, depriving citizens of their sovereignty.

Among the proposals for giving power back to citizens are those that go in the direction of direct democracy, giving electors the possibility to express their opinions on the biggest economic and social choices. In this vein, greater possibilities for referenda are called for, with reduced quorums (for signatures and electors) and increased thematic areas subject to decisions through referenda.

But there is also another vision of democracy, that which normative theory has recently defined deliberative democracy, and which the global justice movement has elaborated and diffused through the social forums as consensus democracy. This conception of democracy is prefigured by the very same *indignados* that occupy squares, transforming them into public spheres made up of 'normal citizens'. It is an attempt to create high-quality discursive democracy, recognising the equal rights of all (not only delegates and experts) to speak (and to be respected) in a public and plural space, open to discussion and deliberation on themes that range from conditions of distress to concrete solutions to specific problems, from proposals on common goods to the formation of collective solidarity and emerging identities.

This prefiguration of deliberative democracy follows a vision that is profoundly different from that which legitimates representative democracy, founded on the principle of majority decision-making. Democratic quality here is in fact measured by the possibility to elaborate ideas within discursive, open and public arenas, where citizens play an active role in identifying problems, but also in elaborating possible solutions. It is the opposite of accepting a 'democracy of the prince', where the professional elected to govern must not be disturbed – at least until fresh elections are held. But it is also the opposite of a 'democracy of experts', legitimised by output, on which European institutions have long relied upon. After the Maastricht Treaty and the introduction of the euro, calls for this kind of legitimation, which appeals to the capacity to produce, apolitically and on the basis of specialist skills, economic successes, have gradually reduced. They are now crumbling under the disastrous results of European policies in the current financial crisis, and the unpopular attempts to impose neoliberal solutions to the crisis – up to 90 per cent of citizens in Spain and Greece express their agreement with the *indignados*. European citizens believe less and less in the road of the past.

Donatella della Porta is a professor at the European University Institute, and is author of several books on social movements and European policies. This piece was first published in English on OpenDemocracy.net. An earlier version of this article, in Italian, was part of the debate on 'The Road to Europe', published in August 2011 at www.sbilanciamoci.info/Forum and www.ilmanifesto.it/archivi/forum-economia.

be in disarray, and are increasingly unable to convince the global public of either their delivery or even capability to solve, manage and control rapidly-changing realities. As the global crisis unfolds daily, it is less and less possible for these formally unquestionable and formidable players to hide their weaknesses and decreasing legitimacy. Public trust is today at its lowest level concerning economic, political and legal institutions, be they on the national, regional or global level (see Figures 4.3 and 4.4). Both markets and democratic legal-political institutions are made by people, and are reflections of public and individual needs, expectations and trust. If the complex consensus and respect that legitimates their existence and functioning is seriously eroded, they become dysfunctional and redundant, and will sooner or later disintegrate.

Except for a handful of nation states, most of these players were born after WWII specifically to give economic, political, legal, and institutional guarantees of democracy, and even of a democratic world order. These partly imagined, partly real guarantees have practically evaporated today. We have arrived at a stage where we need a new, inclusive and decisive debate about different possible interpretations, meanings, institutions and functioning of democracy on all possible levels. The process of deliberation and reinterpretation will neither be rapid nor without conflicts: the harmonisation of regulations and interests on global, regional and local levels is rather a politically correct slogan than a reality today.

The 'fourth wave' of democratisation that started with the revolutions in the Arab world has resulted in a major shift of focus in interest and action. Democracy has been exposed to irreversible global dynamics, initiated and led by unexpected actors who were almost completely out of the scope of the democracy discourse dominated by the politics, media and other institutions of the West. Since most of Western democracies themselves became or are becoming 'no choice democracies' and are therefore losing their legitimacy, democracy is out of joint in the Western world; meanwhile, the idea of democracy, the spirit of freedom and dignity, is rapidly and unexpectedly spreading in 'impossible' regions. This global stretch of the boundaries of possible democratisations not only heralds the end of a set of Western prejudices and racist conceptualisations such as the 'clash of civilisations'; it also begs new methods and approaches to dialogue and analysis. In a conventional sense, following a nineteenth-century paradigm, it is true that democracy assumes congruence between the state, the people and the territory.

But facing the realities of the twenty-first century, such as the formidable increase of migration, the uncontrollable flows of global financial capital and the unaccountability of international and domestic guardian institutions, we need to find new configurations for matching the expectations of an increasingly deterritorialised and growing global public.

Escaping From the Iron Cage of the Nation State

It is widely recognised by recent social and political science literature that in the present era of globalisation we have to face 'a strong growth of transboundary problems' (Tinnevelt and De Schutter 2001: 1). Although deterritorialisation is not at all a new phenomenon, its intensity has reached a critical level today. It is undeniable that our social existence cannot be reduced to territorially bounded units called nation states. As Jan Aart Scholte has observed, social and political space is 'no longer wholly wrapped in terms of territorial places, territorial distances and territorial borders' (Scholte 1999: 3).

This robust and irreversible tendency poses serious and inevitable questions for both the praxis and theory of democracy. Stepping out from the iron cage of the nation state, there are no clear answers to such questions as: who is responsible to whom? Or, where are the boundaries of democracy? Or, can one imagine democracy without boundaries?

According to a powerful argument made by those who believe we need to reconsider the basic assumptions of conventional democratic theory, and consequently the framework and action radius of democracy, 'nation states are no longer able ... to guarantee the successful realisation of their basic principles of justice and democracy' (Tinnevelt and De Schutter 2010: 4).

As a consequence, exposed citizens have to pay for the one-sided decisions of 'sovereign players'. To overcome the democratic deficit of the nation state paradigm, democracy needs to be expanded and established on the transnational and regional, as well as global level. As global and transnational democracy theorists and activists argue, 'whoever is affected by a public decision should be included in the democratic process that makes the decision' (Tinnevelt and De Schutter 2010: 2). This principle again poses new questions about the transnational, global constituency:

- Who are 'we'?
- Who is able to define who is affected?

- What kind of common identity supports global/transnational democracy?
- Must citizens of all kinds of democracies share a common identity, in other words, is it true that a unique identity is the condition sine qua non of democratic self-determination?
- Can democracy bypass the insider versus outsider, friend versus foe assumption? In other words, can democracy become non-exclusive?

As Chantal Mouffe asked quite some time ago, 'why does every definition of "we" imply the delimitation of a "frontier" and the designation of "them"?' (Mouffe 1993: 84).

We won't find clear answers to these profound, new and old, questions rapidly or easily. Most likely blended versions of different forms, frames and content for democracy will emerge on transnational and global levels. The process of hybridisation has already begun in global governance (Jensen 2009), but this does not mean that we can predict what shape effective institutions and mechanisms of global governance will take. What we can say with certainty today is that if we want to shape a new global democratic order, without an exclusionary political character, the divided parts of democracy – that is, human dignity and human rights on the one hand, and well being, 'good life' and economic democracy on the other – need to be reconnected.

Democracy today seems to be lost in the labyrinths of intertwining transformations but, at the same time, it is gaining new strengths and reinventing itself in unexpected and unorthodox ways and forms. In the end, this means that it is not democracy per se, or certainly not the idea of democracy that is lost in transformations, but all of those forms, procedures, power structures and political and financial regulations which have proved to be inadequate to serve not only the local, regional and global public good in all of the increasingly interdependent and intertwined levels of governance, but, more importantly, social existence itself.

References

Archibugi, Daniele, and Montani, Guido (eds) (2011) *European Democracy and Cosmopolitan Democracy*. The Ventotene Papers, The Altiero Spinelli Institute for Federalist Studies. Pavia, Italy.

Blissett, Luther (2002) *Guy Debord is Really Dead*. London: Sabotage Editions.

Blokker, Paul (2009) 'Democracy Through the Lenses of 1989: Liberal Triumph or Radical Turn?', *International Journal of Politics, Culture and Society*, Vol. 22 No. 2: 273–90.

Cavallero, Eric (2010) 'Federative Global Democracy', in Ronald Tinnevelt and Helder De Schutter (eds), *Global Democracy and Exclusion*. Chichester: Wiley-Blackwell, pp. 55–79.

CiSONET (2005) 'Towards a European Civil Society' (CiSONET) Wissenschaftszentrum Berlin für Sozialwissenschaften, Manuscript.

Civil Szemle (2011) 'Változatlanul alacsony szinten a a közbizalom Gyorsjelentés 2010' ('Continuing low level of public confidence. Fast report'), *Civil Szemle* (Civil Review) Nos 26–27, 6 August.

Craig, Campbell (2010) 'The Resurgent Idea of World Government', in Ronald Tinnevelt and Helder De Schutter (eds), *Global Democracy and Exclusion*. Chichester: Wiley-Blackwell, pp. 27–37.

Crouch, Colin (2004) *Post-Democracy*. Cambridge: Polity Press.

Dahl, R. A. (1971) *Polyarchy: Participation and Opposition*. New Haven: Yale University Press.

Diamond, Larry (1996) 'Is the Third Wave Over?', *Journal of Democracy*, Vol. 7 No. 3: 20–37.

Diamond, Larry (2008) *The Spirit of Democracy*. New York: Holt.

Diamond, Larry (2010) 'Why Are There No Arab Democracies?', *Journal of Democracy*, Vol. 21 No. 1: 93–105.

Dobson, William J. (2011). 'Is this the Fourth Wave of Democracy?', *Washington Post*, http://www.washingtonpost.com/blogs/post-partisan/post/is-this-the-fourth-wave-of-democracy/2011/03/22/ABKBatDB_blog.html, 22 March (accessed 26 August 2011).

Edwards, Michael (2004) *Civil Society*. London: Polity Press.

Edwards, Michael (2010) 'Why Social Transformation is Not a Job for the Market', *Open Democracy*, 26 January 2010.

The Economist (2011) 'On the March – Populist Anti-immigration Parties are Performing Strongly across Northern Europe', *The Economist*, 17 March.

Emerson, Michael (2011) 'Dignity, Democracies and Dynasties – in the Wake of the Revolt on the Arab Street', CEPS, 7 January.

Gaon, Stella (ed.) (2009) *Democracy in Crisis: Violence, Alterity, Community*. Manchester: Manchester University Press.

Garton Ash, Timothy (2009) 'Velvet Revolution: The Prospects'. *New York Review of Books*, http://www.nybooks.com/articles/archives/2009/dec/03/velvet-revolution-the-prospects (accessed 12 July 2011).

Gilbert, Jeremy (2009) 'Postmodernity and the Crisis of Democracy', *Open Democracy*, 28 May.

Grand, Stephen R. (2011) 'Starting in Egypt: The Fourth Wave of Democratisation?' The Brookings Institution, http://www.brookings.edu/opinions/2011/0210_egypt_democracy_grand.aspx, 10 February 2011 (accessed 26 August, 2011).

Hauner, Milan (2008) 'Charter 77 and European Peace Movement'. Conference Paper: 'Peace Movements in the Cold War and Beyond: An International Conference', http://www.lse.ac.uk/archived/global/PDFs/Peaceconference/Hauner.doc (accessed 12 July 2011).

Held, David, Kaldor, Mary and Quah, Danny (2010) 'The Hydra-Headed Crisis', *Global Policy Journal*, 28 February, http://www.globalpolicyjournal.com/articles/global-govern-ance/hydra-headed-crisis (accessed 12 April 2010).

Huntington, Samuel P. (1991) *The Third Wave: Democratization in the Late Twentieth Century*. Norman, OK: University of Oklahoma Press.

International Center on Nonviolent Conflict (2009) http://www.nonviolent-conflict.org (accessed 12 July 2011).

Jensen, Jody (2009) *Whose Rules? Globalizing Governance in a Multistakeholder World*. Saarbrucken: Lambert Academic Publishing.

Kaldor, Mary (2003) *Global Civil Society: An Answer to War*. Cambridge: Polity Press.

Kaldor, Mary (2008) 'Democracy and Globalisation', in Martin Albrow et al. (eds), *Global Civil Society 2007/8*. London: Sage Publications.

Karatnycky, Adrian and Ackerman, Peter (2005) 'How Freedom is Won: From Civic Resistance to Durable Democracy'. Freedom House, http://www.freedomhouse.org/uploads/special_report/29.pdf (accessed 12 July 2011).

Keane, John (2009) 'Why There's No Instant Answer to Democracy's Growing Crisis', *Scotsman*, 3 December 2009.

Keane, John (2010) *The Life and Death of Democracy*. London: Simon & Schuster.

Kurzman, Charles (1998) 'Waves of Democratization', *Studies in Comparative International Development*, Vol. 33 No. 1: 42–64.

Marchetti, Raffaele (2010) 'Interaction-Dependent Justice and the Problem of International Exclusion', in Ronald Tinnevelt and Helder De Schutter (eds), *Global Democracy and Exclusion*. Chichester: Wiley-Blackwell.

McFaul, Michael (2002) 'The Fourth Wave of Democracy *and* Dictatorship: Noncooperative Transitions in the Postcommunist World'. *World Politics*, Vol. 54 No. 2: 212–44.

Meijenfeldt, Roel von (2011) 'Fourth Wave of Democracy Engulfing the Arab World', *The Broker*, http://www.thebrokeronline.eu/Blogs/Current-global-affairs/Fourth-Wave-of-democracy-engulfing-the-Arab-world (accessed 26 August 2011).

Miszlivetz, Ferenc (2010) '"We are in a Situation of Relative Free Will", Interview with Immanuel Wallerstein', *Society and Economy*, Vol. 32.

Miszlivetz, Ferenc and Jensen, Jody (2005) *The Languages of Civil Society – Europe and Beyond*. EUI Working Paper. Badia Fiesole: European University Institute, May.

Mouffe, Chantal (1993) *The Return of the Political*. London and New York: Verso.

O'Connor, Kevin (2003) *The History of the Baltic States*. Westport, CT: Greenwood Press.

Offe, Claus, and Gaines, Jeremy (1996) *The Varieties of Transition: The East European and East German Experience*. Cambridge: Polity Press.

Perez, Carlota (2009) 'After Crisis: Creative Construction', *Open Democracy*, 5 March.

Phillips, Leigh (2011) 'Austrian Far-Right in Fresh Push for EU Respectability', *EU Observer*, 9 June, http://euobserver.com/843/32466 (accessed 29 July 2011).

Plattner, Marc F. (2010) 'Populism, Pluralism, and Liberal Democracy', *Journal of Democracy*, Vol. 21 No. 1: 81–93.

Posner, Richard A. (2010) *The Crisis of Capitalist Democracy*. Cambridge, MA: Harvard University Press.

Preuss, Ulrich (2001) 'The Rulemaking and Policy Actors in the Transition and the Issue of the Strategy of Transformation', *Studies in East European Thought*, Vol. 53: 183–95.

Putnam, D. Robert and Sander, Thomas H. (2010) 'Still Bowling Alone? The Post-9/11 Split', *Journal of Democracy*, Vol. 21 No. 1: 9–17.

Reich, Robert (2008) *Supercapitalism: The Transformation of Business, Democracy and Everyday Life*. New York: Knopf.

Reuters (2011) 'Finnish Election Results', Reuters Online, 18 April, http://www.reuters.com/article/2011/04/18/finland-election-results-idUSLDE73H0J620110418 (accessed 29 July 2011).

Rupnik, Jacques (2010) 'Twenty Years of Postcommunism. In Search of A New Model', *Journal of Democracy*, Vol. 21 No. 1: 105–13.

Sharp, Gene (1973) *198 Methods of Non-violent Action*. Cambridge, MA: Albert Einstein Institution, http://www.aeinstein.org/organizations/org/198_methods-1.pdf (accessed 12 July 2011).

Shaw, Martin (2011) 'The Global Democratic Revolution: A New Stage', *Open Democracy*, 7 March.

Schmitter, Philippe C. (1993) 'Democracy's Third Wave', *Review of Politics*, Vol. 55 No. 2: 348–51.

Schmitter, Philippe C. (2010) 'Twenty- Five Years, Fifteen Findings', *Journal of Democracy*, Vol. 21 No. 1: 17–29.

Schmitter, Philippe C. (2011) 'The Future of Real-Existing Democracies', *Society and Economy*, Vol. 34 No. 2.

Scholte, Jan Aart (1999) *Global Civil Society: Changing the World?* Centre for the Study of Globalisation and Regionalisation, Working Paper No. 31, Coventry: University of Warwick.

Stolberg, Sheryl Gay (2011) 'Shy U.S. Intellectual Created Playbook Used in a Revolution'. *New York Times*, 16 February, http://www.nytimes.com/2011/02/17/world/middleeast/17sharp.html?_r=1 (accessed 12 July 2011).

Tinnevelt, Ronald and De Schutter, Helder (2010) 'Introduction: Global Democracy and Exclusion', in Ronald Tinnevelt and Helder De Schutter (eds), *Global Democracy and Exclusion*. Chichester: Wiley-Blackwell.

Tismaneanu, Vladimir (1999) *The Revolutions of 1989*. London: Routledge.

Tocci, Nathalie (2011) 'Rethinking Euro-Med Policies in the Light of the Arab Spring', *Open Democracy*, 25 March.

Touraine, Alain (2010) 'Strong Democracy to Cope with Economic Crisis'. Speech delivered at the Parliamentary Assembly of the Council of Europe, 21 June.

Traynor, Ian (2010) 'Economic Gloom Fuels Far-Right Growth in Europe', *Guardian*, 17 October, http://www.guardian.co.uk/world/2010/oct/17/far-right-growth-europe (accessed 29 July 2011).

Vasconcelos, Álvaro de (ed.) (2011) *The Arab Democratic Wave: How the EU can Seize the Moment*. Report No. 9, Institute for Security Studies, March.

Whitehead, Laurence (2010) 'The Crash of '08', *Journal of Democracy*, Vol. 21 No. 1: 45–57.

CHAPTER 5

PASSIONATE PUBLICS IN MEDIATED CIVIL SOCIETY

Bolette Blaagaard

Technology of information and communication is a fundamental dimension of civil society in our time (Castells et al. 2006: 283).

New technology is making public communication and deliberation ubiquitous to an extent not previously imagined. Information technology is strategically used to gain access and to inform populations in NGO and activist programmes and in political struggles for information power and domination, as well as in personal, social networking. This has been discussed at length in previous issues of the *Global Civil Society* yearbook, from John Naughton's study of the contested space of the internet in the first yearbook (2001: 147–68) to Sabine Selchow's analysis of our framing of the notion of the internet, in this volume (see Chapter 2). In this chapter I attempt to add to this body of work with an examination of the role that passion plays amidst the technology. I describe how mediated civil society is being infused by the passionate and private voices of citizen journalists, thereby challenging the public and private binary so often invoked as fundamental to the structure of society.

Mediated civil society, today marked by the overwhelming access to and immersion in public spaces of deliberation through technology, brings about a promise of political inclusion and diversity through what has been termed 'citizen journalism' (Allan 2007, 2009). Citizen journalism is here broadly defined as mediated contributions of a political or civic character to the civic space, through (online) broadcasting and print press. Unlike professional journalism's quest for objectivity, citizen journalism does not need to strive for abstract reasoning or unbiased accounts. Citizen journalism makes democratic deliberation more inclusive in that citizens may have their say and be listened to. It is different from public journalism[1] (Glasser 1999) as it builds on a bottom-up approach and on the initiative and action of the citizens. As we shall see, mainstream journalism is often the entity against which citizen journalists react. But citizen journalism also breaks with deliberate democratic formats in that emotions, affect and passion are introduced

into the deliberative space through technology. 'Global civil society', which, as we have acknowledged in the yearbooks, is a highly contested term, here functions as the signifier of these public spaces of deliberation; 'a terrain for developing ideas, investigating issues, and gathering information that does not readily fit existing categories and cannot be found in conventional sources' (Anheier et al. 2001: 3). Mediated civil society is then the journalistically or technologically founded debates that take place in this space, and in this sense, citizen journalism presents a potential for passionate expressions in global civil society.

After a brief discussion of the public/private split and the notions of objectivity and representation that underpin mainstream journalism, this chapter will present three kinds of citizen journalism, which – it is argued – bring to the fore the political potential of the twenty-first century's technological and social developments. I will then discuss how the rise of citizen journalism brings about the political potential for activism in the increasingly merged private and public realms of human life and, in particular, the possibility of using passion as a political action through three interrelated modes of communication: arational and situation-dependent expressions (Flyvbjerg 2001), 'voice' (Couldry 2010) and, finally, through an enhancement of accountability by way of acknowledging the imbrication of the body, the social and the technological. These theoretical modes are ways of defining 'passion' not as the opposite of reason and of 'objective' reporting and deliberation, but as crucial to politics (Hall 2005). Although extensive and diverse in scope, for our purpose in this chapter, these theories serve as ways of highlighting different ways in which public communication plays on, and in, mediated civil society. Together with the three selected types of citizen journalism, they allow us to discuss the ability of the media to change and challenge the relation between the private and the public in mediated global civil society, by letting citizen journalism inject passion into this public space of deliberation.

It is important to keep in mind that although the examples used for this particular analysis show mainly positive expressions and democratic intensions, the internet is neither democratic nor just. It is what the users make of it, and often that is as hateful and biased as it is inclusive and accountable (Blaagaard 2010, Citron 2010, Zuckerman 2010). This fact notwithstanding, the point of this chapter is to show in which ways politics are expressed through citizen journalism and through passion.

The Private in the Public

Citizen journalism questions our perceptions about what is private and personal and what is public and political by introducing private and personal thoughts directly online and into the public realm. Although a widely acknowledged corpus of feminist scholarship contests the legitimacy of the divide between the public and the private spheres as ambiguous and slippery at best, and politically discriminating at worse, many public functions and theoretical writings rely upon the division. Journalism, for instance, is dependent upon the divide, requiring it in order to function as the watchdog of the citizen in relation to public governance, and as a go-between for the two spheres. Traditional journalism is held up as the 'objective' or unbiased organ able to speak for all, plural and subjective, citizens in a given society (Anderson and Ward 2007, Durham and Kellner 2001, Berry 2005). Moreover, the divide is gendered. Historically, the private sphere is the sphere for women, children, slaves and others, and for the emotions; whereas the public and political space is reserved for male, rational deliberation. Feminist research points out the historical and consistent exclusion of women from the public sphere, and therefore from public life and involvement. Thus the private/public divide corresponds to issues of exclusion and inclusion. Importantly, the private and the public spheres are occupied by stereotypically gendered characteristics and qualities: that is, what belongs to the private sphere is seen as feminine, soft, irrational, emotional and passionate, while what belongs to the public sphere is seen to be masculine, rational, abstract and disembodied.

Technology itself is often portrayed and theorised as disembodied and objective (Ess 2009), and therefore belonging to the masculine and public sphere. However, the internet and online citizen activity, such as social networking, permits passionate expressions and personal experiences to merge with public deliberation. This not only challenges the stereotypically gendered division between private and public, but also questions the rule

of Stoic 'professional objectivity' and 'self-abstraction' (Peters 2005), which, as noted above, has been upheld in professional journalism and mediated communication (Habermas 1989, Dahlgren 1985, 2009). The political and social contributions of citizens directly into the mediated centre via the internet challenge that Stoicism by reintroducing personal and political passions penned by private rather than professional writers. Political issues are broadcast through a personal lens, and the journalistic mantra to speak for everybody and from a position of objectivity is no longer defended. In journalistic practices and studies these issues of representation are part of an ongoing debate, which I will attempt to highlight throughout the rest of the chapter and discuss by use of interdisciplinary theories from the fields of journalism, gender, ethnicity and cultural studies.

Publicity, Accountability and Inclusion: Citizen Journalism's Contribution

Young (2001) argues that deliberative democracy (and I would add a functioning civil society) requires publicity, accountability and inclusion. Looking at mainstream journalism in particular, which aims both to be a watchdog and to provide unbiased reporting, it is clear that established journalistic practices have succeeded, to an extent, in providing publicity as well as journalistic accountability. Journalism aims at holding governing bodies and other powerful organisations and individuals accountable to the public by exposing their wrongdoings, and is itself held accountable through journalistic ethics and practices.

However, the introduction of new media has encouraged the growth of inclusion and political diversity, which has been shown to have had far reaching and political implications. Journalism and journalists have often been seen as actors of civil society: representing the people in their quest against corruption, for civil rights, and for justice. New media tests mainstream journalism's privileged role as watchdog and keeper of the truth by making visible the many other possible formations of civil society and their relationship to journalistic practice. It enables citizens to broadcast and publish alternative versions of facts and events, often bringing personal perspectives and experiences into the debate. It has the potential to engender intimate connections, and to foster political and cultural solidarity across the globe through personal as well as political knowledge transfer and debate. New technology has created the possibility for citizens to communicate and deliberate directly, across

Box 5.1
Citizen Journalism in the Arab Spring: Syria

Not long after the events in Tunisia and Egypt that sparked the 2011 Arab Spring, similar uprisings erupted in Syria. On 3 February, activists employed social networking sites such as Twitter and Facebook to call for a Day of Rage, demanding both governmental reform and that President Bashar al-Assad leave office (The Syrian Days of Rage 2011). Such protests continue as this publication goes to press. On 3 June internet access was cut across most of Syria, only to be restored on the 4th. At the same time the refusal of the Syrian government to grant access to the international media has meant that the only information coming out of Syria has come from citizen journalists determined to ensure that the world hears both sides of the story.

One such group is the Shaam News Network, a self-proclaimed 'group of patriotic Syrian youth activists demanding the freedom and dignity for the Syrian people' (www.shaam.org). By all appearances, the group is not affiliated in any way with the Syrian opposition parties or other states that might have stakes in the outcome of the events in Syria. Shaam uploads significant amounts of video content to YouTube depicting the actions of security forces and chronicling violent street protests. They have accumulated more than 10 million views on their various uploads since joining the site on 26 February 2011 (SHAMSNN 2011).

Citizen journalism concerning Syria has not only been contained within the nation's borders. It was revealed in June 2011 that the blog 'A Gay Girl in Damascus' (damascusgaygirl. blogspot.com)[1] was a work of fiction, penned by an American. Tom MacMaster claimed that he used the blog to bring attention to Syria's poor record on human rights and chose to do so in this way due to the country's strict laws surrounding the media (Bell and Flock 2011). However, the 'disappearance' of his fictional blogger led both to anti-government activists within Syria taking considerable risks to find a nonexistent person, and to a global Facebook campaign; once the blog was exposed as a fake, inevitable questions over the legitimacy and reliability of citizen journalism followed.

Speaking for the Disappeared: Nepal

Ram Kumar Bhandari is a human rights activist, scholar and journalist from Nepal; his work focuses on the issue of enforced disappearances. From 1996 to 2006 Nepal was consumed by a civil war that killed over 13,000 and left more than 1,300 missing. Most commonly known as 'the disappeared', these people were victims of human rights abuses perpetrated by both sides. Five years after the end of the conflict, families are still waiting for answers about what happened to their loved ones.

Bhandari's campaign to unite the families of the disappeared has taken him from one end of Nepal to the other. He is a tireless campaigner and journalist, writing for both local and national newspapers. He makes regular contributions to the *Nepali Times*, a paper that targets the international NGO community, and aims to incorporate the voices of people on the ground into the national debate (Bhandari 2008). In addition, he harshly criticises the instrumentalisation of victims by Nepal's NGO and human rights community in fulfilment of donor agendas (Bhandari 2011).

The majority of Nepal's population lives in remote villages without regular access to television or newspapers. Recognising the importance of reaching out to these remote communities, Bhandari established Radio Marsyangdi in his hometown of Besisahar, Lamjung. Launched in 2007, Radio Marsyangdi is Lamjung's first and only community radio station, broadcasting a radius of 50 kilometres and reaching roughly 300,000 people. The station runs a wide variety of programming, including advocacy and participation programmes that take phone calls from people in the community wishing to share their stories. The station has created a distinct sense of community for people separated by considerable distance. It has also succeeded in bringing together families of disappeared citizens, providing a crucial platform from which to deal with such difficult issues.

Bhandari's own father disappeared in December 2001. In the years since he has made it his mission to unite the families of the disappeared in search of justice, and his personal passion and use of different media has given crucial agency to a distinctly marginalised community.

Erik Wilson is an MSc candidate in Development Studies at the London School of Economics. Previously he worked with civil society in Nepal, and has recently returned to the region to conduct research on transitional justice.

[1] All content was removed on 15 July 2011.

vast spaces, and in a format which is well incorporated into the daily lives of many – that is, than through more traditional forms of news reporting, which now typically incorporate the Tweets and blogs of citizen journalists into their own coverage. However, it is important to note that the character of today's mediated world, in which we tend to live online as well as offline simultaneously (see Chapter 2) and in which mainstream media and online news outlets make use of each other, support each other, and are sometimes owned by the same corporation, blurs the boundaries between what is citizen-led and what is professional journalism. New technology has provided a previously unimagined and powerful tool to gain access to mediated spheres of deliberation; the question is how this deliberating communication is presented, and how it differs from the representation of public deliberation by professional journalism.

The Grounded Experience and Multiple Truths of Citizen Journalism

Here I want to divide the idea of citizen journalism into three groups or formats (Blaagaard 2010), both in an attempt to define the emerging and often slippery field, and in order to extract the different ways in which this kind of politico-journalistic communication contributes to public speech.

Group One: Engagement with Crises

Citizen journalism is often used in times of crisis. From 9/11 to the tsunami in the Indian Ocean in 2004 and the Iranian election demonstrations of 2009, the practice of 'ordinary citizens using the web, [has] fostered a heightened sense of personal engagement for "us" with the distant suffering of "them"' (Allan 2009: 23). However, these crises also occur 'closer to home'; for Britons, for instance, reports from the London bombings in 2005, the G20 demonstrations in 2009 and the August riots in 2011 in London and elsewhere also fall within the group of citizens' crisis reporting. In these instances, a heightened engagement in local politics and social change is a potential outcome.

The mobile phone footage of Ian Tomlinson's fatal meeting with the London police during the G20 demonstrations in 2009 is one such example. Tomlinson was struck down by a police officer and later died in the street. The citizen recording of the incident which sparked the subsequent media and public attention was a spontaneous occurrence, although the photographer was deliberately trying to show the inside of the 'kettle'[2]

at the demonstration (Greer and McLaughlin 2010). The citizen journalist's actions were based on a critique of the mainstream media representation of the protests, and an attempt to show the other side – the arguments and experiences of the protestors. Although the footage was shot at a protest against a political event of global significance, the mediated story took a national turn when the police officer was shown to knock over Tomlinson unprovoked, possibly causing his death.[3] The story transformed into a local critique of the police and their methods, and the footage created an inversion of public understanding of the London police.

Citizen journalism of this kind, which is borne out of crisis, can be seen to be driven by a desire to show the experience on 'the ground': recontextualising the news and reframing the journalistic truth. Such a critique of mainstream media coverage is implicitly a critique of the abstract and impersonal reporting that focuses on political discourse and police control, and which places demonstrators in the role of irrational and violent instigators rather than political actors. Though the incident was unplanned, the citizen's coverage in the case of Tomlinson was nevertheless successful in changing the primary mediated story from one of riotous demonstrators to the unlawful use of violence by the London police (Greer and McLaughlin 2010). This first type of citizen journalism therefore gives voice to (potential) 'victims', unedited by mainstream media – at least until it is shared with them.[4]

Group Two: Political Debates

The second type of citizen journalism has a political and issue-based focus. Typically, it is expressed via blog sites and discussion forums that explicitly aim to engender political communities, enable debates, and affect potentially radical interventions in mainstream party politics.

When Gavan Titley and his colleagues made a call for *vita active*, and launched Budgetjam in the autumn of 2010 as a response to the Irish budget of 2011, it was again a case of showing an alternative to the story produced by mainstream media, and to base that alternative in personal, professional and political experiences (see Box 5.2). The push towards political change and telling the 'other truth' – the one that is seen from the perspective of the citizens' experience – is shared by Claire Sambrook, who launched End Child Detention Now (ECDN), a citizens' website aimed at changing UK immigration laws and the practice of detaining young children in refugee

Box 5.2
Turning TINA: Budgetjam and the Political-Economic Crisis in Ireland

The global financial crisis, according to Alain Badiou, has played out like a conventional disaster movie, from the 'gradual spectacle of the disaster, and the crude manipulation of suspense' to the resolute appearance on the screen of the 'little squad of the powerful'. The monetary figures at stake occupy the realms of fiction, and the central focus of rescuing the banking system to tackle the global financial crisis takes on the quality of a 'noble, humanist and democratic' mission, evangelized by mainstream politicians and media. Where, in this crisis cineplex, is the real, and where is the spectacle? For the most part, Badiou argues, the audience for this blockbuster, who will ultimately finance it

> watch the astronomical figures go by, and automatically compare them with their own resources, and, in the case of a sizeable proportion of humanity, the complete lack of resources that makes the last years of their lives both so bitter and so brave. I am telling you: that is the real, and we will gain access to it only if we take our eyes off the screen and look at the invisible masses of those for whom, until just before they were plunged into something even worse than what they had already experienced, the disaster movie and its schmaltzy ending was never anything more than a shadow play. (2010: 93–4)

The 'little squad of the powerful' came to Dublin in 2010, and the silent, but not entirely passive, audience watched the specifically Irish iteration of the global crisis enter a new chapter under IMF/EU suzerainty. The rapid implosion of a period of economic growth and complex cultural transformation known as the 'Celtic Tiger' had already raised awkward questions for many institutions and sectors in Ireland, not least the media, academia and NGOs, who had collectively failed to pursue adequate critiques. Now, in the light of 2010's rapid transformation and its socio-political consequences, these lingering, awkward questions informed a pressing need for critique and opposition. It was in this context that the media collective Budgetjam was formed.

Its initial shape was provided by participation in the Carnegie Trust's project on the news, civil society and the media – a part of the 'Making Good Society' project – in early 2010. Departing from a normative commitment to enhancing citizen participation in 'thoroughly mediated democracies', a study conducted for Carnegie by the Goldsmiths Leverhulme Media Research Centre emphasised the new communicative spaces and digital possibilities available to civil society organisations, with particular emphasis on providing a diversity of viewpoints and sources in the face of the general homogenisation of mainstream news content (Witschge et al. 2010). While the media analysis in the study emphasised broadly similar issues in the UK and Ireland, other Commission reports had drawn particular attention to the role of the media and state patronage systems in blunting both the voice and capacity for dissent from within civil society in Ireland (Commission of Inquiry 2010).

On the basis of this finding, and having conducted the media research in Ireland, I was involved in organising an event in May 2010 on 'Media and Civil Society in the Crisis'. This gathering of journalists and bloggers, researchers and activists, and (formerly) state-funded and autonomous organisations and movements provided the network for Budgetjam's subsequent 'communications intervention'. Reactivated from its post-conference slump by the transparent ferocity of the 'austerity' agenda, the network focused on the lead-up to the budget of December 2010, with a strategy best described as 'making them work hard for their eventual victory'. The specific context requires some brief explanation.

Having offered a blind guarantee of what now appears to be €440 billion of bank debt, the government exposed the state to the possibility of sovereign, public default in the event of a private bank 'credit event'. As a remedy, a period of post-sovereignty was ushered in, consolidating the transfer of vast sums of private debt to the public. The EU-IMF loan agreement, signed in late November 2010, involved the transfer of €17.5 billion from the National Pension Reserve and other funds to the loan fund, and was structured through a series of coercive 'policy conditionalities' specifying cuts, tax rises and privatisations (Storey 2010).

While post-sovereignty was narrated as a form of national shame, it quickly became a malleable political alibi. What David McNally (2011) calls the 'neoliberal mutation' – the rapid discursive shift away from the systemic weaknesses of finance capitalism to the 'necessity' of slashing state investment and spending – involves a longer-term project to transform the modern state, and its relationship to society. The affinity of international and national administrations with this mutation was made very clear in the 2010 'austerity' budget, a week after the loan agreement was signed. The task for the communications intervention was to make this mutation transparent, to expose its class politics and deep social costs, and to unsettle the consensus that 'there is no alternative'. The harder question was how to go about doing so.

Jodi Dean has argued that 'democracy that speaks without listening' incorporates vast quantities of oppositional and critical communication by converting 'messages' into 'contributions'. In other words, in deliberative theories of democratic communication, a message has a use value, where 'understanding is a necessary part of the communicative exchange' (2009: 27). Under what she terms 'communicative capitalism', messages are instead defined by their exchange value, by their 'contribution to a larger pool, flow or circulation of content' (2009: 27). The political justifications for further cuts to living standards and essential services, in our evaluation, were based on the circulation of myths calibrated both to the limited form of most mediated inquiry, and more importantly, to the task of filling this fraught time-period with media flow, of democracy speaking incessantly while being explicitly prohibited by external agencies to listen.

Of course, accepting Dean's line of critique does not necessitate relinquishing any form of communicative politics; rather it suggests that communicative strategies need to be forged in and sharpened through this awareness. The Budgetjam network set itself the concerted task, for one week, of contesting and 'jamming' the near-hegemonic circulation of supposedly incontrovertible facts and truths by mainstream media and politicians. We identified five key mantras structuring budget coverage, namely: the country is broke (bankrupt); we're all in this together; we have to move on and move forward; the tough love of the IMF/EU will set us on the straight and narrow; and the Ur-mantra, there is no alternative (TINA). We developed three intersecting strategies of tracking and contesting these invitations to passivity.

A live-blog was maintained for the week, and the live-bloggers were supported by the wider network, who worked to monitor media content and produce targeted responses. At a certain point, the infinite flux of Dean's critique is tempered by scale; mainstream media in Ireland is comparatively limited, and a handful of television and radio programmes wield significant influence in political communications. The live-blog monitored these shows, disseminated their contact details, and worked to provide information and criticism that could be used by activists, or by a wider public. Twitter was used to send specific follow-up questions and critiques to journalists and politicians, and the live feed was disseminated through a range of political blogs in Ireland (and eventually by some mainstream media).

The live-blog drew heavily on the other two strategies. Each key 'myth' was allocated to a working group of activists, researchers and bloggers, and the group worked to produce and gather informative and accessible critiques which could be disseminated through the website and social media platforms. The working group dealing with the IMF, for example, produced and collated material on the failures and corrosive impacts of the IMF's ideological faith in 'expansionary austerity' programmes in the majority world, as well as analyses of the probable future impacts of their policies on employment, health and social cohesion. The live-blog continually related spurious or debatable claims to references and passages in the research and reports being gathered. While this production and collation was aimed at equipping activists and civil society with additional critical material, it was paralleled by a focus on the 'silent audience', on gathering testimonies and evidence of the social and personal impacts of cuts, and of insisting on the irreducible human dimension traduced and patronised by technocratic declarations of TINA.

As the week progressed, the blog flow devoted increasing energy to linking and networking protest actions and mobilisations aimed at the budget. Although the silent audience did little to disrupt the magic of crisis cinema on Budget day, the network and energies gathered together for Budgetjam have been channelled into the more durable, if conventional Crisisjam collective. Having produced a weekly reflection of key dimensions of the crisis from January to June 2010, the collective is now embarking on a different strategy, involving a monthly thematic focus explored both through the production of media content and public meetings with activists and community groups.

Gavan Titley is Lecturer in Media in the National University of Ireland, Maynooth, and co-author of *The Crises of Multiculturalism: Racism in a Neoliberal Age* (2011, Zed Books).

camps (ECDN 2011). Painstakingly prepared, featuring blogs, comments, petitions and Tweets, and promoted in part via appearances in mainstream news which are then subsequently reposted on the internet, ECDN and BudgetJam are examples of political activism and citizens' campaigns that bring personal political motivation into the public realm. Although rooted in national campaigns, these citizen projects reach out beyond borders, encouraging the transfer of knowledge and building solidarity with similar campaigns elsewhere. An example of a more globally-based project is Global Voices, which is a blog site or forum for approximately 300 contributors uploading written as well as video-recorded blogs from around the globe. In their own words: 'Global Voices seeks to aggregate, curate, and amplify the global conversation online – shining light on places and people other media often ignore. We work to develop tools, institutions and relationships that will help all voices, everywhere, to be heard. (Global Voices 2011).

Group Three: The Creative Voice

Finally, the third type of citizen journalism discussed here takes the format of online opinion writing and visual expressions of opinion, as, for instance, in YouTube debates (see Zoonen et al. 2010). Voices don't need to be in written form or in linguistic form, and online broadcasting allows people to engage in debate using emotive and sensorial effects. One example is the online debate that emerged around the release of the ultra right-wing, anti-Muslim short film *Fitna*, created by Dutch politician Geert Wilders in 2008. By editing and uploading mixed pictures, film clips, voice-overs and sounds to YouTube, people took part in the discussion about the film, its portrayal of Muslims, Dutch integration policies, and so on. Most of the videos made in response to *Fitna* were user-replicated; that is, they were 'mix 'n' match' productions of a visual and political character rearranging previously posted footage. Some were personal statements containing arguments for or against Wilders and his film, presented to a camera and uploaded virtually unedited; others were elaborate films. In this public debate, the arguments of different religions had a voice on equal terms (Zoonen et al. 2010).

If the previous case shows citizen journalists in the role of reviewer, a contrasting example of citizen journalists as news-makers and analysts can be seen in the thousands of user-created and replicated versions of the death of Neda Agha-Soltan, a bystander at the uprisings against the Iranian government elections in 2009 (YouTube

2009). Agha-Soltan was shot while witnessing the anti-government demonstrations, and was filmed by an anonymous onlooker with a mobile phone as she struggled in vain to survive. The footage was sent to the Netherlands, where it was uploaded to public websites and emailed to mainstream media corporations. At the same time as the story evolved in the mainstream media, the internet audience developed their own angles and analyses, uploading films, photo collages and other footage which argued for diverse stances, explained contextual matters, and publicly mourned Agha-Soltan's death. In this third group, then, citizen journalism is linked to activist politics in which participants engage in mediated civil society with expressive as well as discursive means (Young 2001).

Passion: Arationality, 'Voice' and Visual Politics

What becomes immediately apparent in citizen journalism is the 'arational' (Dahlgren 2009) motivation behind the political stories. As an antonym to rationality, arationality is that which cannot be counted or analysed with reason but thrives on intuition and experience. Flyvbjerg puts it like this: 'Rationality in the West has become identical with analytical thinking, that is, with conscious separation of wholes into parts. Arational behaviour, in contrast, connotes situational behaviour without the conscious analytical division of situations into parts and evaluation according to context-independent rules' (2001: 22). As an arational form of communication, new media allows citizen journalists to contextualise and situate the news in a personal perspective, and with a bodily experience to back up his or her contribution. It thereby challenges the abstract and analytical, reshaping the relationship between the public and the private in civil society. The first group of the described citizen journalistic manifestations, in particular, exhibits this sort of arational behaviour. The Tomlinson footage was captured by a participant in the demonstration who was showing his or her experience from inside the 'kettle'; it was a grounded perspective, motivated by a political position and a need to voice concern about the particular situation.

The first two groups differ in that the second consists primarily of thoroughly planned political arguments and commitments that sustain the involvement of participants, whereas the first relies on the spontaneous filming of events. However, what the two groups have in common, in addition to the arational, is the 'listening mode'. Rather than making a rights-based claim, such as, for example,

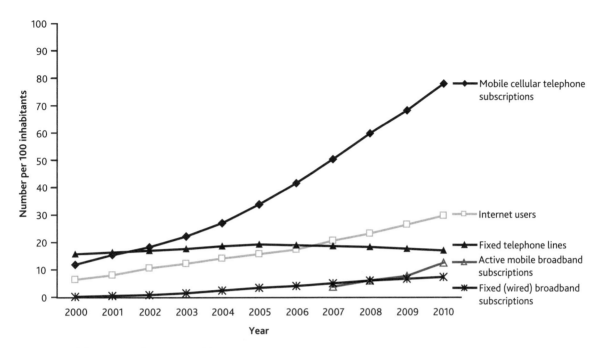

Figure 5.1   Global ICT Developments, 2000–10

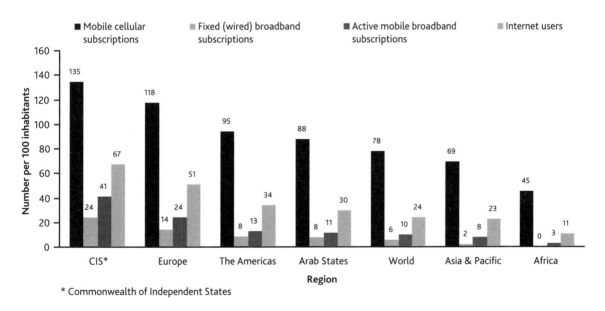

* Commonwealth of Independent States

Source for both figures: ITU World Telecommunication/ICT Indicators Database (http://www.itu.int/ict/statistics).

Figure 5.2   ICT User and Subscription Rates by Region, 2010

the right to free speech, what Titley, Sambrook, Global Voices and others urge through their citizen journalism is an obligation to others, with responsibility as its starting point. As Silverstone (2006) argues, obligations strive for communication; they presuppose a receiver or a partner in communication, and are not simply an outlet of self-expression but must also sustain the conditions of communication. These examples of citizen journalism are a 'communicative norm of receptivity' (Peters 2005: 22). Whereas mainstream media may allow for comments and suggestions, the journalistic ideology of inhabiting the role of editor and gatekeeper is minimised in citizen journalism.

This listening mode is an important aspect in the engenderment, through citizen journalism, of a political 'voice'. In recent work, Nick Couldry (2010) discusses voice as a process, and posits the term against the rationality of neoliberalism. Voice, he writes, is socially grounded, a form of reflexivity, embodied, and requires a material form which cannot be exclusively individual. Voice in Couldry's terminology 'is people's practice of giving an account, implicitly or explicitly, of the world within which they act' (2010: 7). 'Giving an account' is a form of necessary narrative which is seen as a basic feature of human action and which 'involves, from the start, both speaking *and listening*' (2010: 9, italics in original). Citizen journalism, in the three groups presented above, can be seen as an expression of Couldry's 'voice' insofar as the political and social passions expressed through new media are socially grounded and embodied, and reflexive both on media and on their own role in politics and society. Reflexivity is here a form of responsibility and accountability, which citizen journalists practice. Finally, citizen journalism as discussed here is part of a larger flow of political narratives. In Couldry's work, voice as a process and as a value is always more than discourse; it also bears intrinsic links to a wider field of human actions because it perceives democracy as social cooperation rather than deliberation or speech, in the Aristotelian sense of speech (logos) (2010: 8).

Through giving 'voice', citizen journalism introduces an alternative mode of engaging in civil society. Titley et al. write: 'please get involved. We are not looking for political or ideological unity. We are simply looking to broaden the political debate' (Politico 2011). This act of broadening the political debate is based on multiple voices and, importantly, on the seriousness with which these voices are heard. Group Two citizen journalism expresses a considered contribution to civic debate, while all groups give voice to 'the other', who is traditionally under- or misrepresented in mainstream media.

In Group Three in particular, explicit expressions of emotive and affective characteristics are introduced in addition to political, religious and personal motivations. Moreover, citizens make use of creative modes of communication. In this group, perhaps even more than the other two, citizen journalism exhibits passion as a driving force, and creativity as a means to invigorate the deliberative democracy aimed for in normative conceptions of civil society. It is not merely grand public affections that are displayed. As Hall explains, 'passion is the enthusiasm for and commitment to an envisioned good ... Passions are an important part of a political debate about the values that should guide the polity's actions' (2005: 23). Citizen journalism makes personal and political motivations explicit, which fly in the face of Stoic objectivism and self-abstraction (Peters 2005). It motivates and empowers people in terms of giving them the access and the ability to act not only in their private lives, but in their public lives as well. (Hall 2005: 125). In this way, the death of Ian Tomlinson at the G20 demonstrations was called into question because of personal engagement and passion for subverting media representation. The Irish election and budgetary cuts were continuously questioned by those who personally believed in an alternative to the dominant discourse. Citizen journalism about Agha-Soltan broke taboos about public mourning, and spontaneous debates about *Fitna* gave religion a place in public spaces and debates (incidentally, strengthening the position held by some that we are living in a postsecular age; see Braidotti 2008, Habermas 2009).

Passionate Publics, Technological Times

A post-phenomenological analysis of new media leads to an interesting embodiment of technology. Because technology is the means through which this new development is taking place, its promise of mechanical objectivity (Daston and Galison 2007) is brought into question. Rather than a tool of journalistic practice and of democratic deliberation, technology becomes an extension of the lifeworld and of narrative (see also Chapter 2). We are shown the world not only from the perspective of another individual, but as if we were inside that person's body, seeing the world with his or her eyes. This is particularly apparent in visualised citizen journalism, in which the poor quality and visibly unprofessional aspect of mobile phone footage makes

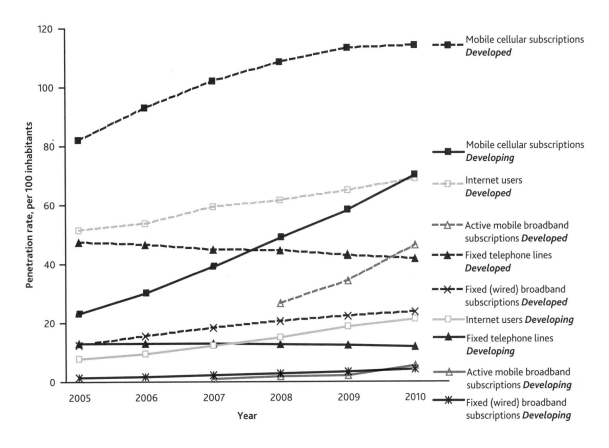

Legend:

- ■ - - Mobile cellular subscriptions *Developed*
- ■— Mobile cellular subscriptions *Developing*
- □ - - Internet users *Developed*
- △ - - Active mobile broadband subscriptions *Developed*
- ▲ - - Fixed telephone lines *Developed*
- ✕ - - Fixed (wired) broadband subscriptions *Developed*
- □— Internet users *Developing*
- ▲— Fixed telephone lines *Developing*
- △— Active mobile broadband subscriptions *Developing*
- ✱— Fixed (wired) broadband subscriptions *Developing*

Note: The 'developed'/'developing' country distinction is one that both the author of this chapter and the yearbook editors find problematic; however, it comes from UN M49, which is used extensively by the ITU. See: http://www.itu.int/ITU-D/ict/definitions/regions/index.html

Source: © INTERNATIONAL TELECOMMUNICATION UNION, 2010.
http://www.itu.int/ITU-D/ict/statistics/at_glance/KeyTelecom2010.html.

Figure 5.3   Key ICT Indicators for Developed and Developing Countries (Penetration Rates per 100 Inhabitants)

that footage even more 'compelling', and suggests to us that the story is true (Slade 2003: 36). As Susan Sontag writes: 'Pictures of hellish events seem more authentic when they don't have the look that comes from being "properly" lighted and composed' (2003: 23–4). Although we – the informed audience – know that television is not necessarily true, and that simply because it can be observed it is not necessarily objective, we still seem to be partial to an image that speaks to our emotions and to our real life – or bodily – experiences. Remarking on the power of photography, Sontag notes that the connection between the visual and the sensory makes imagery neither fact nor fiction. 'This sleight of hand [the connection between eyes, brains and emotions] allows

photographs to be both objective record and personal testimony, both a faithful copy or transcription of an actual moment of reality and an interpretation of that reality' (2003: 23). What we acknowledge as the truth is imagery that speaks to our emotions on a personal level. However, due to a highly mediated contemporary world, our experiences of real-life events are already mediated and fictionalised. Therefore, shaky framing, wobbly camera movements and scattered narrative seem to mimic documentary filmmaking, which in turn is enmeshed in fictional screenplays and vice versa (Renov 1993). Our social imaginary is fraught with Hollywood imagery so that what once 'felt like a dream' today feels 'like a movie' (Sontag 2003: 19).

Box 5.3
Campaigning for the Environment: China

Chinadialogue (www.chinadialogue.net) promotes itself as the world's first bilingual website devoted to creating open and inclusive discussion on environmental issues which impact both China and the rest of the globe. Founded in 2006, with offices in London, Beijing and San Francisco, the website focuses on the impact of China's rapid development on the environment. The ideology that was once termed 'development-at-all-costs' is now being curtailed due to the country's alarming environmental problems, and as China depletes its own resources, the government will begin to look to other regions of the world to fulfil these needs (Barrionuevo 2011). The implications are global and require global recognition and strategy; however, the mainstream Chinese media appears to be ignoring the issue. In 2005, for example, an explosion at the Jilin Petrochemical Company spilled more than 100 tons of chemicals into a local river. Chinese newspapers diverted the public's attention by discussing the impact of an earthquake that never happened (Yardley 2005).

Chinadialogue aims to substitute for this lack of mediated debate, acting as a platform for open discussion. To achieve this, the site uses a myriad of media, including podcasts, books, and a blog, in addition to publishing five regular columnists and a plethora of contributing authors. It should be noted however,

that Chinadialogue was founded by a Scottish journalist and receives funding from the British government's Department for Environment, Food and Rural Affairs (DEFRA), raising questions of accountability and representation.

Another active voice on the environment is photographer Lu Guang. Guang documents environmental calamities resulting from China's rapid development. He won the W. Eugene Smith Grant for Humanistic Photography (Key 2009a) with his series entitled 'Pollution in China', which depicts the impact of industrial factories on surrounding farmlands and the extent of pollutants dumped into China's rivers. In July of 2010, Guang was commissioned by Greenpeace to document the fallout from an oil spill in the Chinese city of Dailin. In an interview, Guang argued that the villagers are left to deal with the consequences of bad business practices, victims of the driving concern with profit. Guang claims that Dailin is a small part of the larger environmental picture in China, and that there is more work to do with regard to helping those most negatively impacted by bad business practice (Key 2009b). While Guang does make his living as a commercial photographer, he pursues his environmental projects on the side, making him another example of the blurred line between citizen journalism and commercial media.

Citizen Journalism in Exile: Malaysia

Radio Free Sarawak (RSF; www.radiofreesarawak.org) is an independent radio station operating in London and broadcasting to the Malaysian state of Sarawak. Run by Peter John Jaban, a former Sarawak state employee who was deported for speaking out against the government, RFS seek to provide news, interviews and reports to the people of Sarawak, free from the influence of government. The station is also part of a growing global campaign against the current chief minister of Sarawak, Abdul Taib Mahmud. Mahmud has gained support for reelection over the years by improving Sarawak's logging and palm oil industries, but has become embroiled in controversy along the way. This is due in large part to the impact that these industries have on the Malaysian rainforests, one of the countries most prized natural resources.

Another active voice in the debate is Sarawak Report (www.sarawakreport.org), a website run by a group of 'concerned citizens and onlookers'. Opposition parties in Sarawak have no voice, with little to no access to the state-controlled media. Sarawak Report seeks to provide a platform for inhabitants

to air their grievances, and bring to light the environmental exploitation and corruption that they believe to be destroying their homeland. For example, the writers point out that only 3 per cent of the state's rainforests remain uncut, which negatively impacts the indigenous populations who rely on the forests for subsistence. Other stories focus on the inequality which they believe has been brought about by the corrupt regime: Sarawak is Malaysia's richest state, and yet most of its inhabitants remain in poverty.

For those at Radio Free Sarawak and Sarawak Report, the ability to appeal to concerned communities outside Sarawak presents an opportunity that is not available within the state itself. Yet their passionate global outreach has a local goal. When asked about his plans for the future of RSF, Jaban stated that he would continue his broadcasts in the hope of returning home. 'It's my land, my people, my family, I miss my home so much and of course I want to go back' (ABC 2011).

Erik Wilson

This argument is enhanced by theoretical discussions on the topics of bodily materialism (Braidotti 2002) and political physiology (Protevi 2009). These discussions encourage us to think about how our bodies, minds, and social settings are intricately and intimately linked (Protevi 2009) and 'offers complex models of analysis for interrelations between the self and society, the "inside" and the "outside" of the subject ... Politics in this framework has as much to do with affectivity, memory and desire as it has with consciousness and resistance' (Braidotti 2002: 20). This implies that online debate can be experienced as internal to our understanding, desire and drive to change the world; as such, technology allows us to experience the private and the public simultaneously without imploding the two. The intensity of the potential presence of other – not just minds, but bodies and emotions – in our private sphere, in our online as well as offline spaces, is changing the relationship encapsulated in the idea of the public and private spheres. The passion relayed by citizen journalism may be recognised by the viewers and listeners as personal and political simultaneously, making the issue at stake appear both true and engaging.

However, as noted before, it is important to bear in mind that this direct connection between the visual and the sensory also allows for debates to become derailed into dichotomous and hateful trenches. Both the online debates of *Fitna* and the Danish cartoon controversy in 2005–08 displayed this kind of conflict (Blaagaard 2010). New technology is not democratic, nor is it neutral. Democratic conduct belongs to subjects, not machinery. Passion may bring about political awareness, but may likewise close the minds of participants in a debate. Indeed, online communities are often made up of people who know each other offline or share political and personal interests (Zuckermann 2010; see also Box 2.3).

Conclusion

Mediated civil society is a platform for engaged citizens who are trying to make their voices heard and their feelings acknowledged in a political and economic world which has long devalued voice as a political actor and process (Couldry 2010). The traditional divide between the private and the public realm is challenged through citizens' mediated engagement in civil society, an engagement previously privileged to journalistic representation. The three types of citizen journalism presented in this chapter illustrate that, firstly, citizen journalism reacts against objective journalism by publicising arational commentaries. Secondly, citizen journalism allows for

'voice', in Couldry's use of the term, by emphasising the listening mode of communication. Finally, passions are made explicit in citizens' contributions to journalism through the imbrications of the body and technology.

Through arational expressions, voice and passion, citizen journalism puts the concerns of real – as opposed to representations of – people on the agenda, implicitly demanding that the cloak of objective journalism be removed. It produces situated and embodied political actors, and in doing so, this author believes that it marks a starting point for a turn in mediated civil society's forms of deliberation, as well as a breakthrough for a possible return of the personal in the political. This may be for the better or the worse: as noted at the beginning of this chapter, information technology is used strategically to gain access to and inform populations of NGO and activist programmes, as well as in political struggles for information power and domination. Passions can provide swift access to the personal space and convictions of the public, and have perhaps the potential to derail democratic deliberation as much as they hold the key to its invigoration.

Notes

1. Public journalism is an American-based idea and movement that was discussed widely in the 1990s. Its basic idea was to engage citizens through grassroots journalistic projects, but the initiative itself was journalistic and academic. In contrast to public journalism, citizen journalism is fragmented and citizen-initiated.
2. 'Kettling' is a term used to describe the attempts by London's police to control crowds at anti-government demonstrations. It consists of containing demonstrators in closed spaces and only releasing a few people at a time. In this way the police hope to contain the violence that may occur during these demonstrations.
3. An inquest into the circumstances of Tomlinson's death has determined that he was unlawfully killed.
4. Citizen journalistic mobile phone footage is rarely shown unedited when it is broadcast in the mainstream press. Circumstances surrounding media production will always play a role in the framing and therefore editing of the footage. However, it goes beyond this chapter to discuss the idea of authenticity and framing in new media.

References

Allan, Stuart (2007) 'Citizen Journalism and the Rise of "Mass Self-Communication": Reporting on the London Bombings', *Global Media Journal, Australian Edition*, Vol. 1 No. 1.

Allan, Stuart (2009) 'Histories of Citizen Journalism', in Stuart Allan and Einar Thorsen (eds), *Citizen Journalism: Global Perspectives*. New York: Peter Lang.

Anderson, Benedict (1991) *Imagined Communities*. London and New York: Verso.

Anderson, Peter J., and Ward, Geoff (eds) (2007) *The Future of Journalism in the Advanced Democracies*. Aldershot: Ashgate.

Anheier, Helmut, Glasius, Marlies and Kaldor, Mary (2001) 'Introduction' in Helmut Anheier, Marlies Glasius and Mary Kaldor (eds), *Global Civil Society 2001*. Oxford: Oxford University Press.

Arendt, Hannah (1958) *The Human Condition*. Chicago and London: Chicago University Press.

Australian Broadcasting Corporation (ABC) (2011) 'The Fight for Sarawak', segment on the *7.30* current affairs programme, broadcast 14 April, http://www.abc.net.au/7.30/content/2011/s3191901.htm (accessed 26 August 2011).

Badiou, Alain (2010) *The Communist Hypothesis*. London: Verso.

Barrionuevo, Alexi (2011) 'China's Interest in Farmland Makes Brazil Uneasy', *New York Times*, 26 May, http://www.nytimes.com/2011/05/27/world/americas/27brazil.html?pagewanted=all (accessed 26 August, 2011).

Bell, Melissa and Flock, Elizabeth (2011) '"A Gay Girl in Damascus" Comes Clean', *Washington Post*, 12 June, http://www.washingtonpost.com/lifestyle/style/a-gay-girl-in-damascus-comes-clean/2011/06/12/AGkyH0RH_story.html (accessed 26 August, 2011).

Berry, David (2005) 'Trust in Media Practices: Towards Cultural Development' (2000), in David Berry (ed.), *Ethics and Media Culture: Practices and Representations*. Oxford and Burlington, MA: Focal Press.

Bhandari, Ram Kumar (2008) 'Families of the Disappeared want Truth and Justice', *Nepali Times*, 24 July, http://www.nepalitimes.com.np/issue/2008/07/18/Nation/15056, (accessed 26 August 2011).

Bhandari, Ram Kumar (2011) 'The Politics of Memory', *Nepali Times*, No. 538, 28 January – 3 February, http://www.nepalitimes.com/issue/2011/01/28/Comment/17895, (accessed 26 August 2011).

Blaagaard, Bolette B. (2010) 'Media and Multiplicity: Journalistic Practices and the Resurgence of Xenophobia in Europe', in Mark Maguire and Gavan Titley (eds), *Translocation: Migration and Social Change*, Vol. 6 No. 2.

Braidotti, Rosi (2002) *Metamorphoses*. Cambridge: Polity Press.

Braidotti, Rosi (2008) 'In Spite of the Times. The Postsecular Turn in Feminism', *Theory, Culture & Society*, Vol. 25 No. 6: 1–24.

Castells, Manuel, Fernandez-Ardevol, Mireia, Linchuan Qiu, Jack and Sey, Araba (2006) 'Electronic Communication and Socio-Political Mobilisation: A New Form of Civil Society', in Marlies Glasius, Mary Kaldor and Helmut Anheier (eds) *Global Civil Society 2005/6*. London: Sage.

Citron, Danielle K. (2010), 'Civil Rights in our Information Age' in Saul Levmore and Martha Nussbaum (eds), *The Offensive Internet*. Cambridge, MA and London: Cambridge University Press.

Commission of Inquiry into the Future of Civil Society in the UK & Ireland (2010) *Civil Society: Enabling Dissent*. Carnegie Trust UK.

Couldry, Nick (2010) *Why Voice Matters. Culture and Politics after Neoliberalism*. London: Sage Publications.

Dahlgren, Peter (1995) *Television and the Public Sphere*. London: Sage.

Dahlgren, Peter (2009) *Media and Political Engagement*. Cambridge: Cambridge University Press.

Daston, Lorraine and Galison, Peter (2007) *Objectivity*. Cambridge, MA: Zone Books.

Dean, Jodi (2009) *Democracy and Other Neoliberal Fantasies*. Durham, NC: Duke University Press.

Durham, Meenakshi Gigi, and Kellner, Douglas M. (eds) (2001) *Media and Cultural Studies: KeyWorks*. Oxford: Blackwell.

End Child Detention Now (2011) http://ecdn.org/ (accessed 7 March 2011).

Ess, Charles (2009) *Digital Media Ethics*. Cambridge: Polity Press.

Flyvbjerg, Bent (1998) 'Habermas and Foucault: Thinkers of Civil Society?', *British Journal of Sociology*, Vol. 49 No. 2.

Flyvbjerg, Bent (2001) *Making Social Science Matter: Why Social Inquiry Fails and How it can Succeed Again*. Cambridge: Cambridge University Press.

Glasser, Theodore L. (ed.) (1999) *The Idea of Public Journalism*. New York: Guilford Press.

Global Voices (2011) http://globalvoicesonline.org/ (accessed 7 March 2011).

Greer, Chris and McLaughlin, Eugene (2010) 'We Predict a Riot?', *British Journal of Criminology*, Vol. 50: 1041–59.

Habermas, Jurgen (1989) *Structural Transformation of the Public Sphere*. Cambridge: Polity Press.

Habermas, Jurgen (2009) 'What is Meant by a "Postsecular Society"? A Discussion on Islam in Europe', in Jurgen Habermas, *Europe: The Faltering Project*. Cambridge: Polity Press.

Hall, Cheryl (2005) *The Trouble with Passion*. New York: Routledge.

Key [pseudonym] (2009a) 'Amazing Pictures, Pollution in China', *China Hush*, 21 October, http://www.chinahush.com/2009/10/21/amazing-pictures-pollution-in-china/ (accessed 26 August 2011).

Key [pseudonym] (2009b) 'Interview with Lu Guang, the Photographer of "Pollution in China"', *China Hush*, 11 November, http://www.chinahush.com/2009/11/11/interview-with-lu-guang-the-photographer-of-pollution-in-china/ (accessed 26 August 2011).

McElwee, Charlie (2008) 'China's Media Coverage of Environmental Issues', *China Environmental Law* blog, 8 April, http://www.chinaenvironmentallaw.com/2008/04/08/chinas-media-coverage-of-environmental-issues/ (accessed 26 August 2011).

McNally, David (2011) *Global Slump: The Economics and Politics of Crisis and Resistance*. Oakland, CA: PM Press.

Naughton, John (2001) 'Contested Space: The Internet and Global Civil Society', in Helmut Anheier, Marlies Glasius and Mary Kaldor (eds), *Global Civil Society 2001*. Oxford: Oxford University Press.

Peters, John Durham (2005) *Courting the Abyss*. Chicago and London: University of Chicago Press.

Politico (2011) http://politico.ie/index.php?option=com_content&view=article&id=7100&Itemid=1068 (accessed 2 September 2011).

Protevi, John (2009) *Political Affects*. Cambridge: Polity Press.

Renov, Michael (ed.) (1993) *Theorizing Documentary* (AFI Film Reader). New York and London: Routledge.

SHAMSNN (2011) http://www.youtube.com/user/SHAMSNN#p/a (accessed 26 August 2011).

Silverstone, Roger (2006) *Media and Morality*. Cambridge: Polity Press.

Slade, Christina (2003) *The Real Thing*. New York and Oxford: Peter Lang.

Sontag, Susan (2003) *Regarding the Pain of Others*. New York: Picador/Farrar, Straus and Giroux.

Storey, Andy (2010) 'The IMF and Ireland: What We can Learn from the Global South', AFRI (Action from Ireland), http://www.scribd.com/doc/55212430/Afri-Report-on-EU-IMF-Loan-Deal (accessed 12 September 2011).

The Syrian Days of Rage (2011) https://www.facebook.com/SyrianDayOfRage?sk=info, (accessed 26 August 2011).

Witschge, Tamara, Fenton, Natalie and Freedman, Des (2010) *Protecting the News: Civil Society and the Media*. Carnegie UK Trust.

Young, Iris M. (2001) 'Activist Challenges to Deliberative Democracy', *Political Theory*, Vol. 29 No. 5: 670–90.

YouTube (2009) http://www.youtube.com/results?search_query=neda+agha-soltan&aq=f (accessed 2 September 2011).

Yardley, Jim (2005) 'Spill in China Brings Danger, and Cover-Up', *New York Times*, 26 November, http://www.nytimes.com/2005/11/26/international/asia/26china.html (accessed 26 August 2011).

Zoonen, Liesbet van, Hirzalla, Fadi, Muller, Floris and Vis, Farida (2010) http://www.lboro.ac.uk/departments/ss/research/FITNA/index.html (accessed 7 March 2011).

Zuckerman, Ethan (2010): *Listening to Global Voices*. TED Talk, http://www.ted.com/talks/ethan_zuckerman.html) (accessed 28 April 2011).

PART III

Peace and Justice

CHAPTER 6

A DECADE OF THE WAR ON TERROR AND THE 'RESPONSIBILITY TO PROTECT'

Mary Kaldor[1]

Debating Military Intervention

In 2001, before 9/11, it seemed as though the world was moving inexorably towards a new humanitarian norm of military intervention in cases of massive human suffering and, in particular, genocide, ethnic cleansing and large-scale human rights violations. Several reports were published in 2000–01 that strengthened the case for humanitarian intervention. The Independent International Commission on Kosovo concluded in 2000 that the NATO intervention in Yugoslavia aimed at preventing the ethnic cleansing of Albanians was 'illegal but legitimate' and that there was a need to take measures to close the gap between legality and legitimacy (IICK 2000). The same year the *Report of the United Nations Panel on Peace Operations* (UNSC 2000), also known as the Brahimi Report, put forward practical proposals to improve the capacity of the UN to respond to crises. And in 2001, the International Commission on Intervention and States Sovereignty (ICISS) came up with the concept of 'Responsibility to Protect' (R2P) – the idea that the international community has a responsibility to protect civilians where their own states fail to do so (ICISS 2001).

In *Global Civil Society 2001* I argued that this emerging norm was an expression of global civil society, the outcome of a global political debate, that included humanitarian and human rights NGOs, individuals such as Bernard Kouchner, who founded Médécins sans Frontières (MSF), and various think tanks and commissions like the Carnegie Endowment for Peace and the International Crisis Group, as well, of course, as the traditional and new media (Kaldor 2001). In particular, the genocides in Rwanda (1994) and Srebrenica (1995) had shocked the 'conscience of the world', in the words of then UN Secretary-General Kofi Annan, and had led to a new determination among policy-makers and policy-shapers that these tragic episodes should never be allowed to be repeated.

The attacks on the World Trade Center and the Pentagon on 11 September 2001 shook the kaleidoscope of global civil society debate. 9/11 marked the beginning of the War on Terror and of muscular interventions in Iraq and Afghanistan, in addition to indirect or less overt interventions in Pakistan, Somalia and Yemen. The rhetoric of the War on Terror was used to justify Israeli attacks on Palestinians and Russian intervention in Chechnya, as well as other uses of military force. And in many countries, including the United States, the War on Terror was associated with a range of measures increasing surveillance and restricting human rights. In particular, President Bush acquired far-reaching powers that allowed him to detain suspects for indefinite periods and establish the notorious prison at Guantanamo Bay. The consequence was a polarisation of opinion between those who supported the War on Terror and those who were against. This debate divided the human rights and humanitarian community and squeezed the space for those who favoured the norm of humanitarian intervention. Nevertheless, this was also a period when R2P and associated concepts such as human security, peace-building, and stabilisation were increasingly adopted by international institutions and governments, even in the United States, and the momentum of the ideas of the 1990s was carried forward.

In what follows, I describe the debates around the main interventions of the twenty-first century, as well as the development of new concepts like Responsibility to Protect and Human Security. I then analyse the changing composition of the global civil society actors engaged in the debate and how this might influence what happens in the next decade.

Debating Interventions in the Twenty-first Century

Afghanistan

Within a month of the attacks on the World Trade Center, the United States had intervened in Afghanistan. The official justification was not humanitarian; it was self-defence. On 7 October 2001, the United States informed the United Nations Security Council that it was launching airstrikes against al-Qaeda as unilateral action in self-defence.

The debate about intervention in Afghanistan was muted in the aftershock of 9/11. Those who strongly favoured the intervention were largely that group around President Bush known as neoconservatives (neocons) who had joined the administration from think tanks such as the American Enterprise Institute and the Heritage Foundation. In particular, the Project for a New American Century vociferously campaigned for increased defence spending and in support of the War on Terror, arguing that the United States needed to take advantage of its unipolar moment to push for the global spread of American principles and values – if necessary by force. Its first report suggested that the process of what it called 'defense transformation' was likely to be slow unless there were to be some 'catastrophic catalysing event – like Pearl Harbor' (Donnelly 2000). There was also widespread support among Western governments for the intervention.

There were minor demonstrations against the war by the left and by peace groups in the United States, Spain, Greece, Italy and Britain, particularly after the bombing had begun. The main argument against the war was the human suffering caused by bombing, especially because humanitarian convoys were prevented from reaching those in need.

The human rights and humanitarian community were divided. One very important line of argument was that there should have been a legal rather than military response to 9/11. The attacks on the World Trade Center should have been described as a crime against humanity rather than an attack by a foreign enemy on the United States; this would have implied that Osama bin Laden should be treated as a criminal rather than an enemy, and the appropriate response would then have been to try to locate and arrest him using the methods of intelligence and policing (Howard 2002). In fact, a poll carried out by Gallup in September 2001 showed that in most countries this was the dominant view. 'Apart from the US, Israel and India a majority of people in every country surveyed preferred extradition and trial of suspects to a US attack' (Bradford Stop the War Coalition 2001).

However, there were also many who argued that military force was needed to capture bin Laden if the Taliban refused to extradite him. An interesting argument in favour of the war was put forward by Richard Falk, the distinguished international lawyer, who had actively opposed the Vietnam War and other military interventions. He criticised the legalistic approach on the grounds that the capture and trial of bin Laden, even if it were possible, would give bin Laden counterproductive publicity. 'A public platform would give Bin Laden and his associates a platform to rally further support among a large constituency of sympathizers and conviction and martyrdom would certainly be viewed as a kind of legal martyrdom' (Falk 2001). He favoured a limited 'just war'.

With the help of the Northern Alliance, a collection of warlords who had earlier been defeated by the Taliban, the intervention succeeded in ousting the Taliban from power. This was celebrated in Kabul and gave rise to humanitarian justifications for the war. The Afghans had, after all, been freed from tyranny. Laura Bush (2001), for example, emphasised the importance of the intervention for women's rights. In the aftermath of the intervention, the United Nations authorised the International Security Assistance Force (ISAF) under NATO command to maintain security in and around Kabul. Later, ISAF's mandate was extended to the whole of Afghanistan. Nevertheless, security continued to deteriorate and after the election of Barack Obama as President of the United States, a big increase in troops was authorised.

The continuing war has been accompanied by a continuing debate about the conduct of the war. On the one hand, there are those who support the war as a way of defeating terror, in the form of the Taliban and al-Qaeda. In both the United States and Britain, the justification for the war is to 'make our streets safer'. Within this line of reasoning, some favour an effort to stabilise Afghanistan, to assist with governance, justice and development, as a means of defeating the terrorists. This group, which includes General Stanley McCrystal, the architect of the Afghan 'surge' strategy, and General Petreaus, his successor, see no contradiction between what they call 'population security' and continuing offensives against the Taliban. Another group, which includes Vice President Joseph Biden, favours a focus on counter-terror, with fewer troops on the ground and more of an exclusive emphasis on drone attacks, which are thought to have been very successful in killing Taliban and al-Quaeda leaders.

On the other hand, there are those who support a continuing international presence, including military forces, in order to bring security and democracy to Afghanistan not as a means to defeating terrorism, but as a goal in itself. This group is concerned both with the human suffering caused by the continuing conflict with the Taliban, and the human rights violations inflicted by a predatory government composed largely of former warlords. Favouring fewer troops and more emphasis on justice and governance, they fear that continued offensives against the Taliban, even those such as drone attacks that

Box 6.1
Civil Society in Afghanistan

The author has made several trips to Afghanistan in the last two years as part of a research and dialogue project on Afghan civil society for the London School of Economics. Quotes in the piece come from interviews and a civil society workshop held in Kabul in February and March 2011.

For the past nine years, the international community and Karzai-led government have set Afghanistan's political, economic and social agenda while largely ignoring the voices of ordinary Afghan citizens. Despite a rather rare consensus among policy-makers that progress in Afghanistan requires greater political inclusiveness, accountability and bottom-up engagement, international strategies continue to rely nearly exclusively on the very people – corrupt government officials, local strongmen, and a small clique of politically-connected actors – who have deepened the predatory and exclusionary political economy that has alienated ordinary citizens, marginalised moderate voices and energised the insurgency.

From the Bonn Agreement of December 2001 to the recent Parliamentary elections of September 2010 and the much-anticipated Bonn II peace negotiations planned for December 2011, the space for civil society and moderate political forces has contracted, even as the number of NGOs, self-organised groups, and new political groups has mushroomed. This paradox can be partly explained by post-2001 donor engagement approaches, as well as the nature of the country's persistent conflict. Firstly, most groups act as private contractors for service delivery, competing with one another and private enterprises for donor funds rather than assuming a more political role. As one young female teacher put it:

> Civil society is manipulated by everyone, but mostly by the international community. The work that gets done is based on project goals, not for the advancement and betterment of civil society in Afghanistan. The biggest problem is that even the best proposal for your community gets nowhere if it does not fit the donors' priorities.

Even when civil society inclusion has been officially sanctioned in decision-making processes, representatives have either become 'auxiliaries to a pre-established program' (Foschini 2011) or are confined to parallel meetings at a venue distant from where the actual decision-making took place.

Secondly, much of Afghan civil society mirrors the splits and cleavages that previous decades of conflict produced. This is further compounded in today's environment, where civil society finds itself once again caught in a complex system of violence,

squeezed between the various military-political actors in the conflict, as targeted assassinations increase and an attendant climate of fear expands.

Despite these grave challenges, many Afghan civil society actors have managed to continue to play important roles, using their own resources to influence policy and bridge sectarian divides, as well as to foster opportunities for conflict resolution at local levels. Women's groups, such as the Afghan Women's Network (AWN) and the Afghan Women's Educational Center (AWEC), are probably the best organised, having developed innovative ways to cooperate under the Taliban regime. Some Afghan organisations are breaking through client networks, strengthening urban-rural links, and working with and through traditional institutions. The Cooperation for Peace and Unity (CPAU), for example, engages with local communities, setting up local peace shuras and working with them to strengthen their capacity for conflict resolution (Borchgrevink and Harpviken 2008). Other forms of cooperation have been less formalised: in one district in the eastern province of Nangarhar, village elders have come together with farmers, religious leaders, teachers, drivers and businessmen to publicise some of the most egregious examples of government corruption and abuse, as well as to form ad hoc consultation groups to resolve local problems (Theros and Kaldor 2011).

In the post-Taliban political scene, a new current has also emerged from underground and exile – what Afghan analyst Thomas Ruttig refers to as the 'new democrats' (Ruttig 2006). Common to these groups is their desire to transcend the old but prevailing political fault lines pitting leftist, Islamist and ethno-nationalist groups against one another – most of which remain armed, complete with large militias, and exploit ethnic difference to build up political support. Comprised predominantly of young activists who took no part in the bloodshed of the past, political activists formerly of the leftist camp, and Mujahedin wishing to cross ideological divides, these groups include, among others, Hezb-e Kar wa Tause'a-ye Afghanistan (Afghanistan Labour and Development Party, ALDP), Hezb-e Hambastagi-ye Melli-ye Jawanan-e Afghanistan (HaMJA) (National Solidarity Party of Afghanistan's Youth), the Republican Party, and Nohzat-e Azadi wa Demokrasi-ye Afghanistan (Afghanistan Freedom and Democracy Movement, AFDM). Initially formed within certain ethnic communities, these groups actively try to broaden their base and explore different ways of coalition building and unification to become more of a national party (Ruttig 2006).

For one young activist from Kabul, only the collective efforts of all Afghans could stem the current cycle of insecurity and violence:

As a nation we have suffered from conflict at all levels and through each fabric of our lives. Everybody should be involved in a peace process: tribal elders, Imams, local councils, women's groups, family representatives and youth representatives. We must reach those who are holding up arms against each other, we may even have to talk to the wives of the fighters to discourage their husbands from fighting anymore.

But overcoming societal and physical divisions remains almost as large a problem for civil society mobilisation as the lack of a safe political environment. Over the last two years, different efforts to strengthen and mobilise civil society have developed, gaining increasing urgency as momentum shifts towards a negotiated settlement and transition.

One such example is the recent establishment of a platform for Afghan citizens, civil society activists, and community leaders that aims to bring together communities from across the country and mobilise grassroots efforts around a shared vision for peace and unity. In March 2011, prompted by a collaboration between the Civil Society Development Centre in Afghanistan and the London School of Economics, more than 140 Afghan citizens – community, religious, and tribal leaders; activists; teachers and educators; students and youth leaders – came together from across the country to share their experiences of managing life under conflict and discuss strategies for overcoming common obstacles in their daily lives. Given the widespread perception that self-serving elites and extremists dominate the political space,

they desired a permanent platform able to catalyse and support the energies of activists and groups countrywide. Above all, they wanted to overcome their isolation and to create a movement, as opposed to a project-based organisation. This movement, they insisted, was to be focused on: the national interest as opposed to personal political and economic ambitions; and the security of every individual Afghan, not just the security of the government or the West. Foremost, they demanded back their dignity.

By the end of the conference the participants declared their commitment to create a 'Civic Platform on the National Interest and Human Security' that could provide the means and structure for Afghan citizens from all corners and ethnic communities to interact, exchange ideas, and increase their voice in the debates and decisions that currently affect their lives. As one young Afghan woman explained:

Since 2002, civil society has articulated over and over again the problems we face but the government and the internationals do not listen to us. Rather than presenting them a list of demands and grievances that are already well-known and ignored, we must instead find ways to work together to overcome both societal divisions and the obstacles faced in our daily lives. We must now take responsibility ourselves to create a peaceful and stable Afghanistan.

Marika Theros is a research officer and PhD student in the London School of Economics Department for International Development.

minimise civilian casualties, will provoke counterattacks and provide an argument for the further recruitment of young men into the Taliban, many of whom are already frustrated and alienated by lack of opportunity.

This group includes many European governments and organisations, notably the former EU Special Representative, Francesc Vendrell, as well as civil society groups inside Afghanistan. (See Box 6.1.) Many in this group, particularly United Nations officials, favour talks with the Taliban as a way of ending the conflict although, of course, there are fears that bringing back the Taliban into government will lead to even worse human rights violations – even if it stops the killing caused by continuing conflict. In March 2011, the Report of a Task Force chaired by Lakhdar Brahimi, the former UN Special Representative and Thomas Pickering, former US Ambassador, set out a roadmap for such negotiations (Brahimi and Pickering 2011).

Finally there are those who oppose the war and favour the withdrawal of international forces. This is the position of the anti-war groups. Unlike the opposition to the Iraq war, the call for the withdrawal of troops, by and large, does not stem from a principled opposition to the intervention. As one sympathetic commentator put it: 'The call to "bring the troops home" stems from a sense that their presence can only make a horrific mess worse. This is a world away from saying that they should never have been there at all.' (Black 2009)

Perhaps one of the most well-known individuals who has taken this position is the British Conservative MP Rory Stewart, who wrote a book about walking across Afghanistan and founded an NGO there, Turquoise Mountain, before becoming the Director of the Carr Center for Human Rights at Harvard. He argues that the war is unwinnable and that Western governments are pursuing illusory goals: 'After seven years of refinement, the policy seems so buoyed by illusions, caulked in ambiguous language and encrusted with moral claims, analogies and political theories that it can seem futile to present an alternative' (Stewart 2009). He is particularly vitriolic about the inefficiency of the huge international effort:

The thing that drove me up the wall and made me Conservative was the experience of dealing with the international donor organisations. All these organisations from the World Bank to the UN, all these people in international development are living in a crazy world of form-filling, box-ticking, report-writing. You end up where you are trying to get money to clear

a path of rubbish and you say: 'Could I employ some people to move the trash?' And they say: 'Well, maybe if you describe it as a gender project we can get dollars through the gender pool.' (quoted in Sands 2009)

Iraq

The invasion of Iraq in March 2003 was much more polarising of outside opinion than the war in Afghanistan. In support of the war was a combination of neocons, who argued that the quick and relatively painless intervention in Afghanistan had offered a new model of defence transformation, and the so-called liberal intervention-ists, that part of the humanitarian and human rights community who had most enthusiastically embraced military intervention as a response to humanitarian crisis.

The liberal internationalists included people close to the British Prime Minister, Tony Blair, those like former Ambassador to Croatia, Peter Galbraith, who had supported the Kurdish cause, and liberal commentators such as Michael Ignatieff and Christopher Hitchens. Hitchens, a well-known former left-wing journalist, engaged in numerous debates with anti-war luminaries like Noam Chomsky or the far-left politician George Galloway. Hitchens published a collection of his essays in support of the war entitled *A Long Short War: The Postponed Liberation of Iraq* (Hitchens 2003).

Although the formal justification for the war was based on the removal of weapons of mass destruction, both groups used humanitarian and democracy arguments. Thus Robert Kagan and William Kristol, co-founders of the Project for a New American Century, wrote:

It is fashionable to sneer at the moral case for liberating an Iraqi people long brutalized by Saddam's rule. Critics insist mere oppression was not sufficient reason for war, and in any case that it was not Bush's reason. In fact, of course, it was one of Bush's reasons, and the moral and humanitarian purpose provided a compelling reason for a war to remove Saddam … For the people of Iraq, the war put an end to three decades of terror and suffering. The mass graves uncovered since the end of the war are alone sufficient justification for it. (Kagan and Kristol 2004)

Arrayed against these 'bellicose intellectuals'[2] was probably the largest and most global anti-war movement in history. On 15 February 2003, some 11 million people demonstrated against the war all over the world, from Australia to Brazil. The biggest demonstrations were in those countries participating in the war – London, Rome, Madrid and New York. As we reported in GCS 2003:

A general feature of the 15 February demonstrations everywhere was that no particular profile of 'the marcher' could be given, they were of all generations, classes, and races, and many had never been on a demonstration before. In particular, the anti-war movement brought together North and South, Western and Islamic communities, offering the potential for a new cosmopolitan approach which integrated immigrant and developing-country communities into the global political process for the first time. (Kaldor et al. 2003: 28)

The anti-war movement included a number of coalitions such as United for Justice and Peace, Win Without War, Act Now to Stop War and End Racism (all based in the US), and Stop the War Coalition (UK). In the United States, the anti-war movement was supported by every mainstream religious community, and some, like the Friends, or Catholic pacifist organisations, played a major organising role (see Cortwright 2005). A particularly important aspect of the anti-war movement was the use of the internet. Move On was an online organising network founded in 1998 to oppose the impeachment of President Clinton; in the six months leading up to March 2003, its network jumped from approximately 700,000 to more than 2 million (Cortwright 2005). Equally significant was the role played by the World Social Forum (see Chapter 10 this volume), where the idea of a simultaneous day of action was conceived. And as the war in Iraq developed, veterans groups and their families began to play an increasing role.

The anti-war movement failed to prevent the war, but it did undoubtedly influence the United Nations Security Council. The United States and Britain were unable to mobilise support for a resolution authorising support. It was opposed not only by Russia, China and France, but also by six non-permanent members – Chile, Mexico, Cameroon, Guinea, Angola and Pakistan. Indeed, while the divisions over Iraq had devastating consequences both for the United Nations and the European Union, one salient aspect of the debate over Iraq was the way that it propelled the United Nations Security Council into the global public consciousness, with widely watched dramatic televised sessions. In Turkey, civil society groups, including the Helsinki Citizens Assembly, lobbied Members of Parliament so that it voted against the war,

and the US forces were unable to use Turkey for transit and bases as originally planned.

The main focus of the anti-war movement was opposition to both war and to Western imperialism. Some felt that there should have been more emphasis on ending tyranny, and a minority were explicit about their opposition to both Saddam Hussein and war.

The humanitarian and human rights communities were deeply divided. Some saw themselves as liberal internationalists. Others were opposed to both Saddam Hussein and to war. This was, for example, the position of Bernard Kouchner, the foremost advocate of humanitarian intervention, who co-authored a manifesto in February 2003 entitled 'Neither War Nor Saddam'. Big human rights organisations such as Human Rights Watch (HRW) and Amnesty International were initially neutral, although both stressed the importance of respecting human rights and international humanitarian law in the conduct of the war. However, Amnesty International later put out a press release arguing that the war in Iraq was associated with a 'backlash' against human rights, including the repression of anti-war demonstrators in places such as Egypt, Sudan, Turkey, Spain, Greece, Germany and Belgium, and new restrictions on asylum rights (Amnesty International 2003). And in its 2004 Annual Report, HRW argued that the war in Iraq could not be classified as a humanitarian intervention:

In considering the criteria that would justify humanitarian intervention, the most important, as noted, is the level of killing: was genocide or comparable mass slaughter underway or imminent? Brutal as Saddam Hussein's reign had been, the scope of the Iraqi government's killing in March 2003 was not of the exceptional and dire magnitude that would justify humanitarian intervention. We have no illusions about Saddam Hussein's vicious inhumanity. Having devoted extensive time and effort to documenting his atrocities, we estimate that in the last twenty-five years of Ba'th Party rule the Iraqi government murdered or 'disappeared' some quarter of a million Iraqis, if not more. In addition, one must consider such abuses as Iraq's use of chemical weapons against Iranian soldiers. However, by the time of the March 2003 invasion, Saddam Hussein's killing had ebbed.

There were times in the past when the killing was so intense that humanitarian intervention would have been justified ... But on the eve of the latest Iraq war, no one contends that the Iraqi government was engaged in killing of anywhere near this magnitude, or had been for some time. 'Better late than never' is not a justification for humanitarian intervention, which should be countenanced only to stop mass murder, not to punish its perpetrators, desirable as punishment is in such circumstances. (HRW 2004)[3]

In a speech in London introducing the report, Kenneth Roth, the Executive Director of HRW, said that as the arguments about weapons of mass destruction were fading away, the only way left for politicians to justify the war was as a humanitarian intervention (MacAskill 2004).

As in Afghanistan, the initial intervention was quick and involved almost no casualties. Actually, most Iraqi soldiers took off their uniforms and went home when the Americans entered Iraq. And as in Afghanistan, it was after the invasion that security deteriorated, culminating in a deadly civil war in the years 2005–07. The number of casualties is hotly disputed, but perhaps as many as 1 million people died as a result of the invasion and the subsequent hostilities. Some 4 million people were displaced from their homes, and tens of thousands of young men were detained.

The positions that characterised the initial invasion were by and large sustained throughout the war. The pro-war groups favoured increased commitments to Iraq and in particular supported the 'surge' of 2006. The anti-war groups favoured withdrawal. And the human rights organisations focused on the conduct of the war and the treatment of detainees. Of particular importance was the backlash among humanitarian NGOs against humanitarian intervention as a result of this war. Crucial to this backlash were the attack on UN Headquarters in Baghdad in August 2003, which killed the hugely admired UN diplomat Sergio De Mello, and on the International Red Cross compound in October 2003. These events crystallised a growing opposition to what was seen as the militarisation of humanitarianism, accompanied by a growing insistence on the need to restate the principles of neutrality and impartiality. As David Rieff, one of the foremost critics of humanitarian intervention, put it:

Dissenting figures, notably in French humanitarian circles, argue that humanitarianism needs to remain a world apart, no matter how worthy the larger goals of advancing human rights, resolving conflict, and fostering development. Thus many of the most influential figures from Medecins Sans Frontieres (MSF) and other like-minded agencies insist that such projects take humanitarianism beyond the role for which it is suited. (Rieff 2002)

Largely excluded from the global public debate was civil society inside Iraq. Many of those who supported the war had links with the exiled opposition or with Kurdish groups. But a number of civil society groups did spring up inside the country after the invasion; some drawn from the underground opposition to Saddam Hussein. These groups (students, women, oil trade unions, humanitarian and human rights groups, artists and intellectuals) were initially ambivalent about the invasion, describing it as liberation/occupation. Many were targeted during the civil war and lost their lives. But it can be argued that it was Iraqi civil society, including the Sunni Muslims who broke with al-Qaeda and others who insisted on an Iraqi national identity, that was key to the public backlash against all warring parties which led to the decline in violence after 2008 (Said 2011).

Darfur

During this period, the other major public debate about intervention concerned the conflict in Darfur in Western Sudan. The latest round of hostilities began in February 2003 when a rebel group called the Darfur Liberation Front seized the town of Gulu. This was the beginning of an extremely complicated conflict, in which a government-led counter-insurgency campaign that included regular soldiers using disproportionate military force; militias, often known as *janjawijd*, composed of nomadic groups without access to land; as well as bandits, outlaws and criminals (some deliberately released from prison), was pitted against rebel groups largely composed of sedentary farmers and intellectuals. The former were construed as 'Arab' and the latter as 'African', although anthropologists have shown that both groups were highly mixed. The conflict has been described as the first 'climate change' conflict, since the lengthy drought in the area and growing desertification contributed to the tension between nomads and settlers. It has both been attributed to the 'turbulent state' of Sudan (Waal 2007) and explained in terms of both regional (Chad and Libya) and global dynamics.

Most violence has been directed against civilians and it has involved large-scale population displacement and brutal atrocities. Again, casualty figures have been hotly disputed; numbers for the years 2003–05 vary from 50,000 to 500,000.

Unlike other conflicts in Africa, the Darfur conflict has been the subject of major public debate, especially in the United States. The Save Darfur Coalition started as a student outreach campaign by the Holocaust Museum. Formally founded at New York University in July 2004, it rapidly developed into a mass advertising campaign, involving celebrities such as Meryl Streep, Angelina Jolie and Brad Pitt.

A rally in 2006 in Washington DC brought together the American Jewish World Service, the American Society for Muslim Advancement, the National Association of Evangelists, the US Conference of Catholic Bishops, the US Holocaust Memorial Museum, the American Anti-Slavery Group, Amnesty International, Christian Solidarity International, Physicians for Human Rights, and the National Black Church Initiative. Mahmoud Mamdani, a fierce critic of the Save Darfur campaign, suggests that the movement was a substitute for the debate over Iraq; it was apolitical and moral. 'Only a campaign targeting an issue where American power was not *directly* implicated could bring together in a unified chorus forces that are otherwise adversaries on most important issues of the day; at one end of the scale the Christian right and the Zionist lobby; at the other, African-American groups born of the civil rights struggle and a mainly school-based and university-based movement' (Mamdani 2009: 60).

Among the achievements of the campaign were a resolution in Congress on 24 June 2004 declaring that Sudan had committed genocide in Darfur, and a statement by President Bush on 30 June 2004 that 'the violence in Darfur is clearly genocide' (Mamdani 2009: 24). Mia Farrow branded the Beijing Olympics of 2008 the 'genocide Olympics' and Steven Spielberg threatened to resign as artistic director because of Chinese support for Sudan; this does seem to have modified the Chinese position. Yet despite all this mobilisation, only a small African Union (AU) force was deployed to Darfur in 2004; not until July 2007 was a larger hybrid UN/AU force agreed upon, and it has been plagued with difficulties.

The debate about Darfur turned on whether the conflict could be described as a genocide or a civil war. This obsession with calling the conflict a genocide is due to the assumption that only a genocide can legally trigger a military intervention. Even though the norm of humanitarian intervention is increasingly recognised, and the term 'Responsibility to Protect' was approved by the United Nations Summit in 2005, there remains no legal recourse to intervention except through the United Nations Security Council. In the case of Rwanda, the Clinton Administration had tried to argue that there was no genocide, so as to avoid the responsibility of intervention. To prove that the Darfur conflict was a genocide, it was necessary to exaggerate civilian deaths and to demonstrate racial intent – hence the emphasis on Arab and African identities.

Those who opposed military intervention argued that the Darfur conflict was a civil war and that the best approach was a negotiated settlement. Critics such as Mamdani claimed that shrill calls for military intervention and the one-sided application of international criminal law, as in the indictment of Omar al-Bashir, the President of Sudan, were really a justification for a new imperialism. 'More than anything else, the "Responsibility to Protect" is a right to punish without being held accountable – a clarion call for the recolonisation of "failed states" in Africa. In its present form, the call for justice is really a slogan that masks a big power agenda to recolonise Africa' (Mamdani 2009: 300).

Yet the Darfur conflict is not easily characterised as either genocide or civil war. It is clearly not genocide, even though like other contemporary conflicts it involves ethnic cleansing and massive human rights violations – good enough reasons for outside intervention. It is difficult to describe the conflict as a civil war as it involves many external actors, and since numerous attempts to reach a negotiated agreement have failed. Because it took so long to authorise a substantial mission and because of the obstacles to protecting civilians, the people of Darfur are still suffering. The real problem has been that the terms of the debate left no room for a serious analysis about how to protect civilians: whether military intervention actually helps or makes things worse, and what sort of justice and outside help is required. As Iavor Rangelov has put it:

> The Save Darfur movement, in particular has prioritised political will over other important questions such as ideas, instruments and capabilities for resolving conflict. Publicising the plight of civilians in Darfur was useful in eliciting global debate about the need to respond but not at the expense of a debate about the means to respond and the efforts needed to mobilise the range of international and local actors with stakes in a sustainable solution to Darfur. (Rangelov forthcoming 2012)

Libya[4]

The most recent intervention to be the subject of a global public debate is the intervention in Libya in 2011. United Nations Security Council Resolution 1973 was a considerable achievement, adopted on 17 March 2011 just in time to prevent Qadhafi forces from overrunning the eastern town of Benghazi, which pro-democracy protestors had liberated. For the first time, the goal of humanitarian

Box 6.2
Libya: The Revolution of the People

The Libyan revolution could quite aptly be described as a 'revolution of the people'. From the National Transitional Council (NTC) to the fighters on the frontline – all were part of a huge groundswell and uprising of civil society. As a result, the discourse on civil society has become central and is directly integrated into the political debate.

The Growth of Organised Civil Society

Prior to February of this year, regulations and the previous legal framework (for example, Law 19 on freedom of association) under Muammar Qadhafi's regime heavily discouraged the emergence of civil society organisations (CSOs), severely limiting their scope of activities and freedom of expression and constituting a permanent threat to activists. The situation in eastern Libya changed drastically immediately following the civil uprising on 17 February 2011. Numerous CSOs and new media suddenly emerged,[1] willing to take an active part both in the war and aid effort as well as in the debates.

If we consider the type of activities and the sectors of intervention of these CSOs, they are in practice difficult to differentiate. Nominally they focus on many things including: humanitarian aid for IDPs, refugees and vulnerable families; education, youth activities and psychosocial support to children; information campaigns (creation of newspapers and radio broadcasts); medical care; human rights; advocacy on political and other issues; reconciliation; DDR (disarmament, demobilisation and reintegration); and even environmental and cultural heritage protection. However, despite such a broad scope of activities, the vast majority of these CSOs are in reality still responding to the crisis, involved in relief activities or social aid and labelled 'charity organisations'. Libyan civil society is still in a phase of gestation, and what the longer-term missions and objectives of these CSOs will be when the situation continues to normalise remains largely unclear; nor is it clear how many will continue to operate post-crisis.

However, despite such questions, the level of organisation is quite impressive. Two major NGO coalitions, representing approximately 60 and 100 national NGOs respectively (recorded August 2011), were established in eastern Libya directly after February 2011. As well as providing an umbrella structure under which the NGOs can operate, these coalitions are also delivering capacity building and training to their members, as well as instigating collaborative NGO projects. There are also many more CSO platforms, groups and coordination mechanisms that have organically flourished throughout the country. Furthermore, within the NTC's Ministry for Culture and Communities, the Office for CSOs is currently drafting a new legal and regulatory framework for CSOs and INGOs operating in Libya (though this regulatory framework remains very unclear).

It is notable that the membership of these CSOs is based on territorial solidarities (at the neighbourhood or the city levels) and/or socio-professional networks (engineers, lawyers, scholars, students, and so on) – but not on traditional linkages, such as evident tribal affiliations. It is also worth noting that Islamist movements, particularly the Muslim Brotherhood, are indeed influencing some of these new organisations. However, many others are led by intellectuals and scholars opposed to the influence of religion in politics. Although the future direction of these civil society groups is uncertain, it is evident that the debate is currently cast in a western frame of reference; the good will of INGOs (ready-made projects supporting the emergence of a 'democratic civil society') and the influence of the Libyan diaspora are certainly strengthening these stereotypes.

Most importantly, however, this is a society in progress; the main common denominator amongst groups and citizens is the willingness to change, and to overcome the mental structures inherited from both Qadhafi's regime and tribal allegiances.

The Popular Uprising and Humanitarian Intervention

At the start of the uprising in February 2011, and in the days leading up to the Western military intervention outside Benghazi on 19 March, civil society was still largely disorganised and voiceless.[2] Despite this, the Libyan public was aware of the political conversations and expectant of the passing of UN Resolution 1970, the creation of a no-fly zone and the promise to 'protect civilians and civilian-populated areas'. Mid-March, with pro-Qadhafi forces pressing on Benghazi, there were loud public cries for international military air protection, even though the sheer scale of the looming attack was not fully known.

The French-led air intervention was critical and timely. A large poster of Nicolas Sarkozy, crossed out by a vibrant 'Thank you France', still dominates Freedom Square in Benghazi, the epicentre of the civil uprising, where the crowd continues each night to maintain the enthusiasm of the revolution. Flags of France, Britain and other supportive countries are commonplace on the streets of eastern Libya.

1   More than 200 NGOs were registered in Benghazi between February and July; during the same period, 80 news and other media titles were registered.
2   There were a couple of early civil movements that formed, such as the February 17th Coalition, a group of lawyers initially demanding political reform, as well as diaspora groups which formed very quickly around the revolution.

Yet despite such public feelings, the official declaration from the revolutionary forces and the NTC, as well as the majority of the voices of civil society in 'Free Libya', remained united against any form of ground intervention by an external military force. From the outset this was an issue of sovereignty and independence – to call for this was to be a traitor to your country. This defence of sovereignty is reinforced by the widespread suspicion, fed by years of propaganda, that the West remains a potential enemy. The traumatic and humiliating experience of the war in Iraq and incidents such as abuse at Abu Ghraib prison have had a catalytic effect on this perception by the Libyan population of the dangers of a Western military intervention.

Within Libyan NGOs and youth organisations, debates raged as to what level of intervention from NATO forces was acceptable. Although all options are discussed, opinion remained fairly united, even after six months of conflict: air intervention was seen as critical, weapons-drops and training warmly accepted, but full-scale ground intervention was not welcome.

However, some groups expressed a slightly paradoxical opinion, suggesting that the direct removal of Qadhafi was paramount. From this point of view, a limited internationally-led special operations ground intervention, purely aimed at removing Qadhafi, would have been publicly acceptable – although it would never have officially been endorsed by the NTC.

And the fact that there was evident mission creep on the side of NATO from the early phases of the intervention was not only accepted, but somewhat expected by Libyan public opinion in the 'Free Libya' areas. Many, in fact, generally assumed that NATO's 'true' ambition was regime change; it seemed that anything less would have been unacceptable. Moreover, it was popularly suggested that NATO must in fact do more to support the rebels through air strikes and weapons support. NATO seemed to progressively provide such direct support – particularly leading up to the attack on Tripoli.

Few in eastern Libya expected such a protracted conflict, and the dismay was evident. On one hand, the fact that Qadhafi may have been supported by a segment of the Libyan population was unthinkable for most of the civil society groups in eastern Libya. On the other, many people, informed by Hollywood movies,

did not believe that NATO did not have the ability to rapidly defeat Qadhafi's resistance. Suspicions at times even turned to alternative Western agendas; suggestions ranged from attempts at political control to disagreements over oil revenues – even to the desire of Western forces to see Libya damaged further before fighting ceased.

Such rumours were commonplace, such has been the inaccessible nature of reliable information in this conflict. Joining these concerns were genuine fears from Libyan civil actors that NATO would run out of funding, or lose the will to continue to support the rebels. To add to this fear, despite negotiations being a formal option from both sides, they were barely even a consideration for a vast majority of people residing in the 'Free Libya' areas who simply argued: 'We will not accept that Qadhafi remains in power; Qadhafi will not accept giving power up.'

The debate on intervention within civil society remained complex and volatile up until Qadhafi's death and NATO's announcement of a formal end to their mission. What was clear is that the Libyan groups that emerged post-17 February framed and directed this debate. The consensus throughout demanded increased NATO air support, but still refused any form of full-scale ground intervention; the battle for Tripoli certainly seemed to include ever closer NATO air support. Finally, there was an evident desire from the Libyan civil society to engage with Western civil society on this debate.

Francis Ward graduated with an MA from King's College London War Studies department in 2010. Having worked in Afghanistan from 2010–11, he is currently based in Libya, working with an INGO and focusing on humanitarian response and post-conflict recovery.

Remy Reymann graduated from the University Pantheon-Sorbonne in Paris in Economic and Social Studies in 2005. He worked in Central Asia and Afghanistan from 1988 to 1996, and has been based in Serbia since 2000, working with a Serbian Consulting Company and specialising in regional development and cross-border cooperation.

intervention moved beyond a Euro-American preserve. It was pushed by the Arab League and both Russia and China abstained. The resolution called on member states and regional organisations to 'take all necessary measures … to protect civilians and civilian populated areas under threat of attack in the Libyan Arab Jamahiriya, including Benghazi, while excluding a foreign occupation force of any form on any part of Libyan territory' (UNSC 2011). Moreover, Resolution 1973 was preceded by Resolution 1970, which referred Libya to the International Criminal Court (ICC) and imposed sanctions.

However, the means adopted, air strikes, were inappropriate for protecting civilians on the ground. As in Kosovo in 1999, the international community relied entirely on airstrikes. In effect, NATO became the air force of the rebels. The airstrikes did prevent an attack on Benghazi and helped the rebels to take control of Tripoli. But at the time of writing there are still pockets of resistance, with the rebels divided among different regional militias; there is still the risk of a long conflict.

In the case of Libya, those in favour of the intervention regarded the removal of Qadhafi as proof of the validity of their position. Those against argued that airstrikes kill not only soldiers but also the very people who are supposed to be protected; however precise, there is always collateral damage – especially since Qadhafi was using human shields. Even if collateral damage was minimised, the conflict itself has generated much civilian suffering. Airstrikes also seemed to validate Qadhafi's narrative about Western imperialism; they polarised opinion inside Libya so that a future democracy will be more difficult to establish. Some even suggested that the opposition should not be viewed as democrats; rather they echoed the (warlike) views of the son of the dictator, Saif al-Islam Qadhafi, who claimed this was not about democracy but tribal conflict. It was pointed out that many of the opposition leaders were defectors rather than dissidents, having themselves participated in the particularly brutal Qadhafi regime. It was also argued that Western interests in oil were a main motivation, explaining why there was intervention in Libya but not Syria.

During the conflict, those who opposed military intervention favoured negotiations with Qadhafi, urging him either to stop fighting or to step down. At a meeting of the African Union in Ethiopia on 30 May 2011, African leaders stated that airstrikes had exceeded the terms of the UN resolution and President Zuma of South Africa was sent to negotiate. In an article in the *London Review of Books* entitled 'Here We Go Again', Rory Stewart repeats his scepticism of intervention but argues for 'a humanitarian no fly-zone' (Stewart 2011).

A few voices, including my own, suggested an alternative approach. A humanitarian intervention, as opposed to a war, would have focused on protecting civilians throughout Libya and guaranteeing their right to peaceful protest. The first task should have been to declare Benghazi and the liberated areas a UN Protected Area or safe haven. It would have been necessary to deploy international peacekeepers to help protect the liberated areas. Humanitarian and reconstruction assistance and support for a democratic political process would also have to be provided so that the liberated areas could provide poles of attraction for other parts of the country. The peacekeepers would defend the protected areas robustly; they would not attack Qadhafi forces but, given the opportunity, they would try to arrest those indicted by the ICC, including Muammar Qadhafi and his son Saif. They would, of course, need air protection, and indeed what has happened already helps to provide conditions for a safe haven. But this is different from relying on military attacks from the air alone. There was an EU proposal along these lines, for a small ground force to protect humanitarian assistance provided to Misrata; however, it did not receive UN authorisation.

A similar argument was put forward by the Director of the European Union Institute for Strategic Studies, Alvaro de Vasconcelos. He insisted that the divide is not tribal 'but rather one between a minority who has plundered oil and gas revenues, essentially in Tripolitania, and those who have consistently been robbed of the country's wealth throughout the country, who were consistently downtrodden and have now vowed to put an end to political and economic tyranny' (Vasconcelos 2011). He argued for ground troops to protect Misrata, which, as part of Tripolitania, would be critical to prevent the conflict being framed as tribal or geographical.

It is true that the Security Council resolution excludes 'foreign occupation forces', and the rebels themselves said that they did not want foreign occupation. But the deployment of an international peacekeeping group of military, police and civilians, especially if drawn from Arab and Africans countries as well as from Europe and America, could not be construed as such. The aim would have been to damp down violence so that protests could be peaceful, rather than to support one side militarily, thereby creating the conditions for possible long-term violence.

Responsibility to Protect and Other Stories

While Afghanistan, Iraq and Darfur dominated the global public debate during the first decade of the twenty-first century, there were many other interventions in crisis

Box 6.3
Gareth Evans and the Responsibility to Protect

Gareth Evans, co-chair of the international commission responsible for instigating the Responsibility to Protect (R2P), and President Emeritus of the influential INGO Crisis Group (www.crisisgroup.org), has described Cambodia's successful elections in 1993 as one of the best moments of his life. The former Australian Foreign Minister has attributed the country's turn towards stability to the United Nations' deepened involvement in the stalled peace talks, and to a period of intense shuttle diplomacy by his small team (Evans 1991). This episode continues to influence Evans's thinking and, in turn, the policies of states and civil society organisations seeking to prevent conflict in the contemporary international system.

Before entering politics, Evans was an academic lawyer specialising in constitutional and civil liberties law. Combined with his experiences in Cambodia, this background proved pivotal in his appointment by the Government of Canada to co-chair the International Commission on Intervention and State Sovereignty (ICISS) in September 2000. The Commission's report the following year argued that although states have the primary responsibility to protect their people from mass atrocity crimes, when this responsibility is abused or neglected 'the principle of non-intervention yields to the international responsibility to protect'. Where possible, international efforts to prevent mass-atrocity crimes should be led by the UN using whatever measures – economic, political, diplomatic, legal, security or, in the last resort, military – become necessary (ICISS 2001).

Evans viewed this as a complete reconceptualisation of the normative right to intervene, and argued that three elements would be needed to install a new framework for conflict prevention within the international community: an 'early warning' system to recognise the potential of mass atrocities during a crisis; a 'preventive toolbox' of conflict prevention techniques for policy-makers; and political will within the international community to act when required (Evans 2001). He is a vocal advocate of the ability of global civil society to contribute to this framework, particularly through research and advocacy. He describes his own organisation, Crisis Group (www.crisisgroup.org), as a small and relatively inexpensive method of engaging in the vital, but often unnoticed, enterprise of conflict prevention and containment. Formed in 1995 with an office staff of two, the fledgling NGO strived to combine the analysis of professional researchers with the influence of a board of global personalities,

giving it the ability to act as the worlds 'eyes and ears' for impending conflicts (International Crisis Group 2011). Today it encompasses around 130 staff drawn from 49 nationalities, and operates in 60 countries. Evans steered the Crisis Group from 2000 to 2009, guiding its influential reporting, advocacy and alarm-bell ringing on numerous conflicts throughout the last decade. He has stated that the human and economic costs of war, viewed against the low price and moral arguments in favour of such organisations, make the intelligence they produce invaluable to the international community.

Since releasing 'The Responsibility to Protect' report in 2001, Evans has been working tirelessly to make the 'idealism' he identifies with the concept's agenda into an international security mainstay for states, intergovernmental organisations and global civil society (Evans 2007). In response to the ongoing crisis in Gaza, for example, he has argued that Israel, as an occupying power with sovereign responsibility for the Palestinian people, is breaching its responsibilities; while, following the Burmese Cyclone in 2008, he has echoed the comments of Bernard Kouchner encouraging the UN Security Council to consider invoking R2P to allow for robust relief operations. Most recently, he has written of the responsibility of the international community in reaction to the unfolding crisis in Libya (Evans 2011). Yet his reluctance to frame the 2003 Iraq conflict as a case of legitimate intervention demonstrates the strict logic of preventing mass-atrocity crimes underpinning R2P (Evans 2003).

Recognising the reluctance of some to accept R2P for fear that it could justify Western imperialism or hasten the use of military means, Evans brought out his own detailed book on the concept (2008). Moreover, he has publically suggested that the principle requires continual refinement, citing the problematic use of its language by the Sri Lankan and Russian governments to justify their actions (see Box 6.4). Evans has also discussed the need for a rethinking of the posture of standing militaries to allow for preventive interventions short of full scale conflict, and for the role of new technologies in alerting the international community to unfolding crises.

Thomas Kirk is a PhD candidate at the London School of Economics. His work investigates the role of civil society in creating the conditions for peace in contemporary conflict, with particular reference to Afghanistan and Pakistan.

Table 6.1   Foreign Interventions Involving More Than 10,000 Troops: 2000–Present

Country	Purpose	Dates	Troops Involved	UNSC Authorisation
Afghanistan – Operation Enduring Freedom	The destruction of terrorist training camps and infrastructure and the capture of al-Qaeda leaders.	October 2001–present	Initially US and UK troops and the Afghan Northern Alliance. Joined by a coalition of forces that moved to ISAF (International Security Assistance Force)/NATO leadership in 2003; the US command remains active in certain areas of Afghanistan.	On 7 October 2001, the US informed the United Nations Security Council (UNSC) that it was launching airstrikes against al-Qaeda in self-defence.
Afghanistan	Peace enforcement mandate under Chapter VIII of the UN Charter, support of Afghan forces.	2001–present	ISAF – 130,695 troops from 48 nations, as of August 2011, under NATO leadership since 2003, and under mandate with UNAMA (UN Assistance Mission in Afghanistan) and the Afghan Transitional Authority.	The mission was agreed at the Bonn conference of December 2001 and was authorised in UNSCR 1386 the same month. Later ISAF's authority was extended beyond Kabul.
Liberia	Oversee the ceasefire and train national police and justice institutions. Assist the transitional government and the preparation of elections.	2003–present	UNMIL (UN Mission in Liberia) – 15,071 troops from 48 nations.	UNSCR 1509 (19 September 2003).
Iraq	Stated goal was the removal of 'Weapons of Mass Destruction'.	2003–present	100,000–150,000 troops from 32 nations.	No authorisation; UNSCR 1441 (8 November 2002) warned 'serious consequences' for Iraq's refusal to comply.
Côte d'Ivoire	Facilitate the implementation of peace process and DDR (Disarmament, Demobilisation and Reintegration) programme. During 2011 crisis UN/French moved towards protection of civilians and installation of the winner of the elections into power.	2004–present	UNOCI (UN Operation in Côte d'Ivoire) – 11,142 authorised personnel.	UNSCR 1528 (27 February 2004).
Sudan (Darfur)	Monitor and observe compliance with the Humanitarian Ceasefire Agreement of 8 April 2004, secure delivery of humanitarian relief and ensure return of IDPs. Protection of civilians as core mandate.	2004–present	AMIS (African Union Mission in Sudan) – 7,000 troops, mainly from Rwanda and Darfur. Became UNAMID (AU/UN Hybrid operation in Darfur) – originally with over 25,000 troops and police.	AMIS authorised by UNSCR 1564 (18 September 2004); merged into UNAMID on 31 July 2007, under UNSCR 1769.
Sudan (Civil War)	To support the Comprehensive Peace Agreement (CPA) of 2005, give humanitarian assistance and support human rights.	2004–9 July 2011	UNMIS (UN Missions in Sudan) – 10,352 troops and personnel.	UNAMIS (the Advanced Mission) established 11 June 2004 with UNSCR 1547 and given responsibilities in Darfur with UNSCR 1556 (30 July 2004); UNMIS authorised following the CPA in 2005, under UNSCR 1590 (24 March 2005).
Democratic Republic of Congo (DRC)	Monitor ceasefire, protection of civilians, humanitarian personnel and human rights defenders; intervention concentrated in eastern DRC.	MONUC (UN Organisation Mission in the Democratic Republic of the Congo) established 1999. Renamed MONUSCO in 2010.	MONUSCO (UN Organisation Stabilisation Mission in the Democratic Republic of Congo) – 22,016 troops and personnel.	UNSCR 1279 (30 November 1999) established MONUC. MONUSCO authorised by UNSC 1925 (28 May 2010).

situations throughout the world. Indeed, the Stockholm International Peace Research Institute database of multilateral peace operations includes nearly 600 such missions between 2000 and 2009 (SIPRI 2011). Table 6.1 lists the main military interventions of the first decade of the twenty-first century that involved more than 10,000 troops. Particularly important were the UN and EU interventions in the Democratic Republic of Congo, where the conflict, sometimes described as Africa's World War, claimed directly or indirectly up to 5 million lives and yet has elicited very little global coverage. The interventions in Somalia, including the anti-piracy mission, and the Libya intervention are not included because they involve fewer than 10,000 troops. At the time of writing, some 100,000 troops are engaged in UN operations worldwide. Other organisations undertaking missions include the OSCE, the CIS, ECOMOG and the OAS, to name but a few.

Both within international institutions and among governments, there has been a growing effort to mainstream concepts like Responsibility to Protect (R2P), stabilisation and human security, and to develop or at least to conceptualise appropriate capabilities. R2P was adopted by the United Nations General Assembly in 2005. Since his appointment as Secretary-General in January 2007, Ban Ki-moon has said that 'he will spare no effort to operationalise Responsibility to Protect' (Orford 2011: 17). He has appointed special advisors on the topic, and established a $2 million Responsibility to Protect Fund supported by Sweden, the UK and Australia. In January 2009 he produced a report for debate at the United Nations General Assembly setting out strategies for implementing R2P, and on 14 September 2009, the United Nations General Assembly authorised the Secretary-General to seek further financial and institutional resources for implementing and mainstreaming R2P within the United Nations.

It is now standard for United Nations Security Council resolutions to refer to the protection of civilians, although the Libya resolution is the first to name the protection of civilians as its main goal. Furthermore, almost all current UN peacekeepers are now mandated to protect civilians. However, an independent report undertaken for the United Nations on the protection of civilians in UN operations finds that there is still insufficient clarity of mandates, lack of planning, training and preparation, and lack of appropriate structures, resources and tools despite the perseverance of 'many dedicated and creative individuals' (Holt and Taylor 2009: 8).

In the European Union, the new European Security and Defence Policy (ESDP – now the Common Security and Defence Policy, CSDP) was developed following the Anglo-French summit in St Malo during the Kosovo War. ESDP has been designed for the so-called St Petersburg tasks, that is to say, multilateral interventions in crisis situations, rather than classic defence of borders. The European Union has incorporated the concept of human security, understood as upholding human rights, and has been developing combined military/civilian capabilities. Indeed, it is the first institution to have a combined military/civilian planning cell, and has pioneered civilian crisis management, largely consisting of missions aimed at restoring or establishing a rule of law and system of justice. Some 25 missions have been undertaken, including EU NAVFOR, the current mission to counter piracy in Somalia, and the missions to the DRC, which were considered, if too short, at least successful in using a robust approach to preventing massacres and maintaining order (Martin 2010).

And in Africa, the African Union (AU), which succeeded the Organisation of African Unity (OAU) has institutionalised a 'right of humanitarian intervention' in 'grave circumstances', namely war crimes, genocide and crimes against humanity, in Article 4h of the Constitutive Act. It has established a Peace and Security Council and an African Standby Force. This represents a considerable change from an earlier insistence on non-interference. Several African countries, including Botswana, Ghana, Lesotho, Nigeria, Rwanda, and Tanzania, have formally endorsed the Responsibility to Protect.

A particularly significant development in the twenty-first century has been the establishment of the International Criminal Court, which came about as part of the general pressure for humanitarian norms that followed the war in Bosnia and the Rwandan genocide (Glasius 2006). Indeed, both by enthusiasts and critics, the ICC is increasingly bracketed together with the R2P. The Rome Statute, the legal basis for the court, was adopted by 120 states on 17 July 1998 and entered into force on 1 July 2002. As of September 2011, some 117 states have signed and ratified the ICC (those who have neither signed nor ratified include the United States, China and India – indeed, the US 'unsigned' the Treaty). This new emphasis on crimes against humanity has generated a whole new machinery of transitional justice (Rangelov and Teitel 2011). So far, three state parties have referred situations in their territories to the ICC – Uganda, the DRC and the Central African Republic – and, in addition,

Box 6.4
The Use of the Responsibility to Protect in Sri Lanka

In May 2009, the Government of Sri Lanka (GoSL) armed forces annihilated the Liberation Tigers of Tamil Eelam (LTTE), completing the Island's own version of the 'War on Terror'.

While the Sri Lankan conflict is very complex and cannot be analysed lightly, it highlights some of the contradictions inherent in the Responsibility to Protect (R2P) and the danger that lies between rhetoric and actions or lack thereof. The Sri Lankan case illustrates the ways in which R2P – the use of which sets up a framework to intervene in situations where 'peaceful means are inadequate and national authorities are manifestly failing to protect their people from genocide, war crimes' – simultaneously works against its own purpose by the arbitrary and opaque nature of its language and processes. It illuminates the grey area that lies between definitions: the difficulty in determining what constitutes the protection of civilians, and at which point in an internal conflict, a legitimate, democratically elected government could be viewed as 'failing to protect its own civilians'.

In the final months of the war, the LTTE and civilians from the Vanni were pushed towards a sliver of land between the sea and advancing GoSL forces. During this period, human rights organisations and the 2011 UN advisory panel report on the last stages of Sri Lanka's war estimate that thousands of civilian deaths occurred due to government shelling on 'no-fire zones' in which the LTTE used civilians (over 200,000 according to some estimates) as human shields. Bernard Kouchner and David Miliband made a last-minute visit to the Island on behalf of the international community in order to negotiate a ceasefire until a humanitarian corridor for civilians could be established. However, beyond this failed effort, the international community sought no options for a humanitarian intervention. In this case, the GoSL was attacking the LTTE, proscribed by many as a terrorist organisation. As such, civilian deaths (of which there was no official death toll released by the GoSL) were considered collateral damage, rather than a direct attack on unarmed civilians – whose deaths fell outside the realm of an R2P intervention.

The example of Sri Lanka highlights another limitation in the application of R2P: geopolitics. The GoSL played into the vested interests of the powerful countries, who viewed stability and security in Sri Lanka as integral to the larger political economy frameworks of their vision. The relevance of Sri Lanka's location in the Indian Ocean to China's 'string of pearls' strategy, and India's precarious relationship with the US, Pakistan and China at the time, ensured the support of stronger, regional allies to help ward off the 'West' while it finished its internal war .

In 2008, the GoSL cracked down on local NGOs who raised the issue of R2P – to the extent that visas of its proponents were cancelled overnight. In doing so, GoSL cited the dangers of a 'bullying, imperialist West' using the rhetoric of 'humanitarian intervention' to interfere and redefine the 'sovereignty' of a nation. Yet, by 2009, the GoSL's sophisticated PR campaign for the war had changed from defining the post-9/11 conflict as a 'War on Terror', to 'a humanitarian rescue mission'. The GoSL not only co-opted the language of humanitarian intervention and 'responsibility' to legitimise its 'peace project', but went further in using LTTE's own doctrine of 'liberation' of the people against itself.

When a 'functioning' democracy, at least on the face of it, invokes its moral obligation to save its citizens by exploiting the flexibility and adaptability of R2P language to legitimise and legalise its actions, it becomes a barrier in applying R2P to the same situation by external actors, even when civilians remain in the firing line. The potential of R2P to be co-opted to pre-empt international intervention or scrutiny (or accountability in its aftermath) is its limitation, just as the process of arriving to the point of intervention itself is fraught with complications that have in the past, cost too many innocent lives.

Anon.

the Security Council has referred the situations in Darfur and Libya to the court, and the ICC Prosecutor has opened an investigation into Kenya. Some 23 people have been indicted to date. In addition to the ICC, the Yugoslav and Rwandan tribunals established in the 1990s continued their work throughout the past decade; the highly public arrests of Vojislav Seselj, the leader of the Serbian radical party, Radovan Kardadzic, the former leader of Republika Serbska, and Ratko Mladic, the general responsible for the Srebrenica massacre, represents a further achievement in institutionalising humanitarian norms.

Alongside these multilateral initiatives, there have been efforts within many countries to reconceptualise security as something broader than national defence. There has been much discussion about new or non-traditional threats or risks and the appropriate capabilities needed to complement military force; even countries like Russia and China refer to non-traditional threats, while the United States has made tentative moves away from classic defence thinking. Members of the Bush Administration argued when they first came to power that it was not the job of the military to undertake constabulary duties or nation-building (see Rice 2000). However, the experience of Iraq and Afghanistan has led to profound rethinking in the Pentagon. General Petreaus produced a new counter-insurgency manual in 2006 that emphasised the protection of civilians, the need for a rule of law and the integration of military and civilian capabilities (Department of the Army and United States Marine Corps 2006). Secretary of Defense Robert Gates has been 'rebalancing' the defence budget so as to give more space to these new roles. And the State Department under Hillary Clinton has introduced a Quadrennial Diplomacy and Development Review to complement the Quadrennial Defense Review and to plan civilian capabilities for crisis management.

However, for most countries these tasks are typically seen as secondary to the core task of defending nations from attack by a foreign enemy. It is argued that the 'high end' of defence spending – advanced equipment and war fighting capabilities – can be applied at the 'low end', but not the other way round. The financial crisis has meant a closing in on core tasks, thereby weakening an already fragile capability for the new crisis tasks. Even as those directly engaged in international operations, especially the military, recognise the need for change, few political leaders are ready to embrace new approaches. After Afghanistan and Iraq and the weakening of the humanitarian consensus there is an increased reluctance to commit resources to difficult and risky missions. For

example, it is not clear whether it was political reluctance to commit ground troops or lack of capacity that explains the reliance on airstrikes in the Libya case.

The terms 'Responsibility to Protect' and 'Human Security' have entered the political lexicon. Of course it is true that they are used to justify interventions undertaken for quite different purposes. Thus the Sri Lankan government used the language of R2P to justify its final bloody defeat of the Tamil Tigers (see Box 6.4) just as the Russian government used both R2P and human security to justify its intervention in Ossetia, a breakaway republic of Georgia, in August 2008. The Russians claimed an 'allegedly ongoing genocide' of Ossetians and that they were protecting Russian citizens, despite the fact that those Russian citizens were actually Ossetians who had been given Russian passports. Although the war was started by Georgia with an artillery attack on the capital, Tshingvali, on the night of 7 August 2008, the Russian response went well beyond the protection of Ossetians. 'Massive and extended military action' reached deep into Georgian territory, accompanied by military control of the major highways and the deployment of navy units on the Black Sea, and resulting in large-scale human rights violations (IIFFMCG 2009).

This is not necessarily an argument against using the terms. The fact that the language is used offers a standard by which such interventions can be judged. In other words, rather than abandoning these concepts because they have been misused, it is important to claim back their meaning and apply them as criticisms of such actions.

The Global Civil Society Kaleidoscope

The consensus around humanitarian intervention at the turn of the century was shattered by the War on Terror. It is possible to identify three positions that run through the debates about the intervention in the twenty-first century. How they apply to Afghanistan, Iraq, Darfur and Libya is shown in Table 6.2.

The first position is that of the warriors – the unqualified supporters of military intervention. They include the neocons and the liberal internationalists and those involved in the Save Darfur campaign. They see the use of force as a neutral instrument, a black box, that can bring about the desired results and they tend to disregard the consequences of the use of military force.

The second position is that of the anti-interventionists. They include pacifists, especially in religious communities, who fear that any use of military force will cause suffering, which is morally unacceptable; they therefore oppose war

Box 6.5
The Devolution of al-Qaeda

The Facebook page set up in honour of al-Qaeda's founder is entitled 'We are all Osama bin Laden'. But it is this reality – the fact that anyone anywhere can commit a violent act using the al-Qaeda brand – which has proved most damaging for the organisation.

After 9/11 and the destruction of al-Qaeda's headquarters in Afghanistan, al-Qaeda fractured into a moving target, a global cadre of autonomous cells which enabled it to continue to both elude and fight its enemies. However, with the globalisation of his jihad, bin Laden's authority was at once far-reaching and fragmented. Ceding command-and-control to self-defined 'al-Qaeda' franchises brought enormous setbacks.

Bin Laden portrayed al-Qaeda as a vanguard group with a clear and simple mandate: to defend Muslims. Every one of his statements made clear that his was a defensive jihad to protect the innocent blood of Muslims from a Crusader onslaught. All of his legal, moral and political arguments rested on this premise. Yet the credibility of bin Laden's claim to be acting in defence of Muslims exploded alongside the scores of suicide bombers dispatched to civilian centres with the direct intention of massacring swathes of (Muslim) civilians.

On the run in Pakistan, bin Laden and his colleagues at 'al-Qaeda central' seemed unwilling, but more likely unable, to control their over-zealous offspring. For example, two letters were sent to the emir of al-Qaeda in Iraq, berating him for his fanaticism, reminding him that scenes of mass slaughter did not help al-Qaeda's cause – and counselling him that to alienate the population would contravene all of the fundamentals of politics and leadership. But Abu Mus'ab al-Zarqawi's savagery did not stop.

Turning the Masses Away From the Cause

Citing Clausewitz, Mao and Giap, al-Qaeda's strategic thinkers had always emphasised the importance of attracting the support of the Muslim masses to the global jihad. The people were the sea in which al-Qaeda's militants were supposed to swim and, without whom, the Mujahidin would be 'crushed in the shadows'. And so, in a remarkably candid audiotape aired on *Al Jazeera* in October 2007, bin Laden advised the 'brothers in al-Qaeda everywhere' not to succumb to extremism. Allegiance to the *umma* – the global community of Muslims – had to be placed above that of tribe and sect.

Bin Laden's aim was to lead a popular and mainstream resistance movement, yet al-Qaeda's reckless affiliates and their fanatical footmen consigned the group to the more radical margins of the *umma*. Their means (massacring Muslims) contradicted bin Laden's stated end (protecting the *umma*).

But it was bin Laden himself who had helped make this possible, by contributing spectacularly to the democratisation of Islamic authority. Extending the arguments which had been made decades before by radical ideologues like Sayed Qutb, bin Laden claimed that the region's rulers and the traditional clergy were too weak and corrupt to protect Muslim blood. Individual Muslims had not only a right but a duty to take matters into their own hands. Reinventing the Islamic legal concept of *fard ayn* (individual duty for jihad), bin Laden eroded the authority of the clergy without being able to claim a monopoly over it himself.

The Future for al-Qaeda

Bin Laden's departure will only accelerate this democratising process. What little unifying power bin Laden still exerted has now been entirely removed. Indeed, his death deals a heavy blow to the old guard in 'al-Qaeda central', and will probably empower loose affiliates who no longer feel the need to answer to anyone.

Some groups, such as those in Pakistan, will continue the descent into nihilistic chaos, killing for killing's sake. Others, such as al-Qaeda in the Islamic Maghreb, will remain primarily preoccupied with lashing out at the Algerian state. Still others, namely al-Qaeda in the Arabian Peninsula (AQAP), will view this juncture as an opportunity to go back to basics.

Indeed, since its emergence in January 2009, AQAP has endeavoured to re-focus the jihad towards striking the West. Their most high-profile operations have been assaults on the US and British embassies in Sanaa, the bid by the 'underpants bomber' to blow up a flight from Amsterdam to Detroit, and the plot to explode cargo planes over western cities. The latest issue of their English-language magazine is dedicated to providing guidance on, and theological justifications for, attacks in the heart of the west.

Certainly, US-born cleric Anwar al-Awlaki's star is rapidly ascending, precisely because of his fluency in English and his appeal among Muslims outside the region. He also takes bin Laden's subversion of Islamic authority to its logical extreme: on 8 November 2010 he stated that no *fatwa* or prior consultation with Islamic experts was necessary to 'fight and kill Americans'. If a Western target is soon hit in revenge for the slaying of bin Laden, AQAP will be the prime suspect. Next on the list could be the Pakistani Taliban who, since last spring, have vowed to launch their own attacks inside Western countries.

Losing the Struggle

Though al-Qaeda will be temporarily re-energised by the killing of bin Laden, it will not be enough to build up the sort of momentum and broad-based sympathy that they enjoyed at the height of the

US-led occupation of Iraq. Between 2003 and 2006 in particular, bin Laden's poetic narrative of resistance resonated even beyond the Muslim world. A German student in my halls at Oxford once returned from a trip home sporting a bin Laden T-shirt. George W. Bush's 'War on Terror' did not win the struggle for hearts and minds – fortunately, however, al-Qaeda lost it.

Most of the victims of al-Qaeda related violence since 9/11 have been the Muslims of bin Laden's cherished *umma*. At the same time, the global jihad has been left twisting in the breeze of the Arab Spring. An alternative, secular and pro-democracy discourse has emerged as a genuinely popular regional movement which is, crucially, bringing fast results – two tyrants and counting. At a time when millions of Arabs have taken to the streets to cry for freedom, development and the rule of law, al-Qaeda's worldview has never been more marginal, or marginalised. Before he died, the *umma* had stolen bin Laden's thunder.

The covert operation to kill bin Laden confirmed two important points made by critics of Bush's War on Terror. Firstly, it did not involve all-out-warfare against 'enemy' nations. Instead, the surgical, intelligence-led operation was carefully conducted by special forces within a US-allied country.

Secondly, the fact that bin Laden was hiding in an affluent garrison town near Islamabad, a stone's throw from Pakistan's prestigious military academy, supports the long-held suspicion that elements within Pakistan's security establishment have been playing a double-game in the War on Terror. These Islamic militants have been useful pawns in Pakistan's conflict with India, particularly over Kashmir, and they provide potential for strategic depth in Afghanistan.

As for al-Qaeda, it can survive bin Laden's demise because it was designed to do so. Strategically, bin Laden's death was always assumed. The evolution, or devolution, into a diffuse network of affiliate groups guaranteed durability and provided significant tactical agility – but it has been catastrophic for the Muslims bin Laden needed to attract to his cause.

It is unlikely that the re-imagining of bin Laden in the wake of his death can reinvent al-Qaeda's track record of shameful and ultimately pointless bloodshed.

Alia Brahimi is a Global Security Research Fellow at the London School of Economics. This article was originally published as 'Al-Qaeda is its Own Worst Enemy', *Al Jazeera*, 7 May 2011.

Table 6.2 Global Civil Society Positions on the Main Interventions

	Warriors	Anti-interventionists	Humanitarians
Afghanistan	Aim is to defeat the Taliban and al-Qaeda.	Troops should be withdrawn.	Aim should be stabilisation/human security of Afghans.
Iraq	Aim was to destroy weapons of mass destruction by removing Saddam Hussein; later to defeat the Sunni insurgency and al-Qaeda.	War and military intervention is wrong and causes human suffering. Troops should be withdrawn. Humanitarians should be separated from military forces.	War was wrong because there was no immediate humanitarian crisis. Should have been international pressure to remove Saddam Hussein. Need to respect human rights and international humanitarian law and assist transitional justice.
Darfur	Aim is military intervention to stop genocide.	Conflict is a civil war and should be resolved through negotiations.	Need an international presence to protect civilians, including administering justice.
Libya	Aim was initially to protect civilians using airstrikes then Increasingly aimed at regime change, e.g. removal of Qadhafi.	Air strikes cause human suffering and polarise political opinion.	Need for military/civilian capabilities to protect civilians and create space for peaceful political process.

on principle. It includes those who define themselves as left-wing, especially those young people who participate in the World Social Forum. They are sceptical that governments can have humanitarian motives and see the rhetoric of R2P or human security as a cover for a great power, especially the American, neocolonial agenda. A similar view is held by those Islamists who see the main interventions as being directed against Muslims, and argue that the War on Terror is a civilisational clash between the West and Islam, in which concepts like R2P and human security have been co-opted. Neither of these last two groups is pacifist (although many of their members may be), and some support the use of force to resist occupation in Iraq, Afghanistan or Palestine. Finally the anti-interventionists include realists, or what I called in 2001 sovereignists, those who argue that states should pursue their national interests and that the suffering of non-nationals is no concern.

Those who support this position often favour negotiations and tend to be more concerned about the wrongs inflicted by the West than about tyrannical behaviour by non-Western leaders like Saddam Hussein or Muammar Qadhafi. They are also highly critical of the International Criminal Court. The left argues that it is one-sided, concentrating on crimes against humanity rather than war crimes, and on conflicts in poor countries rather than the crimes of Western warmongers. Islamists and cultural relativists argue that that the court imposes a Western conception of justice, and that criminals

should be judged in their local context, according to local conceptions of justice. Pacifists and realists argue that in cases like Bashir of Sudan or Qadhafi in Libya, indictment provides a disincentive to negotiate peace since peace would mean arrest and capture. It is also argued that the cases are very slow, giving a platform to people who espouse extremist ideas.

The third position, the humanitarians, has been pulled apart by this debate. Some, the liberal interventionists, have joined the warrior camp. Others, such as David Rieff, have become disillusioned and cynical about humanitarian intervention and have joined the anti-interventionist camp. Those who remain, largely from the human rights movement, argue that humanitarian intervention is different from war and has to be conducted appropriately. None of the interventions that were subject to public debate, except perhaps the eventual UN/AU mission in Darfur, could be described as humanitarian interventions. In both Afghanistan and Iraq, the use of military force made things worse. In the case of Libya, it is still far from clear whether this will lead to democracy or to a long war. The humanitarians link humanitarian norms to the extension of international law and international justice and argue that states do have an interest in a law-governed world. In response to the criticisms of the ICC they suggest that there should be more emphasis on crimes committed by Western governments, especially the consequences of the use of air power; that international justice supplements local justice and upholds universal norms in situations where local justice can often be subverted by local power brokers (Allen 2006); and that peace negotiations in the context of contemporary forms of violence can never bring sustainable peace unless accompanied by justice mechanisms.

Civil society groups within conflict zones, whether in Afghanistan, Iraq or Darfur, tend to be close to the humanitarian position. It is often civil society that calls for interventions to protect them from violence but, at the same time, they are the victims of the excessive use of force. Yet those who take part in interventions often neglect civil society, focusing on dealing with those responsible for violence or remaining within the protective walls of international compounds. If the humanitarian camp is to regain its influential role, then greater involvement of local civil society in international debates is critically important.

Conclusion

The decade ended with the political death of Osama bin Laden in the non-violent demonstrations that spread throughout the Middle East in the spring of 2011 and the physical death of bin Laden in the American raid on a house in Pakistan on 2 May 2011 (see Box 6.5).

Alongside the debate about humanitarian intervention ran a debate in the Arab world about resistance to occupation: when it is right to use force to resist human rights violations by a state or foreign forces. For many young people, Osama bin Laden and the jihadist movement had discredited Islam. The extraordinary commitment to non-violence in the protests in Tahrir Square and elsewhere is proof of the outcome of that debate.

Despite the visibility of violent conflicts, especially in Afghanistan and Iraq, the number of what the *Human Security Report 2009/2010* calls high-intensity conflicts (more than 1,000 deaths in battle per year) has declined dramatically over the last two decades, by some 78 per cent between 1988 and 2008 (Human Security Research Group 2011). The *Human Security Report* attributes this decline largely to the spread of global norms against war and interventions, and to the greater activism of the United Nations and other multilateral institutions. Nevertheless there has been an increase in the overall number of conflicts in the years since 2000, and the decline of battle deaths may be due to the fact that violence is increasingly directed against civilians – and statistics on civilian casualties are notoriously poor. Additionally, the growing privatisation of violence has

meant that conflicts may be more low-level, but also more pervasive and intractable.

If the norm of non-violence is to be nurtured and protected, especially in the turbulent period ahead, in the context of economic crisis and climate change, then there needs to be a serious debate about the means required to prevent violence and protect people. Perhaps the end of the decade of the War on Terror will open up space for the revival of the humanitarian idea.

Notes

1. I am very grateful to Tom Kirk for research assistance, and to Alia Brahimi, Marika Theros, Iavor Rangelov, Frederick Abrams and Alvaro de Vasconcelos for helpful discussions.
2. 'A band of Wilsonian idealists, cutthroat imperial capitalists, Trotskyists bereft of a cause and neo-patriots traumatised by 9/11' (Cole 2005).
3. See especially Chapter 1, 'War in Iraq: Not a Humanitarian Intervention'.
4. At the time of writing Qadhafi was alive; he was captured and killed in October 2011.

References

African Union/United Nations Hybrid operation in Darfur (2011), http://www.un.org/en/peacekeeping/missions/unamid/index.shtml.

Allen, Tim (2006) *Trial Justice. The International Criminal Court and the Lord's Resistance Army.* London: Zed Books.

Amnesty International (2003) *Report on Iraq – In the Shadow of War: Backlash against Human Rights* (MDE 14/057/2003), available at http://www.amnesty.org/en/library/asset/MDE14/057/2003/en/303beb83-d70e-11dd-b0cc-1f0860013475/mde140572003en.pdf (accessed 6 September 2011).

Black, Tim (2009) 'The Defeatism of the Anti-War Movement', *Spiked*, 15 July, http://www.spiked-online.com/index.php/site/article/7153/ (accessed 6 September 2011).

Borchgrevink, Kaja and Harpviken, Kristian Berg (2008) 'Afghan Civil Society: Caught in Conflicting Agendas'. Paper presented at International Studies Association Annual Convention, San Francisco, 27 March.

Bradford Stop the War Coalition (2001) 'Not In My Name: National Demonstration Against the War', 18 November, http://www.bradfordstopwar.org.uk/events/011118nat/index.html (accessed 6 September 2011).

Brahimi, Lakhdar and Pickering, Thomas R. (2011) *Afghanistan: Negotiating Peace – The Report of The Century Foundation International Task Force on Afghanistan in its Regional and Multilateral Dimensions.* New York: The Century Foundation Press, available at http://tcf.org/publications/2011/3/afghanistan-negotiating-peace (accessed 6 September 2011).

Bush, Laura (2001) *Radio Address to the Nation*, radio programme, The White House, Washington, 17 November, available at http://georgewbush-whitehouse.archives.gov/news/releases/2001/11/20011117.html (accessed 6 September 2011).

Cortright, David (2005) 'The Peaceful Superpower: The Movement against the War in Iraq', in Janie Leatherman and Julie Webber (eds), *Charting Transnational Democracy: Beyond Global Arrogance*. New York: Palgrave Macmillan.

Cole, Juan (2005) 'Christopher Hitchens' Last Battle', Salon.com, 5 September, http://dir.salon.com/story/news/feature/2005/09/05/hitchens/ (accessed 6 September 2011).

Department of the Army and United States Marine Corps (2006) *Counterinsurgency*. Field Manual No. 3-24, Marine Corps Warfighting Publication No. 3-33.5, December. Washington DC: Department of the Army.

Donnelly, Thomas (2000) 'Rebuilding America's Defenses: Strategy, Forces and Resources for a New Century', Project for the New American Century, http://www.newamerican-century.org/RebuildingAmericasDefenses.pdf (accessed 6 September 2011).

Evans, Gareth (1991) 'Cambodia: Past Present and Future', Notes for Address by Gareth Evans at the Tribute Night to Friends of Cambodia, Sydney, 13 February, http://www.gevans.org/speeches/old/1998-1999/130299cambodia_past_present_future.pdf (accessed 21 June 2011).

Evans, Gareth (2001) 'Preventing Deadly Conflict: The Role and Responsibility of Governments and NGOs'. Public Lecture hosted by the Centre for Study of Human Rights, London School of Economics, 2 February, http://www2.lse.ac.uk/humanRights/.../Preventing_deadly_conflict.pdf (accessed 21 June 2011).

Evans, Gareth (2003) Statement of 10 March to the Council on Foreign Relations, http://usiraq.procon.org/view.answers.php?questionID=868 (accessed 21 June 2011).

Evans, Gareth (2007) 'Making Idealism Realistic: The Responsibility to Protect as a New Global Security Norm', http://www.crisisgroup.org/en/publication-type/speeches/2007/evans-making-idealism-realistic-the-respon-sibility-to-protect-as-a-new-global-security-norm.aspx (accessed 21 June 2011).

Evans, Gareth (2008) *The Responsibility to Protect: Ending Mass Atrocity Crimes Once and for All*. Washington: Brookings Institute Press.

Evans, Gareth (2011) 'The Responsibility to Protect Libyans', http://www.project-syndicate.org/commentary/evans3/English (accessed 21 June 2011).

Falk, Richard (2001) 'Defining a Just War', *The Nation*, 29 October 2001.

Foschini, Fabrizio (2011) 'Towards a More United Voice of Civil Society', Afghan Analysts Network, 5 April, http://aan-afghanistan.com/index.asp?id=1601 (accessed 21 August 2011).

Glasius, Marlies (2006) *The International Criminal Court: A Global Civil Society Achievement*. Abingdon: Routledge.

Hitchens, Christopher (2003) *A Long Short War: The Postponed Liberation of Iraq*. New York: Plume.

Holt, Victoria and Taylor, Glyn (2009) *Protecting Civilians in the Context of UN Peace-keeping Operations*. Independent Study Commissioned by the UN Office for the Coordination of Humanitarian Affairs (OCHA) and the UN Department of Peacekeeping Operations (DPKO), 17 November, http://www.peacekeepingbestpractices.unlb.org/PBPS/Pages/Public/viewdocument.aspx?id=2&docid=1014 (accessed 6 September 2011).

Howard, Michael (2002) 'What's in a Name: How to Fight Terrorism', *Foreign Affairs*, Vol. 81 No. 1, January/February.

Human Rights Watch (2004) *World Report 2004: Human Rights and Armed Conflict*. New York: Human Rights Watch, available at http://www.hrw.org/legacy/wr2k4/ (accessed 6 September 2011).

Human Security Research Group (2011) *Human Security Report 2009/2010*. Oxford: Oxford University Press, available at http://www.hsrgroup.org/human-security-reports/20092010/overview.aspx (accessed 6 September 2011).

Kagan, Robert and Kristol, William (2004) 'The Right War for the Right Reasons', *Weekly Standard*, 27 February, http://www.newamericancentury.org/iraq-20040217.htm (accessed 6 September 2011).

Kaldor, Mary (2001) 'A Decade of Humanitarian Intervention: The Role of Global Civil Society', in Helmut Anheier, Marlies Glasius and Mary Kaldor (eds), *Global Civil Society 2001*. Oxford: Oxford University Press.

Kaldor, Mary, Anheier, Helmut and Glasius, Marlies (2003) 'Global Civil Society in an Era of Regressive Globalisation', in Helmut Anheier, Marlies Glasius and Mary Kaldor (eds), *Global Civil Society 2003*. Oxford: Oxford University Press.

Independent International Commission on Kosovo (IICK) (2000) *The Kosovo Report*. Oxford: Oxford University Press.

International Commission on Intervention and State Sovereignty (ICISS) (2001) *The Responsibility to Protect: Report of the International Commission on Intervention and State Sovereignty*. Ottawa: International Development Research Centre, available at http://www.iciss-ciise.gc.ca/ (accessed 6 September 2011).

International Crisis Group (2011) http://www.crisisgroup.org/en/about.aspx (accessed 28 June 2011).

International Fact-Finding Mission on the Conflict in Georgia (IIFFMCG) (2009) *Report of the Independent International Fact-Finding Mission on the Conflict in Georgia*, September, http://news.bbc.co.uk/1/shared/bsp/hi/pdfs/30_09_09_iiffmgc_report.pdf (accessed 6 September 2011).

International Security Assistance Force (2011) http://www.isaf.nato.int/.

MacAskill, Ewen (2004) 'Iraq War Unjustified Says Human Rights Group', *Guardian*, 27 January, http://www.guardian.co.uk/politics/2004/jan/27/uk.humanrights (accessed 6 September 2011).

Mamdani, Mahmoud (2009) *Saviours and Survivors*. London: Verso.

Martin, Mary (2010) 'The European Union in the Democratic Republic of Congo – A Force for Good?', in Mary Martin and Mary Kaldor (eds), *The European Union and Human Security: External Interventions and Missions*. London: Routledge Studies in Human Security.

Orford, Anne (2011) *International Authority and the Responsibility to Protect*. Cambridge: Cambridge University Press.

Rangelov, Iavor and Teitel, Ruti (2011) 'Global Civil Society and Transitional Justice', in Martin Albrow and Hakan Seckinelgin (eds), *Global Civil Society 2011: Globality and the Absence of Justice*. Basingstoke: Palgrave Macmillan.

Rangelov, Iavor (forthcoming 2012) 'Transnational Civil Society', in Adam Lupel and Ernesto Verdeja (eds), *The International Politics of Genocide*. Boulder, CO: Lynne Rienner Publishers.

Rice, Condoleezza (2000) 'Campaign 2000: Promoting the National Interest', *Foreign Affairs*, Vol. 79 No. 1, January/February.

Rieff, David (2002) 'Humanitarianism in Crisis', *Foreign Affairs*, Vol. 81 No. 6, November/December.

Ruttig, Thomas (2006) *Islamists, Leftists – And a Void in the Center: Afghanistan's Political Parties and Where They Come From (1902–2006)*. Afghanistan: Konrad Adenauer Stiftung.

Said, Yahia (2011) 'The Iraq Surge 2007–2008 – What does Human Security have to Say about it?', openDemocracy, 15 January, http://www.opendemocracy.net/yahia-said/iraq-surge-2007-2008-%E2%80%93-what-does-human-security-have-to-say-about-it (accessed 6 September 2011).

Sands, Sarah (2009) 'Rory Stewart: The PM Knows We Shouldn't Be In Afghanistan', *Evening Standard*, 12 August, available at http://www.thisislondon.co.uk/standard/article-23731157-rory-stewart-the-pm-knows-we-shouldnt-be-in-afghanistan.do (accessed 6 September 2011).

Stewart, Rory (2009) 'The Irresistible Intervention: Why are we in Afghanistan?', *London Review of Books*, Vol. 31 No. 13, 9 July.

Stewart, Rory (2011) 'Here We Go Again', *London Review of Books*, Vol. 33 No. 7, 31 March.

Stockholm International Peace Institute (SIPRI) (2011) SIPRI Multilateral Peace Operations Database is available at http://www.sipri.org/research/conflict/pko/multilateral.

Theros, Marika and Kaldor, Mary (2011) *Building Afghan Peace from the Ground Up. A White Paper for the Lakhdar Brahimi-Thomas Pickering Task Force on Afghanistan in its Regional and Multilateral Dimensions*. New York: The Century Foundation.

United Nations Assistance Mission in Afghanistan (2011) http://unama.unmissions.org/.

United Nations Mission in Liberia (2011) http://www.unmil.org/.

United Nations Mission in the Republic of South Sudan (2011) http://www.un.org/en/peacekeeping/missions/unmiss/index.shtml.

United Nations Mission in the Sudan (2011) http://www.un.org/en/peacekeeping/missions/unmis/index.shtml.

United Nations Operation in Côte d'Ivoire (2011) http://www.un.org/en/peacekeeping/missions/unoci/index.shtml.

United Nations Organization Stabilization Mission in the Democratic Republic of the Congo (2011) http://www.un.org/en/peacekeeping/missions/monusco/index.shtml.

United Nations Security Council (UNSC) (2000) *Report of the United Nations Panel on Peace Operations* (A/55/305–S/2000/809), available at http://www.un.org/peace/reports/peace_operations/ (accessed 6 September 2011).

United Nations Security Council (UNSC) (2011) 6498th Meeting. Resolution 1973. Available at http://daccess-dds-ny.un.org/doc/UNDOC/GEN/N11/268/39/PDF/N1126839.pdf?OpenElement (accessed 6 September 2011).

Vasconcelos, Álvaro de (2011) 'Save Misrata – and help Libya set itself free', Analysis, European Union Institute for Security Studies, 18 April, http://www.iss.europa.eu/uploads/media/Save_Misrata_01.pdf (accessed 6 September 2011).

Waal, Alex de (2007) 'Sudan: The Turbulent State', in Alex de Waal (ed.), *War in Darfur and the Search for Peace*. Cambridge, MA: Harvard University Press.

CHAPTER 7

PRO-ROMA GLOBAL CIVIL SOCIETY: ACTING FOR, WITH OR INSTEAD OF ROMA?

Angéla Kóczé and Márton Rövid

Over the past two decades, in the wake of post-communist transition, the emergence of Romani activism has been an important development accompanying political changes in Central and Eastern Europe. Alongside the emergence of Romani associations, international NGOs have been increasingly involved in the struggle against the discrimination of Roma. A special microcosm has developed within global civil society that is specialised in the so-called 'Roma issue', comprising non-governmental and inter-governmental organisations, expert bodies, foundations, activists and politicians.

Who the Roma are, and how many they are, is a matter of considerable debate (see Map 7.1 and Box 7.1). In this chapter we refer to 'Roma' as a category of ethnopolitical practice. We analyse the processes through which it has become institutionalised and entrenched in a segment of global civil society – in the descriptive sense of the term, that is 'the emerging sphere of social and political participation in which citizen groups, social movements and individuals engage in dialogue, debate, confrontation, and negotiation with each other and with various governmental actors as well as the business world' (Anheier et al. 2001: 3).

Activists and scholars alike commonly argue that persons perceived as 'Gypsy' (cigány, cikan, and so on) face a range of prejudices and racism in contemporary Europe and beyond. Physical, symbolic, and epistemic[1] forms of anti-Roma violence are persistent in both Eastern and Western Europe and have deep historical roots (Clark 2004, Hancock 2002, Heuss 2000, Kóczé 2011).

It is similarly widely accepted and documented that the transition from state socialism to capitalism had dramatic consequences for most Roma (Ringold et al. 2005, Ivanov 2003, Szelényi and Ladányi 2006). With the collapse or privatisation of state companies, masses of Roma lost their legal and stable source of income and sank from working-class living conditions (with secure jobs, access to education and other social services) to the margins of society. Their impoverishment was coupled

with the strengthening of anti-Roma sentiments, further increasing their segregation in education and housing, and even resulting in physical violence.

Pro-Roma civil society developed over the past 20 years in response to this extraordinary deterioration of the social situation of Roma. This chapter discusses the emergence of the pro-Roma global civil society, its divisions and controversies, and, finally, draws theoretical lessons from the case study.

Emergence of the Pro-Roma Microcosm

The roots of Roma political activism can be traced back to the early twentieth century. By the 1920s and 1930s, Romani organisations started to function in Bulgaria, Yugoslavia,[2] Romania and Greece. These organisations published their own periodicals, offered mutual assistance in sickness and death, or promoted the education of Gypsy youth (Marushiakova and Popov 2004, Klimova 2002). Generally the founding moment of the international Romani movement is considered to be the first World Romani Congress, held in 1971 in London.

Three phases in the emergence of the pro-Roma microcosm can be distinguished with three respective (dominant but not exclusive) focuses: (1) 1970s–1980s: self-determination; (2) 1990s–early 2000s: human rights violation; (3) from late 2000s: social and economic inclusion.

The Focus on Self-Determination

The origins of the international struggle for the self-determination of Roma can be traced back at least to the 1960s, when the United Nations inspired the creation of a number of international Romani umbrella organisations to promote the interests of the world's Roma through UN instruments and structures. These organisations worked towards the legitimisation of Roma as a nation with the right to a state by creating and promoting national culture. Although the goals of improving living standards and cultural and moral uplifting of the Roma were usually declared, they have always remained secondary to nationalist aspirations (Klimova-Alexander 2005: 16).

By the 1970s, these attempts had crystallised into the First World Romani Congress, which attracted participants from Western, Central and Eastern Europe, as well as from Asia and North America.[3] The Congress was formally organised by the Comité International Rom (an organisation that had been founded in Paris in 1965), and was funded by the World Council of Churches[4] and the Indian government.

The delegates of the Congress adopted a national flag and a hymn, and agreed on the dissemination of a new ethnic label. Hence the term 'Roma' was constructed as the official name to encompass a variety of communal-based identities across different countries. The leading concept was the principle of *amaro Romano drom* (our Romani way), and the phrase adopted was 'our state is everywhere where there are Roma because Romanestan is in our hearts' – expressing a clear disaffiliation from earlier claims for a territorial state.

In addition, commissions for social affairs, war crimes, language standardisation and culture were established. It was also decided that 8 April, the date on which the Congress had opened, should become Roma Day, henceforth to be celebrated annually. A single slogan summed up the Congress: 'The Roma people have the right to seek out their own path towards progress' (Fosztó 2003, Liégeois 2007, Acton and Klimova-Alexander 2001).

Since 1971, another six World Romani Congresses have been held. Of particular importance is the Fourth Congress, held in Poland in 1990, which saw the adoption of the 'Declaration of Nation' manifesto. This confirmed and detailed the claim for non-territorial nationhood and international recognition. Moreover, the manifesto claimed that the Romani nation offers to the rest of humanity a new vision of stateless nationhood that is more suited to a globalised world than is the current affiliation to nation states.

The Focus on Human Rights

The 'Roma issue' boomed after the collapse of the state socialist regimes, which had limited rights of assembly and association. After 1989, Roma could themselves establish various associations, foundations, political parties (for example, in Romania), and minority self-governments (for example, in Hungary).

At the same time, pro-Roma NGOs, run by non-Roma but advocating on behalf of Roma, burgeoned. After the fall of the Berlin Wall, well-established NGOs such as Amnesty International[5] and Human Rights Watch[6] began publicising the violations of Romani people's human rights. By the mid 1990s, national human rights NGOs had emerged – such as the Human Rights Project in Bulgaria, the Citizen's Solidarity and Tolerance Movement in the Czech Republic, the Union for Peace and Human Rights in Slovakia, and the Office for the Protection of National and Ethnic Minorities in Hungary.

Many of these were founded by returning non-Roma dissidents who spoke English and could develop contacts with Western philanthropic organisations. Their determination to pursue legal cases has led to dismissals and criminal proceedings against corrupt or abusive policemen and other officials, to the prosecution of those responsible for attacks against Roma, and the like (Barany 2002b).

A key pro-Roma actor is the Open Society Institute (OSI). The OSI provides financial and institutional support for Roma-related activities and organisations, operates its own programmes aimed at directly building Romani representation and leadership, and plays a key role in such international initiatives as the Decade of Roma Inclusion and the EU Roma Framework Strategy (both discussed below).

The leading international NGO to specifically combat the human rights abuse of Roma, the European Roma Rights Centre (ERRC), was founded with the financial support of OSI in 1996. Their activities comprise strategic litigation to reverse patterns of human rights abuse, organising various forms of human rights education, and submitting shadow reports to international bodies monitoring international conventions. In particular, ERRC submits shadow reports to the Committee on the Elimination of Racial Discrimination, the Committee on the Rights of the Child, and the Committee on the Elimination of Discrimination Against Women within the UN, as well as to the European Commission, reviewing the progress of candidate countries with large Roma populations.

The US-based Project on Ethnic Relations (PER), operating in Eastern European countries, has organised roundtable discussions on key issues (self-government, governmental policies, migration, and so on), brought together activists, experts, and politicians, and thus played a vital role in the emergence of pro-Roma global civil society.

Due to both the advocacy activity of the strengthening pro-Roma microcosm and the fear of westward mass migration of Roma, international organisations have turned their attention to the 'plight of Roma' as well.

First to take action, the Council of Europe (CoE) and the Organisation for Security and Co-operation in Europe (OSCE) produced reports and formulated recommendations from the early 1990s, and established special bodies to tackle the 'Roma issue'.

Initially so-called expert bodies were created, such as the Contact Point for Roma and Sinti Issues within OSCE, and the Group of Specialists on Roma within the Council of Europe – both founded in 1995. Later attempts were made to create more 'representative' bodies comprising Roma themselves; thus the European Roma and Traveller Forum in 2004 was created under the auspices of the Council of Europe and the Platform for Roma Inclusion within the EU.

Local, national and international NGOs, alongside the special bodies, formed a transnational advocacy network aimed at influencing government policies vis-à-vis Roma. In the past 10–15 years, the engaged international organisations have produced myriad reports, declarations, recommendations and resolutions in relation to Roma (or nomads – as they were called until the 1990s) (Majtényi and Vizi 2006, Marchand 2001).

These often inconsistent[7] documents attempt to identify the specific problems that Romani communities face and make non-binding propositions and general recommendations to remedy these problems. However, one international organisation, the European Union, has had a more significant leverage on Eastern European governments, as it measured 'the progress' of Eastern European candidate countries against the Copenhagen criteria.[8]

NGOs prepared well-researched and focused submissions on the situation of Roma communities for the European Commission, which sometimes transposed verbatim passages from the NGO reports to the so-called EU country reports.[9] More importantly, the Commission explicitly formulated the improvement of the situation of Roma communities as criteria for joining the EU. As a response, the Eastern European governments produced medium- and long-term 'Roma strategies'[10] as a sign of political commitment; however, in the daily lives of Roma, little has changed.

Relying on the by-now classic schema of Risse-Ropp-Sikkink (1999), Figure 7.1 recapitulates the flow of norm socialisation in the case of Hungary.

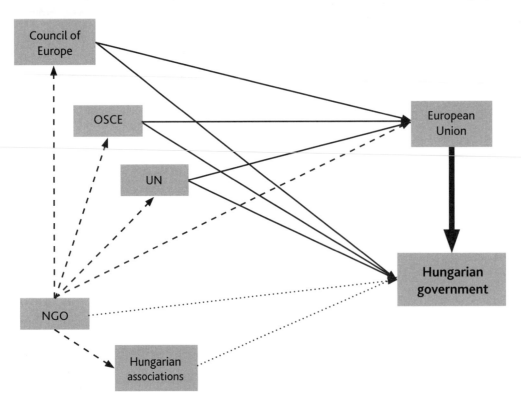

Figure 7.1 The Flow of Norm Socialisation From Civil Society to Government and Inter/Supranational Bodies, Using Hungary as an Example

Box 7.1
Who are the Roma?

Who are the 'Roma'? Several scholars and activists argue that Romani people form a stateless dispersed nation, potentially embracing 9–12 million people from all over the world, who trace their origins (based on linguistic evidence) to the Indian Subcontinent (Gheorghe 1997; Guy 2001). Others dispute that Romani people form such a diaspora and argue that certain allegedly Roma groups (such as Egyptians, Sinti, Travellers and Gitano communities) do not belong to or identify with the Roma nation (Gay y Blasco 2002, Okely 1997).

The roots of the nation-building project unifying various ethnic groups under the label 'Roma' can be traced back to the first World Roma Congress held in 1971 near London. Although the term is not used – in general or in specific contexts – by several allegedly Roma groups, it still commonly employed by activists, politicians, and various institutions to replace such typically pejorative appellations as Cigány, Cikan, Gypsy, and so on.

Furthermore, the group of those who identify themselves as 'Roma' do not usually overlap with the group of those stigmatised with 'Gypsy'. In general, the number of persons *perceived* as Roma is much higher than the number of those who *self-identify* themselves as such (in the context of sociological research and official censuses). The ethnic boundaries are more rigid in certain countries: in Bulgaria almost three-quarters of those perceived as Roma also identify themselves as Roma, whereas in Hungary only one-third do so (Szelényi and Ladányi 2001).

It has to be noted that although in several countries Roma are still associated with an itinerant way of life, only 5 per cent of all 'Roma' have a nomadic or semi-nomadic lifestyle. Furthermore, such administrative, occupational and legal categories as Travellers, Gens du Voyage, Camimanti, Nomadi who are ethnicised under the umbrella term of 'Roma' nowadays embrace sedentary communities as well. For instance, Italian authorities label immigrant (sedentary) Eastern European Roma 'nomads' and put them in caravans in so-called *campi nomadi*.

Angela Kóczé and Márton Rövid

Map 7.1   Who are the Roma?

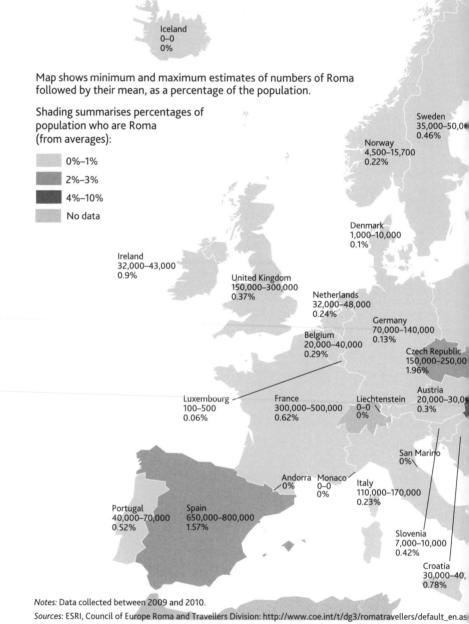

Iceland
0–0
0%

Map shows minimum and maximum estimates of numbers of Roma followed by their mean, as a percentage of the population.

Shading summarises percentages of population who are Roma (from averages):

- 0%–1%
- 2%–3%
- 4%–10%
- No data

Sweden
35,000–50,0(
0.46%

Norway
4,500–15,700
0.22%

Denmark
1,000–10,000
0.1%

Ireland
32,000–43,000
0.9%

United Kingdom
150,000–300,000
0.37%

Netherlands
32,000–48,000
0.24%

Germany
70,000–140,000
0.13%

Belgium
20,000–40,000
0.29%

Czech Republic
150,000–250,000
1.96%

Luxembourg
100–500
0.06%

France
300,000–500,000
0.62%

Liechtenstein
0–0
0%

Austria
20,000–30,0(
0.3%

San Marino
0%

Andorra
0%

Monaco
0–0
0%

Italy
110,000–170,000
0.23%

Portugal
40,000–70,000
0.52%

Spain
650,000–800,000
1.57%

Slovenia
7,000–10,000
0.42%

Croatia
30,000–40,
0.78%

Notes: Data collected between 2009 and 2010.

Sources: ESRI, Council of Europe Roma and Travellers Division: http://www.coe.int/t/dg3/romatravellers/default_en.as

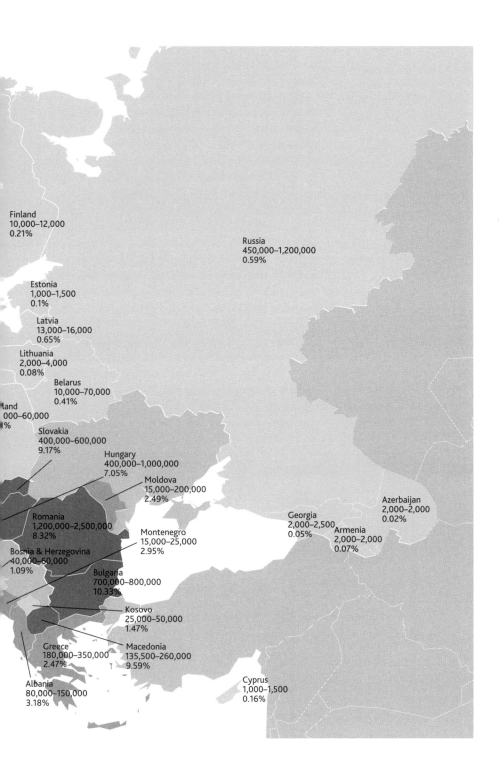

Finland
10,000–12,000
0.21%

Russia
450,000–1,200,000
0.59%

Estonia
1,000–1,500
0.1%

Latvia
13,000–16,000
0.65%

Lithuania
2,000–4,000
0.08%

Belarus
10,000–70,000
0.41%

...land
...000–60,000
...%

Slovakia
400,000–600,000
9.17%

Hungary
400,000–1,000,000
7.05%

Moldova
15,000–200,000
2.49%

Azerbaijan
2,000–2,000
0.02%

Romania
1,200,000–2,500,000
8.32%

Montenegro
15,000–25,000
2.95%

Georgia
2,000–2,500
0.05%

Armenia
2,000–2,000
0.07%

Bosnia & Herzegovina
40,000–60,000
1.09%

Bulgaria
700,000–800,000
10.33%

Kosovo
25,000–50,000
1.47%

Greece
180,000–350,000
2.47%

Macedonia
135,500–260,000
9.59%

Albania
80,000–150,000
3.18%

Cyprus
1,000–1,500
0.16%

The Focus on Social and Economic Inclusion

In a paradoxical way, after their adhesion to the EU, the influence of pro-Roma global civil society on Eastern European governments decreased. To maintain governments' and international bodies' commitment, the Decade of Roma Inclusion 2005–2015 programme (hereafter referred to as 'Decade') was launched by the OSI and the World Bank. The Decade is a unique international initiative formulated by the most important non-governmental and inter-governmental actors,[11] which states were encouraged to join on a voluntary basis.

Member states of Decade have to demonstrate their political commitment to improve the socio-economic status and social inclusion of Roma by developing their own national 'Decade Action Plans', specifying goals and indicators in four priority areas: education, employment, health and housing. Learning from the failures of the national Roma strategies that Eastern European governments had drafted in the enlargement period, the Decade incorporated a 'transparent and quantifiable' review of the progress of Decade Action Plans.

However, the Decade Secretariat realised halfway through the programme that 'the lack of data about Roma communities remains the biggest obstacle to conducting any thorough assessment of how governments are meeting their Decade commitments, despite widespread agreement among participating governments about the crucial need to generate data disaggregated for ethnicity in order to assess and guide policies'.[12] Moreover, research has revealed deterioration, not progress, in certain priority areas in Decade countries.[13]

By 2008–09 the very limited achievements of the Decade became apparent[14] (Popkostadinova 2011) and the pro-Roma microcosm turned its attention and hopes towards the EU once more. The most influential NGOs in this field[15] – with the support of the OSI – formed the European Roma Policy Coalition and called for more active involvement on the part of the EU.

The EU, as a sui generis international actor, possesses legal and financial means like no other international organisation to coordinate and facilitate common policies. After several resolutions and recommendations under the Hungarian EU presidency in 2011, the main EU bodies (the Parliament, the Commission and the Council) launched an EU Framework for National Integration Strategies up to 2020.

These recent efforts represent the third wave of Roma strategies developed by Eastern European governments under the pressure of pro-Roma global civil society and the EU. Similar to the first EU pre-accession phase, joining the recent initiative is quasi-mandatory of Eastern European states, but at the moment it seems unlikely

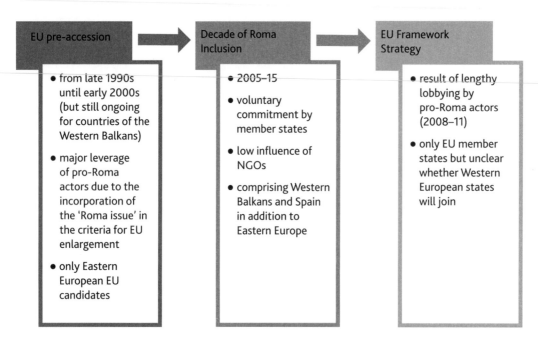

Figure 7.2 Putting Pressure on European Governments to Tackle the Plight of Roma – Three Strategies

that Western European states with significant Roma populations (the UK, France, Italy, Spain) will get on board. The EU Framework strategy can be seen as a revival of the Decade of Roma Inclusion, which now will be transformed into an EU policy agenda (Rövid 2011).

Divisions and Controversies within the Pro-Roma Microcosm

As with other segments of global civil society, within the pro-Roma microcosm there are tensions between moderate service providers and radical activists, small grassroots associations and big international NGOs, formal political parties and civil actors that criticise the establishment.

However, such divisions take a different form in the case of the pro-Roma microcosm, since the major international actors (such as the ERRC and the OSI) are often labelled 'white' or 'gajo' (meaning non-Roma) by their critics. Accordingly, 'white civil society' is contrasted with the Romani subaltern (Trehan 2009). The former is criticised on at least three grounds:

1. 'White' NGOs are accused of promoting a hegemonic discourse on human rights, thus downplaying both macro-economic and macro-sociological processes (such as the enormous rise of unemployment after the fall of state socialism and the retrenchment of the welfare state), as well as the local sources and context of inequalities and conflicts.

   Focusing exclusively on discrimination imposes a very simplistic vision of social relations, blaming only the prejudiced majority. Such an approach is insensitive to the diversity of local inter-ethnic relations, as well as to human rights violations within Roma communities, such as domestic violence, human trafficking and usury. Furthermore, extreme (and even moderate) right wing political forces may exploit such simplifying approaches, turn it inside-out, and blame the Roma for increasing crime, aggression and other social ills.

2. International actors are accused of being accountable to their donors and not to the Roma communities that they work for. In particular, a good number of Roma and pro-Roma NGOs are financed by the OSI so they have to align to OSI's priorities. Membership-founded and voluntary-based Roma associations – especially in Eastern Europe – are almost non-existent.

   Moreover, international advocacy efforts are very remote from the daily struggles of many Roma. Professional NGOs are often perceived as technocratic

and removed from such traditional civic values as altruism, community service and cooperation (Trehan 2001).

In brief, pro-Roma actors often patronise Roma in their desire to help them and impose patterns of development which they consider the best for them. Such a patronage could 'in the long run kill the natural mechanisms of community preservation, thus turning the community into a constant social customer of professional benefactors' (Marushiakova and Popov 2004: 96).

3. International NGOs create a kind of brain-drain, offering high salaries and attracting the brightest Roma from local associations, further weakening grassroots initiatives. Several 'traditional' Roma activists or leaders argue that Roma working for international bodies are detached from their roots and live a 'gajo' way of life.

   However, such 'traditional Roma leaders' (*vajda*, *bulibasa*, and so on) have, in the past, been empowered by non-Roma leaders in order to control and tax Roma communities. Therefore, although they may be able to resolve some local conflicts, such authoritarian, non-elected leaders/mediators also are, to an extent, responsible for preventing Roma from becoming autonomous equal citizens.

We certainly agree with the importance of strengthening grassroots Roma associations. However, we also recognise the invaluable work NGOs undertake in specific fields of human rights violations, such as police abuse, domestic violence, educational segregation or the recent mass expulsion of Roma from France.

The hegemony of 'white' NGOs is not the only reason for the weakness of Romani grassroots mobilisation. At least three other factors can be mentioned: historical, organisational and socio-psychological.

Roma communities in most societies have been pushed to the margins of society. They have never been part of the community of equal citizens, and in certain epochs even faced systematic exclusion, slavery or extermination. The example of African-Americans demonstrates that such a historical disadvantage is gradually surmountable; however presently in most societies a Roma middle class (including not only activists and politicians but also engineers, doctors, lawyers, teachers, and so on) exists only in embryonic form.

'Internal' organisational weaknesses also contribute to the fragility of Roma grassroots. Roma associations

Box 7.2
Romani Women's Rights Activism

As integral parts of the human rights regime, women's rights and gender issues became gradually recognised and accepted by local NGOs and donor organisations in the Central and Eastern European (CEE) countries. Romani women's activism gained impetus through the international gender discourse and emerging civil society in the region.

Romani women's issues first gained visibility in public discourse at the Congress on the EU Roma/Gypsies organised by the European Commission Against Racism and Intolerance in Seville, Spain, in 1994. One of the most striking results of this Congress was the publication of the 'Manifesto of Roma/Gypsy Women', the first publicly printed material which specifically referred to the situation of Romani women in Europe. One year later, in September 1995, the Council of Europe organised the 'Hearing of Roma/Gypsy Women' in Strasbourg as part of the Steering Committee for Equality between Women and Men. The purpose of this hearing was to identify problems and conflicts concerning equality and human rights encountered by Romani women. Although it was the first attempt by intergovernmental organisations to meet with Romani women activists and to bring visibility to their issues, the report issued by the European Commission Against Racism and Intolerance (ECRI) notes that the hearing emphasised economic hardship and educational discrimination against Roma in general, that is, it paid less attention to the specific concerns of Romani women.[1] Nevertheless, it was the first political recognition of Romani women's issues on an international level, and, as such, it allowed them to set up a network to exchange information and foster contacts with other women activists.

In 1998, the Open Society Institute (OSI) organised an International Conference of Romani Women in Budapest, Hungary, attended primarily by delegates from CEE. The meeting was unique because it focused on sensitive issues such the tradition of Roma culture versus women's rights. It is noteworthy that, at the conference, some Romani women challenged the existing male-dominated power structure in the Roma movement itself. In 1999, OSI established the Romani Women Initiative (RWI), which has since worked to develop, link and catalyse a core group of committed young Romani women leaders, in an effort to improve the human rights of Romani women. In 2003, with the assistance of the Council of Europe, Romani women activists from 18 European countries launched the International Romani Women's Network (IRWN), with a leadership that is older and more traditional, in terms of fetishising 'the Roma culture', than that of the RWI. The main focus of IRWN activities, and one that has been consistently encouraged by the Council of Europe, is the health of Romani women. Under the auspices of European Monitoring on Racism and Xenophobia (EUMC), IRWN produced the landmark report, 'Romani Women and Access to Public Health Care' in 2003 (Council of Europe 2003, Kóczé 2008).

On the transnational level, the presence of these Romani women's networks under the wing of international organisations created political leverage. Romani women activists developed a gender-based discourse within the Romani movement itself. However, those educated English-speaking Romani women who are active in developing this discourse may be detached from their local community and do not necessarily represent the local NGOs dealing with Romani women's issues.

In addition to influencing the male-dominated Romani movement, Romani women activists are also impacting the mainstream women's organisations. For example, several local Romani women organisations (SZIROM, Association of Roma Women of Szikszó, Hungary; Coloured Beads Association of Roma Women in Southern Hungary; Association of Roma Women in Public Life, Hungary; Romani CRISS, Romania; Federation of Kalé, Sinti and Manouche Women, France; Center Amalipe, Bulgaria; National Roma Centrum Manuse-Slovo21, Czech Republic; Kultúrne združenie Rómov Slovenska, Slovakia, Asociación Gitana de Mujeres Drom Kotar Mestipen, Spain) came together with the European Women's Lobby (EWL) and Hungarian Women's Lobby in a joint effort to organise a conference on Romani women's issues on 7 April 2011.

Angela Kóczé, excerpted from her PhD thesis, Central European University, Budapest (forthcoming).

---

[1] ECRI played a significant role in exposing the human rights situation of Roma in Europe; this report was instrumental. *Activities of the Council of Europe with Relevance to Combating Racism and Intolerance* (ECRI 2004).

are criticised for lack of transparency and poor internal democracy. Their sources of funding, and details of the members of their boards are often not public. The organisational structure is typically highly hierarchical, dominated by an authoritarian leader who appoints family members or close friends (Rostas 2009).

Many of them 'tend to be rigid and unadaptable; have simple structure and few, often ill-defined, objectives; and are marked by disunity' (Barany 2002a: 292). The majority of Roma associations are 'poorly organised and have difficulty getting along with each other, let alone working together – in large part because of their intense competition for scarce resources' (Barany 2002: 294).

Consequently, it is no surprise that 'amongst Roma the level of trust in NGOs is generally low, a common opinion being that these organisations benefit of [sic] their difficulties' (Rostas 2009: 119).

The weakness of Romani mobilisation can also be attributed to the fragmented and stigmatised nature of Roma identity. On one hand, there is no strong overarching pan-Roma identity: individuals perceived as Roma/Gypsy belong to diverse groups (such as Kalo, Romungro, Boyash, Vlax, Kelderash, Gitano, Manoush, Romanichels, Traveller, Sinti, Caminante, and so on) speak different languages, belong to different religions, and have different citizenships (see Box 7.1).

On the other hand, being perceived as 'Gypsy' is in most contexts a stigma. Non-Roma frequently associate 'Gypsies' with crime, laziness, filth, shouting and aggression. Such stereotypes have deep historical roots, and are reproduced both by public education and the mass media. Extreme-right parties are joined by 'moderate' governing right-wing parties (think of Sarkozy's Union pour un Mouvement Populaire and Berlusconi's Il Popolo della Libertà) in stigmatising 'Gypsies.'

Consequently, the strong desire for (voluntary) assimilation amongst most Roma comes as no surprise. Leaving behind or hiding one's Roma origin[16] makes life a great deal easier: one has a better chance to get into decent schools, take up reasonable jobs, have access to standard health care or simply to do the shopping without being humiliated by security staff.

In brief, there is no strong and unified Roma identity on the basis of which a transnational ethnic movement may emerge.

The Hungarian Influence

In addition to the extensively criticised predominance of 'white' international NGOs, a less oft mentioned form of hegemony has to be discussed. The conception and design of the two above-mentioned flagship initiatives (the Decade and the EU Framework) was largely conceived and implemented by Hungarian or Budapest-based actors.

In particular, the OSI and its Hungarian founder George Soros played a central role in the launching of the Decade, and the only Roma Member of the European Parliament, Lívia Járóka, and the Hungarian Member of the European Commission, László Andor, initiated and gained support for the EU Framework Strategy by all the main EU bodies (Parliament, Commission, Council).

The hegemony and generalisation of the Hungarian perspective marginalises other, especially 'Western European' voices. Both the Decade and the EU Framework are insensitive to the difficulties of Traveller communities in finding stopping places in the UK, for example, or to the plight of immigrant Roma in *campi nomadi* in Italy.

In general, from the emergence of the 'Roma issue' in the 1990s, international actors have turned their attention to Eastern European Roma and assumed that their recommendations and declarations are also suitable for Western European Gypsies, Sinti, Travellers, Gitano, Manoush, Caminante, and other communities. By the early 2000s, the 'Roma' of Western Europe almost disappeared from the discussion on Roma in general. The whole stage was occupied by Eastern European Roma, with the issues of poverty and segregation in the centre (Simhandl 2006, Gheorghe forthcoming).

Conclusions and Theoretical Implications

The pro-Roma global civil society has a mixed record. On one hand, it has managed to raise the attention of international organisations and national governments to the plight of Roma communities; on the other hand, their social status has not improved significantly, with a large proportion of Roma still living at the margins of society.

Roma are increasingly seen as an avant-garde non-territorial stateless nation, offering the rest of humanity a model of political organisation that is more suited to a globalised world than affiliation to traditional nation states.[17] In reality, most Roma cultivate loyalty to the state in which they live, as well as to the specific alleged 'Roma subculture' to which they belong (such as the Boyash, Vlax and Romungro cultures in Hungary). The majority of Roma cannot afford to travel abroad, or even to visit the capital city of their country. The cosmopolitanism of Roma appears to be the class consciousness of the minuscule frequent traveller Roma elite (Calhoun 2002).

Professional NGOs dominate pro-Roma civil society, often speaking in the name of 'Roma', while grassroots Romani associations remain weak and fragmented. The case of the pro-Roma movement demonstrates that solidarity can easily turn into hegemony. A very thin layer of transnational Romani activists and professional elite has emerged, but an educated and well-off Roma middle class that could serve as the backbone of an autonomous Roma civil society is hardly perceptible.

On the basis of this case study, three common critiques of the concept of global civil society can be reflected upon in an attempt to develop a more nuanced understanding.

First, global civil society is frequently conceptualised as a progressive response to economic (neoliberal) globalisation and to the hegemony of the United States. Pro-Roma global civil society, in contrast, is often perceived as being under American influence (namely US foundations), supporting the neoliberal agenda by focusing on human rights violations and downplaying more complex social economic processes that have pushed a vast number of Roma to the margins of society.

However, by the early 2000s the human rights approach proved insufficient and even backfired as it reinforced anti-Roma prejudices. Pro-Roma global civil society and the involved international organisations recognised that the misery of large numbers of Roma could not entirely be explained by racism. Consequently, the most recent efforts of the EU[18] centre on the struggle against the economic and social marginalisation of *all* vulnerable and deprived groups.

The case study demonstrates that the agenda of a segment of global civil society is dynamic: it is not fixed on a one-dimensional, anti-neoliberal programme. The focus of pro-Roma global civil society shifted from a focus on self-determination to human rights violations, and finally to social and economic inclusion. Each reflects upon an important segment of reality; however, none of them are sufficient in themselves. For instance, the most recent focus on social exclusion identifies Roma exclusively with misery, thus – unintentionally – it reproduces stereotypes that hinder the social integration of Roma.

Second, global civil society is often conceived as political agency outside the mechanisms of state and international law. Accordingly, global civil society associations are criticised for running after problems and reacting to crises, although their ability to anticipate, plan, prevent and redistribute lags far behind that of the state (Walzer 2004: 181). Pro-Roma global civil society, by contrast, recognises its limits in terms of the redistribution

and implementation of nationwide policies; that is why, instead of 'running after problems', they are the catalyst of change and attempt to influence national governments by – amongst other means – developing a regime of soft international law pertaining to Roma.

Third, the democratic credentials of global civil society actors are often questioned (Anderson and Rieff 2004). However, it seems, in general, that it is theorists who assign a representative function to such organisations, rather than the NGOs themselves. Amnesty International and Greenpeace never claimed to represent *anyone*; rather, by providing expertise as consultative members of various international organisations, they represent a *cause*.

The case of Roma is peculiar, as they can also be seen as a non-territorial stateless nation whose interests are not represented sufficiently by their respective states. The International Romani Union (IRU) does claim to represent all Roma of the world, and demands a seat in the UN General Assembly.

The self-appointed 'delegates' of IRU lack democratic legitimacy; however, their main message cannot be dismissed. The Roma are second-class citizens in their home countries and within the EU: they are not equal before the law as their human dignity and fundamental rights are violated on a daily basis without any sanctions; they are not equal members of the political community as their values and interests are not represented at either the local, national or international level; and the noble principle of an equally motivated and gifted Roma having the same chance of realising his or her life plans as non-Roma (in terms of profession, living conditions, leisure, and so on) remains a utopia.

Pro-Roma global civil society plays a crucial role in raising awareness of the legal, political and social marginalisation of Roma. However, Roma actors must lead the struggle for equality. Pro-Roma allies may support them in various ways, but replacing or outweighing Roma activists is counterproductive; it can only result in the further marginalisation and demobilisation of Roma.

Notes

1. Gayatri Chakravorty Spivak, the post-colonial theorist, evoked the term 'epistemic violence' to refer to the domination of Western ways of understanding in contrast to non-Western ways of knowledge production. The destruction and marginalisation of one's way of understanding is always distorting the subaltern reality. Spivak's concept is based on Pierre Bourdieu's notion of symbolic violence, accounting for the tacit, almost unconscious, modes of cultural/social and gender domination or racism occurring within everyday social spaces (Spivak 1988).

2. Officially the 'Kingdom of Serbs, Croats and Slovenes' at that time.

3. According to Acton and Klimova-Alexander (2001), representatives of 14 countries participated, whereas Marushiakova and Popov (2004: 78) argue that 'documents of the congress listed delegates from 8 countries, 2 out of which from Eastern Europe (Yugoslavia and Czechoslovakia) and observers'.

4. The first congresses were organised 'with the support of Evangelical churches working among the Gypsies, the Pentecostal church in particular. Later on the different Evangelical churches lost interest in the world Romani movement though they are still active among the Gypsies' (Marushiakova and Popov 2004: 79).

5. *Torture and Ill-treatment of Roma*, 1993; *Bulgaria: Turning the Blind Eye to Racism*, 1994; *Romania: Broken Commitments to Human Rights*, 1995.

6. *Struggling for Ethnic Identity: Czechoslovakia's Endangered Gypsies*, 1992; *Struggling for Ethnic Identity: The Gypsies of Hungary*, 1993.

7. Early documents, such as the 1995 Report for the Council of Europe, contained romantic and essentialist views such as 'the increasing mobility since 1990 … is merely a return to the normal mobility of Gypsies'. Later documents were more balanced, although they also talk about Roma in general (usually recognising their heterogeneity in only a footnote).

8. The Copenhagen criteria are the rules that define whether a country is eligible to join the European Union. The criteria require that a state has the institutions to preserve democratic governance and human rights, has a functioning market economy, and accepts the obligations and intent of the EU. These membership criteria were laid down at the June 1993 European Council in Copenhagen, Denmark, from which they take their name.

9. The ERRC continues to prepare submissions for the European Commission on the situation of Roma in EU candidate countries such as Bosnia-Herzegovina, Croatia, Macedonia, Montenegro, Serbia and Turkey.

10. For instance, every Hungarian government since the democratic transition has produced such Roma strategies in the form of government resolutions setting up various coordinating mechanisms and bodies, and outlining action plans in priority areas.

11. Namely the Open Society Institute, the World Bank, the United Nations Development Programme, the Council of Europe, Council of Europe Development Bank, the Contact Point for Roma and Sinti Issues, the European Roma Information Office, the European Roma and Traveller Forum, and the European Roma Rights Centre.

12. *No Data – No Progress*, Open Society Foundations, 2010.

13. For instance, a survey carried out by the OSI in 2009 suggests that in some member states, only a limited number of Roma children complete primary school. According to the research Roma children tend to be over-represented in special education and segregated schools. *International Comparative Data Set on Roma Education*, Open Society Institute 2008.

14. Although George Soros, the founder of the OSI, and one of the initiators of the Decade, identified the following achievements of the Decade in 2011: 'It has elevated the importance of tackling the interrelated problems of poverty and discrimination. The Decade has involved the Roma communities and provided a forum to discuss what works and what doesn't. It has encouraged civil society to provide independent evaluation. And it has attracted other states and international organisations to join' (Speech at the International Steering Committee of the Roma Decade held in Prague, 27 June 2011).

15. Amnesty International, European Roma Rights Centre, European Roma Information Office, Open Society Foundations, European Network Against Racism, Minority Rights Group International, European Roma Grassroots Organisations Network, Policy Center for Roma and Minorities, Roma Education Fund, Fundación Secretariado Gitano.

16. In different societies, non-Roma identify 'Gypsies' in different ways. In most (but not all!) countries, darker skin colour is considered as an important marker limiting the possibilities of voluntary assimilation. Furthermore the boundaries between Roma and non-Roma are more rigid in some countries than in others. For instance, in Hungary only about one-third of those perceived as Roma identify themselves as Roma, whereas in Bulgaria the figure is nearly three-quarters (Szelényi and Ladányi 2001).

17. This claim is formulated in the manifesto 'Declaration of Nation' that was circulated in the First World Romani Congress in 2000. The concept of Roma being a non-territorial stateless nation has gradually been adopted by all major international actors.

18. The EU Framework for National Roma Integration Strategies up to 2020 was accepted by all EU bodies (Parliament, Commission, Council) in 2011.

References

Acton, Thomas, and Klimova-Alexander, Ilona (2001) 'The International Romani Union. An East-European Answer to West European Questions?', in W. Guy (ed.), *Between Past and Future: The Roma of Central and Eastern Europe*. Hatfield: University of Hertfordshire Press.

Anderson, Kenneth, and Rieff, David (2004) 'Global Civil Society: A Sceptical View', in Helmut Anheier, Marlies Glasius and Mary Kaldor (eds), *Global Civil Society 2004/5*. London: Sage.

Anheier, Helmut, Glasius, Marlies and Kaldor, Mary (2001) 'Introducing Global Civil Society', in Helmut Anheier, Marlies Glasius and Mary Kaldor (eds), *Global Civil Society 2001*. Oxford: Oxford University Press.

Barany, Zoltan (2002a) 'Ethnic Mobilization without Prerequisites: The East European Gypsies', *World Politics*, Vol. 54 No. 3: 277–307.

Barany, Zoltan (2002b) *The East European Gypsies: Regime Change, Marginality and Ethnopolitics*. Cambridge: Cambridge University Press.

Calhoun, Craig (2002) 'The Class Consciousness of Frequent Travelers: Toward a Critique of Actually Existing Cosmopolitanism', *South Atlantic Quarterly*, Vol. 101 No. 4: 869.

Clark, Colin (2004) '"Severity has Often Enraged but Never Subdued a Gipsy": The History and Making of European Romani Stereotypes', in S. Nicholas and T. Susan (eds), *The Role of the Romanies: Images and Counter-images of 'Gypsies'/Romanies in European Cultures*. Liverpool: Liverpool University Press.

Council of Europe (2003) *Breaking the Barriers – Romani Women and Access to Public Health Care*, joint report by the Office of the OSCE High Commissioner on National Minorities, the Council of Europe's Migration and Roma/Gypsies Division and the European Union's European Monitoring Centre on Racism and Xenophobia. Luxembourg: Office for Official Publications of the European Communities.

Fosztó, László (2003) 'Diaspora and Nationalism: an Anthropological Approach to the International Romani Movement', *Regio*, No. 1.

Gay y Blasco, Paloma (2002) 'Gypsy/Roma Diasporas: Introducing a Comparative Perspective', *Social Anthropology*, Vol. 10 No. 2.

Gheorghe, Nicolae (1997) 'The Social Construction of Romani Identity', in T. Acton (ed.), *Gypsy Politics and Traveller Identity*. Hatfield: University of Hertfordshire Press.

Gheorghe, Nicolae (forthcoming) 'Choices to be Made and Prices to be Paid: Potential Roles and Consequences in Roma Activism and Policy-making', in *Price of Roma Integration*.

Guy, Will (2001) 'Romani Identity and Post-Communist Policy' in W. Guy (ed.), *Between Past and Future: The Roma of Central and Eastern Europe*. Hatfield: University of Hertfordshire Press.

Hancock, Ian (2002) *We are the Romani people = Ame sam e Rromane dzène*. Hatfield: University of Hertfordshire Press.

Heuss, Herbert (2000) '"Anti-Gypsyism" is Not a New Phenomenon. Anti-Gypsyism Research: The Creation of a New Field of Study', in T. Acton (ed.), *Scholarship and the Gypsy Struggle*. Hatfield: University of Hertfordshire Press.

Ivanov, Andrey (2003) *Avoiding the Dependency Trap. The Roma in Central and Eastern Europe*. Bratislava: United Nations Development Programme.

Klimova, Ilona (2002) 'Romani Political Representation in Central Europe: An Historical Survey', *Romani Studies*, Vol. 12 No. 5.

Klimova-Alexander, Ilona (2005) *The Romani Voice in World Politics*. Aldershot: Ashgate.

Kóczé, Angéla (2008) 'Ethnicity and Gender in the Politics of Roma Identity in the Post-Communist Countries' in Bahun-Radunovic, S. and Rajan, V.G.J. (eds), *The Intimate and the Extimate: Violence and Gender in the Globalized World*. Farnham: Ashgate Press.

Kóczé, Angéla (2011) 'Gender, Ethnicity and Class: Exposing Contemporary Romani Women's Issues and Political Activism', *Sociology and Social Anthropology*, Budapest: Central European University.

Liégeois, Jean-Pierre (2007) *Roma in Europe*. Council of Europe.

Majtényi, Balázs, and Vizi, Balázs (eds) (2006) *A Minority in Europe. Selected International Documents Regarding the Roma*. Budapest: Gondolat Kiadó.

Marchand, Anna (2001) *La protection des droits des Tsiganes dans l'Europe d'aujourd'hui: éléments de l'approch internationale*. Paris: Harmattan.

Marushiakova, Elena, and Popov, Vesselin (2004) 'The Roma – a Nation without a State? Historical Background and Contemporary Tendencies', *Mitteilungen des SFB 'Differenz und Integration'* 6: Segmentation und Complimentarität. Orientwissenschaftliche Hefte 14.

Okely, Judith (1997) 'Some Political Consequences of Theories of Gypsy Ethnicity', in A. James, J. Hockey and A. Dawson (eds), *After Writing Culture*. Abingdon: Routledge.

Popkostadinova, Nikoleta (2011) 'Little to Celebrate Halfway through Europe's "Roma Decade"', *Balkan Insight*.

Ringold, Dena, Orenstein, Mitchell A. and Wilkens, Erika (2005) *Roma in an Expanding Europe: Breaking the Poverty Cycle*. Washington DC: World Bank.

Risse, Thomas, Ropp, Stephen C. and Sikkink, Kathryn (1999) *The Power of Human Rights: International Norms and Domestic Change*. Cambridge: Cambridge University Press.

Rostas, Iulius (2009) 'The Romani Movement in Romania: Institutionalization and (De)Mobilization', in N. Trehan and N. Sigona (eds), *Romani Politics in Contemporary Europe: Poverty, Ethnic Mobilization, and the Neo-liberal Oorder*. Basingstoke: Palgrave Macmillan.

Rövid, Márton (2011) 'One-size-fits-all Roma? On the Normative Dilemmas of the Emerging European Roma Policy', *Romani Studies*, Vol. 21 No. 1: 1–22.

Simhandl, Katrin (2006) '"Western Gypsies and Travellers" – "Eastern Roma": The Creation of Political Objects by the Institutions of the European Union', *Nations & Nationalism*, Vol. 12 No. 1: 97–115.

Spivak, Gayatri Chakravorty (1988) 'Can the Subaltern Speak?', in C. Nelson and L. Grossberg (eds), *Marxism and the Interpretation of Culture*. Urbana and Chicago: University of Illinois Press.

Szelényi, Iván, and Ladányi, János (2001) 'The Social Construction of Roma Ethnicity in Bulgaria, Romania and Hungary During Market Transition', *Review of Sociology*, Vol. 7 No. 2.

Szelényi, Iván, and Ladányi, János (2006) *Patterns of Exclusion: Constructing Gpysy Ethnicity and the Making of an Underclass in Transitional Societies of Europe*. New York: Columbia University Press.

Trehan, Nidhi (2001) 'In the name of the Roma? The Role of Private Foundations and NGOs', in W. Guy (ed.), *Between Past and Future: The Roma of Central and Eastern Europe*. Hatfield: University of Hertfordshire Press.

Trehan, Nidhi (2009) 'The Romani Subaltern within Neoliberal European Civil Society: NGOization of Human Rights and Silent Voices', in N. Trehan and N. Sigona (eds), *Romani Politics in Contemporary Europe: Poverty, Ethnic Mobilization, and the Neo-liberal Order*. Basingstoke: Palgrave Macmillan.

Walzer, Michael (2004) 'Governing the Globe', in M. Walzer, *Arguing about War*. New Haven: Yale University Press.

CHAPTER 8

CIVIL SOCIETY AND CLUSTER MUNITIONS: BUILDING BLOCKS OF A GLOBAL CAMPAIGN

Thomas Nash

Introduction

The international process to ban cluster munitions, often referred to as the 'Oslo Process' after the city in which it was launched, is an example of a diplomatic initiative in which civil society played a highly involved role. States remained the ultimate decision-makers, with a Norwegian-led core group of seven states launching the process in Oslo in February 2007, and 108 states signing the Convention on Cluster Munitions in the same city in December 2008. However, civil society, organised under the banner of the Cluster Munition Coalition (CMC), was able to influence many of the decisions along the way, both at the national level and within international negotiations. The entire process, from the formation of the CMC to the signing of the Convention, took little more than five years; it has arguably been one of the most successful civil society campaigns of the past decade.

This chapter sets out ten insights gleaned from the efforts of civil society in dealing with the problem of cluster munitions. These insights may or may not be applicable to other coalition campaigns, and there were almost certainly other lessons learned during this campaign that are not captured here (Atwood et al. 2009). But by reflecting on these ten building blocks behind the campaign, this chapter seeks, from a practitioner's perspective, to tell the story of how the movement against cluster bombs was able to achieve many of the goals it set for itself – and in doing so suggest some foundations for the future.

Global Civil Society Coalitions – Transnational Advocacy Networks

Since the 1990s, much has been written on the role of civil society in global politics, and on the phenomenon of global civil society coalitions, or what are often called transnational advocacy networks (Keck and Sikkink 1998: 43–4, Finnemore and Sikkink 1998). There is also a burgeoning academic literature on the collaboration between these transnational advocacy networks and

middle power states; the process to ban cluster munitions has itself begun to be the subject of such analysis (Bolton and Nash 2010, Petrova 2010, Wisotzki 2009, Cooper 2011). This chapter seeks to provide a contribution to this literature by providing a specific example of international civil society work.

Ten Insights

The following ten points are reflections drawn from the author's experience as Coordinator of the international non-governmental Cluster Munition Coalition, the central NGO partner throughout the process to ban cluster bombs.

1. Believe that change is possible

The idea that one has to be convinced of something oneself before one can convince others is fairly obvious, but it assumes all the more importance when one is trying to rally a range of different NGOs, each with diverse interests and cultures, around a particular cause. This was certainly the case in the effort to prohibit cluster munitions. At the end of 2005 – two years after the CMC was established – few people believed (or at least expressed a belief) that any kind of ban on the weapon was possible. Indeed many observers stated that even a specific law restricting their use would be impossible. Three years later, in December 2008, 94 countries signed a treaty prohibiting cluster munitions.

Thus, even when critics and mainstream observers say the task is impossible, including perhaps some allies, it is crucial that a campaign has a leadership that genuinely believes that the goal is achievable and necessary. Having a group of people who are somehow infected with the will to achieve what they believe is possible is a powerful unifying force: for the CMC, this group of individuals within the leadership kept each other motivated when the campaign faced setbacks, and presented a united front to other campaigners and external partners, including governments.

It is also true, however, that a campaign's goal can change over time. In the early years, the CMC did not make public calls for a prohibition on cluster munitions. So while the early group of campaigners on cluster munitions believed change on this issue was possible, they retained enough flexibility to shape and react to the different possibilities that evolved over time.

2. Be ready

When progress on the political front is difficult and it is not yet possible to get traction for advocacy efforts, a campaign can make good use of time by building the strength and reach of its network, deepening the case behind the campaign and refining the intellectual framework underpinning it.

During the early period of the CMC, from its launch in November 2003 through to the Review Conference of the Convention on Certain Conventional Weapons in November 2006, the coalition doubled the size of its NGO membership from around 90 to 180.[1] A number of key reports on cluster munitions were published by coalition members that began to present evidence, shape the debate and reframe the issue at hand. With others, Brian Rappert, Richard Moyes and this author undertook a rather intensive process of discussions in order to determine the optimal intellectual framework with which to pursue a prohibition on cluster munitions. These reports included 'Out of Balance' (Rappert 2005), which questioned the value of the proportionality assessments of International Humanitarian Law in relation to cluster munitions, given the British government's failure to gather data on humanitarian harm; 'Failure to Protect' (Rappert and Moyes 2006), which moved beyond IHL to set out a case for the prohibition of cluster munitions based on the pattern of harm caused, and drawing on precautionary approaches; and 'Foreseeable Harm' (Nash 2006), which was the first report produced on the use of cluster munitions during the conflict between Israel and Hezbollah in 2006. During this period individual NGOs and other actors were also undertaking a range of other work to document the problem and shape the discourse; these included CMC members such as Human Rights Watch (HRW) and Handicap International (HI) as well as other partners such as the International Committee of the Red Cross (ICRC) and the United Nations (UN) (Borrie 2009).

Additionally, a number of informal meetings took place between key players from NGOs, progressive states and international organisations during these early years. Two meetings held in 2006 were particularly significant, the first hosted by the Geneva Forum and the second by the Diana, Princess of Wales Memorial Fund. Both meetings brought together a relatively small group of key actors from the aforementioned groups to discuss strategy on what was then still only a potential process to ban cluster munitions. These two gatherings were important in helping to develop and strengthen the strategic partnerships between, for example, Norway (a key state supporter of the process) and the CMC. They also helped to build a 'community of practice' (as discussed in Borrie and Thornton 2008), on the cluster munitions issue, allowing the key drivers of the process to feel part of a group that was engaged in a shared enterprise, in which they could learn from each other and solve problems together (Borrie 2005).

'Being ready' means that once the foundations are in place, a campaign can take full advantage of opportunities when they arise. The CMC was faced with a number of such opportunities in 2006. When a close collaboration between Belgian civil society activists and progressive parliamentarians led to a process to prohibit the weapons in the Belgian national parliament in 2005 and 2006, the CMC had an early chance to mobilise and motivate its membership. An email in December 2005 from Kasia Derlicka, a campaigner working with HI in Belgium, asking CMC campaigners to urge Belgian parliamentarians to support a draft bill banning cluster munitions, highlighted the global impact that an active, international coalition could make via national politics:

> If Belgium adopts the bill it will be the first country to ban cluster munitions, which may have a domino effect on other countries and hopefully can bring us to a global ban. Therefore we believe it is very important if we can show international support for the current developments in Belgium.

Belgian campaigners urged CMC members around the world to contact parliamentarians on several further occasions during the draft law's passage through parliament, which was eventually passed in early 2006. This was the first major success for campaigners on cluster munitions.

Similarly, the widespread use of cluster munitions during the Israeli bombardment of southern Lebanon in 2006, which again occurred towards the end of the early period of the CMC, saw significant mobilisation by a range of actors, who, 'being ready', were already engaged

Box 8.1
History of the Cluster Munition Coalition

Public disquiet about cluster munitions dates back to their use during the US bombardment of Vietnam, Cambodia and Lao PDR in the 1960s and 1970s. At a conference hosted by the International Committee of the Red Cross (ICRC) in Lucerne in 1974, 13 countries proposed a prohibition on cluster munitions. However, it was not until the late 1990s that attention was refocused on the weapon. The International Campaign to Ban Landmines (ICBL) successfully campaigned from 1992 to 1997 for the adoption and signature of the Mine Ban Treaty, which prohibits anti-personnel landmines (Williams et al. 2008). Many ICBL member organisations were also concerned about the impact on civilians of explosive remnants of war, cluster munitions in particular. This concern intensified with the use of cluster munitions in Serbia and Kosovo in 1999, in Afghanistan in 2001–02 and in Iraq in 2003.

At a meeting of experts on explosive remnants of war in Dublin in April 2003, a group of NGOs met to discuss the way forward for collective action on cluster munitions. Following further NGO discussions at a landmine meeting in Bangkok in September 2003, the Cluster Munition Coalition (CMC) was established in The Hague in November 2003. That same month, states adopted the Protocol on Explosive Remnants of War at the UN Convention on Certain Conventional Weapons (CCW), which set out obligations regarding the recording of information and clearing up of explosive weapons used or abandoned in armed conflict (Harrison and Moyes 2009).

Civil society groups, the ICRC and UN agencies widely considered this to be inadequate as a response to the cluster munitions problem. From 2004 until 2006, the CMC worked on building up its network of members, initially drawing from the ICBL's membership, and building up the evidence and arguments to support new international rules on cluster munitions. The CMC's part-time coordinator, employed by Mines Action Canada, became a full-time employee in 2005 when Landmine Action took over the housing of the CMC.

The CMC's advocacy during this period centred around the CCW, whose 'Group of Governmental Experts' continued to meet at the UN in Geneva to discuss possible further action to deal with explosive remnants of war and cluster munitions. The key turning points occurred in 2006 when Belgium passed a law banning cluster munitions, the Austrian parliament resolved to negotiate an international instrument on the issue and Israel undertook a massive bombardment of southern Lebanon with cluster munitions. These events, and the reactions to them by states, international organisations and the CMC, changed the political landscape substantially.

At the CCW's Third Review Conference in November 2006, the CMC put increasing pressure on states to launch negotiations on cluster munitions, but a number of countries, including the US, Russia and China, opposed a proposal by 27 states for a negotiating mandate. As a result, Norway invited like-minded states to a conference in Oslo in February 2007, initiating the so-called 'Oslo Process', which culminated in the negotiation of the Convention on Cluster Munitions in Dublin in May 2008 and its signature in Oslo in December of the same year.

Thomas Nash

on the issue. Human Rights Watch, together with UN personnel on the ground, confirmed that cluster munitions had been used. From that moment on, and as information on the scale of the use and contamination became available, the CMC issued regular updates to members based on communications with UN mine action staff in the country.[2] The campaign prompted and facilitated the involvement of states, independent researchers and in particular the global media who all played important roles in the discussions on the use of cluster munitions. The CMC and many of its members regularly briefed the media on the issue to help shape and boost coverage.

3. Move fast and make the goal inevitable

Having an external deadline for a campaign and a framework for the process can help keep up the pace and foster the sense that the outcome being sought is going to happen no matter what. Together with other events in 2005 and 2006, the developments described above provided a platform for the CMC from which to drive forward its ambition to prohibit cluster munitions. The campaign and its partners maintained a sense of urgency and intensity through to the signing of the treaty in December 2008.

There was a definite sense of humanitarian urgency throughout the entire process. Not only were campaigners responding to the continued casualties from unexploded cluster bombs dropped 40 years ago in South-east Asia, they witnessed their massive use in Lebanon and could envisage the devastation should the billions of submunitions stockpiled around the world ever be used. A common refrain used by CMC campaigners and other progressive actors was that 'we are not going to spend years in negotiations while people are being killed and injured on a daily basis and millions of cluster munitions sit in ammunition depots waiting to be used'.

This sense of urgency was successful in pressing a remarkable pace in diplomatic terms: the period from the Lebanon conflict in July and August 2006 to the adoption of the Convention on Cluster Munitions in Dublin in May 2008 was less than two years. The seeds of this hectic pace were sown in the Oslo Declaration, adopted at the initial meeting of likeminded states in Oslo in February 2007. The key line of this political declaration stipulated a deadline of 2008, by which states should 'conclude' a legally binding instrument[3], a controversial inclusion that a number of states sought to remove. However, the value of this deadline should not be underestimated, and it has not gone unnoticed in related circles: the negotiating

mandate adopted in 2009 for the Arms Trade Treaty, for example, included a deadline of 2012 for the conclusion of that instrument.

When a campaign has momentum on its side and its leadership is able to control, or at least regulate the tempo, a sense of the inevitability of the outcome may start to spread. If those involved in a process feel that events are moving fast and that they are struggling to keep up with the schedule of meetings and the pace of developments, it can become easier for them to believe that the outcome being pursued by those driving the process is unavoidable. Once this change in attitude occurs amongst more peripheral members or potential members, the political decision emerges as to whether it is better to get on board early and take a share in the credit, or hold out and risk being dragged on board at the last minute, perceived as a reluctant participant. To use a sporting metaphor, a campaign with momentum behind it can stay on the front foot and keep opponents on the back foot.

4. Dominate the data

Being able to command the information available on a particular issue is a very powerful asset to a campaign. Throughout the discussions on cluster munitions, NGOs provided substantial information on the humanitarian harm of these weapons, and on global policy and practice with regard to them.[4] In contrast, states published very little information. This imbalance had a number of implications. States found themselves less effective at rebutting NGO claims about the impact of cluster munitions or the inadequacy of the IHL proportionality rule, given that they had gathered no data on humanitarian harm against which to balance the anticipated military advantage. States and other pro-cluster munition parties also failed to provide a case for military necessity. An ICRC meeting of experts from states, NGOs and the UN, held in Montreux in April 2007, provided a ready-made opportunity for military experts to demonstrate that cluster munitions were essential, but, as the meeting's Irish rapporteur on military aspects noted, these experts did not deliver (ICRC 2007: 66–9). Instead, NGOs came out of the meeting having presented data demonstrating a pattern of humanitarian harm over 40 years and – at least in the view of the NGO representatives at the meeting – having not received clear answers from the state-appointed military experts as to when cluster munitions had ever been a battle winner.[5]

Through their use of data, NGOs also became seen as authoritative. Government representatives from African and Latin American states, and from other states affected by cluster munitions, regularly came to CMC campaigners for advice in the negotiations. These government officials were often stretched for time, having to cover a wide range of issues on the diplomatic agenda, so that many came to see the CMC as a key resource in this particular debate. Their trust in, and reliance on, the CMC was in part possible because the coalition's interests were perceived as clearly humanitarian rather than motivated by factors such as the military and commercial interests of producer and stockpiling states, who were also providing briefings on the issue.[6]

It may not have been obvious to those involved on the NGO side at the time, but, looking back, many campaigners may have overestimated the information and the expertise of those responsible for policy decisions. Whilst one possible perception is that governments are all powerful, well-resourced machines capable of outgunning campaigners, in the case of the CMC, the NGO sector arguably had at its disposal significantly more resources than any given government in terms of the number of people with expert knowledge who were able to research and discuss an issue when needed. Campaigners often know far more about the issues concerned than the people that they are talking to in governments. This is likely to be true regardless of the field of work. A lesson here is that campaigners should never underestimate their strength in regard to the data and arguments at their disposal.

Furthermore, the coalition and many of its key members made a point of not overstating the case. This was considered essential in order to maintain credibility; on the issue of cluster munitions, a highly conservative picture of the case was bad enough. There was a culture of scepticism and rigour within the CMC, and it was well understood that questionable use of data would only have given opponents an opening to criticise the campaign. Given the not-infrequent questioning of civil society legitimacy (see, for example, Anderson and Rieff 2004) it might also be argued that the use of data is one of the only tangible metrics for NGO legitimacy – although this would rely on some objective criteria for monitoring the use of data by NGOs (Bolton and Nash 2010: 181).

5. Set the terms of the debate

Campaigners can win powerful advantages by framing the issue at hand in the way that suits them best, rather than struggling to win a debate whose terms have been set by those promoting the status quo. The CMC put a great deal of effort into framing the issue of cluster munitions as a humanitarian problem; based on an observed pattern of harm over many years, the starting position was that the weapon should be banned, putting the burden of proof on governments to argue that they should be permitted.

Prior to this, the prevailing wisdom was that cluster munitions were legitimate weapons that were not overly problematic if used in accordance with existing rules of international humanitarian law. Any concern over humanitarian harm caused by the weapons had to be balanced against the distinct military advantage they allegedly gave to armed forces. Rather than engage with this argument in terms of military utility and the adequacy of international humanitarian law, the CMC worked to reframe the problem in a way that gave campaigners the upper hand. The critical questioning approach adopted here involved scepticism, precautionary approaches and shifting the burden of proof.

The role of scepticism played an important part throughout the campaign, but in particular in response to the arguments focused on the essential military utility of the weapon. As noted above, the CMC regularly asked for specific examples of the military utility of cluster munitions, but users of the weapon were not able to provide any convincing material.[7] Precautionary approaches were also important. The CMC asked user governments what information they had on the humanitarian harm caused by the use of cluster munitions. In the case of the UK, for example (and the UK was by no means an outlier), the answer was none (Rappert 2005). In that case, the coalition then pointed out, it was impossible for the UK government to make a judgement on the permissibility of the weapon using a proportionality assessment that balanced humanitarian harm against military advantage. The CMC also emphasised the need to move beyond a strictly legal approach based on IHL and to shift the burden of proof onto governments. Given the demonstrated humanitarian harm over four decades and on the basis of precautionary approaches, users were asked to justify the use of cluster munitions rather than NGOs having to justify their prohibition.[8] Crucially, the core group of states managing the negotiations on the text, in particular New Zealand, which was responsible for the definition of a cluster munition, was supportive of this approach.

6. Constantly focus on the human impact

Another key element in reframing the debate was to emphasise the pattern of human suffering from cluster munitions as unacceptable.[9] The humanitarian evidence

Box 8.2
'What Remains'

'What Remains' is an exhibition of film and photography examining the impact of cluster bombs on the lives of civilians in affected countries around the world. Documenting the damage to both individual civilians and their social infrastructure, this two-year project was created for a very specific purpose – to support the international campaign to ban cluster bombs.

Between 2006 and 2008, Alison Locke and Chris Anderson travelled to affected regions to document the harm caused to civilians by these indiscriminate weapons. In remote regions and often without reliable statistical information, they were obliged to do research in-country, searching for survivors, often many years after their injury, and for the bereaved. In some cases, this research and the subsequent interviews undertaken by Locke and Anderson led to the identification of individual survivors who became active advocates in the movement against cluster bombs.

With images from Lebanon, Laos, Afghanistan, Tajikistan, Western Sahara, Kosovo, Nagorno Karabakh and Ethiopia, 'What Remains' presents a moving collection of stories told by people who are witnesses to suffering through injury and loss. The exhibition uses photographs and film to give voice to their experiences, which are mirrored and repeated throughout the decades in which cluster bombs have been used.

Initially focusing on the physical and visual impact of the consequences of these weapons, Locke and Anderson became increasingly concerned with the possibility that the photographic representation of physical injury might also describe people's mental anguish and psychological trauma. Working in the field in the documentary tradition, it was important that their subjects spoke as witnesses to their experience of war in a way that was visceral and immediate. The use of combined media, creating both formal photographic portraits and video footage which allows people the space to speak of their experience, gives the raw documentary material a resonance that is difficult to achieve in a static exhibition, as subjects are revealed in a dialogue between still images and film. 'What Remains' reflects on the fact that external injury is only the visual marker of the deeper consequences of cluster munitions.

The film and photography that was eventually exhibited in Dublin in May 2008 and in London in August 2010 was also used extensively throughout the campaign to ban cluster munitions. The material was exhibited at the initial meeting to launch the process in Oslo, and at subsequent diplomatic conferences in Peru, Austria, Serbia and New Zealand, culminating in a major exhibition at the Dublin Gallery of Photography during the final treaty negotiations. The material was also used in the campaign materials developed by the Cluster Munition Coalition (CMC), including brochures, posters, short films, and so on. The presence and prominence of these images throughout the diplomatic process was a constant and powerful reminder of the purpose behind the initiative to prohibit cluster bombs.

Alison Locke is a London-based documentary photographer.

that member organisations of the coalition could gather through their fieldwork in areas affected by cluster munitions was important here.[10] This approach appealed to the moral sensibility of all those involved in the process. It was consistent with the concept of human security focused on protecting the lives of people and communities, rather than traditional security focused on protecting the nation state.

This human focus was maintained in all campaign arguments, in communications to the media and to governments, in the representatives sent to meetings with government officials and politicians (where survivors of cluster munitions played a prominent role), and in audio-visual materials (see Box 8.2). Striking photographic images of individuals and communities affected by cluster munitions were a regular feature at the regional and international meetings throughout the process. This unrelenting focus on the human impact helped the campaign to occupy the moral high ground, foster a sense of urgency and maintain pressure on delegates; it also kept the standard of ambition high during the negotiations, challenging others to reach the maximum humanitarian protection possible rather than lowering the bar in compromise.

7. Leadership from those directly affected

Some of the most powerful advocates for a cause are those individuals, communities and states that are directly affected by the issue under discussion. Ensuring that campaigning and advocacy processes include these actors can be challenging for all involved, but it is vital in order to ensure legitimacy and relevance, and can be critical to the success of an initiative. Within the CMC individual survivors regularly participated in conferences and spoke out on behalf of the campaign. These campaigners – some of whom had lost limbs, lost their eyesight, or lost their children – not only influenced decision-makers in governments, but also helped to motivate people inside the campaign and to remind all involved why they were working on the issue. Likewise the coalition actively engaged official representatives of affected states, in particular the Lao People's Democratic Republic (PDR) and Lebanon, to play prominent roles during the negotiations. An influential group of affected states emerged during this process, with a meeting for affected states held in Belgrade in October 2007 and key interventions by affected states during the final negotiations in Dublin. Observers (Borrie 2009) have noted the importance of the Belgrade Meeting of States

Affected by Cluster Munitions and highlighted the role of affected states during the negotiating process in 2007 and 2008. There is little doubt that through their lobbying meetings and bilateral consultations, survivors and affected states helped to change minds and win arguments.

However, it is important to recognise the challenges in involving survivors. Above all, any initiative should be based on principles of dignity and respect. A sense of exploitation can easily emerge if campaigns simply bring in survivors to speak at a conference in a wealthy northern capital and then send them home again, where their home might be an impoverished village in Afghanistan or Lao PDR. Some kind of support network, peer-to-peer support structure or buddy system is vital so that these individuals can get around and get through the day, let alone undertake lobbying activities. Individuals who have become involved in the campaign because they are survivors should be supported so that through their work they are seen primarily as campaigners rather than primarily as survivors. This takes training and follow up, including once these campaigners return to their homes. This can mean substantial commitments of funding and staff time. HI ran a project throughout the Oslo Process to develop a group of 'Ban Advocates'. This initiative provided many of the positive elements required to make survivor inclusion in advocacy possible and also confronted many of the challenges outlined above.[11] As a result of intensive lobbying from the CMC, Article 5 of the Convention on Cluster Munitions includes an obligation to include victims in the development of policies and practice on victim assistance (CCM 2008). Implementing this obligation in practice will take some work, but it is an important articulation of the need for those making policy to be inclusive of those directly affected.

8. Build a powerful NGO coalition

The CMC operated as a coalition of NGO members in around 100 countries (see Map 8.1). The significance and influence of these 'transnational advocacy networks' has been discussed from a range of perspectives, both theoretical and practical (Moyes and Nash 2001, Keck and Sekkink 1998). The global reach of these networks is a key aspect of their capacity to influence decision-making at the international level, and the CMC leadership put significant effort into developing and maintaining a network with global reach. Some of the aspects of this work are described below.

- *Coordination*: it was important to have a common message that all members were happy to promote, based on their own values and interests. The coalition leadership ensured that its messages to key partners and external audiences were carefully coordinated. This involved clear documentation translated into different languages and substantial time preparing for major conferences and global actions, including pre-meeting briefings.

- *Diversity*: the CMC was comprised of 400 organisations in around 100 countries, providing diversity across regions, linguistic groups, cultures and interest groups, and worked hard to maintain a gender balance in its representative and decision-making work.

- *Inclusivity*: the campaign sought to listen to the voices of members and maintain a link between the broader membership of the coalition and the governance and leadership. The 'Steering Committee' was made up of 13 organisations from the membership and took a hands-on approach to decision-making on policy, strategy and communications.

- *An affiliative approach*: NGO coalitions can be tricky to manage, given the diversity of actors involved. The coalition's leadership sought to foster a sense of belonging by understanding the interests, approaches and contexts of members and promoting shared interests, rather than laying down the approach all members must follow. The CMC did not experience – at least on a regular basis – conflict or competition amongst NGOs on policy, resources or profile, but where such tensions emerged the leadership sought to deal with them swiftly and openly (Borrie 2009: 274–5). Comprised of a centralised staff that did not represent one particular coalition member, the coordination team sought to promote the interests of the coalition as a whole.

- *Cooperation*: the coordination team sought to share the burden of work, using the skills of the different member organisations and individuals to undertake the tasks required. For example, during the final negotiations in Dublin, regional facilitators and thematic facilitators were appointed to coordinate advocacy work during the meeting. Based on a model adopted from the International Campaign to Ban Landmines (ICBL), internal workshops and campaign meetings were facilitated by campaigners themselves (Moyes and Nash 2011).

9. Foster strategic partnerships

In addition to having its own wide-reaching network of NGO members, the CMC itself was part of a larger group working towards the same goal; the coalition leadership was included in a group of key individuals from states and international organisations very early on in the process. A particularly strong bond developed between the CMC, Norway and the United Nations Development Programme (UNDP). This bond existed both institutionally and personally amongst the individuals involved. These interpersonal relationships were very tight, with information shared on a daily basis ensuring a coordinated approach to problems and opportunities. Relationships also existed with key political leaders, which at times proved to be influential in encouraging those leaders to take risks in pursuit of the prohibition. There are concrete examples of these sorts of relationships, but it is difficult to provide them without exposing politicians and civil servants to claims that they may have been working against their own governments' instructions (see Box 8.3).

Strong partnerships were also forged with key regional players such as Zambia, Mexico, Indonesia and New Zealand, as well as with cluster munition affected countries like Lao PDR and Lebanon. By developing partnerships with parliamentarians, faith leaders, academics, journalists and other interest groups around the world, the CMC was able to take advantage of their existing networks of influence to promote change and apply pressure. Very importantly, the coalition recognised the importance of individuals as well as institutions. Although perhaps more difficult to document and analyse, it became apparent throughout the campaign that often the personalities of individuals and the relationships that they build with one another are more important than the policy positions and institutional interests of any one entity at any one time.

10. Do a lot with a little

The CMC thought carefully about where to place its resources and how to approach its advocacy and campaigning activities in order to get maximum impact. Throughout the Oslo Process, the coalition carved out a space for itself as a significant international campaign with the capacity to influence decision-makers in countries all over the world. The CMC was never a mass grassroots social movement that had the ability to mobilise millions of people; it was a network of organisations, some professional, some voluntary, that could reach decision-

Map 8.1 Cluster Munition Coalition Members and Donors

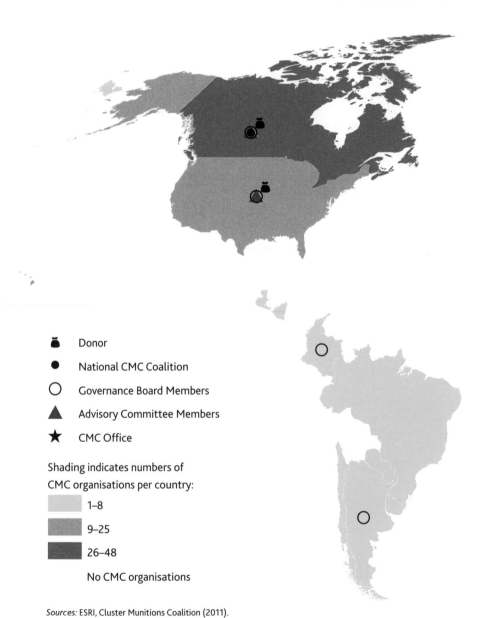

Donor

National CMC Coalition

Governance Board Members

Advisory Committee Members

CMC Office

Shading indicates numbers of
CMC organisations per country:

1–8

9–25

26–48

No CMC organisations

Sources: ESRI, Cluster Munitions Coalition (2011).

...e inset above

Box 8.3
Disclosure, Concealment and Legitimacy

In order to draw lessons from the process that led to the international ban on cluster munitions, it is useful to pay attention to how the exchange of information was strategically managed.

Debate within the Oslo Process and the United Nation's Convention on Certain Conventional Weapons (CCW) was infused with the negotiated exchange of information. While some participants in the coalition have provided a variety of allusions to the types of managed disclosures and concealments enacted (see Rappert et al. 2011), it can be difficult to examine the role of such negotiated exchanges in global campaigns for the very reasons that motivated the information being subject to management in the first place.

For instance, without some government officials deliberately working against their governments' stated position for many years, the campaign against cluster munitions would not have assumed the status that it eventually did in international diplomacy. Commonly, it was those in ministries of foreign affairs working regularly with NGOs and IGOs who took a position contra their colleagues in defence ministries. Officials and campaigners shared materials, ideas, and strategies. A good example was the coordination of timely media stories that criticised pro-retention policies; this then provided additional opportunities for action by progressive officials within what often proved to be risk-adverse bureaucracies.

In addition, at least some campaigners shared strategies with those government officials resisting a comprehensive prohibition, as part of their efforts to engage the latter in constructive discussions. The extensiveness of these types of government-nongovernment collaborations was an open secret for many participants in the Oslo Process, but it is nevertheless an element of the campaign that remains difficult to acknowledge, even today. The pervasiveness of such collaborations owes much to the fact that complex processes such as the negotiation of the CCM, processes that involve many different types of actors, cannot be reduced to simple expressions of national power, or to the interests of abstract international actors. Instead, they are rich with transforming relations of trust (and distrust) between individuals.

But the fostering of debate and dialogue is only one side of negotiated disclosure. Silences were also jointly produced. At times, the negotiated exchange of information worked against those campaigning for a ban. To avoid alerting certain governments of the strategy afoot, there was a lack of overt recognition within the CMC or elsewhere regarding the definition strategy being pursued for cluster munitions in the CCM. This then resulted in tensions within the CMC during the height of the formal proceedings in Dublin. Those who wanted an outright categorical ban with no exclusions and those who were willing to settle for a comparatively limited treaty were troubled by the perceived direction of the formal deliberations.

Additionally, with the initiation of the Oslo Process, overt criticism of states arguably became bounded by the requirement to keep mutual respectful dialogue between those involved. Although it had become increasingly clear that many governments had, for decades, made ungrounded claims regarding the rigor of their understanding of cluster munitions' humanitarian effects, such gross failings of political accountability were rarely mooted as part of the Oslo Process. As a matter of diplomacy between a group of individuals, those partaking in the discussions adopted diplomatic (read: bounded) kinds of criticisms of each other – at least in public.

Professor Brian Rappert, based at the University of Exeter, has written widely on the social and ethical dilemmas associated with scientific and technical expertise. He has contributed to international discussions on weapons issues, including cluster munitions and biological weapons.

makers directly. Although this raises questions of legitimacy and representativeness, which will be addressed below in the examination of some of the criticisms of the process, the success of the campaign suggests that a relatively small network can have significant impact.

For example, the CMC's experience was that one good contact with a strong relationship in a key country can be more important and have more of an impact than a major public campaign in that country. The value of a coalition is that all of these contacts can work together in the same direction. Similarly, strategic media work that targets decision-makers at key moments will amplify the significance of the campaign and make pressure felt where it counts. In the UK, a campaign by Landmine Action in 2007 targeted then Foreign Minister David Miliband with a large advertisement in Westminster tube station that read: 'Cluster bombs: get them Milibanned'. It is always difficult to assess the impact of such campaigns, but the following passage from a US Embassy cable published by Wikileaks is instructive. The passage refers to comments by senior UK Foreign and Commonwealth Office official Mariot Leslie:

> Leslie explained that [Her Majesty's Government] was experiencing much of the same public and political pressure to ban [cluster munitions] that the Norwegians felt. She noted [Foreign Secretary] Miliband had been targeted personally with posters saying 'Cluster Munitions should be Milibanned!' [Her Majesty's Government], therefore, needed to be seen cooperating with the process and 'could not just walk away'. (Wikileaks 2011)

During the final negotiations for the prohibition in Dublin, the CMC undertook an advertising campaign aimed at fostering a sense amongst delegates that the issue that they were there to debate was the most important issue in town. Advertisements were placed in strategic locations along the routes that delegates were most likely to take, around their accommodation and outside the conference venue.

The coalition's budget throughout the campaign was also relatively modest. There was only one fulltime member of staff until the beginning of 2007; at its peak, the coalition had five full-time employees. The campaign never had a budget for mass public mobilisation; rather it focused on supporting member organisations around the world (including through a small grants programme) and maximising strategic moments, in particular the key

negotiating conferences, for which the coalition helped finance the participation of civil society (Moyes and Nash 2011).

Criticisms of the Cluster Munition Ban Process

Almost all of the existing analysis of the international efforts to prohibit cluster munitions, and the 2008 Convention on Cluster Munitions that resulted from it, is broadly positive (Borrie 2009, Rappert and Moyes 2009, 2010, Bolton and Nash 2010, Nystuen and Casey-Maslen 2010). Some have criticised the prohibition of cluster munitions from an ideological standpoint that rejects the constraining of state sovereignty (Heritage Foundation 2011). Others have suggested that the prohibitions on mines and cluster munitions are peripheral to the central challenges of controlling the means of violence (Cooper 2011). The next section considers some of the main strands of criticism that exist, even though this chapter's primary goal is to analyse the workings of the coalition, and not the value of the end result.

The Process

Certain states, such as the United States, Brazil and India, have consistently criticized the Oslo Process for undertaking multilateral negotiations outside the traditional conventional weapons negotiating forum, the Convention on Certain Conventional Weapons.[12] The argument goes that such freestanding initiatives amongst like-minded states risk damaging the existing multilateral system. States that were unwilling to be paralysed by the consensus practice within the traditional negotiating forum, like Norway, were criticised for circumventing the accepted channels of diplomacy and marginalising states that disagreed with them. In fact, looking at the history of initiatives to advance the protection of civilians and the laws of war, it is not unusual for a number of likeminded states working in ad hoc processes with international and non-governmental organisations to develop standards whose norms are then adopted by a wider group of states. From the first Geneva Convention, adopted by only twelve nations in 1864, to the prohibition of antipersonnel landmines in 1997, norm creation has often involved broadening out from an initial group. Similarly, processes such as the negotiation of the International Criminal Court (ICC) have often been instigated and led by groups of 'likeminded' states together with civil society and international organisations.

Box 8.4
From Treaty Text to Shaping Norms

The Convention on Cluster Munitions (CCM 2008) was signed by 94 countries at the Oslo Signing Conference in December 2008. It had been ratified by 30 states by 16 February 2010, and thus entered into force on 1 August of that year. By the end of August 2011, 109 states had joined the Convention.

However, while the text of the CCM is agreed, the real power of the treaty will be determined by how states deal with cluster munitions in the context that this instrument provides. A common criticism of conventions is that their normative aspirations fail to be matched by concrete actions; another is that treaty text can obscure the necessary path to action.

Whilst the definition of cluster munitions in the text of the CMC is rather complex, the basic prohibition is very simple: states commit not to use, develop, produce, stockpile, or transfer cluster munitions. This simplicity has an important communicative power. Although some states remain outside this legal instrument and so are not formally bound by its terms, the treaty's standard – that cluster munitions are illegal – will be a yardstick against which their actions will be judged regardless.

Such communicative power helps to build a 'stigma' against these weapons – the assumption that they are unacceptable. Indications of the broad stigma that has already developed include Thailand's denial that it used cluster munitions in border clashes with Cambodia early in 2011, and the prominence given to Human Rights Watch's evidence of cluster munitions use by Qadhafi's forces in Misrata, Libya, in April 2011, as well as condemnation of this use by others. By immediately denying use of cluster munitions, both the Thai and Libyan authorities indicated that they did not wish to be associated with the use of a weapon that is now seen in the eyes of the media and the public as unacceptable. A similar scenario unfolded during the conflict between Russia and Georgia over South Ossetia in 2008, even before the Convention was ratified: both sides swiftly denied use, despite conclusive evidence against both parties. Georgia later admitted use, but Russia continues to deny using cluster munitions.

Such stigmatising power of the treaty is set against one of the more problematic areas of the CCM. Article 21 deals with the relationship between states that have endorsed the treaty and states not party to it. It was developed primarily to assuage the anxiety of states that expected to be operating in military alliances with the US (which to date has not adopted the Convention, and which was lobbying such states hard from the sidelines). Operating in such alliances might lead to states inadvertently 'assisting' the US in the use of cluster munitions, thus making them liable to prosecution for breaching the terms of the treaty. Although Article 21 does contain positive elements, notably a positive obligation on states to encourage others to join the Convention, it introduces ambiguity into the text – and it is this ambiguity that some states hope will allow them to continue to operate in military alliances without having to be overly anxious about their partner's stance regarding cluster munitions.

However, it remains to be seen if appeals to complicated loopholes regarding the prohibition on 'assistance' will be sufficient to stand up against the broader dynamic of stigmatisation. It may yet be found that the political risks of using cluster munitions in joint military operations are simply too great. Certainly they have not been used in Afghanistan since the initial phases of the conflict there, and they are most unlikely to be used by US forces in Libya. Too much focus on Article 21 risks overlooking the fact that the viability of certain weapons is likely to turn more on broad concepts of what is acceptable or unacceptable in the public conscience than on the detailed text of the treaty itself.

The complete text of the Convention on Cluster Munitions and a full list of signatories can be found at www.clusterconvention.org.

Richard Moyes, former co-chair of the Cluster Munition Coalition, is Head of Policy at Article 36.

Those states opposed to the prohibition of cluster munitions have steadfastly rejected the notion that the normative power of the Convention on Cluster Munitions will constrain their willingness to use, produce and transfer these weapons in the future (see Box 8.4). They have argued that a comprehensive international instrument must include all of the major potential user countries (Khanna 2011). The lesson from the 1997 Mine Ban Treaty, however, indicates the opposite. Even though the US and a number of other major military powers have not joined the treaty, the only governments that resort to the use of anti-personnel landmines today are regimes such as the Burmese junta and, recently, the forces of Colonel Qadhafi.[13]

The Treaty

Others have questioned why there should be a focus on cluster munitions at all; that a focus on single-issue weapons systems misses the point of the broader picture of conventional weapons and that in this context, the relevance of the prohibition of cluster munitions may be limited (Kidd 2008). There are two primary reasons to counteract these claims. Firstly, the Convention on Cluster Munitions provides a specific framework for states and organisations to address a humanitarian problem and to prevent it from becoming even worse in the future. The majority of donor states have joined the Convention and are working together through an Action Plan agreed in November 2010 to 'accelerate' clearance, 'expand' coverage to victims and survivors and 'increase' the resources to affected countries (The Vientiane Declaration 2010). Additionally, the Convention will prevent the use of hundreds of millions of cluster munitions which are now being destroyed by stockpile states that have joined the treaty. Secondly, the treaty represents another example of how small and medium-sized countries can work together successfully to develop new international standards, even when major powers refuse to cooperate (Bolton and Nash 2010).

The Campaign

So far, there has not been a comprehensive analysis of the Cluster Munition Coalition as a civil society coalition. There are certain points, though, that merit consideration briefly here in order to provide some critical inquiry into the way the campaign worked. Certainly the campaign faced challenges that it had to overcome and some of these are set out below.

There were undoubtedly points when the campaign leadership – the staff and certain members of the coalition's Steering Committee – found themselves disconnected from the broader membership of campaigners. Because of the management of information and communications and the fast-moving and complex nature of the negotiations amongst states, a disparity emerged between a leadership apprised of the nuanced strategic and tactical decisions at play, and the broader group of campaigners around the world. The clearest manifestation of this disconnect took place in relation to the final negotiations on the definition of a cluster munition during the Dublin diplomatic conference in May 2008. During a campaign debrief early on in the two-week negotiating session, the team negotiating on behalf of the CMC reacted positively to a proposal that most campaigners considered to be a weakening of the text as it stood. This led to a tense 24 hours during which the coalition risked being divided, with campaigners unwilling to advocate the negotiating group's suggested messages to states. These tensions were addressed the following morning during a meeting in which interested campaigners were able to question the positions being taken by the negotiators. The statement to that day's forthcoming definitions negotiations was placed on the projector screen and edited until the entire group was comfortable with it (see Borrie 2009: 274–5, Rappert et al. 2011).

Another area of potential tension was the fact that the majority of the active individuals within the leadership of the CMC were from wealthy, primarily northern countries. Although there was a concerted effort to promote diversity in the coalition, as noted above, the fact that member organisations in the north had more money and resources, and therefore time, to devote to the campaign made it easier for them to take up key leadership roles. This is frequently raised as a criticism in the literature on civil society and is likely to be a point of tension for any global civil society coalition (Moyes and Nash 2011: ch. 3). The CMC sought to overcome this tension by supporting active member organisations in the south financially, including through the allocation of grants of up to £6,000 per organisation. In 2008 the CMC's Steering Committee of 13 organisations included members from Latin America, Africa and the Middle East, as well as from Europe and North America.

The coalition's close relationship with Norway also provided a potential bone of contention for some observers. Such criticism was not often articulated publicly, but a US State Department official did make the following oblique reference during a paper in 2008: 'NGOs were allowed to heckle state delegations in plenary and surrounding venues, using funds provided by one state participant to attack the positions of other state participants. Is this the kind of international system that any administration wants to work in?' The 'one state participant' was Norway (Kidd 2008: 119). From late 2006 to the date of writing, the campaign has received significant funding from the government of Norway. In addition, the CMC and the Norwegian government shared a very close political alignment in relation to the protection of civilians, human security and the importance of civil society as a key actor in international affairs. As the Norwegian government had placed a significant political priority, domestically as well as internationally, on the achievement of a ban on cluster bombs, it was logical for senior political leaders in Norway to consider the global coalition as an important and powerful tool in the achievement of this political objective (Borrie 2009). For its part, the CMC was quite transparent about its funding relationship with Norway, acknowledging all of its donors on its website. Since the majority of Norway's funding to the coalition was so-called 'core funding', provided to the institution itself rather than to specific projects, the CMC maintained flexibility to use those funds within a broadly agreed framework. Norway was also not the only donor; a number of other governments, including Ireland, Austria, Switzerland, Canada and Australia, contributed at various stages of the process, as did the Macarthur Foundation and the Diana, Princess of Wales Memorial Fund.

Legitimacy and Representation

These questions of relationships with funder governments also relate to the potential concern with issues of legitimacy and representativeness. Critiques of civil society typically flag up funding from governments as a counter to independent legitimacy, placing constraints on the recipient organisation's willingness to criticise the actions of donor governments. However, in this case, the CMC did not hesitate to criticise Norway when it took up positions that were in conflict with the coalition, and Norway was listed by the CMC as one of the countries of concern during the negotiations on the definition.[14] It was not only funding relationships that raised legitimacy concerns. There is a wider question, often asked in the literature, of which

citizens a transnational advocacy network represents, and on whose behalf it is advocating (VanTuijl and Jordan 1999). As discussed above, the CMC was not a mass movement supported by signed-up members of the public, but rather a network of organisations that represented a broad range of humanitarian, human rights, development and disarmament interests, with support from key sectors of society including women's groups, youth groups, faith-based groups, parliamentarians and others. NGO legitimacy will undoubtedly remain a contested area, but campaigners would be wise to be mindful at all times of their own legitimacy and representativeness. It has been suggested elsewhere that the degree to which data is used with rigour and caution might be one useful measure of legitimacy and accountability:

> As NGO involvement in international decision-making processes increases, so too will the level of scrutiny applied to their legitimacy and accountability. The way NGOs manage themselves and their data and communicate with their constituencies could be deciding factors in measuring their legitimacy and, thus, the legitimacy of the NGO–middle power coalition itself. (Bolton and Nash 2010: 181)

Global civil society coalitions can have an important role to play in bringing about positive change in international affairs. Each coalition may have to find its own way to deal with criticisms, but the experience of the CMC shows that, with the help of existing partnerships, a global campaign with long-lasting implications can be built on limited resources.[15] Those involved with civil society activism – practitioners or observers – may need to accept that there will always be challenges related to NGO legitimacy and representativeness and criticisms over the role of middle-power civil society partnerships. It is important to keep addressing these challenges and criticisms, but it may also be time to move beyond some of these debates, which have been central elements of the literature on global civil society for the past decade. Emerging coalition work to address the impact of explosive weapons when used in populated areas and collective NGO work to promote a commitment by states to record and recognise every casualty of armed violence may well provide further evidence on the importance and effectiveness of civil society coalitions at changing law and policy around the world.[16]

Table 8.1 Chronology of the International Movement to Ban Cluster Bombs

1999	
16 December	In a memorandum for Convention on Conventional Weapons (CCW) delegates, Human Rights Watch (HRW) calls for a moratorium on the use of cluster munitions.
2000	
June	International Committee of the Red Cross (ICRC) issues report, *Cluster Bombs and Landmines in Kosovo*.
2001	
14 June	Norwegian parliament adopts a resolution urging the government to work to achieve an international ban on cluster munitions.
2002	
18 December	HRW issues report, *Fatally Flawed: Cluster Bombs and Their Use by the United States in Afghanistan*.
2003	
23–25 April	Ireland convenes a meeting on ERW in Dublin that is hosted by Pax Christi Ireland. NGOs decide to establish an international coalition to tackle cluster bombs.
13 November	The Cluster Munition Coalition (CMC) is launched in The Hague, Netherlands.
27 November	United Nations (UN) Inter Agency Standing Committee calls for a freeze on the use of cluster munitions.
2004	
28 October	European Parliament calls on EU member states to enact moratoria on the use, stockpiling, production, transfer and export of cluster munitions, and negotiate an international legally binding instrument on the use of cluster munitions.
2005	
June	Norwegian Government Pension Fund excludes eight foreign companies involved in the production of cluster munitions from the fund's investments.
Autumn	Handicap International (HI) Belgium mobilises in Belgium to support the parliamentary process to ban cluster munitions. CMC campaigners support efforts through a global letter-writing campaign to Belgian parliamentarians.
2006	
16 February	Belgian parliament passes first national law in the world banning cluster munitions.
July	Austrian parliament passes a resolution urging the government to support the preparation of a CCW Protocol on cluster munitions and bombs.
25 October	Austria, Holy See, Ireland, Mexico, New Zealand, and Sweden propose a CCW mandate to negotiate a legally-binding instrument to address the humanitarian concerns posed by cluster munitions.
7 November	UN Secretary-General Kofi Annan calls for a 'freeze' on the use of cluster munitions in populated areas and the destruction of 'inaccurate and unreliable' cluster munitions.
17 November	At the CCW, 25 countries issue a joint declaration calling for an agreement that would prohibit the use of unreliable and/or inaccurate cluster munitions in civilian areas.
2007	
22–23 February	Norway hosts the Oslo Conference on Cluster Munitions, where 46 states agree an 'Oslo Declaration'.
2 March	Belgium passes first law in the world to specifically prohibit financing of cluster munitions.
5 November	The CMC calls its first Global Day of Action to Ban Cluster Bombs, in which campaigners in 40 countries take action.
November	CCW states parties fail to agree on a mandate to negotiate a legally binding instrument on cluster munitions and instead agree to 'negotiate a proposal'.
5 December	UN Secretary-General Ban Ki-moon calls for a prohibition on cluster munitions that cause unacceptable harm to civilians.
2008	
19 April	The second Global Day of Action to Ban Cluster Bombs is held, with actions taken by campaigners in 53 countries.
30 May	A total of 107 states adopt the 2008 Convention on Cluster Munitions on the final day of the Dublin negotiations. The CMC and Mines Action Canada launch the 'People's Treaty' petition.
August– September	CMC members protest Georgia and Russia's use of cluster bombs in South Ossetia.
27 October	The CMC calls its first Global Week of Action to Ban Cluster Bombs, in which campaigners in 74 countries take action.
3–4 December	Norway hosts the Oslo Signing Conference for the Convention on Cluster Munitions, attended by 122 states. A total of 94 states sign the Convention in Oslo in front of a CMC delegation of 250 campaigners.
2009	
11 March	President Obama signs into law a permanent ban on nearly all US cluster bomb exports.
18 March	DR Congo signs and Lao PDR ratifies the Convention on Cluster Munitions during a special event held at UN headquarters in New York.
1 May	Cluster bomb survivor Branislav Kapetanovic accepts the Tipperary International Peace Award in Ireland on behalf of the CMC.
29 May	The CMC calls its second Global Week of Action Against Cluster Bombs, with campaigners in 58 countries taking action.
25–26 June	Germany hosts the Berlin Conference on the Destruction of Cluster Munitions, attended by 87 treaty signatories.
2010	
1 August	CCM enters into force with campaigners undertaking actions in 82 countries to celebrate.
9–12 November	First Meeting of States Parties to the Convention on Cluster Munitions held in Vientiane Lao PDR.

Source: This is an abridged chronology; for a full list of regional conferences and reports produced over this time period, see the full chronology at http://www.stopclustermunitions.org.

Notes

1. The membership doubled again from 2007 to 2008 during the key period of the treaty negotiations.
2. Emails from Thomas Nash to the CMC international email distribution list in July and August 2006, on file with the author.
3. See Oslo Conference on Cluster Munitions (2007).
4. For a list of relevant publications see the website of the Cluster Munition Coalition (http://www.stopclustermunitions.org/campaign-resources/reports/).
5. Author's notes from the Expert Meeting on Humanitarian, Military, Technical and Legal Challenges of Cluster Munitions, Montreux, Switzerland, 18–20 April 2007.
6. This respect for the CMC can be seen in the statements from a wide range of governments which praised the CMC during the closing debate at the Dublin Diplomatic Conference in May 2008, and during the Oslo Signing Conference in December 2008. In June 2011, the Lao Assistant Minister of Foreign Affairs referred to 'the great CMC' when introducing the CMC Director, Laura Cheeseman.
7. For more discussion on the treatment of military utility in the negotiating process on the Convention on Cluster Munitions, see Rappert (2008: 21–3) and Borrie (2009: 330–33).
8. For an early discussion of this reframing, see Rappert and Moyes (2006).
9. Whilst the campaign kept a focus on the human suffering from cluster munitions, there was a recognition amongst many campaigners that, in line with interpretations of international humanitarian law, certain civilian deaths and injuries would happen. The key to the concept of 'unacceptable harm to civilians', which underpinned the diplomatic negotiations, was that cluster munitions were exceptional in the harm they caused to civilians.
10. See for example King et al. (2007).
11. See the website of the Ban Advocates at http://www.banadvocates.org/.
12. The Landmine and Cluster Munition Monitor (2010) notes that: 'at the November 2010 meeting, Brazil referred to the Convention on Cluster Munitions as an "illusory achievement" and criticized the "trend" of what it described as "aristocratic multilateralism" amongst like-minded countries'.
13. For up to date details on the use of anti-personnel landmines see Landmine Monitor at http://www.the-monitor.org.
14. See internal CMC lobbying documents from Wellington (February 2008) and Dublin (May 2008), on file with author.
15. For recent work on the mechanics of global civil society coalitions, see Moyes and Nash (2011). An online version of this document is available at http://www.globalcoalitions.org and will be updated and expanded on an ongoing basis.
16. See the International Network on Explosive Weapons at http://www.inew.org and the Every Casualty network http://www.everycasualty.org for more information on these two initiatives.

References

Anderson, Kenneth, and Rieff, David (2004) 'Global Civil Society: A Sceptical View', in Helmut Anheier, Marlies Glasius and Mary Kaldor (eds), *Global Civil Society 2004/5*. London: Sage.

Atwood, D. et al. (2009) 'Learn, Adapt, Succeed: Potential Lessons from the Ottawa and Oslo Processes for Other Disarmament and Arms Control Challenges', *Disarmament Forum*, Vols 1 and 2: 19–25.

Bolton, Matthew and Nash, Thomas (2010) 'The Role of Middle Power-NGO Coalitions in Global Policy: The Case of the Cluster Munitions Ban', *Global Policy*, Vol. 1 No. 2, May 2010: 181.

Borrie, John (2005) 'Rethinking Multilateral Negotiations: Disarmament as Humanitarian Action', in J. Borrie and V. Martin Randin (eds), *Alternative Approaches in Multilateral Decision Making: Disarmament as Humanitarian Action*, May, United Nations.

Borrie, John (2009) *Unacceptable Harm: A History of How the Treaty to Ban Cluster Munitions was Won*, December, United Nations.

Borrie, J. and Randin, V. Martin (eds), (2006a) *Thinking Outside the Box in Multilateral Disarmament and Arms Control Negotiations*, December, United Nations.

Borrie, J. and Randin, V. Martin (eds), (2006b) *Disarmament as Humanitarian Action: From Perspective to Practice*, May, United Nations.

Borrie, J. and Thornton, A. (2008) *The Value of Diversity in Multilateral Disarmament Work*, December, United Nations.

Convention on Cluster Munitions (CCM) (2008) Diplomatic Conference For the Adoption of a Convention on Cluster Munitions, CCM/77, Dublin, 30 May, available at http://www.clusterconvention.org/

Cooper, N. (2011) 'Humanitarian Arms Control and Processes of Securitization: Moving Weapons along the Security Continuum', *Contemporary Security Policy*, Vol. 32 No. 1: 134–58.

Keck, Margaret E. and Sikkink, Kathryn (1998) *Activists beyond Borders: Advocacy Networks in International Politics*. Ithaca and London: Cornell University Press.

Edwards, Michael and Gaventa, John (eds) (2001) *Global Citizen Action*. Boulder: Lynne Rienner Publishers.

Finnemore, Martha and Sikkink, Kathryn (1998) 'International Norm Dynamics and Political Change', *International Organization*, Vol. 52 No. 4, Autumn: 887–917.

Florini, Ann M. (ed.) (2001) *The Third Force: the rise of transnational civil society*. Washington DC: Brookings Institution.

Harrison, Katherine and Moyes, Richard (2009) *Ambiguity in Practice: Benchmarks for the Implementation of CCW Protocol V*. London: Landmine Action.

Heritage Foundation (2011) 'The US Should Not Join the Convention on Cluster Munitions', Backgrounder 2550, 28 April.

International Committee of the Red Cross (ICRC) (2007) *Humanitarian, Military, Technical and Legal Challenges of Cluster Munitions*, Montreux, Switzerland, 18–20

April, http://www.mineaction.org/downloads/1/ICRC%20 expert%20meeting%20report.pdf (accessed 30 August 2011).

Kidd, Richard (2008) 'Is There a Strategy for Responsible U.S. Engagement on Cluster Munitions?', *DISAM Journal*, September, http://www.disam.dsca.mil/pubs/Vol%2030_3/Kidd.pdf (accessed 30 August 2011).

King, C., Dullum, O. and Østern, G. (2007) *M85: An Analysis of Reliability*, Norwegian People's Aid.

Khanna, Melanie (2011) 'U.S. Statement at First Round of Negotiations for a Protocol on Cluster Munitions in the CCW', 21 February, http://geneva.usmission.gov/2011/02/23/2011-ccw/ (accessed August 30 2011).

Landmine and Cluster Munition Monitor (2011) 'Statement of Brazil, CCW Meeting of the High Contracting Parties, Geneva, 25 November 2010', Brazil country profile, http://www.the-monitor.org/custom/index.php/region_profiles/print_profile/231 (accessed 30 August 2011).

Moyes, Richard and Nash, Thomas (2011) *Global Coalitions: An Introduction to Working in International Civil Society Partnerships*. London: Action on Armed Violence.

Nash, Thomas (2006) *Foreseeable Harm: The Use and Impact of Cluster Munitions in Lebanon: 2006*. London: Landmine Action.

Nystuen, Gro and Casey-Maslen, Stuart (2010) *The Convention on Cluster Munitions: A Commentary*. Oxford: Oxford University Press.

Oslo Conference on Cluster Munitions (2007) *Declaration*, 23 February, http://www.regjeringen.no/upload/UD/Vedlegg/Oslo%20Declaration%20(final)%2023%20February%202007.pdf (accessed 30 August 2011).

Petrova, M. H. (2010) *Banning Obsolete Weapons or Reshaping Perceptions of Military Utility: Discursive Dynamics in Weapons Prohibitions*. Barcelona: Institut Barcelona d'Estudis Internacionals (IBEI).

Price, Richard (1998) 'Reversing the Gun Sights: Transnational Civil Society Targets Landmines', *International Organisation*, Vol. 52 No. 3: 613–44.

Rappert, Brian (2005) *Out of Balance: The UK Government's Efforts to Understand Cluster Munitions and International Humanitarian Law*. London: Landmine Action.

Rappert, Brian (2008) *A Convention Beyond the Convention*. London: Landmine Action.

Rappert, Brian and Moyes, Richard (2006) *Failure to Protect: A Case for the Prohibition of Cluster Munitions*. London: Landmine Action.

Rappert, Brian and Moyes, Richard (2009) 'The Prohibition of Cluster Munitions: Setting International Precedents for Defining Inhumanity', *Non-proliferation Review*, Vol. 16 No. 2: 237–56.

Rappert, Brian and Moyes, Richard (2010) 'Enhancing the Protection of Civilians from Armed Conflict: Precautionary Lessons', *Medicine, Conflict & Survival* 26(1) January–March: 24–47.

Rappert, Brian, Moyes, Richard and Other, A. N. (2011) 'Statecrafting Ignorance: Strategies for Managing Burdens, Secrecy, and Conflict', in Susan Maret (ed.), *Part III: Government Secrecy: Current Policy (Research in Social Problems and Public Policy, Vol. 19)*, Emerald Group Publishing Limited, pp. 301–24.

Tarrow, Sidney (1998) *Power in Movement: Social Movements and Contentious Politics*, 2nd edn. Cambridge: Cambridge University Press.

The Vientiane Declaration (2010) 'No Cluster Munitions; From Vision To Action', adopted at the First Meeting of States Parties to the Convention on Cluster Munitions, November, http://www.clusterconvention.org/files/2011/01/V-declaration.pdf (accessed 30 August 2011).

Van Tuijl, Peter and Jordan, Lisa (2009) 'Political Responsibility in Transnational NGO Advocacy', October, http://www.bicusa.org/en/Article.138.aspx (accessed 30 August 2011).

WikiLeaks (2011) 'International Security Discussions with Hmg', Diplomatic Cable from the US Embassy in London, 6 March, printed in the *Telegraph*, http://www.telegraph.co.uk/news/wikileaks-files/london-wikileaks/8305077/INTERNA-TIONAL-SECURITY-DISCUSSIONS-WITH-HMG.html (accessed 15 August 2011).

Williams, Jody, Goose, Stephen D. and Wareham, Mary (2008) *Banning Landmines: Disarmament, Citizen Diplomacy, and Human Security*. Lanham: Rowman & Littlefield.

Wisotzski, S. (2009) *Between Morality and Military Interests: Norm Setting in Humanitarian Arms Control*. Frankfurt am Main: Peace Research Institute Frankfurt.

PART IV

Economy and Society

CHAPTER 9

GLOBAL CIVIL SOCIETY AND THE RISE OF THE CIVIL ECONOMY

Robin Murray

A New Millennium

Ten years is a long time in economics. The decade opened with the Nasdaq crash and finished with a world financial crisis, which hit first the banks, then national governments, and is now calling at the doors of the international financial institutions. The world's mass production continued its move to the East, with the result that by the end of the decade China alone had doubled its share of world GDP (gross domestic product – from 7 per cent to 13 per cent in relative purchasing power) and had become the world's largest manufacturer, its largest exporter and, by 2011, its second largest economy. That growth has darkened further another shadow: climate change. The past decade has witnessed the highest average temperatures on record, with the Arctic ice cap melting to an all-time low.

At the same time over these ten years, the Web economy has taken off. Google was only two years old at the start of the millennium. At that point it had developed an infrastructure of 6,000 web servers and indexed 1.3 billion webpages. It now runs 1 million servers in data centres globally, has an index of 46 billion webpages and processes 1 billion searches a day. And this is just one marker of the growth of a new economy of the ether, one that operates in cyberspace and makes its connections by airwaves and spectrums rather than roads and railways.

This is a discordant symphony, with its powerful global contraflows of creation, crisis and destruction. Yet it had its counterpart in the continuing and ever expanding response to globalisation from civil society – part-political, part-cultural, part-economic. From time to time this response has made the headlines, but for the most part it has spread through a multitude of initiatives that, taken together, may shape the nature and direction of the world's economic future.

Global Civil Society

Ten years ago, in the launch volume of the *Global Civil Society* yearbook, the editors defined civil society as 'the sphere of ideas, values, institutions, organisations, networks and individuals located between the family, the state and the market and operating beyond the confines of national societies, polities and economies' (Anheier et al. 2001: 17). It was autonomous and interstitial and challenged both the state and the multinational corporate economy.

In its twentieth-century conceptual origins and in the studies that the yearbooks have contained, the notion of civil society is first and foremost a political one. Developed within the context of dictatorial states, and in what was increasingly experienced as an absolutist global market economy, civil society created both spaces of survival and platforms for contesting the existing order. How this contest has developed since the first yearbook is one strand of the story of the past decade.

The economy is a central theme of that story. The chapters in the yearbooks have discussed the various positions taken by civil society movements in relation to the great contemporary economic issues: international money and trade, aid and the environment, and the many global dimensions of labour – wages, trade unions, the insistent surge of international migration. On these issues, and in specific sectors like water and food, or the media and sport, the movements have mounted a political challenge to the policies and practices of states and the corporate global market. They have contested how others run the economy.

This chapter is about another side to the story, a second strand closely linked to but distinct from the first. It is about the innumerable cases all over the world where people have taken matters into their own hands and set up for themselves. It is a kind of productive democracy, and as such is part of a long-term shift. For much of the twentieth century, the main alternative economic projects were state-driven national ones; however, since 1989 and the fall of the Berlin Wall, there has been a surge in these micro-economic initiatives. It is as if the energy that had been focused on creating alternative national economies has been redirected towards creating new versions of the economy from below.

In some cases these initiatives have been a matter of economic survival. In others, their creators aim to show that another way is possible; a kind of propaganda of practice. There are a growing number of areas where neither the private market nor the state are providing adequate services, and where social initiatives are proliferating as a result. All of these different types have intensified in the past decade, and been further extended by developments in the internet. Taken together, they amount to another form of economy: one that is driven by social and environmental rather than financial imperatives, and is fuelled by a mixture of necessity and enthusiasm. I refer to this as the civil economy.

The Civil Economy

One of the issues in civil society theory is whether or not the concept includes the civil economy. For the civic humanists of the Italian Quattrocento, as for Adam Smith and his Neopolitan contemporary Antonio Genovese, the civil economy was a central element in civil society.[1] It was considered a market economy with autonomy from the state, but embedded within social norms and marked by the principles of trust and reciprocity. For these authors the market was both subordinate to society and helped to reproduce it. As a means of connecting small scale producers it had not yet been coupled to the imperative of capital accumulation, nor the tendency to erode social ties rather than strengthen them.

Once industrial capitalism took off and the market economy was seen more in Hobbesian than in civic terms, a civil society that encompassed the market economy came to be thought of either as grounds for a state that represented the general interest (Hegel), or, later, when the state was clearly imbricated with private capital, as a cultural and political space separate from the economy (Gramsci). It is this latter view which has remained predominant in contemporary analyses of civil society.[2]

The experience of the past 20 years suggests that we need to revise these approaches. First, the civil economy as it has developed is both a cultural and a political space. It is not just an idea or a demand, but an alternative realised in practice. As such it carries political and cultural weight whether or not it is part of a wider social movement. Second, while it may engage both with the market and the state, it is an autonomous productive force, a 'sphere of ideas, values, institutions, organisations, networks and individuals' applied directly to economic production and circulation. It is a significant element in the concept of civil society.

Figure 9.1 shows the civil economy as a subset of a hybrid social economy. The key distinction underpinning

the diagram is not between the market, the state, and some notional third sector, but between those parts of the economy that are driven by social goals (the social economy) and those which are subject to the imperatives of capital accumulation. I see this as the major distinction in contemporary political economy.

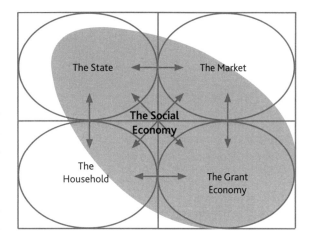

Figure 9.1   The Social Economy

The social economy, represented by the shaded egg-shape in the diagram, overlays the four sub-economies shown in the diagram. These sub-economies are each distinct in how they are financed, in who has access to their outputs and on what terms, what social relations they entail, how any surplus is distributed, and what forms of economic discipline are exercised over them. We can describe them as governed by reciprocity (the household), the gift (the grant economy), the exchange of equivalents (the market), and the combination of levies and bounties (the state). They are not separate economies, but rather represent distinct, semi-autonomous but inter-related economic force fields.

In some cases the state may be functionally integrated into the requirements of capital accumulation, just as the grant economy may act as a subaltern to private corporations or to an incorporated state. But there is nothing intrinsic within the nature of the state, the grant, or the household economies that drives them towards capital accumulation. As economies they are oriented to their own social goals; each can operate in the market in pursuit of their goals without being drawn into the vortex of accumulation.

I have drawn the shaded egg-shape of the social economy (optimistically) large. All the grant economy

Box 9.1
Co-operatives and Global Growth: The Case of Mondragon

Co-operatives are one of the longest established and resilient forms of the civil economy. Having taken off in Europe in the mid nineteenth century, they spread to North America and then to Russia, as part of a thriving civil society that existed before the Soviet revolution (Chayanov 1991, Dowler 2010). There was further expansion during the Great Depression, particularly in the US. In some cases – as in post-colonial Africa – their development has been top-down, driven by states seeking a new form of democratic economy. However, for the most part they have been grassroots reactions to the workings of the mainstream economy.

Having started small, and due to their democratic structure, there has been an underlying resistance to the loss of control that accompanies size. In this sense, co-ops are emblematic of the civil economy. Set against this are the counter-pressures of scale, scope and systemic coordination that are strong drivers of corporate expansion and of globalisation. 'As large as is necessary, as small as is possible' is a motto of the Dutch credit unions, encapsulating the tension between the two.

Globalisation has been a force making the 'necessary' larger. It has pulled many co-ops beyond their home boundaries, particularly those involved with finance and industry. The long-established credit unions or *caisse populaire* – notably in Holland, Germany, France, Austria and the Canadian provinces of Quebec and British Columbia – have had to strengthen their collective bodies and engage internationally (see Figures 9.6, 9.7 and 9.8). There have been similar pressures on industrial co-ops engaged in world markets. The Mondragon group of co-ops – now the seventh largest industrial group in Spain, with €15 billion annual sales – responded to the liberalising of the economy in the 1980s and Spanish entry into the EU by strengthening its central corporate bodies and expanding overseas. Capital goods co-ops established plants close to their clients, and some processes were passed over to subsidiaries in areas of cheaper labour. The 120 Mondragon co-ops (www.mcc.es) now operate 250 plants in 16 countries, including two plants in India and 13 in China (Sanchez Bajo and Roelants 2011).

There is a danger that scale and globalisation leads to the loss of the civil essence of co-operation. In some of the insurance or building society mutuals there is no real sense of ownership by members, with cooperative governance formal rather than real; these are the ones most vulnerable to threats of demutualisation. And even at Mondragon, a former manager described the post-liberalisation group as 'too large, too multinational and too capitalist' (Ramesh 2011); only 50 per cent of Mondragon's 85,000 employees are themselves members.

Yet, even with these limitations, Mondragon, like similar industrial co-ops in Europe, remains distinctly civil. The group's primary interest is the collective welfare of its members and surrounding communities. It has an uncapitalist loyalty to place and social equity. The pay ratio between bosses and shop floor workers is 5:1. Losses in one unit are covered by profits in another. Divisions cannot be sold nor members made redundant. If a plant is forced to close, its workforce has to be re-employed within a 31-mile radius. Workers save a portion of their share of profits, which they realise as a pension. Like all such co-ops, governance is by its members and their primary organisations.

It is striking how many co-operatives have been able, like Mondragon, to couple competitiveness with a civil purpose. Their local rootedness and ethical commitment have been a key part of the trust and consequent commercial success they have enjoyed. Credit unions encourage the local investment of their surpluses, as do the retail co-ops. This explains why they have often become key players in their local and regional economies, as well as proving remarkably resilient in the face of financial crisis.

Other parts of the civil economy have much to learn from how co-operatives have developed such complex capillary systems that marry the economies of scale and specialisation with the benefits of decentralised autonomy. Co-operatives can equally learn from the way in which many of the new actors in the civil economy – particularly in the software, cultural and environmental fields – have developed strong interactive cosmopolitan networks, as well as new forms of productive democracy.

Robin Murray

is included since nominally it is defined as serving social goals. So is a minor segment of the market representing social enterprises, co-operatives and petty producers, such as those small farmers and artisans who operate according to the model of the civic humanists. Some parts of the state are excluded (such as the military), while from the household economy I include all those activities that involve inter-household collaboration, whether of mutual support, common projects, or the voluntary economic activities of social movements.

The civil economy is a subset of this wider social economy. It is represented by those shaded parts of the social economy egg that are autonomous from the state. In some countries and in certain periods, the distinction is minor: there is a close relationship between the state and the other parts of the social economy; they share goals and pool resources. But in other cases – and notably in the global arena – the distinction is significant, particularly where the state or states have been subordinated to the requirements of accumulation. We then have the kind of turbulence that results when two currents run against each other.

What the intersecting figure suggests is that the civil economy is far from homogeneous. It includes enterprises established by professional associations and by intentional communities; inspired by environmentalism or social exclusion. There are charities and foundations, civic associations and numerous other forms of formal and informal cooperation. Many institutions, whether religious organisations, guerrilla movements, prisons, or schools, have their own internal economies. The goals of these diverse organisations may be different, but what is shared is that they are driven by top-line social or institutional goals rather than bottom-line financial ones.

The Re-Emergence of the Civil Economy

The mass production paradigm that dominated twentieth-century economies had little space for the civil economy. The role of the household was to provide labour on the one hand, and a demand for commodities on the other (the $5 day). The home, whose associated daily tasks were themselves revolutionised by the new mass-produced goods, was redefined as a site of passive consumption rather than active production. Wider social provision – from social insurance to health, education and housing – which in the nineteenth century was provided by the civil economy or the private market, was now supplied on a mass basis by the state.

But side by side with the process of globalisation, there is evidence of a surge in new civil economic activity. The expansion of NGOs picks up pace from the mid 1970s and by 2005 the Johns Hopkins Project estimated that the non-profit sector of its 40 sample countries had an operating expenditure of $2.2 trillion and accounted for an average of 5.6 per cent of the workforce. Historical data for five of the countries showed non-profit institutions growing at twice the rate of national GDP (Salamon 2010: 187, 201).[3] There has been a parallel expansion of philanthropic funding: the number of US foundations more than trebled between 1980 and 2009 (from 22,000 to 77,000), with grant-giving rising by nearly a third in real terms from 2000 to reach $45.7 billion in 2010.[4]

These data reflect the US emphasis on the non-profit element of the civil economy. There is an even larger sphere of civil 'for profit' enterprises. One sizeable group are co-operatives, which are estimated to have a worldwide turnover of $3 trillion (ICA 2011). Both nationally and sectorally they have been expanding (see Box 9.1 for more details, and Map 9.1 for a selection of co-operative activity around the world). The number of credit unions, a specific type of financial co-op, went up from 37,000 to 53,000 between 2000 and 2010, their membership grew by two thirds to 188 million, and their total savings more than doubled to $1.2 trillion (see Figures 9.6, 9.7 and 9.8).

While in Europe there is a strong tradition of industrial and consumer co-ops, in the developing world it is agricultural co-ops that have been in the forefront of the movement. In Latin America they were promoted by governments in the early 1980s, then contracted as a result of neoliberal policies. Over the past decade they have revived and expanded not least because of the growth of another recent civil economic movement, fair trade (see Box 9.2). Fair trade global sales trebled between 2005 and 2009 to €3.4 billion, with the UK accounting for over £1 billion (see Figures 9.2, 9.3, 9.4 and 9.5). Three quarters of fair trade is sourced from co-ops, and this has helped to expand and establish new farmer co-ops not only in Central and Latin America, but in Africa and Asia.[5]

There are many social enterprises that are not co-ops. The data have not kept pace with the experience of their growth, social enterprise being only recognised as a category in the early 1990s. An official estimate put their number in the UK in 2010 at 62,000, of which only 8 per cent were co-ops, and evidence from continental

Map 9.1   A Selection of Co-operative Activity Around the World

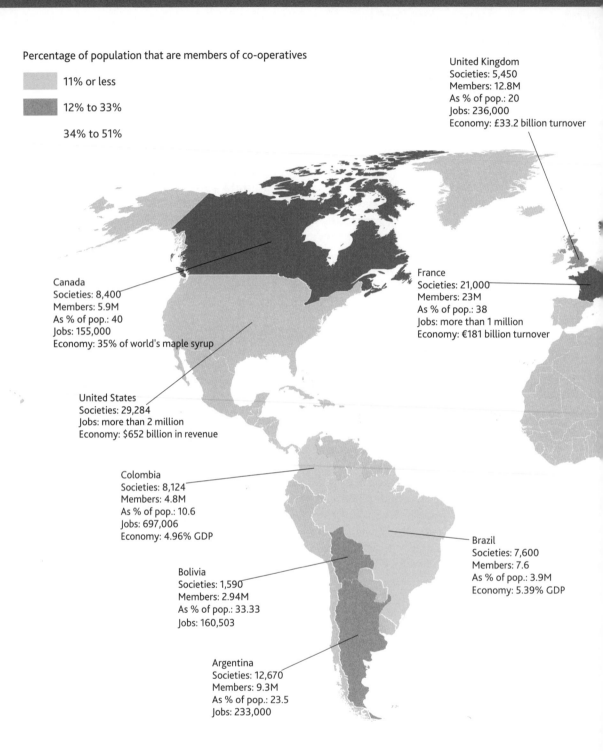

Percentage of population that are members of co-operatives

11% or less

12% to 33%

34% to 51%

United Kingdom
Societies: 5,450
Members: 12.8M
As % of pop.: 20
Jobs: 236,000
Economy: £33.2 billion turnover

Canada
Societies: 8,400
Members: 5.9M
As % of pop.: 40
Jobs: 155,000
Economy: 35% of world's maple syrup

France
Societies: 21,000
Members: 23M
As % of pop.: 38
Jobs: more than 1 million
Economy: €181 billion turnover

United States
Societies: 29,284
Jobs: more than 2 million
Economy: $652 billion in revenue

Colombia
Societies: 8,124
Members: 4.8M
As % of pop.: 10.6
Jobs: 697,006
Economy: 4.96% GDP

Brazil
Societies: 7,600
Members: 7.6
As % of pop.: 3.9M
Economy: 5.39% GDP

Bolivia
Societies: 1,590
Members: 2.94M
As % of pop.: 33.33
Jobs: 160,503

Argentina
Societies: 12,670
Members: 9.3M
As % of pop.: 23.5
Jobs: 233,000

Note: Data on co-operatives are not always comprehensive, and are generally based on the best information available to umbrella organisations in each country. Most of the data here are from 2008 or 2009.

Source: ESRI; The International Co-operative Alliance (http://www.ica.coop/coop/statistics.html), or the websites of their members, accessed in 2011.

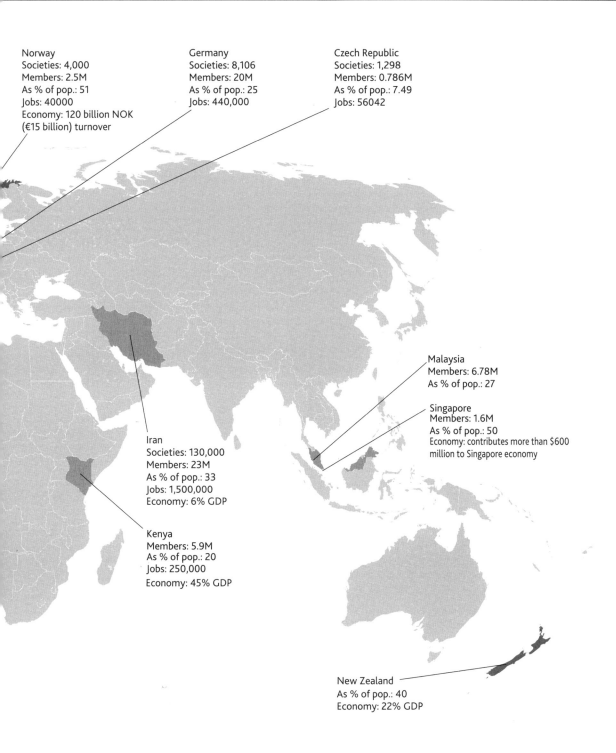

Norway
Societies: 4,000
Members: 2.5M
As % of pop.: 51
Jobs: 40000
Economy: 120 billion NOK
(€15 billion) turnover

Germany
Societies: 8,106
Members: 20M
As % of pop.: 25
Jobs: 440,000

Czech Republic
Societies: 1,298
Members: 0.786M
As % of pop.: 7.49
Jobs: 56042

Malaysia
Members: 6.78M
As % of pop.: 27

Singapore
Members: 1.6M
As % of pop.: 50
Economy: contributes more than $600 million to Singapore economy

Iran
Societies: 130,000
Members: 23M
As % of pop.: 33
Jobs: 1,500,000
Economy: 6% GDP

Kenya
Members: 5.9M
As % of pop.: 20
Jobs: 250,000
Economy: 45% GDP

New Zealand
As % of pop.: 40
Economy: 22% GDP

Europe suggests that there is a similarly large body of social enterprises in addition to formal co-ops.[6]

These data do not cover many of the less formal associations, nor the informal collaborations whose growth has been one of the most striking features of the past decade. But they bear out the general proposition of growth of the civil economy, and help explain the recognition that is now being given to it as a source of human-centred production, employment, and social innovation.

In 2006 the Labour government in the UK established an Office of Third Sector – now the Office of Civil Society. The Obama Administration created an Office of Social Innovation in 2009 and the European Union followed suit by launching Social Innovation Europe from its Enterprise and Industry Secretariat in 2011. The United Nations meanwhile has declared 2012 the International Year of Co-operatives. Having been marginalised and at times attacked during the twentieth century, the civil economy is now being officially promoted on the public stage.

Causes of the Expansion

What accounts for this striking upsurge, what Louis Salamon calls a 'global associational revolution'? One view is that it is the result of globalisation and the neoliberal restructuring of the state (Pawel Zaleski 2006). Another is that it is part of a wider global movement for economic democracy and social justice; a third that it represents a search for identity and meaning by an expanding class of knowledge workers (Drucker 1989). In this chapter I want to identify three forces that I believe have particular relevance:

The Counter Movement of the Marginalised

If we understand the period of globalisation as one of intense creative-destruction in the Schumpeterian sense, the counter movement can be framed in a Polanyian one. Karl Polanyi argued that market liberalism was an unsustainable and utopian project, because it threatened to destroy the social and environmental conditions necessary for a market society to flourish. State-led attempts to impose unregulated liberalism by treating labour, land and money as commodities would provoke a counter movement for the 'self protection of society' led by those suffering at market liberalism's hands. Drawing on the first instance of such an uninhibited liberal project, the 1830s in industrialising Britain, he cites as the counter movement the political campaign of the Chartists, the economic alternative of Owenism and the remarkable growth of co-operation from the 1840s onwards.

There is such a counter movement to global neoliberalism now taking place. La Via Campesina is in many ways a contemporary parallel to the Chartists. It was formed by peasant movements in 1993 and has grown and strengthened in the past decade, its members now representing 500 million peasants and family farmers from both the developing world and North America, Europe and Japan. Their platform has strong echoes of Polanyi. 'We do not own nature – it is not a commodity' (La Via Campesina 2011). They demand domestic food sovereignty as a means of protecting a peasant life based on reciprocity and rural ecology against the unregulated and unequal power of international markets. It is a political movement on a global scale. It is also an economic one, the rural equivalent of Owenism. It has involved the strengthening of peasant co-operatives and of ecological farming practices and the expansion of control by these co-operatives of the food chain nationally and internationally (through fair trade).

Many similar responses are found in towns and communities, all over the world, hit by structural adjustment and liberal trade policies. In the south, Argentina – hit by the default crisis of 2001–02 – exemplifies the growth of civil economic initiatives provoked by crisis. They range from the development of local currencies to the takeover of 200 abandoned industrial plants (the *fabricas recuperadas*) by worker co-operatives, all but four of which are still operating.[7]

In the north, a flourishing movement for community economic development sprung up in Canada. It was concentrated in those places hit by industrial decline after the introduction of the North American Free Trade Agreement in 1990, as well as among marginalised areas such as declining fishing communities or people from the First Nations. In Europe, a strong current in the expansion of the civil economy has been the so-called 'work integration social enterprises' that are geared towards creating jobs for those excluded from the labour market.[8]

What runs through these counter movements is a spirit of self-reliance, a strong sense of human (and in many cases ecological) well-being as the starting point for any economy, and an opposition to neoliberalism. In the words of the Landless Workers Movement (the MST) in Brazil, 'the enemy is the model'.

Economic alternatives

Although counter movements have traditionally sprung from the marginalised, what is striking in the current era is that there is a second counter movement that is lodged

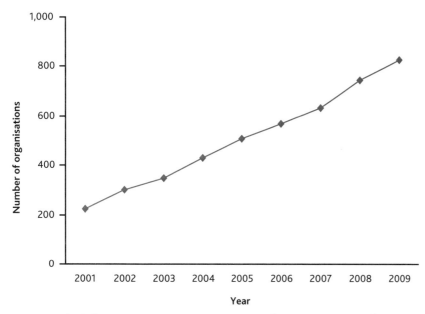

Source: Fairtrade Labelling Organisations International Annual Reports (2007 and 2009–10 reports).

Figure 9.2   Numbers of Fair Trade Certified Producer Organisations Worldwide, 2001–09

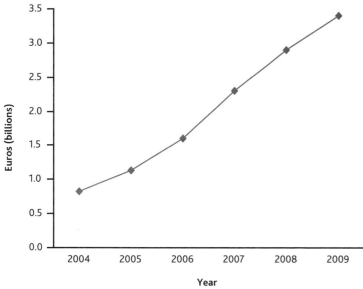

Source: As Figure 9.2.

Figure 9.3   Estimated Global Fair Trade Retail Sales in Billions of Euros, 2004–09

Box 9.2
The Rise and Rise of Fair Trade

Fair trade has risen as a counterpoint to neoliberalism. The term 'fair trade' was first used in 1988, a year that saw a sudden surge of new solidarity trading projects. They took a variety of forms and followed different economic paths. What has been common to them all is the attempt to resocialise the market, to make it an instrument for the redistribution of power and resources and redraw the institutional architecture of international trade.

Initially the contacts were contingent and direct. Fair trade in Japan, for example, began with drama. A group of dispossessed sugar workers from the island of Negros in the Philippines were invited to Japan to perform their story to the members of a large consumer co-operative. As a result of their tour, Altertrade (www.altertrade.co.jp) was founded in 1988 to provide a market for whatever the sugar workers were able to produce. Finding artisan sugar a difficult product to sell at the time, they then switched successfully to an unusual local variety of organic bananas. Twenty years later they export $30 million of these bananas annually (see Figure 9.5 for a comparison of the growth of fair trade sugar and bananas).

The secret of Altertrade's success has been the direct link between the producers and the consumer co-op. They refer to this as 'people to people trade' and support it with a programme of mutual visits and exchanges. Other products from neighbouring countries have since been added (notably shrimps and coffee). In each case the aim has been to provide export earnings to finance the development of the kind of self-reliant agriculture that La Via Campesina has campaigned for at the global level.

Such an approach requires three things: farmer co-operatives, some form of consumer organisation, and an accountable intermediary to organise the trade. Together they allow the goods to bypass mainstream retail chains, the consumer network acting as a retail bridgehead for multiple fair trade products. Altermercato (www.altromercato.it), the largest fair trader in Italy with a turnover of $48 million, is another version of this model. Also founded in 1988, it is a network of 125 solidarity co-ops that run 300 *botteghe del mondo* (world shops). They jointly own CTM, a co-operative wholesale importer, which sources the products sold in the shops and acts as a connector between its co-operative suppliers and consumers.

We could say that these shops carry within them the political economy of the world in one hundred objects. The products each have their own narrative – a bunch of bananas comes from a Costa Rican co-op established after Chiquita's closure of its plantations; a packet of spaghetti is produced by a co-op of people with learning difficulties on land confiscated from the Mafia in Sicily. The shops act as centres of such storytelling, stories that those coming to the shops can then play a part in, whether simply as shoppers, or as champions of the products and their producers. And whether the visitors are schools, municipalities, local businesses, or simply passing individuals, the shops offer a site for engagement. Run on the basis of enthusiasm by 6,000 volunteers, with the support of 400 paid staff, Altermercato is a movement that takes the form of shopkeeping.

In North America, such direct trade originated with religious groups like the Mennonites and the Church of the Brethren, who had for some time been selling crafts through churches, bazaars and shops supporting the developing world. Oxfam and Traidcraft had similar craft origins in the UK; Traidcraft also established a mail order catalogue, on similar lines of Pueblo to People in the US. Initially at least, these were alternative traders, independent of the mainstream.

As fair trade took root, there was pressure, not least from the producers, to engage directly with the mainstream. One path, exemplified by Twin Trading (www.twin.org.uk) in the UK, has been to develop fair trade brands. The economic rationale behind this was that it was in branding that the main surplus was to be found; producers therefore needed to have their own brands. Twin had been founded in 1985 to help post-revolutionary countries in the South, but in 1989 switched direction to support Mexican coffee co-operatives hit by the collapse of the International Coffee Agreement and the slump in prices.

After two years of successful green coffee trading, Twin and the producer co-ops decided to establish their own coffee brand. In co-operation with other fair trade sales networks, they formed Cafedirect (www.cafedirect.co.uk), which became a flagship for fair trade in Britain. It was sold predominantly through mainstream supermarkets and coffee shops and by 2005 had become the sixth largest coffee brand in the UK. The brand profits meant that Cafedirect could pay up to three times world market prices and fund an extensive programme of technical support for the producers. It was a model aimed at reversing the direction of power in the supply chain, and Twin extended it into cocoa (Divine; www.divinechocolate.com), fresh fruit (Agrofair UK), and nuts (Liberation; www.chooseliberation.com) all of them, including Twin itself, co-owned by the producers.

Branding lacked the direct connection with consumers but it widened the market. Its product range, however, was limited, for it took seven to ten years to establish a successful producer-led brand. The major market widening came through another channel, the generic mark. The first fair trade mark was established in Holland in 1988 by the liberation theology group Solidaridad (www.solidaridadnetwork.org) and a Dutch priest, Fritz van der Hoff, who had been working with small coffee farmers in Mexico.

It was an immediate success. It could be carried by any coffee that met the set criteria, and over the next nine years the idea spread to many products and countries. In 1997 the national marks combined to form the Fair Trade Labelling Organisation (FLO; www.fairtrade.net) – an international body that ensures consistency of the criteria and the main product lines of the mark's global expansion (see Figure 9.2).

While solidarity groups had pioneered the concept and the practice of fair trade, and continued to grow (their current turnover is some $200 million), the mark radically extended it. FLO registered sales rose from €220m in 2000 to €3.4billion in 2009 (see Figure 9.3). Of the sales total, a third is in the UK, where all the main supermarkets carry fair trade products and 70 per cent of consumers recognise the mark.

Has the mark diluted fair trade by its engagement with the mainstream, or significantly changed the mainstream by drawing it into fair trade? This is the point of tension. On the one hand, there are pressures to weaken fair trade criteria. Rival labels like Rainforest Alliance and Utz Kapeh have sprung up which lack the small farmer focus, the price guarantees and advance credit requirements of FLO. They have come to dominate some continental European markets, putting pressure on FLO, while Transfair, the US fair trade label, has sought to modify FLO criteria to meet the requirements of major multinationals. When multinational brands like Nestlé, Cadbury, Starbucks and even Chiquita register some of their products as fair trade, it threatens to drain the concept of its meaning.

On the other hand, fair trade has expanded its own autonomous economy. In the South it has strengthened small farmer co-operatives against the forces of the world market. Some have developed joint marketing organisations, as well as their own processing capacity. They are increasingly providing each other with consultancy and advice. There are international co-operative groups of small farmer co-ops dealing with coffee, fresh fruit and nuts, and regional groups of small farmer co-ops in Latin America, Africa and Asia. The principles of 'commercio justo' have now been taken up by Latin American governments through the Bolivarian Alliance for Peoples of the Americas (ALBA), which provides for minimum price guarantees, advanced credit, and development financing for small farmer co-ops exporting within the nine-country alliance.

In the North, fair trade has spilled over from the checkout. In Britain, trade justice campaigners declared the small town of Garstang a fair trade town in 2000. The idea spread with the force of a fire. There are now nearly 500 fair trade towns in the UK and 336 in other countries, including in Costa Rica and Brazil. In Britain there are also 60 fair trade universities, 1,500 fair trade schools and 4,000 fair trade faith groups. Wales has even announced itself as the first fair trade country. They are drivers in the growth of ethical consumption – in the proposition that there is a politics in what you buy.

The core idea of fair trade remains strong. It represents a form of globalisation from below. Its extension into the mainstream market, and now via ALBA into government policy, is a mark of its success. Many of the studies of its impact focus on the economic gains for producers, but its significance goes well beyond that. It has enhanced the power of producer co-operative organisations. It has developed institutions that provide markers for new forms of global economic governance. And it has issued a general invitation to look beyond the appearance of commodities and inquire into the conditions of their production – part of a wider trend towards a new era of economic transparency.

Robin Murray

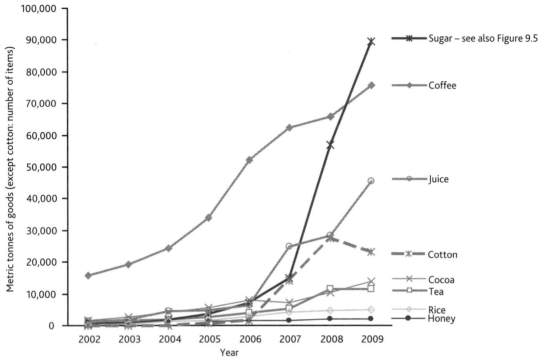

Source: Fairtrade International's annual reports, from 2003/04–2009/10. http://www.fairtrade.net/annual_reports.0.html.

Figure 9.4   Growth in Volumes of Fair Trade Labelled Products, 2002–09

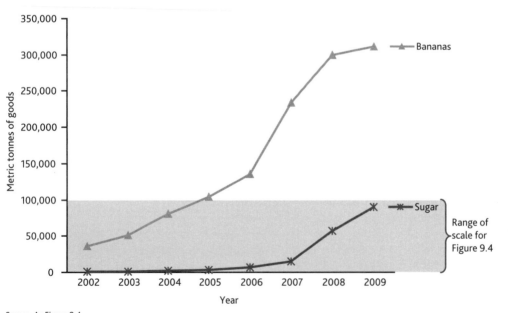

Source: As Figure 9.4.
Notes: 2010 figures not available at time of going to press. Cotton figures only published from 2005.

Figure 9.5   Growth in Volumes of Fair Trade Labelled Products, 2002–09: Bananas and Sugar

at the heart of the mainstream. It argues for alternatives not just for those people and places abandoned by the market, but for the core structures of the mainstream itself. The alternatives that it promotes are not, as in the 1930s, about national models of economic management – more or less central planning – but about the very models of production and consumption that prevail in the world economy, whether private or public, planned or unplanned.

The leading challenge to the status quo has come from the environmental movement, not only in the field of resources – energy, water, waste, forests and farming – but also against the oil-based, resource-intensive and hazardous character of the economy as a whole. The challenge has been at the same time particular and universal, directed at both the policies of governments and the practices of corporations. In each case successful campaigners have recognised that they first needed to develop their own alternatives. Some have established laboratories to show that products could be made without the use of hazardous chemicals; others started solar companies and local wind co-ops. Many countries saw the growth of community recycling networks, and social companies have built zero-energy housing. In Brazil there were remarkable social innovations in low-powered rural electrification. A recent catalogue listed 110,000 environmental initiatives of this kind.

Similar stories are increasingly common in other fields: in the media there are leading newspapers owned by trusts (like the *Guardian*) and a growing number of community cable channels; in the field of finance, there has been the widespread growth of credit unions (see Figures 9.6, 9.7 and 9.8) and socially-driven micro credit enterprises. Football fans are not only fighting the finance-driven ownership of football, but are starting their own clubs or taking over ones in difficulty; Real Madrid, Barcelona and Benefica are all co-operatives. Campaigns against industrial food chains have generated a remarkable alternative food economy, from organic farming and local processing to consumer food co-operatives; in Japan, for example, the latter have 12 million members (ICA 2011). In health and personal services there has been a flowering of campaigns and development of alternative services, from birthing to education and on through each stage of life, to the care of the aged and to dying and mourning.

This remarkable growth of civil alternatives can, at least in part, be seen as a Polanyian counter movement to the commodification of labour, nature and money. He no doubt would have felt his propositions confirmed by the rise and strength of opposition to the industrial destruction of nature and to the inequalities to which that gives rise, as he would by the growth of alternative finance. But many of these alternatives go beyond Polanyi's categories. They concern alternative forms of consumption, of ways of living and caring, of being human in the widest sense. And they are also a counter not only to the impact of a disembedded market, but also to the limitations of a particular model of the administration of the state.

The ICT Revolution

It is one thing to develop counter movements and civil alternatives; quite another for them to have more than marginal significance or to shift the structure of economic control. It is striking that some of the civil innovations are taken up by private corporations (zero-energy housing for example, or fair trade) or adopted by the state (the hospice movement in palliative care, for example); one way in which the civil economy and its significance is now being viewed is as a source of social innovation for the private market and the state.

What this reflects is the emergence of problems for which neither the market nor the state, in their current forms, has persuasive answers. Multiple environmental issues are such an example; the twenty-first-century epidemics of diabetes and obesity, another. Chronic disease more generally, together with issues of funding and caring for an ageing population, are described as time bombs for health care and public budgets. Then there is the incessant widening of the gap between rich and poor, exacerbated by the crisis of private and public finance. The civil economy has been a laboratory for alternatives on all these issues.

The question is whether these alternatives can be incorporated into the forms of the private market and the state as they stand, or whether there will have to be a change in those forms. Does the civil economy have a long-term place in the next economic phase, rather than being merely a pressure valve, a provider of first aid, and a source of innovative prototypes?

The answers may be found partly in the counter movements and the extent to which they can reshape the mainstream. But there are also significant forces that are expanding the civil economy that have arisen from within the womb of the mainstream itself. This is a departure from Polanyi, because these forces are less about the 'self protection of society' from erosion by the market, than the creation of new productive relations from within capitalism itself. Put schematically, the last decade has

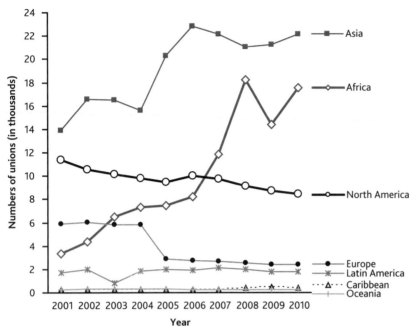

Source: 2010 Statistical Report, World Council of Credit Unions.

Figure 9.6   Numbers of Credit Unions, by Region, 2001–10

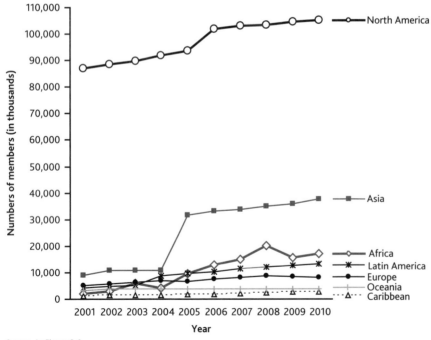

Source: As Figure 9.6.

Figure 9.7   Numbers of Members of Credit Unions, by Region, 2001–10

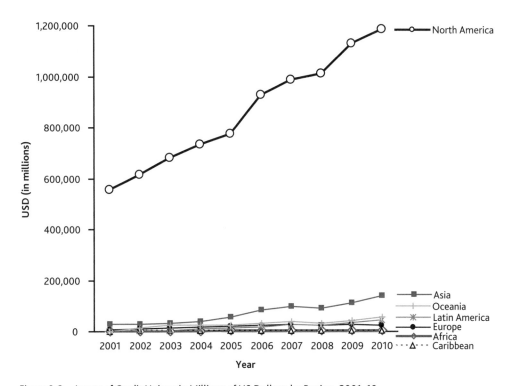

Figure 9.8　Assets of Credit Unions in Millions of US Dollars, by Region, 2001–10

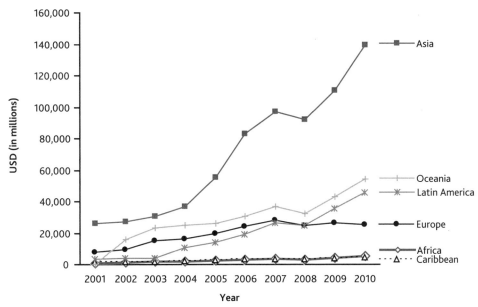

Source: 2010 Statistical Report, World Council of Credit Unions.

Inset: Assets of Credit Unions in Millions of US Dollars, by Region, excluding North America

shown, in outline, how the ICT revolution is opening a space for the civil economy to play an active and in some cases a leading role in production.

I want to touch on three aspects of this revolution:

1. The return of the micro. The ICT revolution underpinned a paradoxical feature of globalisation. On the one hand, it has allowed corporations to manage complex systems on a much wider scale. Retailers, who along with banking and the military, were pioneers in the use of the new technology, are now managing up to 80,000 product supply chains to as many as 10,000 stores worldwide with the aid of modern information systems. Such a capacity has been a major factor in corporate global expansion from the 1980s onwards.[9]

On the other, the technology has led to the return of the micro. At the heart of ICT is micro-electronics. Its characteristic capital good is not the large 'satanic mill' of the industrial revolution but the micro-computer, so small that it has now become available to any consumer who can afford a 'smart' phone. In energy generation, solar panels, heat pumps and mini combined heat-and-power boilers turn the home into a power station. The latest machinery used for industrial production can be sized to fit into a garage. Mini-mills have sprung up for the production of steel and for paper. Small is being rendered not just beautiful but economic.

Some of these micro-technologies realise the Gandhian dream of a technology that is open to local control. In brewing, for example, the consumer movement that campaigned against mass-industrialised beer has been able to start up numerous micro-breweries, some owned by their consumers.[10] In other cases these micro-capital goods are part of larger systems: locally-generated domestic energy, for example, may be connected to other micro-suppliers via smart grids; local convenience stores are linked together through retail networks.

This model of distributed systems potentially increases the autonomy of those on the front line as workers, users and communities, by distributing complexity to the margins. It also involves profound institutional and technical changes, calling into question the role of the old, administration-heavy, central institutions (whether corporations and central states or utilities, hypermarkets and hospitals). In many areas it is these 'systems economies' that are more important than 'scale economies', with power and control passing to so-called 'systems integrators'. The key question then becomes who controls the design and management of the systems.[11]

In many parts of the private economy, giant corporations have designed their systems to increase control from the centre. While this allows for a degree of outsourcing, the micro-producers are merely part of a modern, often global, putting out system. But as often it is the micro-producers who have formed and control the systems, enabling them to combine the benefits of autonomy – creativity, flexibility, and motivation – with the advantages of scale, which are provided in this case by inter-firm federations and consortia, and by local intermediary institutions such as banks, colleges, and specialist research centres.

This explains the continued resilience of the Italian and Spanish co-operative industrial districts, the food and livelihood co-ops in Japan, and the small-scale shoe-producers in Brazil; the dominance of the credit unions in Quebec, and the success of the Mittelstand in Germany. Up until the 1980s these were regarded as relics of the past.[12] Within 20 years they have been taken up as a model for the future.

The civil economy is at the heart of these systems, involving the household and the local state along with co-operative and family firms, and bound together by strong social bonds – or 'social capital', as it has come to be called. It is a model being adopted in other fields, by energy co-ops, in social care and among networks of co-operative schools, providing an alternative way of governing complex systems.

2. The new consumer. The passive consumer of the mass production age is now being recognised as an active producer – or 'prosumer' – in the present one. Of course this has long been the case; it is just that domestic work has not been acknowledged within a market economic model. But now the work of the market is crossing the domestic threshold. One factor is the availability of the micro-capital goods mentioned above. The home is becoming not just a power station but the new workshop: an office, a print works, even a recording studio.

Another factor is the incorporation of consumers into industrial and service production. New flexible production systems are involving consumers in co-design and co-production. Toyota have been a pioneer of these new forms of mass customisation. As a purchaser of a Toyota house – and the company produces 10,000 houses a year – you can spend a weekend with an architect, designer and a whole park of model houses, parts and visualisations, deciding on everything from your new home's shape and size to its decoration and fittings. This becomes an I-house, just as a Dell computer is an

I-computer. Lego even helps its consumers to design their own models.[13]

Much of this relates to individual households being drawn into the world of private market production – that part lying outside the shaded egg-shape in Figure 9.1. But this type of active consumption cannot be contained. Clubs form. Home workers attach themselves to hubs. A social market arises for training, support, advice, and troubleshooting – the things that are required for anyone involved in production.

These trends of prosumption apply even more in services. In expanding environmental services, like recycling, or household energy and water management, the householder plays a key part in the productive cycle. The same is true of relational services, such as health, education, and in many aspects of social care in which the 'user' is both the subject and object of production.

Relational services have three characteristics: first, relationship and trust are central to the efficacy of the service; second, there are limits to the extent that labour can be substituted by machinery, since it is the human relationship that remains central; third, each involves not only the user but the voluntary help of those around them. They have been called 'I-services', with packages of support assembled around the particular requirements of the user. These packages are often most effective when they are drawn from all the four economic spheres shown in Figure 9.1, with the user and the volunteer working side by side with a supportive professional.[14]

Both the private and public sectors have provided such services, and have sought to adapt to the relational requirements of, say, elder care or higher education. One strand of public sector reform, for example, has been to try and incorporate those involved in the decision-making process. Health and social services have been 'co-created' and 'co-produced'. Greater weight has been given to users, both individually, through personal budgets, or collectively, through feedback websites such as Patient Opinion (http://www.patientopinion.org.uk).

It is no accident that these services are the ones that have seen a rapid growth in the civil economy. Social services and early years education have formed the majority of social enterprises in many European countries. In Italy, there are over 7,000 social care co-ops. In the UK there has been a sudden upsurge of co-operative schools. In North America there are long established health co-operatives, and in Japan the food co-operatives have diversified into livelihood co-operatives that include social and elder care.

This new wave of social and educational co-operatives is multi-stakeholder in governance, involving both the users and those providing the service. A typical UK co-operative school, for example, will have members drawn from parents, staff, pupils, a local further education college, the local authority providing the funding, and so on. In this case, as with the Italian and Canadian social co-ops, the civil economy is not separate from and rival to public provision, but rather provides a structure that allows the state to participate, through funding and engagement, alongside the many other civil parties involved.

Multi-stakeholder co-operatives of this kind are emerging as the adequate organisational structure for relational services and they are set to expand. For it is these services which are threatening to overwhelm public budgets; in a number of post-industrial countries, spending on relational services is approaching 25 per cent of GDP and is forecast to increase further. It is the civil economy, not the state, that is expanding in response.

3. *Information.* The ICT revolution has, above all, enabled people to collaborate, both as 'prosumers' and citizens. The big change came in 2003, when Silicon Valley realised that the future was less in content than in platforms. As the newspaper industry realises only too well, content is costly. Platforms, on the other hand, create a space for the content of others. These platforms can be 'enclosed' and administered as if they were property; the issue for such web platform companies as Facebook or YouTube has been that of any landlord: how to maximise the usage of resources, and then raise a rent on the basis of that usage. With the rise of web-based platforms, capitalism has shifted its axis: from the capturing of profit through control of production to the generation of rent from its informational property. Battles become ones over intellectual property as much as distributional struggles between profit and wages.

That is one way of looking at it. From another perspective, capitalism has provided the infrastructure for a massive increase in the civil economy. The most striking example is the production of knowledge itself. This can no longer be constrained within the traditional structures of property; households are collaborating directly in a new economy of sharing that is treating creativity and knowledge as a social resource, voluntarily developed and freely distributed.

New legal structures have been developed to ensure that this resource is treated as a commons and not a commodity. The Creative Commons licences are one such

Box 9.3
Health Care Without Harm

Health Care Without Harm (HCWH; www.noharm.org) exemplifies a new model of global civil knowledge economy. A global campaign and coalition, it was founded in 1996 in response to a study that identified hospital incinerators as the principal source of dioxins in the atmosphere. Hospitals, it turned out, were also a major source of mercury pollution. They made use of a large number of toxic chemicals in their building and their treatments. The fact that hospitals, providers of health care and committed to do no harm, are also principal agents of health-threatening pollutants is a paradox that has been the driver of HCWH's development.

Because hospitals are themselves largely part of the social economy, HCWH has sought to change existing institutions rather than set up alternative ones. It works issue by issue, highlighting the problem (and thus the paradox) and developing an implementable alternative in collaboration with partner hospitals. It then documents the results so others can take up the innovation, and so that it can be incorporated into local and national standards (for example, building regulations) or international ones (World Health Organisation protocols).

To reduce dioxins from incinerators HCWH promoted autoclaves – in effect a pressure cooker for hospital wastes – and as a result has succeeded in cutting the number of hospital incinerators in the US by over 90 per cent. It then targeted the use of PVC in hospital equipment and identified non-polluting alternatives. Next it was mercury in thermometers, whose use, as a result of HCWH's work, has been radically reduced globally. HCWH now covers 13 such issues, from the composition of hospital flooring materials to the content and sourcing of hospital food and the impact of any particular hospital on climate change.

Around each of these issues HCWH forms a coalition of the willing: those with the knowledge and expertise to develop the alternatives, and hospitals open to implementing them. The PVC alternative, for example, was developed in collaboration with sympathetic group-purchasing organisations and medical suppliers. The original incinerator initiative was formed as a coalition of 28 different bodies, and the testing of the first autoclave was done in a religious hospital, run by nuns who were convinced that they had to end incineration.

It is therefore a highly distributed model of organisation and finance. Implementation and funding is local – via existing hospitals. But the information and knowledge is generated and circulated through a global network. There are now nearly 500 partners in this network in over 50 countries – hospitals, medical professionals, community groups, health-affected constituencies, trade unions, environmental organisations and religious groups – all of whom share a commitment to the mission and a readiness to work collaboratively. The central core, funded primarily by foundations, is fewer than 40 staff, and includes specialists who act as consultants.

HCWH has created a particular form of open source economy. Structured around projects, it draws on the collective intelligence of the network and then freely distributes the results of its trials and methods. Instead of intellectual property (IP) it follows the principle of intellectual commons (IC), not simply by posting results and methods but by editing, translating and presenting know-how in a way that can further its application.

The campaign is an active host of a global open knowledge network. It institutionalises dialogue through fortnightly conference calls, workshops and discussion groups, both in order to share problems and as a form of reflective practice. An annual conference draws some 3,000 people. It produces handbooks and model documents, translations of regulatory and procedural regimes, legislation updates and key reports; it has built up an online library of 400 downloadable documents.

By breaking through the barriers that a regime of private IP presents to the generation and diffusion of knowledge, and by its attention to application, HCWH provides a model of how innovation and transformation can be advanced throughout the global social economy. It is already inspiring initiatives on climate change, particularly with respect to public procurement and service design, where governments have been restricted by their substantial dependence on private consultancy and supplier know-how. As a civil organisation committed to the common good, HCWH in effect offers a multi-sourced free consultancy and support service whose results are then shared globally.

Robin Murray

example; launched in 2001, they now cover over 400 million works of art (Creative Commons 2011). Similar protection applies to open-source software, a creation of volunteer collaborators that now accounts for two-thirds of the world's basic software.

The primary principle at work is one of openness: open involvement, open access, open source, open knowledge. This has extended the civil economy far beyond the formal structures of NGOs and co-operatives, into a world of informal cooperation. As an idea, it has exploded over the past decade seemingly into every corner of social collaboration. For example:

- common projects (Letsdoit, Mars Mapping and Wikipedia, founded in 2001 and whose 3.7 million entries greatly outstrip the *Encyclopaedia Britannica*)
- giving away (Freecycle, Kiva, Landshare, Jumo)
- sharing (Limewire)
- hosting (roomarama, couchsurfing)
- recommending (Grunhub, Foursquare launched in 2009 with now 6.5 million users worldwide)
- connecting (Diaspora, Gaydar, Netmums, Meet-Up)
- co-consuming (Netflix, zip car)
- co-renting (Zilok, the hirehub, Erento)
- swapping (Thred-up, big wardrobe, swapstyle, Swap.com)
- exchanging (eBay and Craigslist)
- bartering (u-exchange.com, planetgreen)
- financing (Zopa, YES-Secure, Quackle, Profounder, Kickstarter)
- news producing (Reddit).

One of Marx's central theses was that capitalism developed the 'socialisation of labour'. By this he meant the direct organisation of labour within the sphere of production, which he held to be the result of the development of technology.[15] The rise of the Web has seen a remarkable shift into the direct organisation of citizens; in part political, but also increasingly economic. It is a socialisation of civic life, extending the socialisation based on physical proximity to the open medium of cyberspace.[16]

The Civil Economy and Globalisation

How far is this expanding civil economy global? Some of its elements are clearly so, as is the case with fair trade. There has been a steep rise in the number of international NGOs from 1989 (from 5,000 to 27,000 in 1999 and to around 55,000 in 2010), and NGOs now administer an estimated 15 per cent of all overseas aid. Some projects extend overseas through social franchising, as is the case with Freecycle, an Arizona-based project to promote the re-use of products by a form of eBay without payment. Within ten years they have developed 4,000 local chapters in 85 countries with 8 million members (Freecycle 2011). Another example is Habitat for Humanity, with its franchised system for both financing and building low-cost housing.

In contrast, the responses of those marginalised by neoliberal globalisation have been framed in direct opposition to it. Whereas in the 1930s the effects of depression led to demands for more autarchic national economies, the recent post-globalisation crises have sought to develop self-reliant local economies. They emphasise the local against the global. They argue for an economy driven by values rather than value. And they see their projects in terms of an extension of economic democracy that is best realised at a local, micro, level.

There has been a similar emphasis in the environmental and food movements, dissolving the global into innumerable locals, as a means of reducing transport, increasing resilience, and redirecting the appetite for cheap globally-produced commodities towards a richer form of civic life. They have championed everything local: local energy systems, local closed loop recycling, local sourcing and locally-integrated food chains. The remarkable growth of the transition towns movement (www.transitionnetwork.org) which seeks to support each member town or neighbourhood in developing its own self-reliant low-carbon economy embodies this approach. Globalisation of the mainstream economy and the tensions to which it has given rise has in this way provoked its opposite, an intensely local, self-governing, socially embedded alternative.

It is, however, only one side of the story. For while material production may be local, the networks and communications that connect them are uninhibitedly global. The internet has allowed global communities of practice to mushroom. Networks like Zero Waste International (http://www.zwia.org) compare experiences, share information, form research consortia, and develop common curricula and training materials. They mutually diffuse know-how not through cross-licensing or corporate expansion, but through the free circulation of people and information, with a regular round of conferences, workshops, visits, speaking tours, exchanges, and assignments.

Some have developed international advisory networks that act as a 'civil civil service' for projects in the social economy. A striking example is Healthcare Without Harm, an initiative started in the US in the mid 1990s to make hospitals less hazardous to health – initially by closing down incinerators, but then expanding into finding alternatives to the use of PVC medical apparatus, mercury thermometers, and so on (see Box 9.3). It is now an international network of over 500 social organisations sharing a common goal and a network that identifies relevant innovations globally, and gives advice on how they can best be applied.

In many fields, civil projects and their networks have become a principal channel for the local generation and global diffusion of social and environmental innovation. A good example is the Bio Regional environmental group. One of its projects has been to produce local recycled office paper with an input of straw or hemp, but in starting the project the group encountered a global problem: black liquor effluent is produced by this process. Bio Regional has spent 14 years researching a solution, and is now prototyping a mini-mill with the aim of making the technology available worldwide, thus preventing the closure of similar recycling projects in India and China. As with its parallel development, a now iconic model of zero-carbon housing in South London, Bio Regional's process of innovation has involved those from every sub-economy shown in Figure 9.1; and, as with open-source software, the results have been shared freely. Most recently, the group posted detailed building information and blueprints about its zero-carbon housing on the internet (Bio Regional 2011).

The idea of the civil economy as global information applies even more so to the cyber economy. Linux is produced through global collaboration. So is Wikipedia and all the growing number of projects that are based on the 'crowd-sourcing' of ideas. Medical websites for those with common medical conditions are global. Universities are placing their course content and even their recorded lectures on the internet, free to download. Around 20 per cent of the 250,000 students enrolled at the British-based Open University are from overseas, with their own support systems of local tutors and study groups, coupled with virtual conferences, chatrooms and lectures (Open University 2011). As improving language translation programmes remove the barrier of language, we can see these as examples of hyper-globalisation.

The internet has swept away the geographical and property frontiers of information. We now have not just Médecins sans Frontières and 'Engineering sans Frontières', but *information sans frontières* taken to a new level. The traditional environmental slogan 'think globally and act locally' can be rephrased as 'click globally and produce locally'.

The first decade of the twenty-first century has witnessed a historically unprecedented expansion of a civil global information and knowledge economy, side by side with a multiplicity of initiatives that, seen from within, are experienced as local and self-reliant in character, but viewed from without comprise a highly distributed network of material and service production. They are not bound by the chains of ownership or by being a small cog in an interdependent global wheel, but rather connected together through the movement of people and the free circulation of ideas. Because significant parts of this civil economy have developed in opposition to the mainstream and are democratically rooted, these scattered initiatives can be seen as examples of globalisation from below. But we might equally describe it as a globalism of the head and the heart, rather than the hand.

Conclusion

The civil economy is commonly regarded as an economy of small things, marginal to the main action in the economy of the large ones. It is the lamb next to the lion. Yet over the past decade, as the lion has run into difficulties the lamb has grown, and now plays an ever more significant role in the global economy. This is partly due to its distinctive relational and motivational quality, and to its reintegration of the social and the personal with the economic. It is also because of the freedom from the constrictions of property intrinsic to an economy based at least partially on information.

I have described it as a hybrid of force fields rather than as a distinct 'third' sector, with clear boundaries and legal forms. In practice the interfaces between the different spheres of the hybrid are in constant movement, particularly that between the civil economy and the state. One opinion holds that the civil economy is an alternative to the state, another that it is a staging post to privatisation. Neither is inherent. Both the state and the civil spheres are part of a social economy, often in pursuit of common aims but subject to different structural political forces.

Which leads us to one of the major challenges to be met as the social economy grows: how to reintegrate the state and the civil spheres. Some of the projects that I have described in this chapter suggest possible answers:

new forms of public-social partnerships, and the closer involvement of civil society in the shaping of the public economy. Here, it is movements in the global South that have been pioneers, from planning and literacy campaigns in Kerala to participatory budgeting in Brazil. Such initiatives have now spread to Latin America more generally, and are now showing, through their practice, how to heal that conceptual split introduced by nineteenth-century liberal theory – the forced separation of the economic and the political.

Notes

1. On the history of the theory of the civil economy see Bruni and Zamagni (2007); for Adam Smith and moral economy see Phillipson (2010).
2. Bruni and Zamagni (2007) have sought to reintroduce the tradition of civic humanism into the contemporary concept of civil society. They argue that the market economy needs to re-internalise the principles of equity and reciprocity alongside equivalence and efficiency, and re-orient itself from the production of goods to the strengthening of relationships.
3. See also *Princeton Encyclopaedia of the World Economy* (2009).
4. 57 per cent of the active larger US foundations were established since 1990, 26 per cent of the total in the last decade. See Foundation Center (2011).
5. One example is the Kuapa Kokoo Farmers Union in Ghana, started in 1993 with 1,000 cocoa farmers and now grown to 45,000 in 1,200 village societies, and part-owners of Divine, the UK- and US-based fair trade chocolate company. For a recent review of fair trade in its character as a social movement see Bowes (2010).
6. The British data are based on the annual survey of small business. A later study of for profit entrepreneurs found that many of them saw themselves as social enterprises reinvesting their profits to further their social purposes, suggesting that this would increase the number of UK social enterprises to 232,000. See Hidden Social Enterprises, Delta Economics and IFF Research (2010). For Europe see Borzago and Defourny (2001).
7. See Restakis (2010: ch. 9). He also has a striking chapter on the Calcutta sex worker co-operative that started in 1995 as a means of regulating the sex trade, and which now has over 12,000 members.
8. The development of such active labour market policies via social enterprises in 15 European countries is described in Borzago and Defourny (2001).
9. Walmart is an example. It is the world's largest retailer with sales of $422 billion a year, 8,500 stores in 50 US states and 15 countries. By the 1980s it operated a satellite system that enabled communication and electronic scanning throughout the store, supplier and distributor networks. Data from the point of sale could be transmitted to the headquarters or to a supplier's distribution centres instantly, and an Electronic Data Interchange (EDI) system with its 3,600 suppliers enabled a just in time, 24-hour restocking of its shops.
10. The US has now 1716 micro-breweries, the surge in growth taking place since the 1990s. In the UK such steep growth has been over the past decade, with the number of micro-breweries now reaching nearly 700. On micro-brewing as the outcome of a social movement in the US see Rao (2009).
11. See Prencipe et al. (2003) and Davies and Hobday (2005). Their concern is with complex products and systems principally in the capital goods sector, such as flight simulators, electricity network control systems, superserver networks, and electronic retail networks.
12. The first book to alert the English-speaking world to the economic vibrancy of these industrial districts was Michael Piore and Charles Sable (1984). On similar districts in the South see Schmitz (1989) and Navdi and Schmitz (1994).
13. Firms are also turning to their customers for feedback and intelligence. Users have become a key source for innovation (second only to employees, according to the EU's Community Innovation Survey).
14. See Cottam (2011) for the outlines of a new model of welfare services based on this approach, as well as Zuboff (2010).
15. The emphasis on the socialisation of labour in Marx and its forms of commensuration was one of the lasting contributions of Alfred Sohn-Rethel: see Sohn-Rethel (1978) Part III.
16. The trend towards collective consumption is discussed in Botsman and Rogers (2011).

References

Anheier, Helmut, Glasius, Marlies and Kaldor, Mary (2001) 'Introducing Global Civil Society', in Helmut Anheier, Marlies Glasius and Mary Kaldor (eds), *Global Civil Society*. Oxford: Oxford University Press.

Best, Michael (1990) *The New Competition*. Cambridge: Polity Press.

Beynon, Huw and Nichols, Theo (eds) (2006) *The Fordism of Ford and Modern Management: Fordism and Post Fordism*, 2 vols. Cheltenham: Edward Elgar.

Bio Regional (2011) http://www.bioregional.com (accessed 12 September 2011).

Boltanski, Luc and Chiapello, Eve (2005) *The New Spirit of Capitalism*. London: Verso.

Borzaga, Carlo and Defourny, Jacques (2001) *The Emergence of Social Enterprise*. London: Routledge.

Botsman, Rachel and Rogers, Roo (2011) *What's Mine is Yours*. London: Collins.

Bowes, John (ed.) (2010), *The Fair Trade Revolution*. London: Pluto Press.

Bruni, Luigino and Zamagni, Stafano (2007) *Civil Economy*. Bern: Peter Lang.

Carr, Marilyn and Chen, Martha A. (2001) 'Globalization and the Informal Economy: How Global Trade and Investment Impact on the Working Poor'. ILO Task Force on the Informal Economy. International Labour Office: Geneva.

Chayanov, Alexander (1991) *The Theory of Peasant Co-operatives*. London: I.B.Tauris.

Cottam, H. (2011) 'Relational Welfare', *Soundings*, Vol. 48, Summer: 134–44.

Creative Commons (2011) http://creativecommons.org/ (accessed 12 September 2011).

Dale, Gareth (2010) *Karl Polanyi*. Cambridge: Polity Press.

Davies, Andrew and Hobday, Michael (2005) *The Business of Projects*. Cambridge: Cambridge University Press.

Dowler, Wayne, (2010) *Russia in 1913*. Illinois: Northern Illinois University Press.

Drucker, Peter (1989) *The New Realities*. New York: HarperCollins.

European Union (2010) *This is Social Innovation*. Brussels, doi 10.2769/825.

EuroMonitor Blog (2010) 'Top 10 Largest Economies in 2020', 7 July, http://blog.euromonitor.com/2010/07/special-report-top-10-largest-economies-in-2020.html (accessed 12 September 2011).

Foundation Center (2011) *Foundation Growth and Giving Estimates 2011*, New York.

Freecycle (2011) http://my.freecycle.org/ (accessed 12 September 2011).

Freeman, Chris and Louca, Francisco (2001) *As Time Goes By: From the Industrial Revolution to the Information Revolution*. Oxford: Oxford University Press.

Hart, Keith, Laville, Jean-Louis and Cattani, Antonio David (2010) *The Human Economy*. Cambridge: Polity Press.

La Via Campesina (2011) http://viacampesina.org/en/ (accessed 12 September 2011).

Martinez-Torres, Maria Elena and Rosset, Peter M. (2010) 'La Via Campesina: The Birth and Evolution of a Transnational Social Movement', *Journal of Peasant Studies*, Vol. 37 No. 1: 149–75.

Mondragon (2011) http://www.mcc.es (accessed 12 September 2011).

Munck, Ronaldo (2006) *Globalisation and Contestation: The New Great Counter Movement*. Abingdon: Routledge.

Navdi, Khalid and Schmitz, Hubert (1994) *Industrial Clusters in Less Developed Countries*. Brighton: Institute of Development Studies.

Ohno, Taiichi (1988) *Toyota Production System*. New York: Productivity Press.

Open University (2011) http://www8.open.ac.uk/about/main/ (accessed 12 September 2011).

Perez, Carlota (2002) *Technological Revolutions and Financial Capital*. Cheltenham: Edward Elgar.

Petrini, Carlos (2007) *The Slow Food Revolution*. New York: Rizzoli International.

Phillipson, Nicholas (2010), *Adam Smith*. London: Allen Lane.

Piore, Michael and Sable, Charles (1984) *The Second Industrial Divide*. New York: Basic Books.

Polanyi, Karl (1957) *The Great Transformation*. Boston: Beacon Press.

Portes, Alejandro and Haller, William (2005) 'The Informal Economy', in Neil Smelser and Richard Swedberg (eds), *Handbook of Economic Sociology*, 2nd edn. New York: Russell Sage Foundation.

Prencipe, Andrea, Davies, Andrew and Hobday, Michael (eds) (2003) *The Business of Systems Integration*. Oxford: Oxford University Press.

Princeton Encyclopaedia of the World Economy, Volume II (2009) Princeton: Princeton University Press.

Ramesh, Randeep (2011) 'Basque Country's Thriving Big Society', *Guardian*, 30 March.

Rao, Hayagreeva (2009) *Market Rebels: How Activists Make or Break Radical Innovations*. Princeton: Princeton University Press.

Restakis, John (2010) *Humanizing the Economy: Co-operatives in the Age of Capital*. Gabriola Island, BC: New Society Publishers.

Salamon, Lester M., Sokolowski, S. Wojciech, and Associates (2010) *Global Civil Society: Dimensions of the Nonprofit Sector*, 3rd edn, Greenwich, CN: Kumarian Press.

Salamon, Lester M. (2010) 'Putting the Civil Society Sector on the Economic Map of the World', *Annals of Public and Co-operative Economics*, Vol. 81 No. 2: 167–210.

Sanchez Bajo, Claudia and Roelants, Bruno (2011)*Capital and the Debt Trap*. Basingstoke: Palgrave Macmillan.

Schmitz, Hubert (1989) *Flexible Specialisation: A New Paradigm of Small-Scale Industrialisation*. Brighton: Institute of Development Studies.

Sohn-Rethel, Alfred (1978) *Intellectual and Manual Labour*. London: Macmillan.

World Bank (2010). *Shadow Economies All over the World*, Washington DC: World Bank.

Zaleski, Pawel (2006) 'Global Non Governmental Administrative Systems: Geosociology of the Third Sector', in Darlusz Gawin and Pietr Glinski (eds), *Civil Society in the Making*, Warsaw: IFS Publishers.

Zuboff, Shoshana (2010) 'Creating Value in the Age of Distributed Capitalism', *McKinsey Quarterly*, September.

CHAPTER 10

A DECADE OF WORLD SOCIAL FORUMS: INTERNATIONALISATION WITHOUT INSTITUTIONALISATION?

Geoffrey Pleyers

Introduction

The World Social Forum (WSF) celebrated its tenth anniversary in 2011. Each year between 2001 and 2007 and every couple of years since, this alter-globalisation gathering has drawn up to 170,000 activists from all over the world. In spite of its size, very international nature and numerous logistical challenges, the WSF has not become a tamed and institutionalised place. Indeed, recent meetings were far less institutionalised than their predecessors between 2001 and 2003.

Such an evolution contrasts with one of the best established models in social movement studies, asserted by the most prominent scholars in the field (Michels 1911, Weber 1922, Touraine 1973, Tilly 1986, Kriesi 1993, Tarrow 1998, Della Porta and Diani 1999, Kaldor 2003). According to this model, movements either dissolve or become institutionalised. They 'take the familiar path from charisma to regularised routine, from inventiveness and passion to bureaucracy, hierarchy and instrumental reason' (Walker 1994: 677, quoted in Kaldor 2003: 84). Institutionalisation is widely considered as a 'classic stage [of] social movements' natural history' (Touraine 1973: 353). It brings an end to a 'cycle of contention': 'At its height, the movement is electric and seems irresistible, but it then erodes and gets integrated through political process' (Tarrow 1998).

The process of institutionalisation entails internal and external dimensions. Internally, movements evolve from loose structures to professionalised, hierarchical organisations (Tilly 1986, Kriesi 1993), which brings an increasing power to the movement's leaders over its grassroots members, as stated by R. Michels' 'iron law of oligarchy' (1962) [1911]. Externally, movements are progressively integrated into institutional politics (Tarrow 1998) or become self-help networks, whose main purpose is to provide services to their members (Kriesi 1996). Movements usually lose much of their critical stance in the process: 'The more movements become groups of interest, the more they risk losing their historicity [the questioning of society's major orientations]' (Touraine 1973: 354). Indeed, 'taming is not just about access. It is about adaptation of both sides. When authorities accept part of the agenda of protest, the movements modify their goals and become respectable' (Kaldor 2003: 83).

The fact that the WSF has not become an institutionalised organisation relying on strong leaders and professional organisers is even more surprising given that a strong connection between a movement's internationalisation and its institutionalisation has been asserted by eminent scholars. Social movements' internationalisation is supposed to lead to a 'proliferation of organizations, brokers and political entrepreneurs specialized in connecting those populations and coordinating their action' (Tilly 2004: 155).

In the 1990s, the rise of a global civil society was indeed strongly associated with the institutionalisation of many of its actors. That period witnessed the multiplication of international NGOs that relied upon professional activists, able to fulfil the funding applications of international institutions and to conduct international advocacy campaigns (Keck and Sikkink 1998, Kaldor 2003). In the early 2000s, observers thus predicted a quick and massive institutionalisation of the emerging 'global civil society'. Jonathan Friedman (1999) has showed how strongly the 'discreet charm of bourgeoisie' operates on delegates from local indigenous movements, who were progressively transformed into a group of elite global activists after being projected into international arenas by taking part in UN negotiations on the rights of indigenous people. Charles Tilly's future scenarios for social movements directly bind internationalisation, institutionalisation and an increasing power of their elite.

If the scenario of internationalization prevails, we might reasonably expect some further consequences for popular politics. First, given the minimum requirements of large-scale social movements for information, time, contacts, and resources, the existing elite bias of social movement participation would increase ... Second, for this reason and because of uneven access to communication channels ... excluded people would suffer even more acutely than today from lack of means to mount effective campaigns and performances ... Third, brokers, entrepreneurs, and international organizations would become even more crucial to the effective voicing of claims by means of social movements. (Tilly 2004: 155; see also Tarrow 2005)

As both a global and a mass event, the WSF was expected to follow the path of quick and massive institutionalisation. How then can we explain that recent forums were actually less institutionalised than the first forums: less centralised, less dominated by elite activists, with a diminished influence of INGOs and political parties? This chapter suggests that, while a pattern of institutionalisation exists within the WSF process, it has been countered by the political culture of WSF activists; a culture that favours horizontality, internal democracy and the active participation of grassroots actors. The first section focuses on internal dimensions of the institutionalisation process, analysing the evolution of the organisation of WSF panels and the power of a group of intellectual leaders. The second section focuses on the evolution of the place of more institutionalised civil society actors (INGOs and political parties) in successive WSFs. Their number and influence is supposed to increase with an institutionalisation process.

This analysis relies on an extended qualitative research conducted since 1999 at eight World Social Forums, as well as field work conducted in alter-globalisation organisations and at events in Europe and the Americas, including the 2010 US Social Forum in Detroit. The argument presented here also draws on several chapters dedicated to the alter-globalisation movement from previous *Global Civil Society* yearbooks.

From Institutionalisation to Decentralisation

2001–03: Towards an Institutionalised and Hierarchical WSF

Over its first three meetings, all held in Porto Alegre, the WSF process experienced increasing institutionalisation and professionalisation (Desai and Said: 2003). From January 2001 to January 2003, WSF attendance shot up quickly, from 15,000 in 2001 to 50,000 in 2002, reaching the 100,000 mark in 2003 (see Map 10.1). This resulted in major logistical challenges for the organisers, and gave

an increasing power to the professional team employed by the 'Brazilian Secretary of the WSF'. Logistical aspects, including fundraising (Timms 2006), took on a greater importance, despite the fact that some contributors were corporations criticised by some groups of activists.

Charles Tilly (2004) and Sidney Tarrow (2005) maintain that social movements rely far more on 'mobilisation professionals' at the international scale than at the local scale. The alter-globalisation movement was no exception. Initially, its growth largely relied on the prestige and fame of committed intellectuals, on their legitimacy as experts in the analysis of globalisation and on their international networks of affinity. Working as scholars or for NGOs, intellectuals possess the necessary time and resources (economic, cultural and social capital) to attend international forums and their preparatory meetings, which leaders of grassroots movements often lack. They were thus able to attend and connect the protests against corporate globalisation that took place over the world, and to convene convergence meetings (Houtart and Polet 2001).

The burgeoning of civil society and alter-globalisation parallel summits in the late 1990s and early 2000s (Pianta 2001, 2002 and Chapter 11 this volume, Box 11.2) gave rise to informal but very influential global affinity groups of elite and globalised activists, with a clear dominance by older male intellectuals whose activism and world visions are rooted in the 1970s anti-imperialist perspective. As one finds in other sectors of global civil society (Chandhoke 2002: 48), many of the leaders of the International Council (IC), who had the upper hand in deciding WSF guidelines and on the main WSF panels, lacked social constituency and representativeness (Pleyers 2008). In many aspects, the 2001 WSF resembled an academic congress, with intellectuals and scholars monopolising the large panel discussions – and even the majority of the smaller workshops. The IC held its meetings behind closed doors, with security guards at the entrance and, to most activists, the organisation of the forum appeared 'so opaque that it was nearly impossible to figure out how decisions were made or to find ways to question those decisions' (Klein 2002: 204).

In 2001 and 2002, the 'VIP lounge' provided the clearest illustration of the assumed hierarchy between elite and 'ordinary' participants. This concept of a top-down forum became even stronger in 2003. While to many the 100,000-plus member audience was an exciting reflection of the dynamism of the forum, the Brazilian organising team noted at the pre-Forum IC meeting that they were

Box 10.1
Notes on the World Social Forum 2011, Dakar

The 2011 World Social Forum (WSF) took place in Dakar, Senegal, 6–11 February. After a year in which 55 networked events took place right across the globe (see Map 10.1), WSF activists convened once more in a single venue to meet, reconnect, organise, discuss, and to share experiences and imaginations of other possible worlds. Against the backdrop of renewed confidence and the glare of possibility brought about by the events of the Arab Spring, and celebrating ten years of WSF activities, the WSF 2011 was a space of experimentation and reflection on the social forum movement, on its challenges and potentialities, its regional rootedness, its organisational capacity, its ambition and its limitations. It was not an easy forum for its organisers and for many participants. It was a WSF that stretched imaginations but also frustrated expectations, that addressed past challenges and exposed new ones, and that hesitated on problems that have afflicted WSF activists since its inception, and which ten years of experience have not yet fully resolved.

The events unfolding across North Africa and in the Middle East gave the forum an added relevance. Roaming in the lush avenues of the Cheick Anta Diop University campus, activists exchanged views on daily transformations occurring across the Maghreb-Mashreq, and those from the region were courted for news, explanations, analysis, inspiration. Some just wanted to know how they could do the same: bring about democracy, justice, equality, rights in their oppressed countries. And soon the forum became the backdrop of opportunity against which activists came together to project into the future plans and activities of change, imbued with a new sense of hope.

The expectations of organisers, partners and participants varied enormously, but there were commonalities. Inevitable comparisons were made to the previous WSF, held in Belem, Brazil, in 2009; and to the last African WSF, the controversial WSF of 2007 which was held in Nairobi, Kenya (see Map 10.1). For many, the key success of the Belem event was the ability of the organisers to include a wide range of indigenous movements, and the fact that subsequently a close connection was established between the forum and those activists who worked in the region. In this sense, Dakar matched the successes of Brazil, with the significant participation of activists from Senegal, West Africa and, indeed, the whole continent, brought together by a thorough and inclusive pre-event mobilisation.

Nairobi was perceived as problematic for a number of reasons, particularly for its relative exclusiveness, heightened by the difficulties and cost of getting to the venue and by the controversies on the role of some Christian organisations and other large NGOs. In contrast, Dakar was open and accessible, and, as noted during the International Council (IC) meeting that

followed its closure, at the same time militant and assertively political. The event was notable for its inclusiveness and the diversity of participants. At the opening march, tens of thousands of people marched through Dakar, including local minorities and unions, Senegalese peasants and their regional partners. And the outreach continued in the following days: there was an experiment of virtual decentralisation via the internet (the 'Dakar Extended' project allowed remote participation); the organisation of events in the suburbs by groups like the World Assembly of Inhabitants; the visit of a delegation to the unplanned settlement of Baraka. In this sense, Dakar was a confident step along the journey of the African chapter of the WSF.

An important trend in global activism, both highlighted by the Dakar forum and a contributing factor to its success, was that many activists had networked with local partners and other groups in advance, expressing a key concern of strengthening regional and global alliances on shared issues. Those convergences, at the heart of WSF's mission, seem to indicate a clear trend towards the consolidation of transnational alliances. Some took place before the WSF itself, others in its last days. The World Charter of Migrants, for instance, was launched on Goree Island, in Dakar, following two days of meetings with activists from all corners of the planet. A solidarity convergence on Palestine, the first ever to be organised at the forum, attracted hundreds of activists. And media activists converged a communication assembly to take stock of communication activism in the era of Wikileaks, and to examine the influence of social media on street protests as in the Maghreb-Mashreq. Aptly, all computers in the press centre, donated by Oxfam, were running on GNU/Linux to stress the research and practices that many in the WSF are conducting on the common creation and ownership of intellectual rights.

Among the processes that did not work as expected in the Dakar forum was the 'agglutination' of self-organised activities. Part of the event methodology since 2005, this process facilitates the convergence of different workshops and seminar organisers towards shared activities around similar topics in order to foster networking among potential partners. If this process had been more successful, it was argued, a considerably smaller number of events would have had to compete for the limited spaces available in the venue. As an Indian activist put it, instead the open space this year had become a 'grab-a-space space'.

The new university rector did not honour the commitments agreed to by his predecessor, who had promised both the suspension of classes during the forum to allow students to participate to the WSF, and the allocation to the organisers of the forum of the entire campus for their activity. When such an opportunity was denied at the last moment, confusion and a degree of frustration spread among participants. New tents were pitched to host the events and a lot of creative scheduling was hurriedly performed, but it took a while for all to become familiar enough with the spaces and schedules, which were posted daily on notice boards around the campus. It was estimated that, in the end, only 80 per cent of the activities took place as planned.

Whereas creativity, expediency, ingenuity and, most important of all, genuine solidarity marked the trajectory of many lost souls in the avenues of the campus, fiddling with their phones and escorted by welcoming volunteers, a darker side to the initial confusion was raised by many. Competition for spaces and the varying abilities of activists to convene last-minute audiences generated a phenomenon profoundly at odds with the values of the forum. In general, there are great imbalances of connections and social capital among WSF participants. Some network on the basis of their relations, extend their reach and feel more included; others prefer to rely on structured programmes and feel lost when they fail. The last-minute venue confusion in Dakar created a position of privilege among those activists and organisations with tighter networks and larger resources, while it excluded and alienated those who had joined the forum for the first time, or those not closely connected with other activists.

The logistical issues were not the only ones. Outrage was caused by the confrontations between Moroccan activists and supporters of the independence of the Saharawi people from the Moroccan state. There were also problems with the ambitious 'Dakar Extended' web-based project, which failed to implement the programme as planned due to lack of resources and spaces. And there were protests by those who found it unacceptable that Coca-Cola and Danone products were sold at the food stalls or that water was sold at three times the street price. In the same vein, others questioned the extent to which it is coherent with the WSF vision that activists house themselves in expensive hotels, and whether it would have been more appropriate to stress the organisational commitment on solidarity accommodation with local activists.

Yet even these problems were not without value: many reflected on the shortcomings of the forum, and their considerations became sophisticated reflections on causes and responsibility, and on criteria to assess outcome and impact in ways that were coherent with WSF's values. A working group was set up to conduct an open evaluation of the forum, with a preliminary report presented at the IC meeting in Paris in May. And what the organisers could not do, Dakar did. Welcoming people, warm weather and the soft blow of the Harmattan over the sparkling ocean; an enthusiastic IC member stated during the WSF evaluation that it was the friendliest city in which a WSF had ever taken place. Another emphasized that it had been the safest forum for women. This alone would be enough to celebrate Dakar and the 2011 WSF. Then there was the impressive cultural programme, complemented by the many options for inspiration and celebration that the city offers. And there was much cause for celebration: on the closing day of the forum, the news spread that Hosni Mubarak had finally fled in the face of the unrelenting, unintimidated and increasingly confident crowds of Tahrir Square. Despite the many setbacks and problems along the way, a decade of World Social Forums came to a close on an unmistakable high.

Giuseppe Caruso is a post-doctoral researcher at the Centre of Excellence for Global Governance Research – University of Helsinki, and a board member of the Network Institute for Global Democratization, which is a WSF International Council founding member. He writes a blog on the WSF at giuseppecaruso. wordpress.com.

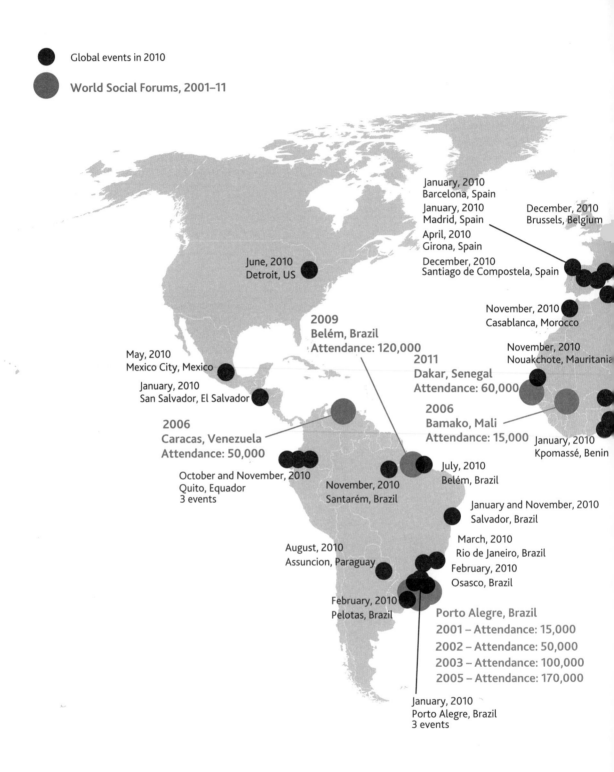

Global events in 2010

World Social Forums, 2001–11

January, 2010
Barcelona, Spain

January, 2010
Madrid, Spain

April, 2010
Girona, Spain

December, 2010
Santiago de Compostela, Spain

December, 2010
Brussels, Belgium

November, 2010
Casablanca, Morocco

November, 2010
Nouakchote, Mauritania

June, 2010
Detroit, US

2009
Belém, Brazil
Attendance: 120,000

2011
Dakar, Senegal
Attendance: 60,000

2006
Bamako, Mali
Attendance: 15,000

January, 2010
Kpomassé, Benin

May, 2010
Mexico City, Mexico

January, 2010
San Salvador, El Salvador

2006
Caracas, Venezuela
Attendance: 50,000

October and November, 2010
Quito, Equador
3 events

November, 2010
Santarém, Brazil

July, 2010
Belém, Brazil

January and November, 2010
Salvador, Brazil

March, 2010
Rio de Janeiro, Brazil

February, 2010
Osasco, Brazil

August, 2010
Assuncion, Paraguay

February, 2010
Pelotas, Brazil

Porto Alegre, Brazil
2001 – Attendance: 15,000
2002 – Attendance: 50,000
2003 – Attendance: 100,000
2005 – Attendance: 170,000

January, 2010
Porto Alegre, Brazil
3 events

Sources: ESRI; http://www.worldsocialforum.info, Pleyers Geoffrey (2007)

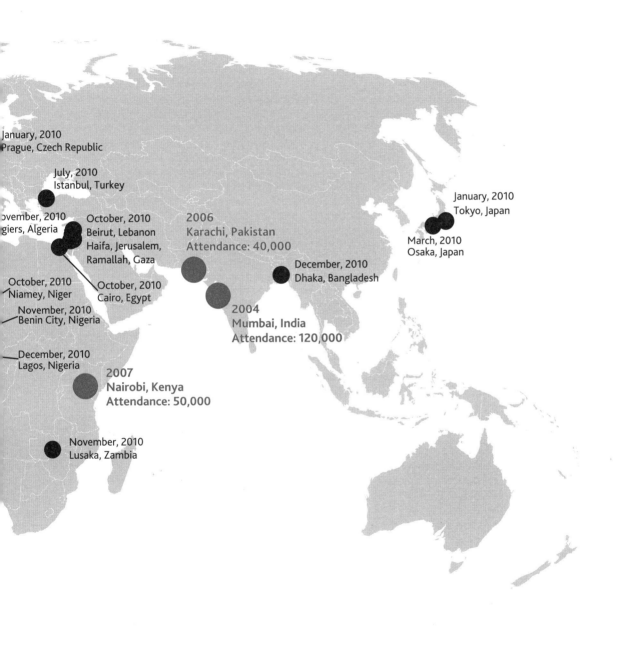

January, 2010
Prague, Czech Republic

July, 2010
Istanbul, Turkey

November, 2010
giers, Algeria

October, 2010
Beirut, Lebanon
Haifa, Jerusalem,
Ramallah, Gaza

2006
Karachi, Pakistan
Attendance: 40,000

January, 2010
Tokyo, Japan

March, 2010
Osaka, Japan

December, 2010
Dhaka, Bangladesh

October, 2010
Niamey, Niger

October, 2010
Cairo, Egypt

2004
Mumbai, India
Attendance: 120,000

November, 2010
Benin City, Nigeria

December, 2010
Lagos, Nigeria

2007
Nairobi, Kenya
Attendance: 50,000

November, 2010
Lusaka, Zambia

Box 10.2
The International Council of the World Social Forum: Illusions and Practices of a Global Open Space

The International Council was set up to give guidance to the Forum. It meets two or three times a year, usually coinciding with a social forum or event. Initially, members were the scholars and leaders of social movements who had been involved in the organisation of the first WSF. Membership of the IC was viewed as an important strategic position, providing members with the chance to affect the direction and organisation of the WSF. Although it grew rapidly, attendance was strictly regulated by its founders and meetings were more or less secret, leading to the perception that it was a meeting of VIPs.

At the first meeting, a text was adopted to clarify IC tasks, its major responsibility being to formulate WSF strategies (see Sen and Waterman 2009: 72). At the IC in Miami in 2003, six commissions – Methodology, Content, Strategy, Communication, Resources and Expansion – were established, which remain in place today. Notably, when the first questions about 'restructuring' the WSF arose after the Mumbai WSF, Chico Whitaker defined the objectives of the IC as promoting the expansion of the WSF process, giving it more visibility and enhancing the transition from event to process.

In practice, the main decisions taken by the IC concern two issues: the structure of WSF and of the IC itself; and the major political controversy behind the movement: is the WSF merely an 'open space' (see Whitaker, 2006: 81), or also a place for action?

At the IC in Barcelona in 2005, the first political debate took place. It was nothing more than a long series of individual statements, every speaker receiving exactly five minutes without any attempt to make a synthesis. It did lead, however, to the first specific debate on the space versus action opposition: more than one hundred written contributions were received on the website and the debate took place at the IC in Abuja in 2008. Unfortunately, what came out of the discussion had very little resemblance to the wealth of opinions that were received.

At the same meeting in Barcelona, a draft road map for the restructuring of the IC was created, to tackle perceived problems of legitimacy. Real power, so it was said, was in the hands of a highly political secretariat. With these plans put into action, the IC evolved into a meeting of many participants, with decisions made by consensus. In order to make this more efficient, an idea grew of constituting a 'Liaison Group'; a technically-minded group of people who would prepare the meetings and coordinate the activities of the different commissions and working groups. This was eventually created at the IC held in Berlin in May 2007. Today, an attempt is being made to better coordinate the activities of the different commissions.

What observations of ten years of IC meetings suggest is that the supposed 'open space' of the WSF is really quite structured, and that further structures are added in order to hide the real power relations behind the Forum, rather than to actually democratise the IC. It has become a highly self-referential exercise. Power remains in the hands of those founders who still attend the IC, and in those of their allies, irrespective of their legitimacy or their practical contribution to the council. Power is informal but real.

A second observation is that decisions are not always respected. Sometimes a group of people succeeds in pushing through an idea, which is then broadly discussed; but once the decision is taken, it somehow disappears … For example, this happened with a document of 'Guiding Principles' for the organisation of WSFs. The principles were adopted in Copenhagen in September 2008, and have never been heard of since.

A third observation is the lack of transparency. The IC is no longer a secret meeting. Members receive a balance sheet after every WSF, so that it is known what was budgeted and what was spent. However, decision-making remains largely opaque.

At every WSF and at every IC it is repeated that one purpose of the WSF movement is to create a 'new political culture'. Yes, the social movements present at the IC have, for the most part, achieved much in the practice of listening to and discussing with each other. But the IC is still far from the democratic and political ideal (see Pleyers 2004, 2007: 121) that it was intended to be.

Francine Mestrum is a researcher, a member of the IC of the WSF for CETRI (Centre Tricontinental), and member of the Global Social Justice association.

worried about how they would be able to 'manage the crowds'. To solve this logistical challenge, they opted for mass lectures: famous intellectuals and political leaders were chosen as speakers while 'ordinary' participants were relegated to the role of a huge but passive audience. Around 11,000 people attended the speeches of cosmopolitan intellectuals like Noam Chomsky and Arundhati Roy. On another day, over 100 panels were cancelled to ensure that 60,000 people would listen to and applaud Lula, the newly elected Brazilian president.

2005: From Critics to Cross-Fertilisation

Two years later, when the WSF returned to Porto Alegre after the 2004 session in Mumbai (Caruso 2010), it could have been expected that the record audience (now over 170,000 people) would lead to even more centralisation and institutionalisation. Yet the 2005 forum actually looked very different. Everything was angled to enable participants to take an active part in meetings and discussions. Instead of massive crowds listening to famous intellectuals, hundreds of tents hosted smaller and more participatory workshops. In many cases, after short introductory talks, the audience split into discussion groups, giving each person the opportunity to express an opinion. The organisation of panels and the choice of the speakers were transferred from WSF organisers and IC members to the participating organisations, which considerably lessened the role of leading intellectuals and IC leaders. This bottom-up dynamic gave the event a new and refreshing momentum. It showed that a 170,000-strong gathering could allow space both for grassroots participation and for autonomous organisation by activist networks.

Activists' reflexivity, and their will to create a more horizontal and participatory forum, had a determinant impact in counterbalancing the institutionalisation patterns that the WSF had previously followed. The organisation and assumed hierarchy of the WSF increasingly came under fire from participants, who insisted on the value of democratic opening and on experimentation with concrete alternatives, and opposed an IC 'that concentrates lots of power but is accountable to no one' (delegate of the Italian trade union COBAS, WSF 2004).

Activists used the 'open space' (Whitaker 2006) provided by the WSF to implement horizontal and participatory processes both within and in the margins of the WSF.[1] Activists in the autonomous spaces within the youth camp, women's movements (Wrainwright

2004, Dufour et al. 2010) and the network of activist interpreters' 'Babels' have been particularly engaged in promoting more participatory models of relations and in stressing the need for consistency between the values defended by the movement and the organisation of the WSF (Pleyers 2010a: part 2). They repeatedly urged members of the IC to adopt horizontal and participatory practices. In 2002, young activists engaged in a festive demonstration that invaded the WSF 'VIP lounge' with the slogan 'We are all VIPs' (see Juris 2008). The VIP lounge was immediately closed, and never reappeared at any other Social Forum.

The 2003 WSF suffered particularly strong criticism. It led leaders of the IC to progressively open themselves to the idea that the WSF needed to become more horizontal and participatory. In January 2004, the message was largely accepted and even relayed by various founding members of the IC: 'The sons and daughters of Porto Alegre are not here ... We have to change the methodology of the Forums. We need a democratic dialogue.'[2] The modalities of a more decentralised way of organising the forum then became the main focus of the fifth WSF preparation process.

While a rising institutionalisation could have paralyzed the 2005 forum, critiques from grassroots activists and interactions with IC leaders opened the way for a more inclusive and participatory event. From this perspective, the tension between different conceptions of the WSF and its organisational form, which is expressed primarily through conflicts and debates among activists, must not be mistaken for a diversion or deficiency of the alter-globalisation movement. On the contrary, it creates cross-fertilisations (Della Porta 2006) and a dynamism spurring the movement to innovate (Pleyers 2010a).

The tension between the trend towards institutionalisation and the wish for open, horizontal and participatory practices is indeed a structural feature of the alter-globalisation movement. It is visible at each and every scale of movement, from the IC to local coalitions and even in discourses and wishes of individual activists, 'We shouldn't have very institutionalised and well-established organisational structures ... But of course, we need some structured organisation to be able to work effectively together' (a young activist from Attac-Germany, in Hurrelmann and Albert 2002: 315).

After 2005: A Permanent Tension

The fight against 'residual forms of avant-gardism' (Glasius and Timms: 2006) was, however, far from over. Even the 2005 WSF reality was not the 'total self-organisation' and '100 per cent horizontal process' that J. Miola, the 'WSF executive manager', claimed it was (interview in *Libération*, 1 February 2005). This was notably highlighted by the process behind the 'Porto Alegre Manifesto', which was written by 19 intellectuals without consultation with other WSF participants and was presented to the press in a five-star hotel.

One year later, the 'Polycentric WSF' (P-WSF) was held in three locations: Bamako, Caracas and Karachi. At least two of these three events were dominated by elite activists. The organisation of the Bamako P-WSF widely relied on a small group of Malian professional activists, well inserted in international networks. In many aspects, they seemed much closer to their European fellows than to their country's grassroots activists. As for the event in Caracas, it was largely appropriated by committed intellectuals who were keen for the forum to get closer to Latin American political leaders, and who gave this P-WSF a clear political orientation. Caracas was, however, also home to various autonomous forums. The open and participatory 'Alternative Social Forum', set up by Libertarian activists, adopted a critical attitude towards the 'vertical' and 'authoritarian' organisation of the 'official' forum. Its limited size allowed deep debates and discussions that had been forgotten in the larger events (cf. Pleyers and Ornelas 2011).

Since 2006, the power of some of the WSF founding leaders has also been eroded[3] by the rise of a new generation of experts and advocacy networks, less based on prominent and mediatised intellectuals and more committed to horizontal relationships both between activists and among member organisations of alter-globalisation networks. The testimony published by Matti Kohonen in *Global Civil Society 2011* provides a vibrant illustration of the new dynamic that they have fostered. Then an LSE postgraduate student, and the international coordinator of the Tax Justice Network and of the Network Institute for Global Democratisation, Kohonen's concept of activist networks allies quality expertise with a decentralised and open way of working.

In other cases, the transition from organisations centred on historic leaders and intellectuals to more decentralised and participatory networks has had dramatic consequences. The confrontation between these two types of structures was particularly vigorous within ATTAC-France, the Association for the Taxation of Financial Transactions and Aid to Citizens. Founded in 1998, its French chapter was the most prominent group of the alter-globalisation movement in that country. In 2006, an electoral fraud was orchestrated at the internal national elections in favour of the organisation's historic leaders (Passet 2006). The latter subsequently lost most of their seats on the board at the new elections, held a few months later. The German chapter of ATTAC had its own shake-up in 2007. Most founding members eventually resigned from the national coordination committee in both countries, and ATTAC evolved towards a less hierarchical, more collegial, more decentralised structure, with a younger and more gender-balanced steering committee: two members of ATTAC-Germany's new national committee were aged 24 and 26, and the new co-chair of ATTAC-France was a 27-year-old woman.

The process of cross-fertilisation between WSF leaders and activists who promoted an open, horizontal and democratic movement organisation intensified after 2006. In the WSF IC, as in many other alter-globalisation networks, much energy has been devoted to discussing and rethinking the forum and its preparatory processes in order to reconcile openness, flat hierarchy and democracy with the efficiency required for an event of its size. Rather than speeches by star intellectuals, grassroots activist networks and more horizontal thematic expertise networks became the dynamic engine behind the world and continental Social Forums. It was particularly clear at the 2011 WSF that the forum owed much of its dynamism to networks dedicated to issues such as housing, climate change or international financial institutions. Moreover, the fact that the WSF has been hosted by different cities after 2005 has prevented the local organising committees from becoming as professionalised and as powerful as the Brazilian committee did between 2001 and 2005, when four WSFs were convened in Porto Alegre.

Grassroots Actors and NGOs in the Social Forum Process

Political Parties

The international nature of the WSF increases the need for resources and organisational capacity, which political parties and INGOs are able to provide. Moreover, the WSF seems particularly vulnerable, as open spaces 'that belong to no one' (Whitaker 2006) and that are dedicated to discussion and debate are 'constantly subject to invasion' (Kaldor 2003: 46): social and political actors want to take credit for the process, to take advantage of its coverage or to seize its political outcome. Many expected that the forum would quickly become dominated by INGOs or be swallowed up by political parties.

Box 10.3
The World Social Forum and the Maghreb-Mashreq Uprisings

A World Social Forum regional chapter, the Maghreb-Mashreq Social Forum (MMSF) has been closely involved in the development of the regional uprisings and in the institutional and social transformations currently under way across North Africa and in the Levantine Middle East. The MMSF gathers dozens of partners, including trade unions, national and regional human rights networks, women's and youth networks, peasants' organisations and development NGOs, all of which were instrumental in supporting the revolution. It was the Union Generale Tunisienne du Travail, to give one notable example, which called for and sustained the general strike that eventually ousted Ben Ali. The initial idea for a MMSF was voiced at the second WSF's global event held in Porto Alegre in 2002. Later that year, a meeting took place in Morocco in which activists committed themselves to network the entire region in a space animated by the values and the vision of the World Social Forum. That initial seed has grown through the committed and painstaking work of Moroccan activists and their regional partners. After successful local events in Morocco which were attended by thousands of activists from across the entire region, the Maghreb Social Forum finally came of age in July 2008, in the city of El Jadida. This first official regional forum saw the participation of 2300 activists from 28 countries.

In the months following the exhilarating experience of El Jadida, activists from the Maghreb and Mashreq networked intensely, working towards a wide regional meeting that would engage activists from Mauritania to Iraq. Such a meeting eventually took place in Rabat, Morocco, in early May 2009. It was then that the MMSF was officially launched. Since that time, the forum has expanded in scope; it has spearheaded, among other events, the recent global thematic forums on Education (Palestine 2010) and on Health, Land and Water (Cairo 2010).

At the same time the regional process has fed back into national forums like the Tunisian Social Forum (TSF), which, oppressed during Ben Ali's regime, is currently blossoming. As would be expected, the social forum framework in the region has been greatly enhanced by the current atmosphere of change, and by the feeling of possibility shared by activists throughout the region and beyond. In early April, following the departure of Ben Ali from Tunisia, the TSF hosted a global delegation of activists convened by the African Social Forum, under a collective decision taken by the International Council of the WSF in Dakar in February (see Box 10.2). Shortly after, a delegation of the MMSF visited Tunisia and held meetings with the local activist on topics of transitional justice, development and activist mobilisation, and to reflect upon the challenges of the democratic transition.

This flurry of solidarity and mobilisation continues to take shape. At the latest International Council meeting of the WSF, held in Paris in May 2011, it was decided that the next WSF, to be held in 2013, will take place in either Tunis or Cairo. In the meantime, a series of regional, continental, national and thematic events will be arranged, starting in July 2011 in Tunisia. A Solidarity Forum with Palestine will be organised in Egypt, and a global seminar on the same topic will take place in Brazil. In Montreal and in Santiago de Compostela, large events will be organised under the aegis of the WSF, focusing on the revolutions and their global effects, and their contribution to the development of alternative civilisational paradigms, patterns of migration and of labour, goods and services markets.

The revolutions of the Maghreb and Mashreq regions are not over; there will no doubt be setbacks and counter revolutionary attempts, as it is common of revolutions. It is in this context that transnational activist networks and global civil society forums could become tools of collaborative activism and spaces of debate and reflection aimed at supporting the democratic transition. The WSF has offered itself as one such space, and, if the successes of the MMSF are anything to go by, it is a space with transformative potential.

Giuseppe Caruso

The WSF Charter states that forums are spaces dedicated to social movements and citizens. Political parties are welcome as a passive audience (see Glasius and Timms 2006). However, at each of the Latin American and Indian WSFs, a few stages and panels have been given to local and national political parties and leaders. In 2001, a stage in the final session was provided to local and national leaders of the Brazilian Workers' Party (PT). Lula took part in each of the WSFs in Brazil, and both Indian Communist Parties were very visible at the 2004 WSF in Mumbai. The peak of the influence of political parties on the forum was reached at the 2006 P-WSF in Caracas, where speakers at the main stage took every opportunity to repeat their solidarity with Hugo Chavez' 'revolutionary process'. This eventually resulted in divisions among the IC, with some members opposing the 'politicisation' of the forum. One year later, politicians and parties were almost invisible at the 2007 Forum in Nairobi and 'politics-oriented activists' have clearly lost ground in subsequent forums. The debate over the participation of progressive political leaders is far from over, and probably never will be. However, ten years after the first WSF and in contrast with many predictions, the WSF has not been overthrown by a single political orientation.

Nairobi 2007: An INGOs' WSF

NGOs have played an important role in the alter-globalisation movement. They have brought new ideas, a repertory of action (including the counter-summits; see Pianta 2001, 2002, and Chapter 11 this volume, Box 11.2) and have helped to finance WSF events and travel costs for African and Asian activists. NGOs and INGOs were very active in the WSF between 2002 and 2006; however, the fact that they largely dominated the 2007 WSF in Nairobi raised a wide range of criticisms.

The 'decentralisation' of organisation that has been in operation at the forums since 2005 has had at least one perverse effect: the number and visibility of panels at each forum has depended less on the relevance of the issue at stake than on the financial resources of the organisation that has proposed it. In order to stage a workshop, it helps to be able to rent a room within the forum, advertise the discussion panel, pay the speakers' fees and travel, and so on; NGOs are usually more able than grassroots movements to play this game. This was particularly evident in Nairobi, where, for example, the US NGO Action Aid alone held 36 workshops. Their

audience was often limited to the NGO's members and partners, for whom it had booked several hotels.

Both the main themes in the 2007 WSF programme and the logistical organisation of the forum reflected this supremacy of NGOs. Far more panels focused on international institutions and on the development aid sector than on local struggles. Moreover, the choices made in the organisation of logistics impeded the participation of poorer local people, with a venue remote from the city centre, expensive water and food sold by private companies on the WSF site, and security guards to prohibit access to those who were unable to pay the entrance fee. The International Assembly of Social Movements in Nairobi and the Kenyan network's 'People's Parliament' fiercely denounced the 'privatisation, commodification and militarisation' of a forum 'squandered by the lack of compassion, compounded by the great arrogance exhibited by the organisers' (Mbatia and Indusa 2011 [2007]).

The Nairobi experience deeply affected many WSF organisers and participants, increasing their suspicions about the excessive participation of NGOs and their will to defend 'the prominence of grassroots social movements' in the forums (a member of the IC, 2007). Consequently, the influence of NGOs has declined considerably in subsequent forums. When the WSF came back to Africa in 2011, it was a very different event, 'open and accessible, and … at the same time militant and assertively political … notable for its inclusiveness and the diversity of participants' (see Box 10.1). Not only was it easier for local people to come to the forum, the forum also went to the people; the World Assembly of Inhabitants, organised in a suburb of Dakar, was perhaps the most notable of the events organised externally (see Box 10.1).

International Networks of Grassroots Movements

The evolution of the relationship between NGOs and social movements within the WSF process has both been fostered by and reflects one of the most significant changes in global civil society in the past decade: grassroots networks have realised that their internationalisation did not necessarily require NGOs.

Critiques against some NGOs' practices have risen within and beyond the forum. African local activists complain that they have been instrumentalised by NGOs: 'Some NGOs use us to hold money and contracts but never listen to us.'[4] They denounce their 'double-talk: they speak about participation, but concretely, associated movements have little or no room to discuss the project'.[5] While NGOs attempted to relay the 'voice of the voiceless', some ended up monopolising access to the international arena. Grassroots movements thus decided to build their own international networks (which often compete with INGOs), as well to develop their own expertise. At the 2006 Bamako P-WSF, Paul Nicholson, a leader of Via Campesina,[6] argued that peasants 'no longer want NGOs to speak in our name to international institutions and about agricultural policy. We want to build our own movement, our own international network and to speak for ourselves.' The creation of the International Alliance of Inhabitants reflected a similar process: 'We are not worth less than NGOs. Actually, I would even say we are worth more, because we have a social constituency … We decided to carry their own destiny, not only in the neighbourhood, but also at the international level.'[7]

From that perspective, the WSF has been a powerful tool. It has facilitated networking and knowledge-sharing and has given a global platform to locally-rooted struggles. Via Campesina has been one of the leading actors of the WSF process from the beginning; since then, dozens of other international networks have been created at the forums, including the Network Institute for Global Democratization, the European and African network for the defence of water as a common good and No Vox, a global network that gathers homeless peoples', landless peasants' and illegal migrants' organisations.

The US Social Forum

The desire to prevent NGOs from taking the lead in the Social Forums is particularly strong amongst the US Social Forum (USSF) organisers. Rather than creating a space equally welcoming to all members of civil society, the USSF founding document states it should 'place the highest priority on groups that are actually doing grassroots organizing with working class people of color, who are training organizers, building long-term structures of resistance'.[8] They consequently excluded North American INGOs and philanthropic foundations,[9] as they wanted to avoid the forum being led by 'policy and solidarity organisations that lacked a base in the most marginalised communities in the US' (Leon Guerrero 2011). This decision resulted in smaller forums (about 15,000 activists at each of the first two USSFs), and in additional organisational and financial challenges. After the first preparatory meeting in 2002, it took five years and dozens of local and national gatherings to set up the first US Social Forum.

Rather than holding the forum in cosmopolitan cities, which would likely have attracted thousands of left-wing intellectuals and the staff of major NGOs, the USSFs are held in cities with major poverty concerns and, to date, large African American populations: Atlanta in 2007 and Detroit in 2010. This has resulted in very multicultural, racially and generationally diverse forums (Karides et al. 2010), with the strong participation of domestic workers and minorities, and with spotlights on issues such as immigrant rights, the right to the city, or racism within movements and civil society organisations. By addressing the informal barriers that prevent certain sectors of society from attending Social Forums (Smith et al. 2008, Pleyers 2004), the USSF has helped to redress the domination of white and middle-class activists (Martinez 2000), perceived previously both within more general alter-globalisation spaces in the US and in many of the WSF.

Weaknesses and Limits

Contrasting with theories on social movement evolution and internationalisation, the WSF has not become a tamed and more institutionalised place. Its historical leaders and committed intellectuals have lost much of their power while grassroots activists have found more space in recent forums. The push towards institutionalisation that dominated the first three WSF has been countered by the will of alter-globalisation activists to maintain an open space, and by their predilection for grassroots movements over political parties and powerful INGOs.

Drawing on a comparative study of 53 American social movements, W. Gamson (1975) showed that the more bureaucratic movement organisations were more efficient and more successful in political struggles, notably thanks to a clear division of tasks. This argument has been contested (for example, Fox Piven 1978) and needs to be nuanced, as new technologies have provided new coordination tools and as social movements relying on loose networks have shown they could be efficient.[10] However, there may indeed be a price to pay for limited institutionalisation. In the case of the WSF, this is particularly notable in terms of the efficiency of the logistical organisation, the lack of cumulative knowledge, in maintaining attendance sizes and in promoting the visibility of the WSF in dominant media and amongst policy-makers.

With exponential experience of previous forums and increasing professionalisation, the Brazilian Organising Secretary became more efficient between 2001 and 2005. As the WSF has, since then, moved to a different country each year, and as it has not become more institutional-ised, each forum constitutes a new logistical challenge for a team that has scant experience in convening such a large international meeting. The logistical organisation of the 2011 WSF in Dakar was indeed a nightmare for all the participants. Many tents remained empty, despite the fact that local organisers were unable to assign venues for hundreds of workshops. Participants spent hours looking for the panel that they planned to attend, as the morning's programme was often only made available that same afternoon.[11]

Limited institutionalisation may also be one of the factors that have led to smaller audiences and a drop in media coverage. Compared to previous social forums, both the USSF and the 2011 WSF in Dakar had lower attendance figures (15,000 and 40,000, respectively). In each case, the IC chose to prioritise geographical and social extension (that is, beyond the usual white middle-class activists) over the size of the audience. The formula for gathering a large number of activists is actually relatively simple and well-known: a professional team to deal with logistical issues, a host city that is easily accessible and which boasts strong local movements and clear political support. Ideally, at least as far as the WSF are concerned, this city would additionally be located in Brazil (120,000 people attended the 2009 WSF in Bélem). It may also help to delegate the central organising role to more institutionalised and richer global civil society actors, such as INGOs, which are able to efficiently advertise the WSF, organise workshops and pay for the flights and fees of guest participants. Professional organisations with clearly identified leaders and members with communication skills and training are also far more efficient in procuring global media attention. Since, within the WSF, historical leaders have lost ground and the alter-globalisation movement has become more horizontal, its visibility has decreased, even in the midst of a major financial and economic crisis.

Moreover, organising self-assessment practices and open decision-making processes are difficult and time-consuming tasks. The WSF ideal of participation by the greatest number often conflicts with the need for efficiency in meetings, when time is short and decisions must be made. Efforts to improve internal democracy and the openness of decision-making processes slow down and make more complex the answers to problems in a changing context (Sikkink 2002: 312). While WSF activists have put much time and energy towards developing a more open and democratic forum, and the USSF has made progress in giving the central role at forums to excluded categories of the population, the answer to global crises – the *raison d'être* of the forum – has seemed slow and unclear.

Conclusion

Civil society internationalisation in the 1990s was characterised by strong institutionalisation and a taming process that quickly transformed new social movements into respectable NGOs (Kaldor 2003). The WSF process and the rise of some international networks of grassroots actors suggest that activists may have developed a new pattern of internationalisation without institutionalisation by focusing on grassroots actors and promoting more participatory and horizontal organisation. While global civil society had a tendency to be assimilated to INGOs in the 1990s, global activists have fostered a diverse global civil society, of which INGOs remain a major component, but where networks of grassroots actors have also found their way.

The ten-year-long experience of the WSF suggests that the strong reflexivity of alter-globalisation activists, along with their promotion of horizontal and more participatory organisation, has had a considerable impact on the forum's structure and organisation. Together with other factors, such as the rising use of new information and communication technologies (NICT) and the culture of networks (Castells 1996–98), this has contributed to building a different model of internationalisation. The example of the WSF compels social movement and global civil society scholars to pay greater heed to the reflexivity and political cultures of activists as a determinant factor in the evolution of social movement organisational forms (Jasper 2010, Goodwin and Jasper 2004: 17–23).

While institutionalisation leads to a homogenisation within a movement and to its integration into mainstream political processes, the WSF has increased its diversity, remaining an open space where tensions between different components and concepts of the forum constitute the engine of its constant evolution and adaptation. The success of the forum lies less in its ability to overcome and close internal debates (for example, 'Should it be a space for movement or a political actor?': cf. Whitaker et al. 2006, Cassen 2006, Glasius and Timms 2006; see also Doerr 2008) than to maintain a constructive tension between different poles of opinion. In doing so, the WSF may, in part, realise what the editors of the first *Global Civil Society* yearbook designated as one of the primary purposes of global civil society: to be 'a supranational sphere of social and political participation in which citizens groups, social movements, and individuals engage in dialogue, debate, confrontation and negotiation with each other and with various governmental actors' (Anheier et al. 2001: 4).

Box 10.4
Alter-Globalisation: Two Ways of Becoming Actors in the Global Age

One root of the alter-globalisation movement – also known as the 'global justice' movement – lies in a reaction to transformations in the field of development NGOs. Since the 1990s, the World Bank and the IMF have relied on what they considered to be the 'comparative advantage' of NGOs in terms of efficiency, cost and output, mobilising them in public–private partnerships (Kaldor 2003). Numerous NGOs were solicited by international institutions to provide social services where the 'strategic adjustment plans' imposed by international institutions impeded states from doing so; between 1990 and 2000, the percentage of NGOs stating that their objective was to provide social, medical and educational services grew by 79 per cent, 50 per cent and 24 per cent respectively (Kaldor, Anheier and Glasius 2003: 15–16).

Far from their utopian beginnings, many NGO activists disliked being reduced to bandaging wounds resulting from the application of the Washington Consensus, while struggling within a competitive NGO market. Some of these activists became convinced that improving the situation of the South would occur primarily through a change in policy and ideology in the North and in international institutions. Many of them thus turned towards the alter-globalisation movement, of which several became founders and leading actors (such as Bernard Dreano, author of Chapter 3 in this volume), transitioning from development aid to the struggle against neoliberal policies and global institutions.

Against the dominant idea that 'there is no alternative' to neoliberal policies (cf. Box 5.2) in the shift to a globalised world (Albrow 1996), alter-globalisation activists have developed two pathways for 'ordinary citizens' to have an impact and become actors in the global age. One focuses on reason and expertise; the other on subjectivity, creativity and experience.

In the 'way of reason', activists believe in more active citizens, familiarised with scientific knowledge and able to get involved in debates on global issues, especially in public economics. They propose alternative policies to the Washington Consensus and produce expert reports to show that neoliberal policies are not only socially unfair but also irrational, according to scientific criteria. They consider the major challenge to be the binding of the sphere of finance and economy to social, cultural, environmental and political standards. While the first operate at a global level, the latter remain largely reliant on nation-state policies.

Therefore, 'way of reason' activists underline the urgent necessity of stronger and more democratic international institutions and supranational regulations, with the power to manage the global economy and to set up redistribution and participation at a global level. Their conception of social change is institutionalised and rather top-down, as it focuses on policy-makers, global institutions and regulations. Correspondingly, their organisations are often hierarchically structured. Although they promote a more participatory society, many alter-activist organisations have been reluctant to implement internal participatory management and have shown little consideration for internal democracy.

In the 'way of subjectivity', activists struggle to defend their creativity and the specificity of their lived experience against the hold of a consuming culture, capitalism and global corporations. Their conception of social change is clearly bottom-up: rather than attempting to change policy agendas, these activists seek to implement their own values and alternative solutions in their daily lives, in local communities and in the organisation of their groups and networks. They insist in consistency between the values defended by the movement and its practices. Indigenous Zapatista communities in Mexico, social and cultural centres across Europe and networks of young alter-activists thus seek to create autonomous spaces 'free from power relations', where they experiment with horizontal networking, alternative consumption and participatory decision-making processes.

A constructive interaction between these two concepts of social change and two types of organisational structuring may overcome some of their respective limits and drifts. The cultural actors' arguments help to limit the power of experts and intellectual leaders within the movement, and counterbalance its institutionalisation process. Conversely, intellectuals and citizens who promote rationality will avoid a withdrawal of the movement into local spaces and communitarian experiences, thus helping some alternative solutions to reach policy-makers. Taken together, these two sets of experimentations offer concrete ways forward for a multidimensional approach to building a global society, which simultaneously acknowledges the key role of self-transformation, local communities, citizen activism, national policies and international institutions.

Geoffrey Pleyers

Notes

1. This was also the case with the European Social Forums (Juris 2006). In several European countries, local social movements have played a major role in connecting activists beyond borders without relying on an institutionalisation process (Della Porta and Mosca 2010).
2. A West European scholar/activist, during the IC meeting before the 2004 WSF in Mumbai.
3. Since 2006, several leading scholar activists repeatedly proclaimed that the WSF had lost most of its purpose and had become useless (for example, Bello 2007). Their position may actually reflect the declining influence of this category of activists in the WSF process.
4. A grassroots activist during a preparation workshop for the 2007 WSF; Durban, 22 July 2006. See also Seckinelgin (2007).
5. A delegate from the grassroots network StreetNet, during the meeting 'The Access of Self-Help Networks to the International Arena', Rambouillet, France, 2009. See also Haringer and Vielajius (2010) and Pleyers (2010b).
6. A network that claims to gather over 100 million small- and medium-size farmers worldwide.
7. A delegate from the International Alliance of Inhabitants, during the meeting 'The Access of Self-Help Networks to the International Arena', Rambouillet, France, 2009.
8. Extract from 'What we Believe', available at http://www.ussf2010.org/about (accessed 1 September 2011).
9. The USSF preparation process also included a critical reflection on the dependency of many social justice organisations on wealthy philanthropists who determine the movement's agenda based on their funding priorities.
10. As the Tunisian and Egytian revolutions have recently shown. See also Castells (1997).
11. Lack of institutionalisation also hinders the development of a movement's historical memory, at which loose and evanescent networks proved to be far less efficient than professional and long-lasting social movement organisations (cf. Pleyers 2010a: 53).

References

Albrow, Martin (1996) *The Global Age*. Cambridge: Polity Press.

Anheier, Helmut, Glasius, Marlies, and Kaldor, Mary (2001) 'Introducing Global Civil Society', in Helmut Anheier, Marlies Glasius and Mary Kaldor (eds), *Global Civil Society 2001*. Oxford: Oxford University Press, pp. 3–22.

Bello, Walden (2007) *World Social Forum at the Crossroads*. Bangkok: Focus on the Global South.

Caruso, Gisueppe (2010) 'Differences and Conflicts in the World Social Forum India: Towards an "Open" Cosmopolitanism?', in Jai Sen and Peter Waterman (eds), *Challenging Empires II*. New Delhi: Open Word.

Cassen, Bernard (2006) 'The World Social Forum: Where do we Stand and Where are we Going?', in Marlies Glasius, Mary Kaldor and Helmut Anheier (eds), *Global Civil Society 2005/6*. London: Sage Publications, pp. 79–83.

Castells, Manuel (1996–98) *The Age of Information*, 3 Vols. Oxford: Blackwell.

Chandhoke, Neera (2002) 'The Limits of Global Civil Society', in Marlies Glasius, Mary Kaldor and Helmut Anheier (eds), *Global Civil Society 2002*. Oxford: Oxford University Press, pp. 35–53.

Della Porta, Donatella (2005) 'Multiple Belongings, Tolerant Identities, and the Construction of Another Politics', in Donatella Della Porta and Sydney Tarrow (eds), *Transnational Protest and Global Activism*. Lanham, MD: Rowman and Littlefield, pp. 175–201.

Della Porta, Donatella and Diani, Mario (1999) *Social Movements*. Oxford: Blackwell.

Della Porta, Donatella and Mosca, Lorenzo (2010) 'Build Locally, Link Globally: The Social Forum Process in Italy', *Journal of World-Systems Research*, Vol. 16 No. 1: 63–81.

Desai, Magnus and Said, Yahia (2003) 'Trade and Global Civil Society: The Anti-Capitalist Movement Revisited', in Mary Kaldor, Helmut Anheier and Marlies Glasius (eds), *Global Civil Society 2003*. Oxford: Oxford University Press, pp. 59–85.

Doerr, Nicole (2007) 'Multilingualism and Global Civil Society', in Martin Albrow et al. (eds), *Global Civil Society 2007/8*. London: Sage Publications.

Dreano, Bernard (2004) 'In Paris, the Global Place Is No longer Saint Germain des Prés: Civil Society and the French Debate', in Marlies Glasius, David Lewis and Hakan Seckinelgin (eds), *Exploring Civil Society: Political and Cultural Contexts*. London: Routledge.

Dufour, Pascale, Caouette, Dominique, and Masson, Dominique (eds) (2010) *Solidarities beyond Borders: Transnationalising Women's Movements*. Montreal: UBC Press.

Fox Piven, Frances (1979) *Poor People's Movements*. New York: Vintage Books.

Friedman, Jonathan (1999) 'Indigenous Struggles and the Discreet Charm of the Bourgeoisie', *Journal of World-Systems Research*, Vol. 5 No. 2: 391–411.

Gamson, William (1975) *The Strategy of Social Protest*. Homewood, IL: Dorsey Press.

Glasius, Marlies and Timms, Jill (2006) 'The Role of Social Forums in Global Civil Society', in Marlies Glasius, Mary Kaldor and Helmut Anheier (eds), *Global Civil Society 2005/6*. London: Sage Publications, pp. 190–238.

Glasius, Marlies, Lewis, David and Seckinelgin, Hakan (eds) (2004) *Exploring Civil Society: Political and Cultural Contexts*. London: Routledge.

Goodwin, Jeff and Jasper, James (eds) (2004) *Rethinking Social Movements*. Lanham, MD: Rowman and Littlefield.

Haeringer, Nicolas and Vielajius, Martin (2011) 'Transnational Networks of Self-Representation: An Alternative Form of Struggle for Global Justice', in Martin Albrow and Hakan Seckinelgin (eds), *Global Civil Society 2011*. Basingstoke: Palgrave Macmillan.

Houtart, François and Polet, François (2001) *The Other Davos*. London: Zed Books.

Hurrelmann, Klaus and Albert, Mathias (eds) (2002) *Jugend 2000: zwischen pragmatischem Idealismus und robustem Materialismus*. Frankfurt: Fischer.

Jasper, James (2010) 'Social Movement Theory Today: Toward a Theory of Action?', *Sociology Compass*, Vol. 10: 1–12.

Juris, Jeffrey (2005) 'Social Forums and their Margins: Networking Logics and the Cultural Politics of Autonomous Space', in Marlies Glasius, Mary Kaldor and Helmut Anheier (eds), *Global Civil Society 2005/6*. London: Sage Publications.

Juris, Jeffrey (2008) *Networking Future*. Durham, NC: Duke University Press.

Kaldor, Mary (2003) *Global Civil Society*. Cambridge: Polity Press.

Kaldor, Mary, Anheier, Helmut and Glasius, Marlies (eds) (2003) *Global Civil Society 2003*. Oxford: Oxford University Press.

Karides, Marina, Katz-Fishman, Walda, Scott, Jerome, Walker, Alice, and Brewer, Rose (eds) (2010) *The United States Social Forum: Perspectives of a Movement*. Chicago: Changemaker Publications.

Keck, M. and Sikkink, K. (1998) *Activists Beyond Borders*. Ithaca, NY: Cornell University Press.

Klein, Naomi (2002) *Fences and Windows: The Front Lines of the Globalization Debate*. Toronto: Vintage Canada.

Kriesi, Hanspeter (1996) 'The Organisational Structure of New Social Movements in a Political Context', in Doug McAdam, John McCarthy and Zald Mayer (eds), *Comparative Perspectives on Social Movements*. Cambridge: Cambridge University Press, pp. 152–84.

Leon Guerrero, Michael (2011) 'The Second US Social Forum: What did we Accomplish?', in Jai Sen and Peter Waterman (eds), *World Social Forum. Critical Explorations*. New Delhi: OpenWord, pp. 107–30.

Martinez, Elizabeth (2000) 'The WTO: Where was the Color in Seattle?', *ColorLines*, Vol. 3 No. 1, Spring: 11–12.

Mbatia, W. and Indusa, H. (2011 [2007]) 'The World Social Forum 2007: A Kenyan Perspective', in Jai Sen and Peter Waterman, *World Social Forum: Critical Explorations*. New Delhi: OpenWord, pp. 70–9.

McDonald, Kevin (2006) *Global Movements*. London: Blackwell.

Michels, Robert (1962) [1911]) *Political Parties: A Sociological Study of the Oligarchical Tendencies of Modern Democracy*. New York: Collier Books.

Passet, René (2006) *Elections ATTAC: synthèse finale des rapports d'experts*, http://hussonet.free.fr/rpasset.pdf (accessed 1 June 2010).

Pearce, Jenny (2004) 'Collective Action or Public Participation? Civil Society and the Public Sphere in Post-transition Latin America', in Marlies Glasius, David Lewis and Hakan Seckinelgin (eds), *Exploring Civil Society: Political and Cultural Contexts*. London: Routledge, pp. 61–70.

Pianta, Mario (2001) 'Parallel Summits of Global Civil Society', in Helmut Anheier, Marlies Glasius and Mary Kaldor (eds) *Global Civil Society 2001*. Oxford: Oxford University Press, pp. 169–94.

Pianta, Mario (2002) 'Parallel Summits of Global Civil Society: An update', in Marlies Glasius, Mary Kaldor and Helmut Anheier (eds) *Global Civil Society 2002*. Oxford: Oxford University Press, pp. 371–7.

Pleyers, Geoffrey (2004) 'Social Forums as an ideal model of convergence', in *International Social Science Journal 2004*, Vol. LVI (4), pp. 507–17.

Pleyers, Geoffrey (2007) *Forums sociaux mondiaux et défis de l'altermondialisme*. Louvain-la-Neuve: Academia Bruylant.

Pleyers, Geoffrey (2008) 'The World Social Forum: A Globalisation from Below?', *Societies without Borders*, Vol. 3 No. 1: 72–90.

Pleyers, Geoffrey (2010a) *Alter-Globalization. Becoming Actors in the Global Age*. Cambridge: Polity Press.

Pleyers, Geoffrey (2010b) 'International NGOs and self-help networks: from critics to complementarity?', in *The Access of Self-Help Networks to the International Arena*. Paris: IRG & Ford Foundation, pp. 69–76, available at http://www.institut-gouvernance.org/IMG/pdf/FORD-IRG-seminare-rambouillet.pdf.

Pleyers, Geoffrey and Ornelas, Raul (2011) 'The World Social Forum Hits New Ground', in Jai Sen and Peter Waterman (eds), *World Social Forum: Critical Explorations*. New Delhi: OpenWord, pp. 45–56.

Seckinelgin, Hakan (2007) *International Politics of HIV/AIDS*. London: Routledge.

Sen, Jai and Waterman, Peter (eds) (2009) *World Social Forum: Challenging Empires*. Montreal: Black Rose Books.

Sikkink, Kathryn (2002) 'Restructuring World Politics: The Limits and Asymmetries of Soft Power', in S. Khagram, J. V. Riker and K. Sikkink (eds), *Restructuring World Politics: Transnational Social Movements, Networks, and Norms*. Minneapolis, MN: University of Minnesota Press, pp. 301–17.

Smith, Jackie, Juris, Jeffrey and the Social Forum Research Collective (2008) 'We are the Ones we have been Waiting For', *Mobilization*, Vol. 13 No. 4: 373–94.

Tarrow, Sydney (1998) *Power in Movement: Social Movements and Contentious Politics*. Cambridge: Cambridge University Press.

Tarrow, Sydney (2005) *The New Transnational Activism*. Cambridge: Cambridge University Press.

Tilly, Charles (1986) *La France conteste de 1600 à nos jours*. Paris: Fayard.

Tilly, Charles (2004) *Social Movements 1768–2004*. Boulder, CO: Paradigm.

Timms, Jill (2006) 'The Social Forum is Not for Sale?', in Marlies Glasius, Mary Kaldor and Helmut Anheier (eds), *Global Civil Society 2005/6*. London: Sage Publications, pp. 232–3.

Touraine, Alain (1973) *Production de la Société*. Paris: Seuil.

Walker, Robert (1994) 'Social Movements/World Politics?', *Millennium*, Vol. 23 No. 3: 669–700.

Weber, Max (1978) [1922] *Economy and Society*. Berkeley: University of California Press.

Whitaker, Francisco, Cassen, Bernard and de Sousa Santos, Boaventura (2006) 'The World Social Forum: Where Do We Stand and Where Are We Going?', in Marlies Glasius, Mary Kaldor and Helmut Anheier (eds), *Global Civil Society 2005/6*. London: Sage Publications, pp. 66–72.

Wieviorka, M. (2005) 'After New Social Movements', *Social Movement Studies*, Vol. 4 No. 1: 1–19.

PART V

Records

CHAPTER 11

BORDERING ON THE UNKNOWN: APPROACHES TO GLOBAL CIVIL SOCIETY DATA

Sally Stares, Sean Deel and Jill Timms[1]

The *Global Civil Society* yearbook programme has always involved efforts to collate and collect data that might inform our understanding of this complex phenomenon. In addition to the empirical evidence used by chapter authors, we have included sections of quantitative data in most editions. These have been compiled from a number of sources and presented in various formats, following a conceptual framework devised by Helmut Anheier (Anheier 2001).

The concepts that are central to the study of global civil society (GCS) do not lend themselves easily to the classical, conventional research methods and methodologies of the social sciences. Anheier and Katz have explored a number of ways in which existing data might be analysed for GCS studies, whilst Timms has managed a pilot study in collecting new data on civil society events through a network of GCS correspondents, and Pianta has collected data on parallel summits and GCS events. At the same time, the evolving literature about the nature of GCS has produced some key theoretical principles from which methodologies for capturing GCS might be further developed. And lastly, technologies enabling citizens to report data themselves have become widely accessible and increasingly used by civil society actors.

In this chapter we outline the nature and challenges of operationalising GCS with empirical data, and propose a new data collection initiative that builds on the latest practical and theoretical contributions to this project.

First Things First

Ten years since the first GCS yearbook, there is still no agreed definition of GCS. This is in one sense a serious problem for data collection: how can we operationalise a concept that is undefined? In another sense, however, a blank page is an advantage, affording the opportunity to trial a range of approaches, to be creative and to avoid the diktats of established methods.

An important element of GCS is understanding the connections between and within local, national and global spheres of activity. There is a fundamental tension between this principle and the lens of methodological nationalism that is so often a straitjacket for the social sciences (Beck 2003). More generally, the contested nature of the concept demands a flexible orientation that considers a range of information sources and data types, acknowledging that they are partial, both in coverage and in motivation. GCS is a field of enquiry in which politics and activism are central, making reflexivity and sensitivity to the nuances of context crucially important. In proposing a framework for 'measuring' GCS, Anheier laid out these premises as four 'assumptions':

1. Any measurement of GCS will be simpler and less perfect than the richness, variety, and complexity of the concept it tries to measure.
2. GCS is a multifaceted, emerging phenomenon, and its operationalisation must take account of this essential characteristic.
3. GCS is essentially a normative concept.
4. The operationalisation and measurement of GCS has a strategic-developmental dimension. (Anheier 2001: 224)

As a first operationalisation of the substance of GCS, Anheier set out a list of variables or indicators that would capture the important phenomena for this study. These are depicted in Figure 11.1.

Element A in the figure covers key background or contextual factors that combine with GCS to constitute the 'drivers' of globalisation (Anheier et al. 2001): globalisation of economies, communication and culture and population movement; and the spread of the international rule of law through treaties, human rights and environment movements, international peacekeeping and displacement of persons, and in contraposition, international crime (such as human trafficking). The data for these concepts are mostly administrative statistics collected or collated by centralised national or

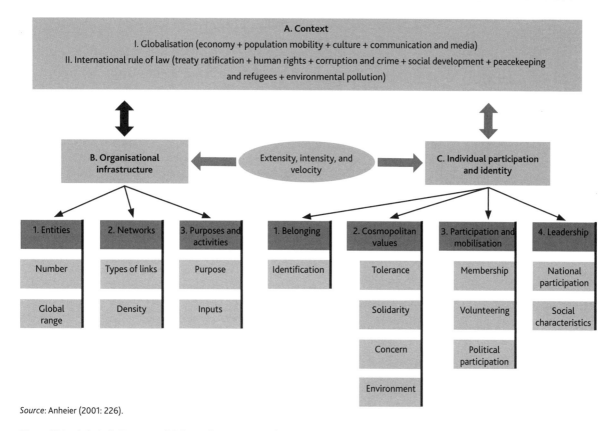

Source: Anheier (2001: 226).

Figure 11.1   Anheier's Conceptual Scheme for Operationalising Global Civil Society

international agencies (in particular the World Bank and United Nations). They typically comprise relatively stable counts or ratios of quantities, such as income per country per year; numbers of telephones per capita in a country at a certain point in time; or numbers of treaties ratified by countries on a given theme at a given point in time. They are not without shortcomings, well documented by their creators – including problems of settling on common definitions across contexts; coverage; accuracy and other aspects of data quality which also often vary widely.

The challenges entailed in measuring these elements of the context of GCS are to some extent common to all of the themes in Figure 11.1. However, there are somewhat different challenges for the concepts that are really central to GCS, which are included in elements B and C of the diagram. 'Organisational infrastructure' refers to the financial, legal, administrative and policy contexts for GCS organisations. For these, we have relied on information from the Johns Hopkins Comparative Non-Profit Sector study (Johns Hopkins 2011), and from the Union of

International Associations (UIA 2011), based in Brussels, which collects data on international and internationally-oriented NGOs and governmental organisations. The UIA maintains an impressively extensive register of organisations, and collects information on a range of their characteristics. These include geographical locations and reaches, interests and numbers of members, and connections between organisations, such as inter-organisation citations in official documents. The UIA has developed its own detailed conceptual scheme and classification for its data (UIA 2011). UIA data are limited to those organisations which are sufficiently connected to register themselves with UIA. Organisations that do not feature in their database include, for example, more local, informally organised groups, who might not be inclined to register with UIA or might lack the means to do so.

Element C of the diagram is 'individual participation and identity', and is operationalised by 'softer' data – for example, those capturing social values relating to such principles as tolerance and solidarity, which are central features of the climate for GCS. For these we have tended to rely on population surveys of social values amongst the public of many countries (World Values Survey 2011), alongside additional data on opinions sought from NGO workers and leaders (Pianta and Silva 2003a), and other relevant actors in GCS. The rich and extensive literature on survey methodology makes clear the challenges of cross-cultural comparability, and critiques of the levels of accuracy and depth that might be gained from these data. Again practicalities always emerge as a concern: drawing good probability samples, on which their validity rests, is a pipe-dream in many countries.

Anheier's framework has played the role of something analogous to a sampling frame for concepts and phenomena in GCS which are relevant to our points of focus in the yearbook. In developing our data programme, we have mostly been trying to map this sampling frame onto pre-existing sources of data collected by other agencies. One of the initial objectives for the yearbook data programme was to emulate the UNDP's Human Development Reports (UNDP 2011), by providing sections of quantitative data to serve as a reference source of relevant statistics for GCS actors. Modestly, we aimed to provide brief commentaries alongside the data on their relevance for GCS, and on notable trends and patterns, without going so far as to propose any grand statistical model of the connections between them. Re-presenting these data in our own format has often been a useful and effective exercise for this purpose. Sometimes this has meant coding and compiling qualitative data – for example, to summarise ratifications of international treaties, or violations of human rights (such as in Kaldor et al. 2007: 247–60). With each new yearbook we have tried to develop our approach, little by little. A first step constituted moving from presenting tables of indicators in per country per annum format, towards an increased use of graphics to highlight trends over time, and to throw into relief comparisons between aggregated units – for example, of countries grouped by geographical region or income (Katz 2008). Hagai Katz has produced numerous maps and network analyses to highlight connections and flows where these are contained in the data. These innovations have resulted from many sources of discussion and feedback: from regular meetings of the yearbook's editorial committee and authors' meetings; from informal feedback to authors from yearbook audiences; and from a few more focused sessions which drew in experts from other fields – these included a yearbook evaluation conference in London 2004, and an expert panel meeting for the data programme in Santa Barbara in 2006.

Analysing GCS Data – Multidisciplinary Innovations

Alongside the data programme, most editions of the yearbook have included a methodology chapter, each time showcasing a new approach to collating and analysing sets of GCS data. The starting point for these thought experiments was a country-level composite index of GCS (Anheier and Stares 2002) using a statistical latent variable model that allowed us to explore the relationships among the various components of GCS. A summary measure such as this invites broad-brush cross-national comparisons of the distributions, or roughly speaking 'amounts' of organisational infrastructure, participation and prevalence of sympathetic social values that together create space for GCS activity. It is then commonly extended to explore the place of the index among other contextual factors; in the chapter we presented a brief analysis of its relationships with a few very rough indicators of economic globalisation and the spread of international rule of law. In many ways an index represents a classic approach to empirical analysis of quantitative data for GCS: identifying the basic unit of analysis as the country; treating countries (statistically speaking) as independent entities, identifying attributes that are common to all and then exploring the patterns of these attributes among them. Indices are popular in the policy world, and a number have been developed that are relevant to civil society. For another example, Box 11.1 describes the GCS 'diamond' developed by the NGO Civicus.

A natural progression from such an approach is to integrate a new attribute into analyses. Anheier and Katz (2003) took up this idea in a creative way: rather than simply add an extra variable to a correlation matrix, they brought in geographical information, and demonstrated the insights that can be gained from mapping 'cases' (again to use statistical terminology) and their characteristics, and drawing out their connections. For example, showing on a map of Europe the distribution of the importance attached to 'tolerance' as a social value among citizens enables the reader to grasp the basic narrative in an instant, rather than reading through and interpreting a large table of statistics (Anheier and Katz 2003: 246). And focusing on the geographical dispersion of phenomena that are central to GCS invites a flexible stance on which unit(s) of analysis to adopt. So Anheier and Katz mapped numbers of NGO secretariats in cities globally, alongside

Box 11.1
The CIVICUS Civil Society Index

The Civil Society Index (CSI) is a participatory, action-oriented research programme. While the research component of the project aims at assessing the strengths and weaknesses of civil society in a comparative way, the action component seeks to strengthen civil society and its positive impact locally through this exercise. For this purpose CIVICUS, an international NGO, cooperates with partners from many countries around the world. Starting with the New Civic Atlas in 1997, the whole programme now comprises a pilot (2000–02, 13 countries) and two main phases (2003–06, 49 countries; and 2008–11, 25 countries).

The CSI is both innovative and one of the most comprehensive attempts of measuring civil society in a comparative way. It uses a multi-level multi-method approach, combining quantitative data from a population survey (micro), an organisational survey (meso), an external perception survey and from different internationally available data sources (Freedom House, World Bank, and so on) (macro) with more qualitative findings from case studies, focus groups, and so on (Mati et al. 2010). Main outputs of the CSI are the international datasets, some volumes summarising the main results (Heinrich and Fioramonti 2008, List and Dörner forthcoming), and, on the national level, the Analytical Country Reports and Policy Action Briefs. Most of the data and extensive descriptions of the methodology and implementation are downloadable from CIVICUS's website at www.civicus.org.

The CSI collects data on four dimensions, based on 53 indicators:

- Civic Engagement (split into social and political engagement)
- Level of Organisation
- Practice of Values
- Perception of Impact (split into internal and external perception).

Additionally, the CSI takes the external environment into account as a fifth dimension (twelve indicators). The national context is assessed in the fields of socio-economic, socio-political and socio-cultural contexts.

Instead of combining all the information into a single figure, as is done, for example, by the Human Development Index, the CSI displays its different dimensions separately. This feature actually makes the CSI an indicator system and not an index. To depict the full information in an easily accessible way, the so-called Civil Society Diamond was developed by Anheier (2004). Each of the four main dimensions builds one of the radiances of the diamond, displaying the scores for each on a scale from 0 to 100. This allows easy comparison across countries and the detection of relationships between dimensions by inspection of the diamond. The external environment is displayed as a circle (see Figure 11.2 for an example).

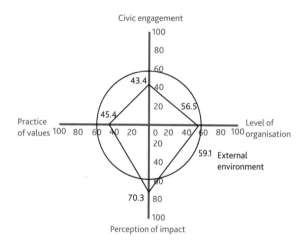

Figure 11.2   The Civil Society Diamond

While the CSI is an invaluable tool for comparing civil society in a broad sense globally, there are also some shortcomings, mainly related to comparability and methodology: although the CSI spans more than a decade now, data is not directly comparable across time, due to substantial changes in the methodology between phases. Comparability across countries might additionally be limited, as quality insurance measures with regard to sampling or to the translation of the English master-questionnaires have been implemented to a different degree. The CSI also initiated a more general discussion as to what extent it is possible to measure such a complex construct as civil society globally (see the contributions in the *Journal for Civil Society* in 2005 and 2006, such as Heinrich 2005).

Michael Hoelscher, University of Heidelberg.

the precise locations of large transnational corporations (Anheier and Katz 2003: 242). Taking up a case study of a single INGO (Friends of the Earth International) they mapped headquarters globally, superimposed onto a map of membership statistics country by country (Anheier and Katz 2003: 244).

This spatially sensitive type of analysis entails a fairly informal treatment of the relative locations of various points. By contrast, network analysis focuses explicitly on the interconnections of points, modelling them in a number of different ways. For example, Anheier and Katz (2005) analysed the organisational links (formal or semi-formal affiliations) amongst a sample of INGOs from the UIA's database, in order to explore how many connections each organisation had with other organisations. They found that very few INGOs had very large number of links, while a very large number of them had a small number of links; on average, an organisation would have ties to roughly seven other INGOs. This implied that the world of (registered) INGOs was fairly sparsely interconnected – existing in pockets or small clusters rather than as one grand densely connected web.

Separate networks can be mapped together in this kind of approach, where each may be structured around a different basic unit of analysis. So Anheier and Katz presented a two-mode network of NGO participation in self-organised events at one of the World Social Forums. One network charted the links between organisations (a link would be formed between two organisations when they participated in the same event), while the other recorded the links between events (two events would be linked by a common participant). The resulting depiction of the 'space for debate' (Anheier and Katz 2005: 217) indicated a rather fragmented sphere, consisting of small sub-networks of organisations, loosely linked by heterogeneous themes, rather than tightly clustered around clear common substantive concerns – perhaps a natural early stage in the development of a complex system.

Moving from overview to case study, Anheier and Katz then focused on describing the 'egocentric' networks surrounding two organisations. They found, in both cases, the networks to be sparse and, globally speaking, Northern-centred, even though one of the networks was framed around an organisation located south of the Sahara. And then adopting once more a wider lens, and this time at a higher level of abstraction, they showed how blockmodel analysis can be used to explore the connections between subgroups of organisations that share similar positions within a network – treating them

as 'joint actors' and exploring their group-level roles. A case study by Anheier and Romo (1999) demonstrated how ties of conflict and support among two sets of NGOs working towards establishing formal coalitions led to quite different structures for their resulting umbrella organisations. In one case the resulting structure had a functionally ambiguous form, with conflict and support connections sitting side by side; in the other, the resulting structure took a hierarchical shape, dominated by a few powerful organisations, with the majority remaining more loosely connected and less influential in the consortium.

In a later chapter, Anheier, Katz and Lam (2008) turned their attention to the theme of how phenomena move around or are spread within networks. They demonstrated the use of diffusion models to represent the spread of protests around the world in response to the publication of cartoons depicting the prophet Muhammad in a Danish newspaper in 2005. The analysis entailed a data set detailing the numbers of protests, protestors, and numbers of reprints of the cartoons, and the locations of these elements. A diffusion model of these data could comprise most simply a timeline showing the dates and frequencies of these elements, or more ambitiously a formal statistical model predicting the chances of a protest occurring in a given country, given some key characteristics theorised to affect these chances. These could afford the opportunity to test various ideas about the spread of ideas and concerns through a number of media sources to particular concerned communities.

One of the attractions of network analysis and diffusion models for social research is that they provide tools for explicitly representing the interconnectedness of organisations, or whatever units of analysis we choose. They directly address 'Galton's problem' – the shortcomings of treating social units and actors as if they are independent of each other. The fundamental interdependency of elements in the network is a central feature of globalisation and GCS (Anheier and Katz 2005).

Developing their thoughts along this line of enquiry, Anheier and Katz shifted their focus on interconnectedness to the time connections or narratives that connect GCS actors and events (Anheier and Katz 2006). Comparative historical analyses provide a middle ground between the very contextually nuanced idiographic depictions typical to historical analyses, and grander nomothetic representations common to social science, which prioritise the inference of general and generalisable trends and patterns, putting local detail to one side. As an illustration, Anheier and Katz applied a formal event structure analysis to a narrative account of the establishment of the International Criminal Court (ICC) (Glasius 2005). The analysis employed a software application to scrutinise the logical connections between events leading up to the acceptance of the ICC statute in Rome, 1998. Once identified as discrete events (an interpretive task in itself) and entered into a database, the task is to clarify which events are prerequisites for others; which are contingencies; which are coincidences; and whether, how and when parallel chains of events intersect. The result is a flow diagram of events (Anheier and Katz 2006: 299) representing a strong set of claims, formally posed and answered, about the causal relationships between events in sequence.

A complimentary approach to causal interpretations can be found in fuzzy sets analysis (Katz et al. 2007). Here the aim is to use a set of attributes to group cases into sets, to determine how 'crisp' or how 'fuzzy' the borders of those sets are, and to understand the relationships or degree of overlap between the sets. Katz et al. used the indicators analysed for the GCS Index to illustrate this approach. Firstly they sought to identify those countries that were variously 'inside' the sets characterised as economically globalised; accepting of the international rule of law; and with a globalised civil society. In a next step they explored the figurative Venn-diagram formation among those sets – for example, are all countries with a globalised civil society themselves economically globalised? The analysis suggested that whereas acceptance of the international rule of law seems to be a necessary prerequisite for GCS, the status of a country's economy is more loosely connected to GCS.

Most recently, Anheier and Katz (2009) proposed a pair of participatory methods that might be valuable to GCS. Forecasting and scenarios are examples of a wide range of 'futures' methodologies, which aim to understand and anticipate potential developments in a particular field. Anheier and Katz sketched out an illustration of forecasting applied to the International Trade Forum's evaluation of different ways of engaging NGOs as trade and development partners (Domeisen and de Sousa 2002). The project recruited experts to discuss this possible future turn in terms of its potential strengths and weaknesses, and opportunities and threats, based on knowledge of present conditions and anticipation of future developments. By contrast, the National Intelligence Council's Global Scenarios to 2025 project (NIC 2008) adopted a more open approach to speculation on future events, recruiting key stakeholders to discuss and describe a number of possible future scenarios around questions of sustainable economic growth in a fast changing geo-political landscape; and possible impacts of shifts in the global balance of power on collaborative policies.

The forecasting and scenario methods described by Anheier and Katz differ in a number of ways from traditional approaches to empirical research. Unlike the majority of statistical methods they seek not to separate system from noise, but to sketch out and explore all the nooks and crannies of possibility. They resonate strongly with GCS studies because GCS is itself such a complex subject, sensitive to the uncertainties and shocks that are key characteristics of globalisation (Anheier and Katz 2009). In addition, these methods are discursive and participatory; they are often used as communication tools among stakeholders as an end in themselves.

Collecting GCS Data – Tracking GCS Events

Alongside the series of methodology chapters, which have introduced readers to novel ways of analysing GCS data, we have published chronologies of GCS events (see, for example, Timms 2009; chronologies in previous yearbooks; and the selected highlights in the chronology of the decade presented by Timms in this volume). The broad objective of this part of the GCS programme is to document a range of civic activity around the world, including, for example, demonstrations, rallies, campaigns, petitions, Social Forums and vigils, as well as landmark legal rulings and other victories and defeats for civil society. These are defined as GCS events if they have a global significance in terms of theme, participants or resonance.

Chronologies of the year published by others usually focus on events and personalities from the North/West and depend on media coverage which tends to be biased against civil society activities, or at least against certain types. Our aim has been to provide a different type of chronology, presenting an insight into the diversity of events taking place around the world; the activities of a vast array of groups and organisations which can be described as part of GCS in the broadest understanding of the concept. Importantly, it includes events that have occurred in places often not reported in the mainstream media, and events which are not necessarily included in statistics on the growth of civil society activities and organisations – because of their unusual nature, because of the difficulty of representing them quantitatively, or because their existence tends not to be formally recorded.

The chronology has always relied on a network of GCS correspondents, developed through a number of avenues:

Box 11.2
Twenty Years of Global Civil Society Events: The Rise and Fall of Parallel Summits, the Novelty of Global Days of Action

In the last two decades global civil society has become a visible force, with events – often with thousands of participants – organised by cross border networks of social movements, associations and international NGOs. From 1990 to 2008, the authors of this box have surveyed 244 parallel summits and similar events, building on the definition devised for the study that opened this line of research in the first edition of the yearbook, *Global Civil Society 2001* (Pianta 2001). We define these types of global civil society events as follows:

- events organised by national and international civil society groups with international participation, independently of the activities of states and firms;
- events that may result from the autonomous initiative of civil society, or may coincide with, or be related to official summits of governments and international institutions;
- events addressing global issues, or the same problems as official summits, with a critical perspective on government and business policies;
- events using the means of public information and analysis, political mobilisation and protest, and alternative policy proposals; and

- events with or without formal contacts with the official summits (if there is one).

Events have been identified by searching the websites of civil society networks and INGOs, as well as websites, newspapers, and magazines that follow such gatherings. While by no means exhaustive, this survey spans a wide range of events, topic and locations, reflecting the evolution of global events.

The Rise and Stabilisation of Global Events

The evolution of global civil society events is shown in Figure 11.3, which reports the number of global events from 1990 to 2008. The early 1990s saw a modest presence of such initiatives, mainly in the forms of parallel summits to IMF-World Bank meetings and other summits of international organisations. The late 1990s saw the emergence of large civil society fora parallel to the major UN conferences on social development, women and other global issues. From 1999, with the protests in Seattle against the WTO, the rise of events is dramatic. First it is driven by the proliferation of protest events against all sorts of gatherings of political and economic institutions. Then, after the first World Social Forum held in Porto Alegre, Brazil, in 2001, there is a proliferation of

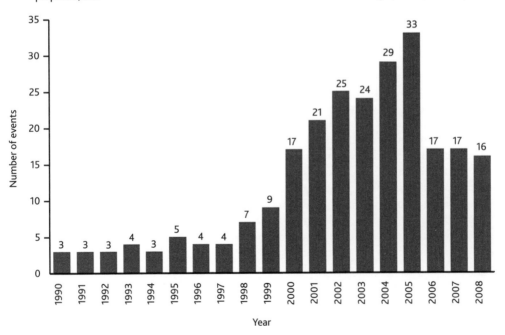

Figure 11.3   Growth of Parallel Summits and Related Events, 1990–2008

events associated with regional or thematic social forums. In 2003, with the start of the US war in Iraq, global protests address the issue of peace. At the same time, there is also a broadening of themes, with specific global gatherings focusing on social, gender, migration and other issues. The peak reached in 2005 is the result of the simultaneous presence of all these types of cross-border mobilisations: parallel summits, social forums, anti-war protests, 'emerging' global issues. From 2006 the wave of global protest – against neoliberal globalisation and war – slows down and global civil society events unfold with the more 'regular' succession of social forums and meetings parallel to the summits of G8/G20, IMF-WB, WTO and UN organisations, with fewer specific cross-border events. Until 2008 we find a stabilisation of events at a level that is about half the frequency found at the peak of global mobilisations.

Events tend to include an international conference, often a street demonstration, and occasional grassroots meetings and media-oriented initiatives. Participation ranges from the millions of people that joined the global days of action against war in Iraq in 2003, 2004 and 2005, to social forums gathering thousands of activists, to conferences of a few hundred activists with more specific interests or events of regional scope, especially in the South.

Global Events Move South

Parallel summits started in the North and have rapidly moved South and all over the world, as shown by Figure 11.4. In the period 1990–2003 almost two-thirds of recorded events were in Europe and North America; in 2004–08 this share is down to a little more than one-third. The move to the South has been led by Latin America and Asia-Oceania, which reached shares of 24 per cent and 20 per cent respectively in 2004–08, with Africa also showing significant increases. Global days of action, with events spread in all continents, are a major novelty, with one-sixth of all cases in 2004–08, as opposed to just 3 per cent in the previous period.

Civil Society Declares Independence

A similar shift is found in the nature of the events that are organised, shown in Figure 11.5. In the period 1990–2003 almost two-thirds of events were parallel summits, evenly divided between those addressing UN conferences; G7, IMF-WB or WTO summits; and other international or regional official summits. In 2004–08 this share had fallen to 40 per cent. Conversely, a major rise is found for the global gatherings of civil society that are independent from international institutions: social forums are now well established in all continents and increased their relevance from 12 per cent to 20 per cent of all events. Even greater has been the rise of events such as global days of action – against wars, trade liberalisation, poverty, climate change, and so on – and international gatherings of activists fighting for 'emerging' global issues such as the rights of women, migrants and indigenous people, labour issues, disarmaments or conflicts. Together they increased their share of global events from 23 per cent to 40 per cent over the two periods.

Key actors in organising such events include activist networks, international NGOs as well as national associations and NGOs, with some presence of trade unions and local groups. In some cases, the number of organisations active in the coordinating bodies of global events (such as social forums) is more than 400; in most cases, however, it is below 50.

The Issues of Global Activism

For each event, the three main fields of activity of the organisations involved have been identified (Figure 11.6). In more than half the events, development and economic issues – such as finance and trade – are prominent; democracy in global governance is relevant in close to 40 per cent of events – typically social forums and G8 or UN summits. The environment, labour and trade unions, human rights and peace follow, with shares between 25 per cent and 30 per cent. Student and youth groups, organisations active in migration issues, humanitarian emergencies, gender, religion

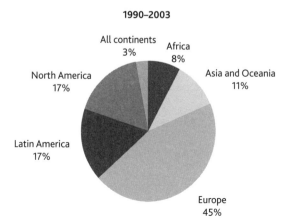

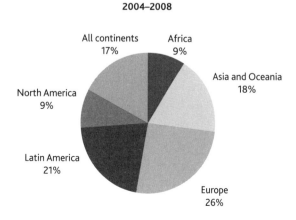

Figure 11.4 Locations of Events for Two Time Periods

Box 11.2
continued

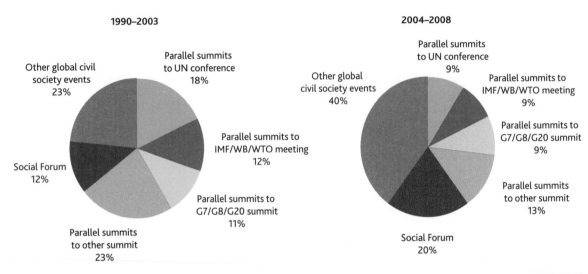

1990–2003

Other global civil society events
23%

Parallel summits to UN conference
18%

Parallel summits to IMF/WB/WTO meeting
12%

Social Forum
12%

Parallel summits to G7/G8/G20 summit
11%

Parallel summits to other summit
23%

2004–2008

Parallel summits to UN conference
9%

Other global civil society events
40%

Parallel summits to IMF/WB/WTO meeting
9%

Parallel summits to G7/G8/G20 summit
9%

Parallel summits to other summit
13%

Social Forum
20%

Figure 11.5   Types of Events for Two Time Periods

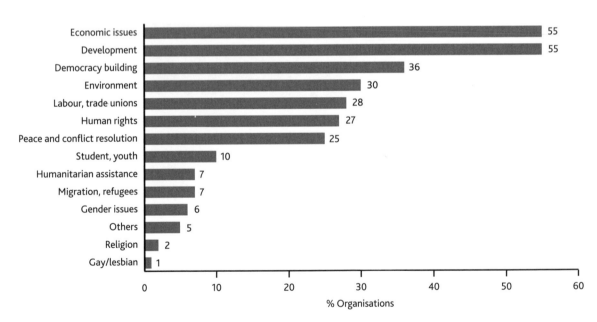

Economic issues	55
Development	55
Democracy building	36
Environment	30
Labour, trade unions	28
Human rights	27
Peace and conflict resolution	25
Student, youth	10
Humanitarian assistance	7
Migration, refugees	7
Gender issues	6
Others	5
Religion	2
Gay/lesbian	1

% Organisations

Figure 11.6   Fields of Activity of Organisations Involved in Events

or gay/lesbian issues follow with shares each below 10 per cent. In the coalitions launching global events, however, one can see a convergence of groups active in disparate fields, especially in the urgency of anti-war protest or in broad-based social forums. This is consistent with evidence from surveys of organisations involved in cross-border activism, showing that they have joined campaigns in fields different from their own when the need arose (Pianta and Silva 2003b, della Porta 2009).

The objectives of global civil society events are multiple, but there is a visible shift from protest against international powers – mainly against the policies of neoliberal globalisation – to the proposal of alternatives, as well as to the creation of permanent networks within civil society. Political confrontation with governments and global powers is important (della Porta 2007). Conversely, lobbying of official summits remains relevant in fewer cases, typically associated with UN Summits (Pianta 2005).

Preliminary evidence on the impact of such events suggests that the strongest effect is on civil society itself, changing the agenda and activities of a large number of organisations and leading to the rise of global activist networks. In some cases the impact is also significant on public opinion and the international media. Much less impact is found on the policies of national governments and international organisations, although global events can be part of longer term mobilisations that may eventually affect the framing of global issues and policy actions on them (see Utting et al. 2012).

The evolution of global civil society events in the last two decades can be understood as the overlapping of two distinct processes. On the one hand, there is a clear cycle of protest, with the rise and fall of parallel summits protesting neoliberal globalisation; it had a long gestation in the 1990s, took off in 1999, peaked in 2005 and rapidly declined in recent years. It is interesting to note that after the global crisis of 2008 widespread protests have emerged, but mainly at the national level; activism perhaps has not yet developed the cross-border networks that are needed for global protests.

On the other hand, there is a slow rise and stabilisation, over the past two decades, of the 'independent' ability of civil society organisations and networks to meet regularly, set their own agenda, deliberate about policy alternatives, beyond the urgency to protest global powers. A consolidation is visible of cross-border structures that make civil society a visible – and permanent – player on the global scene. These activities are first directed at civil society itself, building knowledge, solidarity, common experiences and network links. Such foundations represent the basis for confronting and contesting the power of governments and international institutions on specific global issues.

In the overlapping of the cycle of protest and the rise of an 'independent' global structure of civil society, activists have built shared identities, common framing of issues, joint strategies and forms of action, typical of what have been defined as 'global justice movements' (della Porta 2007).

Global events have reflected the activities of organisations and networks and show three main patterns:

- a *widening* across continents and countries of the actions undertaken, with a declining role of events in Europe and North America, but with rising global days of protests;
- a *deepening* of activists' efforts, moving from protest to the proposal of alternatives, although with a highly uncertain and uneven impact on policies;
- a *convergence* on the priorities of development, economic justice, peace and democratic global governance of groups active on several different themes.

The reaction of civil society to the global crisis of 2008 has so far mainly emerged at the national level, with domestic urgencies – austerity, unemployment, poverty, political turmoil – taking priority over international initiatives. In many countries, organisations – often facing declining resources – appear to have refocused on their 'core issues' of domestic activism, leading to fewer global events. The global nature of the crisis, however, is a new challenge waiting for the response of global civil society.

Paolo Gerbaudo is a social movement and political communication researcher. He has a PhD from Goldsmiths College and is an Associate Lecturer at Middlesex University, London.

Mario Pianta is Professor of Economic Policy at the University of Urbino. He has been visiting fellow at the European University Institute, London School of Economics and Université de Paris 1 Panthéon-Sorbonne.

through the contacts of people involved in the yearbook project and those who have come into contact with it at public lectures, launches, exhibitions and teaching events; and then further enlarged through a 'snowball' process, with connections to the correspondents leading to links with further volunteers. Each correspondent in the network would contribute on a regular basis by submitting qualitative descriptions of events that they knew of, or in which they had participated. Jill Timms remained in contact with members of the network and compiled the final chronology from the entries submitted as well as from additional web-based research.

As well as providing a means for shedding light on activities that might otherwise go unnoticed, the chronology has helped to fulfil a central aim of the research programme: to engage with and contribute to GCS. The correspondent network ensured that the production of the chronology was an interactive project, with many of the reports being sent by activists involved in the events recorded. Input has always therefore been valued from GCS and the readers of the yearbook, and the network and relationships being still built up have great potential for expanding the coverage and depth of the chronology.

It is important to note though, that there are several limitations of the correspondent network and alternative data of the chronology. Firstly, we always stress that each published chronology presents a selection of events, not a comprehensive record of all GCS actions. Secondly, we recognise the problem of definition. What counts as a GCS event is a question of interpretation. We have used a broad criterion, including events which are deemed to be globally significant in theme, participation or resonance. And we have only recorded events that can be located to a particular date or range of dates. There are many long-running campaigns that contribute to GCS that do not easily lend themselves to the format of our chronology. And of course the usual constraints of research time, funding and publication space have always applied.

The correspondent network itself is in no way a representative sample of GCS actors and does not have global coverage. It has been built up informally, and relies on busy volunteers. We have had limited resources to verify reports, and common language is an ever present constraint, as is access to communications technologies for the correspondents.

Over the years we have had many discussions about ways of expanding and improving the chronology (Timms and Stares 2007). These have been concomitant with examples of more focused work that have appeared

within the yearbook. For example, yearbook authors have regularly reported and commented on social forums as indicators of the state of GCS. This commentary has included conceptual work (for example Whitaker et al. 2006) and a range of empirical analyses. Glasius and Timms (2005) elaborated on correspondents' reports of social forums with additional research to map the growth of social forums (2005: 196–7, 200). From interviews with forum organisers and participants, participant observation and analyses of others' reports they charted the range of organisational forms and activities of these spaces of engagement (2005: 199). And from a content analysis of the printed programmes of a sample of world, national and local level social forum workshops, they distilled a summary of the themes which were being debated across this sphere (2005: 212–17). Out of an initial 27 categories, four overall clusters of topics were identified: emancipation; environment/science/health; economy; and politics/law/governance. Over the period 2002–05, politics/law/governance seemed to grow as a focus, economic themes remained a steadily significant concern and environmental topics waxed and waned in different guises. Emancipation appeared as an overwhelmingly prominent theme for the World Social Forum in 2005, with a large proportion of workshops devoting time to reflection on 'the methods of doing politics' (2005: 219), alongside substantive concerns; the related theme of 'culture' made a significant appearance in the local forums studied.

Mario Pianta and colleagues have tracked the prevalence and activities of parallel summits and related GCS events over the last 20 years (Pianta 2001, Pianta and Silva 2003, Pianta et al. 2005). Their cumulative data-gathering has included publications and reports of events from organisations, journals and news media, alongside questionnaires sent to hundreds of civil society organisations. They have produced a wealth of information on trends in frequencies of different types of events; their locations; their organisational forms; the themes that they address; and the orientations, priorities, concerns and aspirations of the civil society actors involved in them. Mario Pianta and Paolo Gerbaudo present a summary and selection of trends in events, including their most recent data (see Box 11.2).

For the chronology, our critical reflections have included a number of aspirations for ongoing work. For example, we have discussed the idea of developing some kind of formal sampling strategy – sampling correspondents, or sampling events. Either approach would require us to define the different strata of GCS within which we would want to sample; strata which might be defined geographically, or thematically, however theory dictates. What data collection techniques should we use to gather information within each stratum? A classical sampling method would in all likelihood be practically unfeasible. But it may also be conceptually inappropriate. We might instead take the aim of collecting a certain quantity of information within each relevant stratum, following the principle of 'corpus construction' (Bauer and Aarts 2000). Under this approach we would continue collecting information within each stratum until such a point at which new data stopped providing new insights, and we achieved 'saturation' of themes.

We have also discussed ways of elaborating the data collected from correspondents, particularly in order to increase the comparability of information. Developing a more in-depth set of prompts for information from correspondents could lead to a coding frame that would allow us to construct a formal database of events information. This would be amenable to a range of analyses, qualitative and quantitative, such as those championed in the methodology chapters. Alternatively, we could opt for a more creative expansion, varying the formats of information to include new media forms. Blogs could generate more detailed narrative-based and interactive kinds of data; audio, video and image files could provide richer representations than written accounts.

Notwithstanding their shortcomings, recent advances in communications technologies have opened up a vast array of data-gathering possibilities – with GCS actors at the forefront of innovations. Two of the text boxes in this chapter describe key innovations: Box 11.3 describes the use of SMS for crowd-sourcing and campaigning in Uganda; Box 11.4 describes the Ushahidi platform, an open source crowd-sourcing tool used extensively already to map events in critical political and humanitarian contexts.

We need a theoretical frame of reference to orient ourselves in such a wide array of ambitions and of possibilities. For this, we take dual leads from Saskia Sassen and from the broad field of qualitative Geographic Information Systems (GIS). These provide flexible yet structured ways of conceiving the analytical contours and borderlines in our conceptual and empirical maps of GCS.

A New Theoretical Orientation to Event Data

Saskia Sassen conceptualises the networks of activists that make up GCS as 'digital assemblages'. In her model, digital assemblages are understood to be a new category

of political grouping which, despite not having the status of a 'legal persona' – that is, a defined territory, jurisdictional rights and subordination to 'conventional state authority' – nevertheless exercise 'particular forms of [political] power' (Sassen 2006: 326) on a global scale. Understanding the nature and potential of that power is complicated and requires grappling with the peculiar characteristics of these assemblages, since they display novel spatial- and temporal characteristics and are partially untrammelled by existing formal structures. They disrupt our existing analytical categories by expressing a litany of apparently conflicting characteristics. They are 'both more and less' than the electronic communications networks which enable them; they are neither fixed nor necessarily mobile; they can be both deeply local and intensely global; they come about with the dismantling of older concepts of spatial and temporal boundaries – that is, the nation state – yet the actors that constitute them still operate within those boundaries (Sassen 2006: 325, 381, 383, 369, 375). It is, in part, these binaries that have complicated most efforts at studying, let alone measuring, GCS. But by redefining them as overlapping and interacting rather than as antithetical, as Sassen suggests, we can start to trace the complex 'imbrications' between persistent historical political organisations and the new political formations – and political imaginaries – that make up GCS (2006: 380, 383).

This approach carries with it a methodological imperative. Sassen's analytical task requires a new cartography[2] of sorts, a way to aggregate the constitutive local actions of GCS assemblages and trace out the new 'analytic borderlands' that emerge, without effacing those older boundaries whose influences persist (2006: 379; 387). In what follows, we will propose such a method for collecting GCS data that uses a mixed-methods approach known as qualitative GIS. We argue that Sassen's model provides a useful heuristic device for guiding the data programme's ambition to generate its own data (Sassen 2006: 365, 383). Furthermore, qualitative GIS methods are capable of accommodating many of the characteristics that this model suggests are necessary for studying the multi-scalar politics of GCS, while also engaging an appropriately diverse range of epistemologies and ontologies (Pavlovskaya 2009: 24, 17, Schuurman 2009: 42).

Scaling the Local

GCS actors are engaged in cross-border political action either through local action 'but with the knowledge

Box 11.3
Crowd-sourcing and Campaigning Using SMS in Uganda

During the Ugandan general elections of 2011, Democracy Monitoring Group (DEMGroup), a coalition of four civil society organisations, developed the platform UgandaWatch in order to provide citizens with a way to share their observations on various issues such as vote buying, registration hiccups, inappropriate campaign conduct, cases of violence and general complaints or positive feedback. With 100 per cent of the country's population covered by a mobile phone network and half the population with a mobile phone subscription, mobile solutions were widely deployed in the run up to the elections. The UgandaWatch initiative was preceded by a national marketing campaign of radio jingles, newspaper advertisements and flyers.

Three thousand unique users sent more than 10,000 messages to the UgandaWatch platform via the dedicated shortcode 6090. The cost of sending a SMS to UgandaWatch was negotiated down to 100 Uganda Shillings, roughly the price of a regular peer-to-peer SMS. Discussions on subsidising the service were held, but the fear was that this would generate a lot of unsolicited messages. The crowd-sourced information was reviewed, validated and geo-tagged by a team of trained volunteers before it was published on the web.

Every message received an automated reply stating:

Thanks for SMSing UgandaWatch. We are independent of any party. Your number remains private. Our volunteers will follow up. Find out more: ugandawatch2011.org.

Many of the messages sent were not very informative, requiring follow up and verification. Marketing a service like this, with directions on how and why to use it, is therefore key and should not be underestimated.

A few weeks after the elections, an SMS questionnaire was sent out to more than 100,000 mobile phone subscribers asking about their awareness of UgandaWatch. Out of these, about 1,000 answered all questions. More than a third of the respondents had, despite the national marketing campaign, never heard of UgandaWatch, and a majority of those who had heard about it had done so via radio. Those who had heard about the service but did not use it said that the main reason was that they had nothing to report. Interestingly, none of the respondents found the service too expensive.

A few (10 per cent) felt it was unsafe. SMS are permanent records and can be accessed by outsiders (for example, by the government). Although it is impossible to know how many did not use the service because of this fear, self-censorship and privacy/security issues are substantial.

Only 3 per cent of the subscribers responded that SMS was their preferred method for democratic participation – a clear majority favoured traditional public meetings. In another SMS survey of a representative sample of election observers using SMS to monitor the elections, one-third listed SMS as their preferred method of democratic participation. What this may indicate is that once mobile technology is being used for a specific cause, its users also see the advantages/benefits in using mobile technologies in comparison with other methods.

Half of the UgandaWatch informants never accessed the ugandawatch2011.org website. This highlights one of the main crowd-sourcing challenges when mostly low-end phones are used: the closing of the feedback loop. However, internet connectivity comes with mobile phone connectivity; of the respondents who did access UgandaWatch, the majority used their mobile phone browser to do so.

When operating in politically sensitive environments it is important to have various backup systems and communication channels in place. On election day, the regulator (under pressure from the government) ordered the operators to filter and block SMS traffic and specific words in messages. Filtered SMSs later on reached the platform but created a serious backlog, and the whole idea of publishing observations in near real-time was lost. A related issue is the fact that running an SMS questionnaire has some limitations too. The format of an SMS is a clear limitation: formulating the question and reply alternatives using 160 characters is difficult. It is also problematic to connect a number to an individual; the same person can answer many times using different numbers, different individuals can answer the questionnaire using the same number, different respondents may answer different parts of the questionnaire, and so on. It is therefore hard to establish correlation and to control the sample size.

Furthermore, the questionnaires used to find out more about UgandaWatch were all free of charge for the respondent, with the cost on the receiver. Designing a questionnaire like this makes it hard to budget for and control the total cost, as all incoming SMS are allowed and spammers are hard to stop.

Johan Hellström, Stockholm University.

and explicit or tacit invocation of the fact that multiple other localities around the world are engaged in similar localized struggles' (Sassen 2006: 372–3), *or* by actively trying to 'engage global actors, for example, the WTO, the IMF, or multinational firms, either at the global scale or in multiple localities' (2006: 372–3). In the first case, a 'combination of multiplication and self-reflexivity contributes to constitute a global condition out of these localized practices and rhetorics'. In the second, 'local initiatives can become part of a global network of activism without losing the focus on specific local struggles' (2006: 372–3). Gathering data on GCS, therefore, requires a method that captures both practice and rhetoric, action and narrative. What's more, it has to be able to capture the actions and narratives of diverse and dispersed local actors, while having a coding frame to collect these words and actions across space and time, and through multiple political, geographical and temporal scales.

Prototypically, this was the ambition of past yearbooks' chronology sections. By engaging with a network of civil society actors and activists around the world, we were able to collect accounts of civil society 'events', or local actions, which were reported by our volunteer correspondents. While this became a valuable appendix, which incorporated some spatial and temporal data, as an aggregate these accounts were patchy, and not comprehensive enough to begin to track the sorts of inter-scalar relationships across time that we aim to study.[3] Nor were they stored or coded in a way to allow any qualitative analysis. In part because of the difficulties of gathering this type of information systematically, many civil society indices to date remain reliant on compiled national records of registered NGOs and CSOs or (cross-)national survey data (see for example the Civicus Civil Society Index and the United Nations' iCSO system) (CIVICUS 2011, UN DESA 2011). The chronology was born of the recognition that these indices were missing important informal, small-scale, and cultural dimensions of GCS, but the tools for capturing these data in all of their ambiguity on the scale necessary simply did not exist.

GIS for GCS

Geographic information systems (GIS) – tools to digitally store and analyse geographically referenced data – have been used as a tool of quantitative spatial science for decades, but their adoption by qualitative methodologies is much more recent. In the 1990s, the representational authority and positivist epistemology of GIS were called into question by critical human geographers, who attacked its inability to accommodate Marxist, feminist, post-structural, and post-colonial approaches to social science (Pavlovskaya 2009: 16). Contemporaneously, the proliferation of GIS software, decreasing hardware costs, and networked access to spatial data and imagery databases opened GIS technologies to wider access, including by 'non-governmental and community-based organisations, minority groups and sectors of society traditionally disenfranchised and excluded from spatial decision making processes' (Rambaldi et al. 2006: 1, Pavlovskaya 2009: 14).

Out of these debates and developments emerged a 'critical GIS', which, when coupled with the broader methodological détente in the social sciences breaking down the strict coordination of ontology, epistemology, and method, has enabled a new and emerging set of research approaches based around qualitative GIS methods (Pavlovskaya 2009: 17). Qualitative GIS aims at intersecting the epistemological stance of mixed methods – that knowledge production is always partial – and the reflexivity of post-structural qualitative methods with the possibilities afforded by the database-driven and spatially referenced data infrastructure of GIS (Elwood and Cope 2009: 5, Knigge and Cope 2009: 96, Warf 2008: 76). Going beyond the reduction of 'people and places' to 'digital dots' (Pavlovskaya 2009: 16), qualitative GIS has been redeployed as a tool capable of capturing multiple identities, narratives and experiences (Elwood and Cope 2009: 8). Efforts to realise GIS's potential for qualitative methodologies have included public participation GIS, where citizens' collaborative input about the spaces that they inhabit is used by policy-makers to influence urban planning decisions; and community-based GIS, in which collective mapping of shared community geographical information helps to reveal the 'identities and meanings that are bound to particular spaces' (Elwood 2009).

Beyond Cartesian Geographies

We suggest that qualitative GIS methods are appropriate for generating GCS data not only for their technical capacities to collect, store, code, and present information, but also because they are premised on disrupting many of the same notions that the emergence of a 'global' civil society demands be interrogated. Among these is the conceptual shift of space as absolute and inert to space as relational and socially constructed, which subsequently opens up new possibilities for mapping GCS data.

Political maps define precisely the territorial boundaries of distinct and exclusive spaces of rights and authority.

Box 11.4
Ushahidi: What Can it Do? What Has it Done?

The rise and convergence of modular open-source programming, web services and increasingly ubiquitous mobile technology has given birth to a powerful platform for collecting, compiling and visualising publically-generated information on the web, known as Ushahidi (www.ushahidi.com). Meaning 'testimony' in Swahili, Ushahidi is an open-source platform developed and deployed initially to track incidents following the post-election violence in Kenya in late 2007 and early 2008. Today, from monitoring crises across North Africa and capturing information about earthquake-affected Japan to tracking crime in Atlanta, the globe-spanning technology toolkit has been applied to a variety of global challenges where 'crowd-sourcing' can help aggregate publically reported information onto a single web-visualisation platform.

What Can the Platform Do?

The group of developers and activists behind the non-profit Ushahidi organisation are primarily based in Kenya, but consist of a global network of users and volunteers. Like other successful open-source web platforms, Ushahidi makes use of the LAMP suite (linux, apache, mysql and php). For full customisation and functionality, Ushahidi must be downloaded and run on a server. However, in addition to the eponymous primary platform, they also have developed CrowdMap, which allows for simple instances to be set up on Ushahidi's own servers, and SwiftRiver, for managing the large flow of information that the platform can yield. The platform can be integrated with another powerful open-source technology tool known as FrontLineSMS to allow for the incorporation of two-way SMS messaging. Beyond the code and technology, savvy and experienced volunteer Ushahidi deployment experts help train and maintain a network of dispersed volunteer members known as the Standby Task Force, who when called upon can help enter, translate, tag and analyse incoming reports. The results can be retrieved and displayed in a variety of formats. Figure 11.7 shows a typical map summarising quantities of reports submitted to the International Organisation for Migration following unrest in Libya.

What Has the Platform Done?

A recent report from the US Public Broadcasting Service explains one of the most prominent deployments of the Ushahidi platform to date. Following the devastating 2010 earthquake in Haiti, an international volunteer community led an effort to develop a way for affected Haitians to report their needs via SMS, or text message. The first step of some volunteers on the ground was to secure an SMS short-code from Digicel, the Haiti telecom. Once the 4636 short-code was broadcast on radio, messages began to come in. The next challenge was translating the texts from Creole into English. Social media such as Facebook helped identify over 1,200 Creole-speaking volunteers in the international diaspora who were able to translate messages in near-real time. These translated messages were then tagged and integrated into the Ushahidi platform by student volunteers at Tufts University in Boston. Conclusive evidence that the platform saved lives and alleviated suffering are hard to come by particularly because the platform developed as it deployed, but first responders from the Red Cross and the US Military have confirmed that they were able to act upon some of the information the platform yielded.

Max Richman is an MSc candidate in Social Research Methods at the London School of Economics.

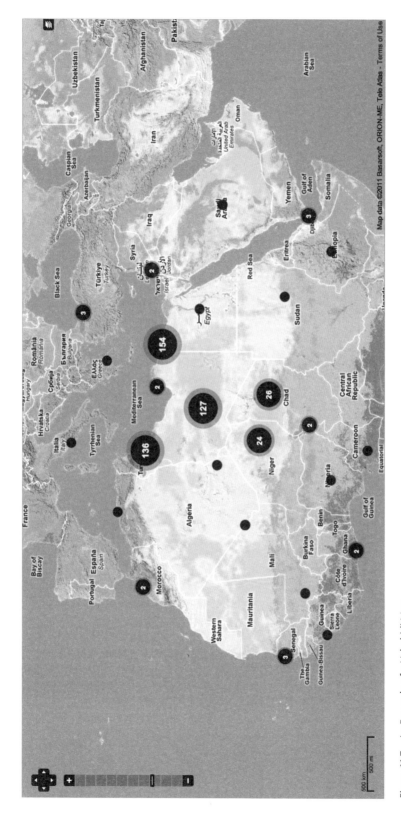

Figure 11.7   An Example of a Ushahidi Map

Accounting for these regimes and the lines that demarcate them is crucial for maintaining analytical specificity when studying GCS, since GCS is constituted by local actors within these boundaries (Sassen 2006: 378). But, while necessary, these analytical divisions are no longer sufficient. Recent mappings have, for example, sought to represent borders as 'networks of flows' and exchanges, or to plot 'geographies of the multitude' that disrupt existing spatial demarcations and the power relations they presume (Cobarrubias and Pickles 2008: 51). The 'critical cartography' of Hackitectura, a Spanish collective of architects, software programmers and artists, exemplifies such efforts at alternative mapping (Hackitectura 2011).

Similarly, in GIS, data is normally understood in terms of absolute Cartesian spatial coordinates, which lend themselves very well to formal spatial analysis. However, since we require a method for redrawing spatio-temporal borders which incorporates the problematic from critical human geography that "relational' space, along with time, is inseparable from social processes' (Pavlovskaya 2009: 25, Warf 2008: 74), incorporating qualitative modes of explanation into GIS becomes critical.[4] Through a research design that is participatory and includes narrative data in several media, we can capture relational flows and social processes that are often obscured in quantitative analysis, without excluding spatial data relevant to localities and jurisdictional boundaries. Or, in Sassen's terminology, qualitative GIS allows us to capture imbrications – 'overlaps and interactions' between old and new political groupings – rather than exclusive spatio-temporal regimes. Qualitative GIS, then, provides the opportunity to capture data that describes both *explicit* (measurable) and *implicit* (discoverable) cross-border exchanges.

Consequentially, we are forced to blur the distinctions between mobility and fixity and admit a conception of scale that explains how civil society actions, even when directed locally, become part of a broader global politics. As before, the challenge for the data programme is in finding ways to capture data which, when analysed in aggregate and in relation to each other, demonstrate the concept of the 'local as multiscalar' (Sassen 2006: 365) and allow us to trace how local actions, as practical or discursive exercises, navigate political and geographical scales.

A Practical Proposal: Participatory Mapping of GCS Events

As Box 11.4 explains, the availability of web-based software applications, like Ushahidi, that allow for the wide-scale sourcing, georeferencing and categorising of time-sensitive event/incident data has led to an adoption of these technologies by some humanitarian and volunteer organisations. Nationally-based civil society groups have used the platforms to monitor political contests, and some humanitarian groups working in crisis contexts – the aftermath of natural disasters and outbreaks of political violence where existing information channels are disrupted, censored, or insufficient – have introduced them to track the scale of unfolding and often chaotic events while maintaining acute specificity. These deployments, inasmuch as they constitute an emerging trend, have stimulated a healthy debate within humanitarian circles, and in a growing scholarly literature, about their utility vis-à-vis existing methods for gathering and exchanging post-disaster information and the politics of their use. Less attention has been given to the potential of these tools for long-term collations of (qualitative and quantitative) social scientific data, however.

We propose that a fruitful next step for the data programme would be to conduct a pilot mapping project by collecting, aggregating and verifying GCS data generated directly by a global correspondent network and input via web and mobile technologies, that would, in the first iteration, generate a 'grounded visualisation' of GCS events (Knigge and Cope 2009: 95–9). Each data 'point' would be linked not only to a set of spatial coordinates but also to a full 'event report' which would include a description, and where available, other qualitative data such as uploaded photographs and video of the reported event. Since each event is also time-stamped, chronologies of events are automatically generated, allowing for the visualisation of trends over space *and* time. Data yielded through this method would be amenable to several of the analytical approaches described above, as well as invite a much wider set of qualitative analytical possibilities.

GIS software also provides an analogous tool for capturing the overlaps between persistent and novel political formations. GCS data can be coded into any number of non-mutually-exclusive categories, and each classification – be it according to the type of organisation(s) involved in the event, the issue(s) being addressed, or the form(s) of political action – can be expressed as a *map layer*. These distinct GCS layers can be stacked in combination with other layers available from public repositories of geo-data on everything from sub-national political districts to transport infrastructure to demographic trends across time. Challenging these more conventional comparisons, GIS tools could also be used to plot visual or narrative data as a basis for qualitative analysis. The GCS map, as its dataset expands, could become a platform for:

1. revealing broad aggregate trends – tracing new 'analytical borderlands' – determined by globally networked civil society action (including by non-digital actors); *and*
2. making apparent the need for further specific research interventions suggested by those broader trends.

Looking Around, and Looking Forward

Data on GCS is elusive, but not because we do not know where to look. GCS is a theoretical hypothesis inductively crafted from a complex of political and social activities that interact across overlapping political and geographical scales. Its emergence is linked to profound changes in the experiences of space and time and the technologies that are responsible for those changes. GCS is not, intrinsically, distinct from existing local or national social and political practices except, crucially, in their explicit or tacit relationship to other such practices around the world. As this chapter has shown, much of the task of detecting GCS through data is one of tracing linkages between individuals, organisations, and everyday social practice. Appropriately – and, indeed, by necessity – we have often relied on proxy indicators to derive insights into GCS, and our ambition has remained methodological innovation. Taking our cues from the broader 'methodological nationalism' debate in the social sciences, we have tried to redefine existing categorical distinctions and move towards capturing, analysing and representing data that help us discern GCS in the skein of contemporary political and cultural expression. In this chapter, we have tried to provide a detailed overview of our efforts to date and reflect on the concomitant challenges. Finally, we presented the theoretical and methodological bases on which we hope to continue in years to come.

Notes

1. The authors wish to acknowledge the contributions of colleagues to this chapter, directly and indirectly through their published work and in conversation: Max Richman, Helmut Anheier, Marlies Glasius, Mary Kaldor, Hagai Katz, Marcus Lam and Mario Pianta.
2. As Cobarrubias and Pickles explain, Gilles Deleuze, with reference to Michel Foucault, also explicated the concept of a 'new cartography'. The Deleuzian new cartography is 'a mode of spatial thinking that [seeks] not to trace out representations of the real, but to construct mappings that refigure relations

in ways that render alternative epistemologies' (Cobarrubias and Pickles 2009).
3. For a more comprehensive account of the *Global Civil Society* yearbooks' chronology as a method for generating alternative data, see Timms and Stares (2007).
4. While there is unfortunately insufficient space herein to explore the (economic, social, theoretical) motivations and implications of this fundamental transformation in concepts of space and the subjectivities they presume, an introduction to the considerable literature bearing upon what is known as the 'spatial turn' in the social sciences can be found in Warf and Arias (2008).

References

Anheier, Helmut (2001) 'Measuring Global Civil Society', in Helmut Anheier, Marlies Glasius and Mary Kaldor (eds), *Global Civil Society 2001*. Oxford: Oxford University Press.

Anheier, Helmut (2004) *Civil Society: Measurement, Evaluation, Policy*. London: Earthscan.

Anheier, Helmut, Glasius, Marlies and Kaldor, Mary (2001) 'Introducing Global Civil Society', in Helmut Anheier, Marlies Glasius and Mary Kaldor (eds), *Global Civil Society 2001*. Oxford: Oxford University Press.

Anheier, Helmut and Katz, Hagai (2003) 'Mapping Global Civil Society', in Mary Kaldor, Helmut Anheier and Marlies Glasius (eds), *Global Civil Society 2003*. Oxford: Oxford University Press.

Anheier, Helmut and Katz, Hagai (2005) 'Network Approaches to Global Civil Society', in Helmut Anheier, Marlies Glasius and Mary Kaldor (eds), Global *Civil Society 2004/5*. London: Sage.

Anheier, Helmut and Katz, Hagai (2006) 'Learning from History? Comparative Historical Methods and Researching Global Civil Society', in Marlies Glasius, Mary Kaldor and Helmut Anheier (eds), *Global Civil Society 2005/6*. London: Sage.

Anheier, Helmut and Katz, Hagai (2009) 'Introducing Futures Research: Forecasting and Scenarios', in Ashwani Kumar, Jan Aart Scholte, Mary Kaldor, Marlies Glasius, Hakan Seckinelgin and Helmut Anheier (eds), *Global Civil Society 2009: Poverty and Activism*. London: Sage.

Anheier, Helmut, Katz, Hagai and Lam, Marcus (2007) 'Diffusion Models and Global Civil Society', in Mary Kaldor, Marlies Glasius, Helmut Anheier, Martin Albrow and Monroe E. Price (eds), *Global Civil Society 2007/8: Communicative Power and Democracy*. London: Sage.

Anheier, Helmut and Romo, F. P. (1999) 'Stalemate: A Study of Structural Failure', in Helmut Anheier (ed.), *When Things Go Wrong: Organizational Failures and Breakdowns*. Thousand Oaks, CA: Sage.

Anheier, Helmut and Stares, Sally (2002) 'Introducing the Global Civil Society Index', in Marlies Glasius, Mary Kaldor and Helmut Anheier (eds), *Global Civil Society 2002*. Oxford: Oxford University Press.

Bauer, Martin W. and Aarts, Bas (2000) 'Corpus Construction: A Principle for Qualitative Data Collection', in Martin Bauer and George Gaskell (eds), *Qualitative Researching with Text, Image and Sound: A Practical Handbook*. London: Sage.

Beck, Ulrich (2003) 'The Analysis of Global Inequality: From National to Cosmopolitan Perspective', in Mary Kaldor, Helmut Anheier and Marlies Glasius (eds), *Global Civil Society 2003*. Oxford: Oxford University Press.

CIVICUS, 2011. 'Welcome to the CIVICUS Civil Society Index', available at http://csi.civicus.org/ (accessed 10 July 2011).

Cobarrubias, S. Sebastián and Pickles, John (2008) 'Spacing Movements', in Barney Warf and Santa Arias (eds) *The Spatial Turn: Interdisciplinary Perspectives*. Oxford: Routledge.

della Porta, D (ed.) (2007) *The Global Justice Movements: A Cross-national and Transnational Perspective*. Boulder, CO: Paradigm.

della Porta, D. (ed.) (2009) *Democracy in Movements: Conceptions and Practices of Democracy in Contemporary Social Movements*. London: Palgrave Macmillan.

Domeisen, Natalie and de Sousa, Prema (2006) 'SWOT Analysis: NGOs as Partners'. *International Trade Centre, International Trade Forum, Issue 2/2006*, www.tradeforum.org/news/fullstory.php/aid/1042/SWOT_Analysis:_NGOs_as_Partners. html (accessed 8 February 2009).

Elwood, Sarah and Cope, Meghan (2009) 'Introduction: Qualitative GIS: Forging Mixed Methods through Representations, Analytical Innovations, and Conceptual Engagements', in M. Cope and S. Elwood (eds), *Qualitative GIS: A Mixed Methods Approach*. London: Sage.

Elwood, Sarah (2009) 'Multiple Representations, Significations, and Epistemologies in Community-based GIS', in M. Cope and S. Elwood (eds), *Qualitative GIS: A Mixed Methods Approach*. London: Sage.

Foucault, Michel (1986) *Of Other Spaces* (translated from the French by Jay Miskowiec), *Diacritics*, Vol. 16 No. 1: 22–7.

Glasius, Marlies (2005) *The International Criminal Court: A Global Civil Society Achievement*. Oxford: Routledge.

Glasius, M. and Timms, J. (2005) 'The Role of Social Forums in Global Civil Society: Radical Beacon or Strategic Infrastructure?', in Helmut Anheier, Mary Kaldor and Marlies Glasius (eds), *Global Civil Society 2005/6*. London: Sage.

Goodchild, Michael F (2007) 'Citizens as Sensors: The World of Volunteered Geography', *GeoJournal*, Vol. 69 No. 4: 211–21.

Hackitectura: ¿Quiénes Somos? (2011) Hackitectura, available at http://hackitectura.net/blog/en/acerca-de/ (accessed 25 July 2011).

Heinrich, Volkhart Finn (2005) 'Studying Civil Society Across the World: Exploring the Thorny Issues of Conceptualization and Measurement', *Journal of Civil Society*, Vol. 1 No. 3: 211–28.

Heinrich, Volkhart Finn and Fioramonti, Lorenzo (2008) *CIVICUS Global Survey of the State of Civil Society: Comparative Perspectives*. Bloomfield: Kumarian Press.

Johns Hopkins Institute for Policy Studies (2011), Center for Civil Society Studies – Comparative Nonprofit Sector Project, http://ccss.jhu.edu/index.php?section=content&view=9&sub=3.

Kaldor, Mary, Albrow, Martin, Anheier, Helmut and Glasius, Marlies (eds) (2007) *Global Civil Society 2006/7*. London: Sage.

Kaldor, Mary, Glasius, Marlies, Anheier, Helmut, Albrow, Martin and Price, Monroe E. (eds) (2008) *Global Civil Society 2007/8: Communicative Power and Democracy*. London: Sage.

Katz, Hagai (2008) 'Indicator Suites of Global Civil Society', in Mary Kaldor, Marlies Glasius, Helmut Anheier, Martin Albrow and Monroe E. Price (eds), *Global Civil Society 2007/8: Communicative Power and Democracy*. London: Sage.

Katz, Hagai, Anheier, Helmut and Lam, Marcus (2007) 'Fuzzy Set Approaches to the Study of Global Civil Society', in Mary Kaldor, Helmut Anheier and Marlies Glasius (eds), *Global Civil Society 2006/7*. London: Sage.

Knigge, LaDona and Cope, Meghan (2009) 'Grounded Visualization and Scale: A Recursive Analysis of Community Spaces', in M Cope and S Elwood (eds), *Qualitative GIS: A Mixed Methods Approach*. London: Sage.

List, R. and Dörner, W. (eds) (forthcoming) *Civil Society, Conflict and Violence*. London: Bloomsbury.

Mati, Jacob M., Silva, Federico, and Anderson, Tracy (2010) *Assessing and Strengthening Civil Society Worldwide. An Updated Programme Description of the CIVICUS Civil Society Index: Phase 2008 to 2010*. Johannesburg: CIVICUS World Alliance for Citizen Participation.

National Intelligence Council (NIC) (2008) *Global Trends 2025: A Transformed World*. Washington DC: NIC.

Pavlovskaya, Marianna (2009) 'Non-quantitative GIS', in M. Cope and S. Elwood (eds) *Qualitative GIS: A Mixed Methods Approach*. London: Sage.

Pianta, Mario (2001) 'Parallel Summits of Global Civil Society', in Helmut Anheier, Marlies Glasius and Mary Kaldor (eds), *Global Civil Society 2001*. Oxford: Oxford University Press.

Pianta, Mario (2005) 'UN World Summits and Civil Society. The State of the Art' , *UNRISD Programme Paper 18*. Geneva: UNRISD.

Pianta, Mario and Silva, Federico (2003a) 'Parallel Summits of Global Civil Society: An Update', in Mary Kaldor, Helmut Anheier and Marlies Glasius (eds), *Global Civil Society 2003*. Oxford: Oxford University Press.

Pianta, Mario and Silva, Federico (2003b) *Globalisers from Below: A Survey on Global Civil Society Organisations*. Rome: GLOBI Research Report.

Pianta, Mario, Silva, Federico and Zola, Duccio (2005) 'Global Civil Society Events: Parallel Summits, Social Fora, Global Days of Action', in Helmut Anheier, Marlies Glasius and Mary Kaldor (eds), *Global Civil Society 2004/5*. London: Sage.

Rambaldi, Giacomo, Kyem, Kwaku, McCall, Mike and Weiner, Daniel (2006) 'Participatory Spatial Information Management and Communication in Developing Countries', *Electronic Journal of Information Systems in Developing Countries*, Vol. 25 No. 1: 1–9.

Sassen, Saskia (2006) *Territory, Authority, Rights: From Medieval to Global Assemblages*. Oxfordshire: Princeton University Press.

Soja, Edward W. (2009) 'Taking Space Personally', in Barney Warf and Santa Arias (eds) *The Spatial Turn: Interdisciplinary Perspectives*. Oxford: Routledge.

Timms, Jill (2009) 'Chronology of Global Civil Society Events', in Ashwani Kumar, Jan Aart Scholte, Mary Kaldor, Marlies Glasius, Hakan Seckinelgin and Helmut Anheier (eds), *Global Civil Society 2009: Poverty and Activism*. London: Sage.

Timms, Jill and Stares, Sally (2007) 'Alternative Data for Studying Global Civil Society: Correspondent Networks, Maps and Chronologies', in *Center for Global, International and Regional Studies, Mapping Global Inequalities*. Santa Cruz, 13–14 December. Santa Cruz: UC Santa Cruz, http://escholarship.org/uc/item/468929x1.

Union of International Associations (UIA) (2011) http://www.uia.be/. See in particular their yearbooks of International Organizations, and their classification of types of international organisations at http://www.uia.be/types-international-organization.

United Nations Department of Economic and Social Affairs (UN DESA), NGO Branch (2011). United Nations: Civil Society Participation (iCSO), available at http://esango.un.org/civilsociety/ (accessed 10 July 2011).

United Nations Development Programme (UNDP) (2011) *Human Development Reports* can be found at http://hdr.undp.org/en/reports/.

Utting, P., Pianta, M., and Elleskirk, A. (eds) (2012) *Global Justice Activism and Policy Reform in Europe: Understanding how Change Happens*. London: Routledge.

Warf, Barney and Arias, Santa (eds) (2008) *The Spatial Turn: Interdisciplinary Perspectives*. Oxford: Routledge.

Warf, Barney (2008) 'From Surfaces to Networks', in Barney Warf and Santa Arias (eds), *The Spatial Turn: Interdisciplinary Perspectives*. Oxford: Routledge.

Whitaker, Francisco, Santos, Boaventura de Sousa and Cassen, Bernard (2005) 'The World Social Forum: Where Do We Stand and Where Are We Going?', in Helmut Anheier, Mary Kaldor and Marlies Glasius (eds), *Global Civil Society 2005/6*. London: Sage.

World Values Survey (2011) http://www.worldvaluessurvey.org/.

A YEARBOOK RETROSPECTIVE

Compiled by Jill Timms

Introduction

An alternative record of global civil society has been included in each yearbook in the form of a Chronology of Events. These chronologies have provided an opportunity to document in qualitative terms the diversity of civil society activity taking place globally, including events such as vigils, social forums, marches, legal challenges, rallies and petitions, as well as particular victories and defeats. These have been defined as global civil society events if they have significance beyond national borders in terms of participants, theme or resonance. Unlike many end-of-year reviews, we attempt to record events that often go unreported in mainstream media due to their location or form. We also record events that can be difficult to include in statistics on the growth of civil society activity and organisation, again because of their form or as they are rarely recorded formally. Therefore, as described in Chapter 11, these chronologies have complemented the other records of the Data Programme, and have only been possible by drawing on the interactive nature of the project.

For each Chronology we have worked with a network of global civil society correspondents made up of activists, journalists, students, academics and interested parties around the world (for details of process and profiles see Timms and Stares 2007: 12–16). The aim has never been to provide a comprehensive list of every global civil society action, which would be (happily) an impossible task. We also acknowledge the problems of using a finite network, the limitations of web-based sources, issues of definition, and language restrictions (see previous Chronology introductions, and Timms and Stares 2007). However, through building up these chronologies each year, we have been able to provide an alternative record that demonstrates the immensely diverse nature of events, and that is able to indicate major themes, directions and sites of struggle for global civil society.

To mark a decade of the Chronology of Global Civil Society Events, we present here a record made up of selected entries from all the yearbook chronologies to date, nine in total. Four points should be noted. Firstly, the aim of this Chronology is to give a sample of the range of events we have been able to record throughout the decade, reflecting particularly the diversity of event type, size and location. This means we are not necessarily including the biggest or 'most important', although some of these have been chosen. Secondly, the chronologies have included many regular civil society events related to annual days marked, such as Women's Day (8 March), Day of Peasant Struggle (17 April), Labour Day (1 May), and Migrant Day (18 December). For the purpose of this retrospective, annual events have not been included more than once for the decade. Thirdly, the reporting of social forums at local, national, regional, thematic and world level made a significant contribution to many of the chronologies. Indeed the importance of social forums has been a key topic for the yearbook (see, for example, Glasius and Timms 2005, and Chapter 10 this volume), and attempts have also been made to track and map their development within and beyond the Chronology (see, for example, the map of social forums by type and year, *Global Civil Society 2007/8*, pp. 328–9). Therefore, for reasons of space, in this Chronology only the annual World Social Forum events have been included. Fourthly, there is some variation in the periods covered and how events are presented in different yearbooks; the last, in particular, was presented within several themed maps, an experiment that we have repeated for the current year (see Chapter 1 this volume, Maps 1.1, 1.2 and 1.3). For clarity, the events selected here are reproductions of the original entries and are divided into sections representing the dates covered by each individual Chronology.

Finally, we would like to offer our thanks again to the network of over a hundred correspondents that have contributed to the chronologies over the last decade, all individually listed in the section below. Many of these have contributed year after year, and we hope that they will continue to do so in the future.

We would also like to offer you an invitation to take part in our research. The Data Programme, including the Chronology, continues to be developed as we build on our experiences and take advantage of new technologies, as discussed in Chapter 11. As part of this, the current Global Civil Society website is in the process of being developed to incorporate various interactive opportunities, which will launch in stages between 2012 and 2013. One way that readers will be able to engage directly with the project will be by contributing to future chronologies, and we hope that you will consider taking part. Further details will be available in due course at the following address:

http://www2.lse.ac.uk/internationalDevelopment/
research/CSHS/Home.aspx

Contributors

Chinwe Achor, Yeshaiahu Ben Aharon, Mustapha Kamel Al-Sayyid, Mulya Amri, Leighton Andrews, Brian Appelbe, Uri Avnery, Leonardo Avritzer, Marcelo Batalha, Baris Gencer Baykan, Andrew Bolgar, Reine Borja, Thierry Brugvin, Nick Buxton, Guiseppe Caruso, Joabe Cavalcanti, Hyo Je Cho, Andrew Davey, James Deane, Sean Deel, Bernard Dreano, Nenad Durdevic, Heba Raouf Ezzat, Andres Falconer, Mary Fischer, Louise Fraser, Uliana Gavril, Marlies Glasius, Nihad Gohar, Habib Guiza, Anil Gupta, Martin Gurch, Stuart Hodkinson, Vicky Holland, Deborah James, Kadi Jumu, Jeffrey Juris, Hagai Katz, Zafarullah Khan, Bjarne Kristoffersen, Svitlana Kuts, Annie Lau, Yung Law, Silke Lechner, Leeshai Lemish, Natalia Leshchenko, Maritza Lopez-Quintana, Ahmad Lutfi, Alejando Martinez, Maite San Miguel, Otilia Mihai, Nuria Molina, Selma Muhic, Mukul Mundy, Esther Nagle, Joseph Nagle, Richard Nagle, Tim Nagle, Alejandro Natal, Monika Neuner, Imogen Nay, Beatriz Martin Nieto, Ebenezer Obadare, Katarina Sehm Patomaki, David Perez, Mario Pianta, Oscar Reyes, Asthriesslav Rocuts, Ineke Roose, Marjanie Roose, Thomas Ruddy, Mohamed El-Sayed Said, Yahia Said, Jasmin San Juan, Trilochan Sastry, Florent Schaeffer, Shameen Siddiqi, Jirina Siklova, Mukul Sinah, Jay Smith, Robert Sommers, Sally Stares, Toralf Staud, Amade Suca, Katharine Talbot, Vanessa Tang, Guy Taylor, Elena Tonkacheva, Kate Townsend, Sunna Trott, Yulia Tykhomyrova, Eduard Vallory, Caroline Watt (nee Walker), Lilian Outtes Wanderley, Aled Williams, Barbara Wisniewska, Sebastien Ziegler, Duccio Zola, Csengeri Zsolt.

Global Civil Society Chronology: Selected Events January 2000–March 2010

January–December 2000 (see *Global Civil Society 2001*, pp. 333–37)

24 January 2000

In an unprecedented event, Somali human rights activists, writers, aid workers, and other civil society figures meet in the port city of Bossasso, Puntland, to discuss the future role of civil society in reshaping Somalia. In contrast to twelve previous failed initiatives which aimed to secure peace among Somali warlords, this peace plan, supported by Djibouti President Guelleh, is based on Somalia's emerging civil society.

29 February 2000

In response to criticism from NGOs, De Beers, the world's largest diamond company, announces that its diamonds will henceforth carry a guarantee that they have not been brought from armed groups in conflict areas.

19 March 2000

Two weeks after a leaking sewer pumped contaminated waste into the Rodrigo de Freitas lagoon, killing more than 30 tons of fish, 10,000 residents of Rio de Janeiro, wearing white T-shirts, link hands around the lagoon to protest against the rising level of sewage in the sea.

15–17 April 2000

Tens of thousands of people blockade the streets surrounding the IMF and World Bank buildings in Washington, DC, where the annual board meetings are held, in protest against the policies of the financial institutions. Meetings are delayed by the blockade, and some delegates fail to make it through. Over 600 demonstrators are arrested.

24 April–19 May 2000

The Review Conference of the Parties to the 1968 Treaty on the Non-Proliferation of Nuclear Weapons (NPT) takes place in New York. 141 NGOs, mainly peace and disarmament groups, monitor the conference.

30 June 2000

Tens of thousands of French farmers and other anti-globalisation protestors gather in Milau, France, where

French farmer Jose Bove stands trial for attacking the local branch of McDonald's hamburger restaurant a year earlier.

14–16 August 2000

The so-called *Observatorio de las Americas* is launched in Morelia, Mexico. It brings together NGOs and academics in an effort to build a monitoring mechanism, based in civil society, to the process of integration of the Americas in a common free-trade area (FTAA). Participants include scholars and NGOs from the whole continent as well as leaders of international agencies such as WTO and WHO.

28–29 August 2000

Over 1,000 representatives of all of the world's major religions, including the Baha'i Faith, Buddhism, Christianity, Hinduism, Islam, Jainism, Judaism, Shintoism, Sikhism, and Zoroastrianism, as well as indigenous religions from nearly every continent attend the Millennium Summit of Religious Leaders in New York. Nearly all sign a declaration entitled 'Commitment to Global Peace', which states that 'there can be no real peace until all groups and communities acknowledge the cultural and religious diversity of the human family'.

26–28 September 2000

Approximately 12,000 activists gather in Prague where the annual IMF-World Bank meeting is held. The meeting is disrupted, and demonstrators clash with the police, leading to many arrests.

25 October 2000

Environmental groups in Russia collect 2.5 million signatures for a referendum that would prevent the country from importing nuclear waste as a source of income. The authorities declare more than 600,000 signatures invalid, however, so that the groups do not reach the required threshold for a referendum.

18 November 2000

Thousands of activists build a dyke around the conference centre where the UN Conference on Climate Change is taking place in The Hague, in order to illustrate the dangers of climate change and rising sea levels. The US negotiator falls victim to the Dutch radical practice of 'taarting': a whipped cream pie is thrown into his face. Governments fail to come to an agreement in limiting CO_2 emissions at the conference.

January–December 2001 (see *Global Civil Society 2002*, pp. 379–86)

25–30 January 2001

The first World Social Forum is held in Porto Alegre, Brazil, as an alternative to the World Economic Forum being held in Davos, Switzerland. 11,000 activists gather to protest against neoliberalism and discuss alternatives to capitalist globalisation under the banner of 'another world is possible'. The event is organised by a number of civil society organisations, including many progressive Brazilian ones such as the Landless Movement and trade union groups, with ATTAC-France also being prominent. It is decided during the forum that the event should be held annually.

22–27 February 2001

Anti-capitalists initiate a series of activities to parallel the regional World Economic Forum (WEF) held in Cancun, Mexico. These include an important encounter between anti-globalists and globalisers as the leaders of the WEF and Mexican authorities meet with 25 civil society organisations, 15 of which are Mexican. Jose Maria Giguerez, director of the Agenda of the World Economic Forum, declares that the encounter is a success for there has been a series of shared arguments around globalisation, such as the demand for inclusion of marginal groups and access to the economy, education, and health for everyone. Representatives of various organisations, unions, peasants, and NGOs take the opportunity to urge President Vicente Fox to conduct a 'real' dialogue and to encourage accountability to civil society for the economic policies of the country. Outside the forum many activist groups come together to protest, and there is a heavy police presence throughout the city as well as in the bay, where Greenpeace moors its Rainbow Warrior ship. More radical activists protest fiercely in the area surrounding the hotels of the WEF participants.

25 February–5 March 2001

The Zapatistas leave their refuges in the highlands of Chiapas to initiate a march to Mexico City called the 'Zapatour'. Passing through several major cities, the Zapatistas raise large numbers of people in protest against the historical oppression of indigenous peoples. The caravan is supported permanently by civil society organisations from Mexico, and participants from all over the world, especially from Italy, take part. They create an enclosure for the leaders, the so-called 'enclosure of peace'.

19 March 2001

Meetings are held at the WTO's headquarters in Geneva to negotiate a liberalising of world trade in services, such as in telecoms, financial services, and tourism. Outside, protesters and anti-capitalist groups gather to voice their opposition, dressed up as business people waving butterfly nets at other protesters dressed up as mobile phones and first-aid kits.

19 April 2001

The court case initiated by pharmaceutical companies against the South African government over the production of generic copies of AIDS/HIV drug treatments is unconditionally dropped. Activists see this as a landmark victory in their attempts to secure medication for the millions of sufferers of the disease in Africa.

19–21 April 2001

The first International Citizens Meeting is held in Barcelona, organised by UBUNTU, the world forum of networks whose president is Federico Mayor Zaragoza. This meeting has the aim of offering a forum for NGOs to analyse and discuss world affairs and to concentrate on issues such as human rights, international disarmament, human development and social justice, ecology, globalisation, peace, and conflict prevention.

2 June 2001

An Arab Women's Forum is held in Tunisia under the headline 'women and politics', calling upon Arab states to promote the political participation of women through literacy campaigns for girls, and the preparation of women to activate their role in political parties.

18–21 July 2001

The G8 Summit is held in Genoa, Italy, and it marked by large-scale protests, marches, and demonstrations as a contingent of 250,000 protesters form 700 groups descend on the city. The majority march in peaceful protests, and many alternative conferences, meetings, and events are organised. However, the police are prepared for violence and use many tactics which an Italian police chief later admits involved excessive force. This includes the raiding of demonstrators' accommodation during the night, unnecessary use of tear-gas, and mistreatment of those arrested. One protester is killed by the police and approximately 200 others are injured. Legal battles continue against the actions of the police.

17 August 2001

Guy Verhofstadt, Prime Minister of Belgium and President of the European Union, writes and open letter to the anti-globalisation movement. Newspapers around the world publish this letter and the responses are collected for publication.

13 September 2001

The Australian government cites the terrorist attacks on the US to justify its hard stance on asylum seekers entering the country. It is claimed that Australia is becoming a target for refugees from a number of countries due to is geographical accessibility, and that a strong line is necessary to discourage the increasing number of refugee boats heading for the country. This and future action is met with fierce resistance by a variety of civil society groups, including Amnesty International, resulting in protests inside and outside many of Australia's detention centres for asylum seekers.

7 October 2001

Air strikes are launched on Afghanistan by the US in the 'war on terror'. Training camps and military installations of the Al Qaeda network are targeted with the objective of capturing those involved in the organisation of the terrorist attacks of September 11, including the leading figure of Osama Bin Laden. Anti-war protesters around the world voice their opposition and step up campaigns to stop the military action.

18 October 2001

After a two-year legal struggle that has been supported by Brazillian organisations and international NGOs such as Greenpeace, the Denie Indians of Manaus in the Amazon win the right to protect their land from illegal logging and industrial practices.

9–15 November 2001

A world Trade Organisation meeting is held in Doha, Qatar. Tight security and the geography of the location prevent protesters from attending in great numbers. Some of the main issues discussed include workers' rights and access to cheap pharmaceuticals. A small contingent of 100 NGOs is invited to attend, with their activities limited to lobbying and quiet protest. Many complaints are made by protesters at the lack of opportunity to voice opinions, and fuel their criticisms of the WTO's undemocratic nature.

5 December 2001

This is International Volunteer Day, and the global closing of what has been the UN-sponsored International Year of the Volunteer. This draws together a year of diverse events held worldwide, such as parades, volunteer fairs, workshops, conferences, and work camps, some of which are aimed directly at young people.

January–December 2002 (see *Global Civil Society 2003*, pp. 395–410)

23 January 2002

In Venezuela, the biggest demonstrations in the country's history commemorate the end of Marcos Perez Jimenez's dictatorship in 1958, which marked the beginning of Venezuelan democracy. Political parties, civil society groups, and trade unions join two rival marches, one supporting and one opposing the current president, Hugo Chavez.

30 January–5 February 2002

In Porto Alegre, Brazil, the second World Social Forum (WSF) is held, with 68,000 participants. Delegates travel from 131 countries and represent more than 5,000 associations. The forum aims to provide a space for the development of alternatives to the current form of globalisation and the neoliberal policies that lead to it, as well as aiming to share ideas for protesting against and resisting current economic and social policies. In the forum's final statement, which is agreed by many of the associations, the activists describe themselves as a 'global movement for social justice and solidarity'. It is also decided that a range of regional and themed forums will be held before the WSF meets again in 2003.

3 February 2002

The first international meeting of ATTAC takes place, facilitated by the WSF in Porto Alegre. Members from 40 countries are able to join the meeting, coming together for the first time to discuss issues of identity and to plan campaigns for the promotion of the 'Tobin tax'.

20 February 2002

In Luanda, the capital of Angola, civil society organisations meet to discuss the continuing violence of the 26-year civil war. These groups, who represent non-political civic interest and include priests, academics, humanitarian officers, and traditional chiefs, call for an immediate ceasefire. In criticising the UN Security Council's handling of the peace process, the coalition requests that a delegation of civil society organisations be allowed to address the Security Council so they can have an input in the process. Although civil society groups have been active in Angola for a number of years, the agreement on a unified position is described as a breakthrough.

27 February 2002

In Israel, 200,000 join a mass peace march in Tel Aviv. This is organised by the Peace Coalition, which brings together civil society groups from Israel, Palestine, and European countries, such as Peace Now, Women for Peace, and Ta'ayush et Gush Shalom. The aim is to strengthen and draw attention to the coalition's campaign against Israeli occupation of the Palestinian Territories and to support Israeli reserve officers who signed a declaration refusing to serve there.

17 April 2002

On the Worldwide Peasant Struggle Day, civil society organisations of farmers, rural workers, and peasants from around the world take part in a variety of activities to mark an international day of farmers' struggle. Co-ordinators of the campaign request that actions focus on the themes of seeds, the problem of patents, and the freeing of partners who are being persecuted or jailed. Actions include a Resistance is Fertile campaign in the Netherlands, involving the planting of eco-potatoes in GM test fields and the erection of DNA scarecrows, and land is taken by activists in Brazil and Guatemala. Other activities take place in Austria, Belgium, Canada, Honduras, India, Italy, Spain, and the USA.

30 May 2002

An international campaign to promote migrant workers' rights in Japan and South Korea is launched to coincide with the FIFA World Cup 2002, to bring attention to the initiative. The campaigners claim that war and neoliberal globalisation have caused an increase in exploitative international migration, and that current policies are anti-migrant and racist.

25–28 June 2002

In Siby, Mali, in West Africa, the first counter-summit to the G8 to be organised by Africans takes place to protest against the dominant neoliberal policies of international financial institutions and the agricultural policies of the World Bank. Participants include organisations of teachers, women, farmers, journalists, youths, and religious leaders, who have travelled from the rest of Mali, Burkina Faso, Niger, the Ivory Coast, and Senegal. The main themes of the summit are strategies for the reduction of poverty in Africa and the New Partnership Agreement for Africa's Development (NEPAD), both of which are also key issues at the official G8 summit. However, the summits differ in most other ways as the participants in Africa are the ones suffering from poverty as well as discussing it. The choice of venue is significant since, in contrast to the luxury of the G8 leaders in Kananaskis, Siby has no transportation system, no clean drinking water, and no access to telephones. The meetings and workshops take place in the open air and in the classrooms of a local school.

1 July 2002

The world's first International Criminal Court (ICC) comes into existence in The Hague, empowered to prosecute individuals anywhere in the world (with the provision that the country has ratified the treaty) for genocide, war crimes, and crimes against humanity. Civil society organisations, including women's groups, religious and human rights organisations, and peace activists, were seen to be instrumental in the drafting of the treaty, and their involvement has been seen as a significant success for global civil society. By this date, 74 countries have ratified the treaty; campaigners continue to put pressure on countries such as the USA, Russia, China, and Israel, which are refusing to do so.

18–28 July 2002

The first Europe-wide 'no border camp' is initiated by the Noborder Network, organised by social movements from several European countries. The camp consists of ten days of workshops and discussions around the central demand for 'Freedom of Movement and Settlement for Everyone'. Strasbourg is chosen because it is home to the central headquarters of the Schengen Information Systems (SIS), the database used to store details of immigrants, terrorists, political protestors, and 'anti-globalisation' protestors. About 2,000 people take park in the camp; and a sit-in of 1,000 protesters outside the European Court of Human Rights is organised under the slogan 'No border! No nation! Stop deportation!'

20 July 2002

To commemorate the anniversary of the death of Carlo Giuliani, who was killed by police during the anti-G8 summit protests in Genoa in 2001, a week of activities culminates in a march of 150,000 people. In the port of Genoa, at exactly the time Carlo was killed, dockers sound their horns, hundreds of balloons are released in Piazza Alimonda, 'illegal immigrants' from Pakistan, Senegal, and Morocco landing at the sea front are welcomed with a brass band and fruit, and activists occupying the Diaz school which was the site of violent police raids the previous year, unfurl banners stating 'This time, please knock before entering!'

18 December 2002

International Migrants Day is celebrated around the world on or around this date by civil society organisations working for labour and migrant rights. A major theme of events is the need to ratify the UN Convention of 1990 for the Protection of the Rights of All Migrant Workers and Members of their Families, Demonstrations to pressure governments into ratifying this are held in Bangladesh, Belgium, Chile, Ireland, Japan, and Indonesia. Forums and conference are organised to promote awareness of this issue and others concerning workers' rights in Canada, Israel, Italy, Malaysia, Nepal, Sri Lanka and the US. Many of these activities and others are highlighted and supported by the web-based portal for the promotion and protection of the rights of migrants, December18.net.

21–22 December 2002

A Global Day of Disobedience is organised in solidarity with the people of Argentina and to protest against consumerist culture, on the retailer's busiest day of the year. In London's Oxford Street, The Wombles with other groups organise a Free Shop where books, CDs, toys, and clothes can be 'bought' for free, a mobile kitchen gives away vegetarian burgers and other food, and free dancing lessons are offered. Similar actions are organised by Disobbedienti in Italy, JNM in Belgium, Yomango in Spain, Black Revolution in Switzerland, and other groups in Jordan, Finland, the US, and Germany.

January 2003–April 2004 (see *Global Civil Society 2004/5*, pp. 350–60)

23–28 January 2003

The Third World Social Forum takes place in Porto Alegre, Brazil, attended by 100,000 people from 123 countries, making it the largest social forum to date. A quarter of participants are young people. Highlights include the speech of the new Brazilian president, Luiz Inacio Lula da Silva (known as Lula), witnessed by 50,000 people, and the controversial visit by Venezuelan president Hugo Chavez, whose rally was kept separate from the official forum in keeping with the WSF commitment to remaining non-governmental.

15 February 2003
This is claimed to be a global day of mobilisation against the war in Iraq. One of the largest demonstrations takes place in Barcelona, with two million people besieging the city centre to protest the war and also the environmental damage caused by the Prestige oil tanker, which sank off northern Spain in 2002. In Dublin up to 100,000 people march to voice their opposition to military action against Iraq. Numerous smaller protests are held in cities and towns throughout Ireland. In Berlin, 500,000 people protest, including some ministers of the federal government, making this the biggest demonstrations in Germany since the Second World War. Throughout France protests are held, including a 600,000-strong march in Paris.

23 February 2003
One million people take part in demonstrations in Madrid, under the banner 'Never Again', to protest against the environmental catastrophe created by the sinking of the Prestige oil tanker. A system of volunteers cleans the coastline on a daily basis and plans to continue doing so until the end of the year.

18 March 2003
In Cuba, 26 independent journalist who established two underground publications, are imprisoned, an action unprecedented in the 44 years of Castro's rule. The international NGO, Reporters Without Borders, mounts a worldwide petition to campaign for their immediate release.

20 March 2003
Despite strong civil society protests internationally, the US-led war to topple Iraq president Saddam Hussein officially starts when American missiles are launched against targets in Baghdad. Around the world, anti-war activities are stepped-up.

16 July 2003
An Internet site is launched for the World Campaign for in-depth Reform of the System of International Institutions, www.reformcampaign.net. The site is intended to collect pledges in support of the Campaign Manifesto, to be submitted at the United Nations General Assembly in 2006, in order to promote reform of the international system.

23 July 2003
Trade unions in Columbia call for a worldwide boycott of Coca-Cola's products amid allegations that the company has employed militias to murder nine trade union members in the past 13 years.

8–9 September 2003
Civil society groups in Mongolia work with international organisations to host the International Civil Society Forum's Fifth Conference of the New or Restored Democracies. This takes place in Ulaan Baatar, the capital of Mongolia.

10–14 September 2003
The Fifth Ministerial Meeting of the WTO is held in Cancun, Mexico, surrounded by thousands of civil society activists. For the first time, the WTO allows the participation of civil society groups, which express their serious concerns about globalisation and free trade; and campaign for neglected rural areas. The WTO is also accused of being undemocratic, anti-development and obsolete. Particularly critical are organisations such as 'Our World is Not For Sale', Public Citizen, and the International Forum against Globalisation, as well as Food First, among many others. Parallel to the formal meeting, several direct action groups rail against the police. A Korean peasant leader, Lee Kyung Hae stabs himself to death. His chest is inscribed with 'The WTO kills peasants'.

21 December 2003
Many protests are organised in Paris against the government decision to ban the wearing of religious clothing in French state schools, including the Islamic Hijab, Jewish jamulke, and 'excessive' Christian crosses. The controversy draws the attention of civil liberties and religious groups around the world.

16–21 January 2004
The Fourth World Social Forum is held in Mumbai, India, the first time the event has been hosted outside Porto Alegre. One hundred thousand people from 132 countries register at the event, with strong representation from groups of all backgrounds across India. For the first time an organised counter-event, Mumbai Resistance 2004, is held directly opposite site of the main forum. Mumbai Resistance 2004 is critical of the social forum process.

4 March 2004
After scientist Hwang Woo-suk's breakthrough in cloning human cells was announced in early February, at least ten civil society groups, including the Citizens' Movement for Environmental Justice, join the campaign against Hwang's nomination for a Nobel Peace Prize.

17 March 2004
Simultaneous demonstrations in seven countries mark South Korean comfort women's 600th Wednesday rally in front of the Japanese Embassy in Seoul. Many Asian comfort women, who were compelled to serve as sex slaves for Japanese soldiers during the Second World War, and their supporters, gather simultaneously in Japan, Taiwan, the US, Germany, Belgium and Spain.

20 March 2004
An international day of action for peace is marked around the world on the anniversary of the start of the war in Iraq. For example, in Italy, a million people participate in a protest organised by the Italian Stop the War committee. There are also several general strike and large trade union demonstrations. The main theme of the action is a call for troops to be withdrawn and for sovereignty to be returned to the Iraqi people.

May 2004–April 2005 (see *Global Civil Society 2005/6*, **pp. 472–80)**

5 May 2004
Thousands of Maori protesters march outside Parliament in New Zealand over plans to nationalise the shoreline, which they claim belongs to them. The action is supported by campaigners for the rights of indigenous peoples and environmentalists.

9 July 2004
Amid much interest from peace activists around the world, the International Court of Justice in the Hague, the Netherlands, rules that the controversial West Bank Barrier, a 425 mile-long wall being constructed by Israel to keep Palestinians out of Jewish settlements in the West Bank, is illegal.

1 September 2004
In Kenya, a campaign is launched by the Masai peoples to win the return of ancestral territory in Laikilia, which was claimed by white farmers under a British colonial treaty of 1904. The campaign is mounted on the expiration of the treaty.

2–30 October 2004
A Monster Tomato Tour takes place in Turkey as part of a European anti-GM campaign, organised by a coalition of 30 Turkish civil society groups, united in the 'No to GMOs Platform'.

5 January 2005
In Sierra Leone, a two-day general strike that has brought the capital of Freetown to a virtual standstill ends after the government agrees to increase the minimum wage to the equivalent of US$13 a month and to cut income tax and fuel duty. The result of collaboration between the major trade unions, the protest is seen as a positive sign that the country is returning to normality after the civil war, which ended in 2001.

17 January 2005
HIV and AIDS campaigners around the world praise Nelson Mandela for revealing that his son, Makgatho, died of an AIDS-related illness and for highlighting the plight of the millions of people living with HIV and Aids in Africa.

26–31 January 2005
The fifth World Social Forum takes place in Porto Alegre, Brazil, with 155,000 participants. The event is organised around several territories, that is, spaces designated for the major themes of the Forum, within which all the events for that theme take place. It attracts the largest number of young people to attend a World Social Form, with 35,000 registering for the youth camp. It is agreed that for 2006, several forums will be held simultaneously in different parts of the world, replacing the single-location format of the WSF will again be in a single venue – in Africa – but the country and city have yet to be confirmed.

12 February 2005
Activist Sister Dorothy Stang is murdered after more than 30 years working for sustainable development in the Amazon, in particular with the Landless Workers Movement. Dressed in white and carrying candles, her supporters throughout Brazil protest against agro-businesses' destruction of the environment and local farmers' livelihoods. The police suspect Stang's murder was a contract killing by local ranchers, and 2,000 officers are sent to track them down.

19 February 2005
The European Court of Human Rights rules that two British environmental campaigners were treated unfairly

when the British government refused to grant them legal aid for their defence against a libel case brought by McDonald's. Helen Steel and David Morris, who have gained international support from environmentalist and anti-corporate activists, are granted £24,000 compensation and costs. The so-called 'McLibel Two' were sued for handing out leaflets containing allegations about the company's unethical behaviour, including low wages, some of which were proved to be true. The firm's action in response to the leaflets and the resulting trial is described by business analysts as one of the worst public relations failures ever, costing the company £10 million in legal costs.

12 March–6 April 2005

To mark the 75th anniversary of the Salt March, when Gandhi led a march to demonstrate the power of non-violence, events take place in Copenhagen (Denmark) and Stockholm (Sweden), with Committees of the Salt March handing over bags of salt with political messages on them to parliamentarians.

9 April 2005

Civil rights organisations condemn the creation of a volunteer force, Minuteman Civil Defence Corps, to patrol the Arizona-Mexico border for 'observation purposes' only. Campaigners accuse them of racism, and point out that they endanger official patrols, which do not coordinate with them, and also raise concerns that some of the volunteers carry guns, the practice is seen to be threatening and contradictory to the force's ostensible purpose of observation.

10–16 April 2005

The largest ever mobilisation of civil society action on trade issues takes place, as more than ten million people in more than 80 countries take part in a Global Week of Action on Trade, part of the ongoing Make Poverty History and Poverty Zero campaigns. Many diverse initiatives against the WTO, IMF, World Bank, and regional and bilateral trade agreements are organised, under the slogan 'Trade Justice, Not Free Trade'.

May 2005–April 2006 (see *Global Civil Society 2006/7*, pp. 363–72)

1 May 2005

International Labour Day is marked around the world with demonstrations in support of workers' rights. In Mexico City, more than 1 million gather for the city's largest ever demonstration. A Euro Mayday campaign organised by several public assemblies of metropolitan workers coordinates 200,000 demonstrators marching simultaneously in 19 European cities, to draw attention to exploitation. In Brazil, the largest ever march organised by the Landless Rural Workers Movement (MST) sees 13,000 protesters set off from Goiania to march the 210 kilometres to Brasilia, calling for government action on agrarian reform and a better deal for rural workers.

13 June 2005

Police use tear gas and batons to break up a protest by Buddhist monks in Sri Lanka who march to the presidential residence in Colombo to demonstrate against a tsunami-aid deal with Tamil rebels. The monks, who hold significant influence in the 70 per cent Buddhist country, claim the deal will bring legitimacy to the rebels rather than aid to those who need it.

2 July 2005

Some 225,000 demonstrators travel to Edinburgh to join the Make Poverty History march, ahead of the G8 Summit in Gleneagles. This protest, the largest ever held in Scotland, coincides with the 10 Live 8 Concerts held around the world, including one attended by 200,000 people in Hyde Park, London. Tickets are distributed free by text lottery for these concerts, which aim to highlight poverty issues and pressurise G8 leaders to implement poverty reduction strategies, twenty years after the original LiveAid concert and campaign.

8 August 2005

Cindy Sheehan, bereaved mother of a US soldier killed in Iraq, begins her vigil outside the Texas ranch of President Bush, during his month-long holiday there. This marks the beginning of more than 1,500 supporting protests and vigils held by anti-war protesters around the country to support Cindy Sheehan and her call for military withdrawal from Iraq.

30 September 2005

The Danish newspaper *Jyllands-Posten* publishes 12 cartoons satirising the Prophet Muhammad, including depictions of him as a terrorist. This results in an eruption of intense global protests by Muslims and their supporters around the world. The images are reprinted in more than 50 countries, with protests leading to deaths, arrests, attacks on Danish and other European targets, and the resignation and arrest of, as well as death threats to, some of the editors who published the caricatures.

14–16 October 2005
An international meeting on minority rights is organised by the Die East West Trans-European Cultural Festival in Drome, south-east France. Residents of the city join with artists and civil society activist from Central and Eastern Europe.

6 November 2005
After sustained protests by international and local NGOs, the Summit of Americas meeting in Argentina fails to endorse the proposed Free Trade Area of the Americas (FTAA). The anti-FTAA campaign worked throughout the 34 countries involved to promote awareness of the consequences of free trade and to lobby governments to reject the deal.

10 November 2005
In the Ogoni region of Nigeria and around the world, events are held to mark the tenth anniversary of the hanging of writer Ken Saro-Wiwa and eight other activists. The men were executed for fighting for rights of the Ogoni people in the Niger Delta, who suffer political oppression and exploitation by the oil industry. Activists draw attention to the political and environmental problems that still blight the area, and call for continued international pressure to improve the situation.

13 November 2005
In Nepal, lawyers stage a sit-in outside the Supreme Court in Kathmandu to demonstrate against King Gyanendra, who sacked the government in February, and the use of torture by government forces in the ongoing war with anti-monarchist Maoist rebels. This action forms part of broader protests and international campaigns to bring about a ceasefire.

19 November 2005
In the largest demonstration yet against election rigging in Azebaijan, more than 30,000 people gather in Baku even though public demonstrations in the city centre without a permit are banned. Even when a permit is granted, protests cannot last more than two hours. The event is peaceful and at the end of the day protesters leave when requested by opposition party leaders, so as to avoid any conflict with police.

3 December 2005
More than 50 protests take place in 32 countries, part of a global day of action to draw attention to the problem of climate change and the urgent need for international cooperation. This coincides with a meeting of world leaders in Montreal to discuss the Kyoto Process. Montreal sees the largest demonstration, which includes many Canadian Inuit protesters. A petition with more than 600,000 signatures is delivered to the US consulate in Montreal by a coalition of NGOs, demanding that the Bush Administration takes action to stop global warming.

27 December 2005
The Russian parliament legislates to increase control over NGOs, amid claims that foreign spies are using charities as a cover for intelligence work.

14–21 January 2006
Protest organisers in Davos, Switzerland, call for activist creativity when officials refuse to grant a permit for public demonstrations. A week of decentralised alternative events is held to protest against policies said to promote corporate interests, as world leaders meet for the World Economic Forum (WEF). In a departure from the centralised protest outside WEF buildings in past years, local actions are organised throughout Switzerland. These include a dance parade event, Dance Out WEF, 'reclaim the streets' theatre, rallies, a funeral march for the right to protest, factory closures, and a spoof 'celebration of capitalism' party, while more militant events involve paint and firework attacks on banks.

19–23 January 2006
The World Social Forum opens for the sixth time, this year in several venues in Africa, South America and Asia. The aim of this polycentric WSF is to spread the scope of the forum, encourage more local action and widen access to participation. This first section of the Polycentric World Social Forum 2006 is held in Bamako, Mali, where 10,000 people take part in more than 160 activities. The forum is launched with a march to the city's Mobido Keita Stadium, where an opening ceremony is held. Danielle Mitterrand, widow of the former French president and campaigner for access to clean water, is among the speakers.

24–29 January 2006
Ten thousand anti-war demonstrators from 54 countries march through the centre of Caracas at the opening of

the Polycentric World Social Forum's Americas venue. Seventy-two thousand participants register for the event, from 2500 organisations. More than 2000 activities take place, and the main themes include social emancipation; imperial strategies and resistance of the peoples; resources and right to life; diversities, identities and cosmo-visions; work and exploitation; and communication, culture and education.

24–29 March 2006
The final section of the Polycentric World Social Forum 2006 takes place in a cluster of venues around Karachi, Pakistan. Although originally planned to coincide with the Americas forum in Venezuela and the African forum in Bamako, this event was postponed due to the earthquakes of October 2005. Initial problems are overcome and the forum creates an alternative space for discussion, with good coverage from mainstream media. More than 30,000 people take part, from 60 countries.

May 2006–April 2007 (see *Global Civil Society* 2007/8, pp. 368–80)

11 May 2006
Families exiled from the Chagos Islands in the Indian Ocean and their international supporters celebrate a victory after the UK High Court rules they were unlawfully removed and should be allowed to return to all but one of the islands. This international campaign has been active since the islanders of the British colony were exiled in the 1960s and 1970s, when the UK government leased the largest island of Diego Garcia to the USA to use as an airbase.

9 June 2006
Over 1,000 anti-violence demonstrators dress in black and line the boardwalk in Copacabana, Brazil. The protestors lie down, playing dead, to represent the number of murders committed in the city so far this year.

19 June 2006
Rallies in over 25 countries mark the birthday of Burmese democracy leader Aung San Suu Kyi.

20 July 2006
Falun Gong adherents and supporters in at least 74 cities across 33 countries and six continents protest on the anniversary of seven years of the spiritual discipline's persecution in China. The demonstrations, torture re-enactments and candlelight vigils calls for the release of all Falun Gong practitioners from labour camps and prisons, and commemorate the 3,000 followers who have been killed.

22 August 2006
International human rights groups call for boycotts of Yahoo, Google and Microsoft after claiming that they have been complicit in politically repressive activities in China.

13 September 2006
A protest against violence in Colombia is led by the wives and girlfriends of gang members. The women in Pereira refuse to have sex with their partners until they commit to giving up violence, as part of the campaign, 'Violence is not sexy'.

13 December 2006
Indigenous rights groups and the Kalahari San Bushmen celebrate victory as the High Court in Botswana rules that their eviction from ancestral lands in the Central Kalahari Game Reserve was both unconstitutional and unlawful. The government had evicted the Bushmen four years ago, and although the case was fought by the poorest citizens of Botswana, it was the longest and most expensive in the country's history.

30 December 2006
The execution of Saddam Hussain sparks protests in many parts of the world, by both his supporters and those who call for an end to the death penalty. Demonstrations include a rally by 3,000 in Jordan, violent clashes in Iraq and India, protests by the Vatican and a hunger strike by an Italian member of the European Parliament.

20–25 January 2007
The seventh World Social Forum takes place in Nairobi, Kenya, under the banner 'People's struggles, people's alternatives'. Over 75,000 people attend from 110 countries and 1,400 organisations take part in the first WSF to be held solely in Africa. A whole range of issues are discussed and experiences shared, aiming to overcome neoliberal globalisation and develop alternatives. Major themes are the principles of forum organisation, the future of the forum and how to ensure it is accessible to as many participants as possible.

8 March 2007
International Women's Day is marked around the world by over 500 events in at least 49 countries. These include

a silent protest in Taipei, a march for equality in Brazil, an assembly of Manitoba chiefs in Canada, and a Right to Play campaign in Tanzania to promote female inclusion in sport. In Iran, a strong police presence disperses women trying to gather outside the parliament in Tehran to demonstrate the arrests of 33 women earlier in the week. These detained women are now on hunger strike over their treatment when they tried to protest against discriminatory laws.

21 March 2007

Anti-racism events are held in cities around the world to mark International Day for the Elimination of Racism on the anniversary of the Sharpeville massacre in South Africa. On this day in 1960, 69 anti-apartheid demonstrators were killed when they stood up against the pass laws which were designed to regulate the movements of black Africans.

May 2007–April 2008 (see *Global Civil Society 2009*, pp. 338–49)

1 June 2007

One million text messages of protest are sent as part of the world's largest ever text message campaign, to stop the building of a chemical factory in Xiamen, China. Together with street demonstrations involving more than 7,000 protesters, the campaign successfully results in the suspension of plans.

10 July 2007

Bedouin activists and their supporters celebrate partial victory as 29 protesters are released. They had been detained during three months of demonstrations against police harassment of the Bedouin people of the Sinai.

4 September 2007

A two-and-a-half-year campaign by peace activists and Palestinian citizens results in the Israeli Supreme Court of Justice ruling that the Israeli Government has to re-route the security barrier which currently divides the village of Bil'in. Villagers and their supporters have maintained weekly protests at the site every Friday throughout the dispute.

17 September 2007

Campaigners celebrate as the UN finally adopts the Universal Declaration of the Rights of Indigenous People after a majority vote, setting out the rights of the 370 million indigenous people throughout the world. However, there is disappointment that Canada, Australia and the US, amongst others, refuse to sign.

18–26 September 2007

Daily pro-democracy protest are held throughout Burma, led by monks, nuns and their supporters, many of whom pin scraps of monks clothing to their own in solidarity. The marches grow to include over 100,000 people, despite the junta's threat and us of violence, leading up to a crackdown resulting in unknown numbers of deaths and injuries, as well as an estimated 3,000 arrests. Protest and vigils are held in support of the Burmese people throughout the world.

14–21 October 2007

A week of Global Action Against Debt and International Financial Institutions is held to demand the immediate cancellation of illegitimate debts across the globe. Throughout the week awareness raising activities and protests are held in 60 countries, with 297 organisations taking park. The initiative grew out of discussions between debt activists at the World Social Forum in Nairobi in January, and has been planned to coincide with annual meetings of the World Bank and IMF in Washington, as well as the annual Day of Global Action Against Poverty.

21–23 November 2007

Street protests are held in Dakar, Senegal, against the government-led eviction of thousands of street traders. Subsequently, the government postpones the action until the new year.

26 January 2008

A Global Day of Action is marked around the world as an alternative to the annual centralised or polycentric meeting of the World Social Forum. Still under the banner of 'Another World is Possible', this global day of action has been designed as part of the experimental process of the World Social Forum, to facilitate global justice activists gathering in their home towns and cities, exchanging information, developing new alliances, and demonstrating for local and global change. The organising committee argue that this is a new form of mobilisation that can promote inclusion and creativity, as well as strengthen global networks. The reporting of actions via the World Social Forum website is described as a form of action in itself, and in order to build a collective memory participants are encouraged to join the 'global reporting team' by collecting and posting photos, articles, pamphlets, media and video clips, and blogs. This shows that 800 actions took place in 80 countries, involving 2,500 civil society organisations, activity that was relayed via 20 press conferences. The number of people involved is lower than predicted, but with noticeably increased activity in Russia and Mexico. In Russia the action across 24 regions is coordinated by the Union of Coordination Council: social and human rights organisations, trade unions, and citizen groups hold rallies, pickets and demonstrations - many cases despite local authority bans. It is reported that the Global Action Day 2008 sees the biggest collective social forum activity in Russia so far. The actions coincide with the start of the Russian presidential campaign, and in some places activists of the Community Party take advantage of the protests. Major themes of the rallies include dissatisfaction with housing and working conditions. In January 2009 the World Social Form will again operate as a centralised meeting, in Belem, in the Amazon region of North Brazil.

20 March 2008

As one of the alternatives to the Olympic torch, a virtual torch relay is launched in the Netherlands by the Play Fair coalition of labour rights organisations. This makes its way virtually East and West around the world, and is eventually taken up by 12,201 people in 99 countries, who all their signatures to the demand that the International Olympic Committee take action on the rights of workers' in supply chains serving the Games.

24 March 2008

The Olympic torch world relay is launched in Olympia, Greece. This year's theme is 'Journey of Harmony' and should last 85,000 miles, the longest route since the relay began in 1936. However, during the torch lighting ceremony, members of Reporters Without Borders breach security to express their support for the Free Tibet campaign, disrupting the official opening speeches which are being broadcast live around the world. Protests are then held in most of the countries visited by the torch relay. Some of the demonstrations relate to national issues or relations with China, but many focus on the Chinese government's domestic human rights record, alleged complicity in the Darfur genocide, and, particularly, the violent treatment of pro-democracy protesters in Tibet. Some celebrities publicly dissociate themselves from the Olympics, and call for a boycott are advanced on online

sites such as YouTube, Facebook and MySpace, as well as websites and blogs dedicated to the Olympics.

April 2009–March 2010 (see *Global Civil Society 2011*, pp. 8–9, 106–7, 136–7)

1–2 April 2009

In the midst of the global financial downturn, the London Summit 2009 brings together the leaders and finance ministers of the G20 countries to discuss institutional and regulatory response and reform. The summit sparks the ire of international protesters who call for systematic change mostly aimed against globalised capitalism, though the date becomes a rally event for other activist groups and campaigners to call attention to anti-war and climate change issues. Violent clashes between London police and protesters lead to hundreds of arrests and injuries as well as the death of an innocent bystander assaulted by riot police.

24 April 2009

Global Justice Action, an anti-capitalist group, organises anti-IMF and anti-World Bank protests during the latter's spring meetings, reacting against the pledged US$1.1 trillion rescue fund agreed by the G20 at the London Summit, whilst highlighting the lack of sufficient aid pledged for Africa.

25 July 2009

A Global Day of Action for Human Rights in Iran is held in more than 110 cities around the world, calling for an end to the persecution of opposition campaigners imprisoned following the disputed presidential elections of 12 June. The global protests are organised by 'United for Iran' and supported by NGOs including Amnesty International, Human Rights Watch, and Reporters without Borders. Appeals are made to the UN to investigate the regime's violent and repressive crackdowns.

8 August 2009

Riot police patrol Rangoon to prevent activists from recognising the 21st anniversary of the pro-democracy demonstrations that brought Aung San Suu Kyi to prominence as the leader of the country's political opposition. The anniversary comes as Suu Kyi awaits sentencing for violating the terms of her house arrest after an American man, uninvited, swam to visit her. The verdict is postponed apparently in order to prevent sparking retaliatory uprisings from Suu Kyi's supporters during the anniversary. However the date is recognised by protesters outside Myanmar embassies in Bangkok, Kuala Lumpur, and Hong Kong. Three days after the anniversary, on 11 August, Suu Kyi is sentenced to a further 18 months' house arrest, which will ensure she is once again unable to stand in the 2010 Burmese general elections.

24–28 January 2010

The World Social Forum celebrates its tenth year by decentralising its annual event in favour of events around the world throughout the year bound together by the theme of crisis, referring not just to the economic crisis but to crises of environment, food, energy and humanitarian crises. The decennial begins with a meeting in Porto Alegre, with further events scheduled throughout 2010.

References

Deel, Sean (2011) 'Chronology of Selected Global Civil Society Events Relating to the Global Financial Crisis', in Martin Albrow and Hakan Seckinelgin (eds), *Global Civil Society 2011*. Basingstoke: Palgrave Macmillan, p. 8.

Deel, Sean (2011) 'Chronology of Selected Global Civil Society Events Relating to Climate Change and Other Environmental Issues', in Martin Albrow and Hakan Seckinelgin (eds), *Global Civil Society 2011*. Basingstoke: Palgrave Macmillan, p. 106.

Deel, Sean (2011) 'Chronology of Selected Global Civil Society Events Relating to Elections', in Martin Albrow and Hakan Seckinelgin (eds), *Global Civil Society 2011*. Basingstoke: Palgrave Macmillan, p. 136.

Glasius, Marlies (ed.) (2001) 'Global Civil Society Events of 2000' in Helmut Anheier, Marlies Glasius and Mary Kaldor (eds), *Global Civil Society 2001*. Oxford: Oxford University Press.

Glasius, Marlies and Timms, Jill (2005) 'The Role of Social Forums in Global Civil Society: Radical Beacon or Strategic Infrastructure?' in H. Anheier, M. Kaldor and M. Glasius (eds), *Global Civil Society 2005/6*, London: Sage.

Timms, Jill (ed) (2002) 'Chronology of Global Civil Society Events', in Marlies Glasius, Mary Kaldor and Helmut Anheier (eds), *Global Civil Society 2002*. Oxford: Oxford University Press.

Timms, Jill (ed.) (2003) 'Chronology of Global Civil Society Events', in Mary Kaldor, Helmut Anheier and Marlies Glasius (eds), *Global Civil Society 2003*. Oxford: Oxford University Press.

Timms, Jill (ed.) (2005) 'Chronology of Global Civil Society Events', in Helmut Anheier, Marlies Glasius and Mary Kaldor (eds), *Global Civil Society 2004/5*. London: Sage Publications.

Timms, Jill (ed.) (2006) 'Chronology of Global Civil Society Events', in Marlies Glasius, Mary Kaldor and Helmut Anheier (eds), *Global Civil Society 2005/6*. London: Sage Publications.

Timms, Jill (ed.) (2007) 'Chronology of Global Civil Society Events', in Mary Kaldor, Martin Albrow, Helmut Anheier and Marlies Glasius (eds), *Global Civil Society 2006/7*. London: Sage Publications.

Timms, Jill (ed.) (2008) 'Chronology of Global Civil Society Events', in Martin Albrow et al. (eds), *Global Civil Society 2007/8*. London: Sage Publications.

Timms, Jill (ed) (2009) 'Chronology of Global Civil Society Events', in Ashwani Kumar et al. (eds), *Global Civil Society 2009*. London: Sage Publications.

Timms, Jill and Stares, Sally (2007) 'Alternative Data for Studying Global Civil Society: Correspondent Networks, Maps and Chronologies', Center for Global, International and Regional Studies, Mapping Global Inequalities. Santa Cruz, 13–14 December 2007. Santa Cruz: UC Santa Cruz. Available at http://escholarship.org/uc/item/468929x1 (last accessed 10 September 2011).